DIOXINS IN THE ENVIRONMENT

Edited by

Michael A. Kamrin
Michigan State University
East Lansing

Paul W. Rodgers
Limno-Tech, Inc.
Ann Arbor, Michigan

● HEMISPHERE PUBLISHING CORPORATION

Washington   New York   London

DISTRIBUTION OUTSIDE THE UNITED STATES

McGRAW–HILL INTERNATIONAL BOOK COMPANY

Auckland   Bogotá   Guatemala   Hamburg   Johannesburg   Lisbon
London   Madrid   Mexico   Montreal   New Delhi   Panama   Paris
San Juan   São Paulo   Singapore   Sydney   Tokyo   Toronto

DIOXINS IN THE ENVIRONMENT

1 2 3 4 5 6 7 8 9 EBEB 8 9 8 7 6 5

Library of Congress Cataloging in Publication Data

Main entry under title:

Dioxins in the environment.

    Sponsored by Michigan State University, Limno-Tech,
and the Cranbrook Institute of Science.
    Bibliography: p.
    Includes index.
    1. Dioxins—Environmental aspects—Congresses.
I. Kamrin, Michael A. II. Rodgers, Paul W.
III. Michigan State University. IV. Limno-Tech (Firm)
V. Cranbrook Institute of Science.
QH545.D55D56   1985   628.5   84-22464
ISBN 0-89116-371-9

Contents

Preface

Dioxins and other closely related chemical compounds have attracted both public and scientific attention. In recent years several incidents have resulted in the enunciation of both fact and fear regarding the extent of dioxin distribution and the unknown human health consequences. These chemicals have been identified in industrial settings following accidents, combustion residues, herbicides, waste disposal sites, fish, soils, and surface waters. It may be that these chemicals have become nearly ubiquitous and we need only to look for them in order to find them. However, their occurrence is often sufficient to raise serious concern regarding human health. Formulation of rational responses to these concerns requires an understanding of dioxins' sources and fate, their toxicological potential, and the critical analytical methods required to measure their presence.

An international symposium and workshop, entitled "Dioxins in the Environment", was held at Michigan State University on December 6-9, 1983. The information herein is divided into two sections. The first section presents the invited papers given at the symposium. These papers were presented before nearly 300 scientists, decision makers, and concerned citizens who were in attendance. The second section reports the conclusions of the workshop sessions which followed the invited papers. The workshop sessions examined the diversity of our relevant knowledge in four concurrent sessions: 1) Sampling and Analytical Techniques; 2) Source, Distribution and Fate; 3) Human Health and Toxicity; and 4) Public Policy. Each of the four workshop sessions included the participation of experienced scientists and/or persons responsible for establishing environmental policy. The workshop participants addressed specific issues relevant to understanding the dynamics and management of dioxins in the environment. The goals of the workshop were to concisely summarize our present knowledge of dioxins, identify research needs and, following the consideration of important areas of concern, to offer concensus regarding the issues. These opinions are offered, unedited, as a part of each workshop report.

Many issues remain in assessing the effects of dioxins in the environment. The information reported here updates our understanding and supplies direction for our continued research and regulatory efforts. The knowledge shared and the understanding gained through the consolidation of this information has demonstrated that our ability to approach the management of toxic chemicals can indeed be proactive and need not be reactive.

We gratefully acknowledge and appreciate the many contributions to this volume. We are especially grateful for the sense of purpose and professional camaraderie expressed by the participants.

Michael A. Kamrin
Paul W. Rodgers

Acknowledgments

The conference on Dioxins in the Environment was a unique collaborative effort between a public institution, Michigan State University, a private consulting firm, Limno-Tech, Inc., and a private institute, the Cranbrook Institute of Science. The success of this meeting was due to the excellent efforts of members of each of these organizations. In particular, the contributions of Dr. Robert Leader of the Center for Environmental Toxicology at Michigan State University and Drs. Dennis Wint and Elliott Smith of the Cranbrook Institute of Science to the development of this conference deserve special recognition. This conference was possible only through the enthusiastic participation of all the speakers and workshop panel members. Their participation and the high quality contributions to this book are greatly appreciated. Recognition and appreciation are also due to the other organizations which supported this conference: Michigan Toxic Substance Control Commission, Michigan State University Lifelong Education Programs, Michigan State University Agricultural Experiment Station, and Michigan State University Cooperative Extension Service. The coordinator of the conference arrangements at Kellogg Center, Joan Martin Alam, did a superb job of facilitating conference events and deserves special recognition. The staff of the Center for Environmental Toxicology at Michigan State University should be commended for their excellent work in the organizational stages of the conference, and also in the preparation of this book. Acknowledgments and thanks are due to Mary Robinson and Carole Abel, as well as the staff of supporting institutions, for their expert word processing and secretarial skills; Dr. Victoria C. Serbia for her excellent editorial assistance, and Steven Johnson for all the tedious checking and proofing that are essential for the finished product. Every effort was made to faithfully reproduce the manuscripts and workshop summaries; however, the editors accept responsibility for any errors.

PART I
INVITED
CONTRIBUTIONS

Section 1
Overview of the Dioxins

Chapter 1

DIOXINS IN THE ENVIRONMENT - INTRODUCTORY REMARKS

John E. Cantlon
Vice President for Research and
    Graduate Studies
232 Administration Building
Michigan State University
East Lansing, Michigan 48823

On behalf of Michigan State University let me welcome you to our campus, and for those from homes beyond our borders, I also welcome you to Michigan and the United States.

This symposium on DIOXINS IN THE ENVIRONMENT is one of a series we have sponsored here at MSU. Earlier we looked at DDT, PCBs, and PBBs. The presence of potentially hazardous materials in environments around research laboratories, points of use, and manufacturing plants has been and perhaps will always be a source of broad public concern and even of fear. At one level such concern is appropriate. Young children who have learned to fear heated stoves are less likely to inadvertently be burned again. However, in today's world, pervasive and dramatic mass media coverage can present exceedingly complex matters in such powerful and simplistic formats as to frighten people far beyond any reasonable level. On other occasions I have suggested to our media friends that they may have made more persons ill with their treatment of these subjects than the chemicals are likely to have done.

This does not, of course, suggest that we can in any way hide real risk from the public. Far from it. As scientists, it is our duty to rigorously assess risk and to make verified information broadly accessible to all , irrespective of whether we work for universities, local, state and federal regulatory agencies, environmental or public interest groups, industry, or state and federal development agencies.

Again, at one level, this is our standard operating procedure. However, each of us with any experience in the field of science knows the problem of achieving this obviously desirable and generally agreed upon goal.

In the case of dioxins, the problems are numerous and severe.

First, sorting out whether one is reporting on 2,3,7,8-TCDD or other dioxins is very costly and requires unusually high levels of expertise and sophisticated facilities.

Second, conducting experiments with animal models poses complex problems with waste disposal, worker protection and organizational support. Resolving these problems has slowed the emergence of good animal data, especially on chronic effects and modes of action.

Third, there appear to be major differences in sensitivity to 2,3,7,8-TCDD among animal models used. This makes the extrapolations of risk to humans more difficult than for other hazardous materials.

Fourth, the levels at which the most sensitive animals show effects are low, and this highly fat-soluble material is known to bioaccumulate. This combination leads to difficulties in establishing the guidelines which an adequate environmental monitoring program should provide.

Fifth, there are studies which suggest there are natural as well as man-made sources for dioxins, although generally knowledgeable researchers agree that primary 2,3,7,8-TCDD contamination sites are from man's industrial, agricultural, construction and sanitation chemicals.

Sixth, the routes by which dioxins move in the environment and the health risk significance of such transport need a great deal of clarification.

Seventh and last, detoxification and degradation of 2,3,7,8-TCDD in natural soils and sediments and options for developing adequate waste treatment processes need much work before we will have answers to what has been going on and what options we might have in the future for ameliorating dioxin-contaminated areas.

As this group is well aware, these seven areas are not an exhaustive list of why our areas of ignorance about 2,3,7,8-TCDD impede our ability to provide a generally agreed upon risk assessment for this hazardous chemical. They are, however, illustrative of the complexity of the issues involved.

Placing 2,3,7,8-TCDD risk in perspective, I suspect from the emerging data on worker chronic exposures and short term exposures from various accidents that risk from that chemical is most likely to be less than that from smoking cigarettes, mining coal, driving autos and a number of other risks the public seems willing to accomodate in return for the perceived benefits from engaging in the activity.

However, when such risk is imposed on highly localized human populations, through ignorance and bad judgment, in placing residental areas on former waste disposal sites, as in Love Canal; or settling road dust with dioxin-containing waste oils, as at Times Beach, Missouri, we should not be surprised that what we don't know can, through mass media hype, significantly disrupt human lives in major ways and lead to governmental decisions which may in calmer times be viewed as questionable as to their cost effectiveness.

Our Center for Environmental Toxicology here at MSU came into being as a result of Michigan's experience when a PBB containing fire retardant was inadvertently mixed into animal feeds and distributed broadly in the state. The event was not discovered for some time and when it was, coping with it followed a trajectory that cold hindsight finds many things to criticize. While Monday morning quarterbacks never lose football games, we also recognize that the well-equipped, well-researched and well-managed team will, on average, prevail over the opportunist or the merely lucky and well-intentioned.

This Symposium has as its objective the sharing both of information and of our areas of ignorance with regard to dioxins in the environment. Participants include a broad range of researchers as well as administrators who are faced with having to make decisions on problems rather than having the opportunity of continuing to study them. There are also representatives of the media present. If we were to achieve the ultimate from the Symposium we would each leave content that we had identified the level of human health and environmental risk from various types of exposure to 2,3,7,8-TCDD and what realistic steps might then be suitable to alleviate or avoid such risk. Undoubtedly, as scientists and administrators we will have to settle for a more modest product, that of better illuminating what we do and don't know about the dioxins. Hopefully this mutual education will speed our research on dioxins and their significance as well as assist administrative officers in coping with perceived dioxin problems in the real world where they demand prompt, tough decisions in the face of uncertainty. The real world also imposes on administrators both accountability with a myriad of critics and second guessing of virtually all decisions from vested interests. The real world further provides oversight by the media -- which makes its living by illuminating things which are unexpected, differences of opinion among experts and the often noteworthy fact that mankind lives in a world which is rich in its diversity of risks. For representatives of the media we must be content to have given them access to experts who can provide a broader and deeper grasp of the complexities of assessing dioxin risks.

Much illumination can come from careful study of research and case histories already completed. However, there are high priority research projects on dioxins that need to be initiated and we must sustain important programs now underway. These continuing investments will provide bases for future opportunities to summarize, to synthesize and to share our areas of knowledge and of ignorance among ourselves and, via media representatives, with the public.

Thank you.

Chapter 2

DIOXINS AND FURANS IN THE ENVIRONMENT: EVALUATING TOXICOLOGICAL RISK FROM DIFFERENT SOURCES BY MULTI-CRITERIA ANALYSIS

O. Hutzinger
Chair of Ecological Chemistry and Geochemistry
Universitaetsstrasse 30, D-8580 Bayreuth, Germany

M. V. D. Berg, K. Olie, A. Opperhuizen
Laboratory of Environmental and Toxicological Chemistry
University of Amsterdam, The Netherlands

S. Safe
Department of Veterinary Physiology and Pharmacology
College of Veterinary Medicine
Texas A & M University

INTRODUCTION

Polychlorinated dibenzodioxins (PCDDs) and polychlorinated dibenzofurans (PCDFs) are present as trace contaminants in several industrial organic chemicals (e.g., chlorinated phenols, phenoxy herbicides, PCBs) which have been identified as environmental pollutants (Rappe and Buser, 1980; Buser, 1975; Rappe et al., 1975, 1979, 1981; Buser and Bosshardt, 1974, 1976; Nilsson et al, 1978; Norstrom et al., 1980, 1982; Heida, 1983). In addition, combustion processes contribute to PCDD and PCDF release to the environment (Lustenhouwer et al, 1980; Olie et al., 1977; Kooke et al., 1981; Hutzinger et al., 1980; Gizzi et al, 1982; Buser and Rappe, 1978, 1979). Despite these two significant routes of pollution by PCDDs and PCDFs, detection of these chemicals in environmental samples is only now being widely reported.

Humans may be exposed to PCDDs and PCDFs as a result of these sources, from occupational exposures or from specific incidents; for example:

1. exposure of U.S. armed forces personnel and Vietnamese civilians; primarily to 2,3,7,8-tetrachlorodibenzodioxin (2,3,7,8-TCDD) which was present as an impurity in the defoliant herbicide, Agent Orange (a mixture of 2,4-D and 2,4,5-T) (Young and Shepard, 1983);
2. occupational exposure of workers to diverse PCDDs and PCDFs in industries preparing or using chlorinated phenols and derived products (Hardell, 1980);
3. exposure to 2,3,7,8-TCDD in factories in which chlorinated phenols (primarily 2,4,5-trichlorophenol) have dimerized to PCDDs during overheating (May, 1983);
4. exposure to 2,4,5-trichlorophenate and 2,3,7,8-TCDD as a result of the Seveso incident (Fara, 1983);
5. Yusho poisoning in Japan and Taiwan (PCBs and PCDFs) (Buser et al., 1978; Chen et al., 1980; Miyata et al., 1979; Kashimoto et al., 1981; Rappe et al., 1983b);
6. exposure to PCDFs during PCB fires (e.g., the accident in the Binghamton Office Building) (Schecter, 1983).

Therefore, both environmental and occupational exposures to PCDDs are significant. This suggests that human risk assessment requires not only a detailed knowledge of the biologic and toxic effects of the individual compounds and mixtures, but also knowledge of their origin, release, distribution, environmental fate and pharmacokinetics. The

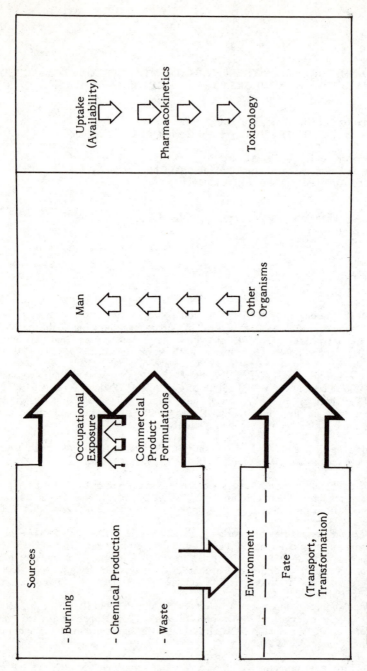

FIGURE I. PCDD/PCDF: Formation to Toxic Effect

overall relationship of these factors is outlined in Figure 1.

PCDD AND PCDF SOURCES

The key sources of PCDD and PCDF are the following:

1. Chemical manufacturing
   a. production processes
   b. end use
2. Burning and other high temperature processes
   a. municipal and chemical waste
   b. natural materials
3. Reservoirs
   a. chemical waste dumps
   b. sludge, contaminated sites

Chemical Manufacturing

The earliest concern about PCDDs in the environment arose in the late 1960s when it was reported that 2,3,7,8-TCDD was a contaminant of phenoxy herbicides such as 2,4,5-T. It was found that this extremely toxic material was formed from 2,4,5-trichlorophenol during the manufacture of these herbicides which were in wide use in the U.S. as well as in Europe. The 2,3,7,8-TCDD was present in ppb to ppm amounts in 2,4,5-T and so significant amounts were released to the environment through herbicide usage (Esposito et al., 1980). Later, PCDFs were also found in 2,4,5-T-related pesticides (Huckins, et al., 1978; Rappe et al., 1978).

Although PCDDs are also found in other pesticides, like 2,4-D, Silvex and Dicamba, the congeners that are present usually contain less than four chlorine atoms. These congeners are of low toxicity to humans and the environment and so are excluded from this article. However, the congeners formed during the production of Silvex, Ronnel, Erbone and Sesone deserve attention, because 2,4,5-trichlorophenol and its sodium salt have been used as key intermediates with 2,3,7,8-TCDD formation a possible result (Esposito et al., 1980).

Furthermore, numerous PCDDs and PCDFs have been identified in pentachlorophenol (PCP) products which are most commonly used as wood preservatives. Generally, commercial PCPs contain the higher chlorinated PCDDs and PCDFs (Cl $\geq$ 6) at ppm levels; the amounts of PCDDs and PCDFs found were in the order $Cl_4 < Cl_5 < Cl_6 < Cl_7 \leq Cl_8$. However, the highly toxic 2,3,7,8-TCDD and -TCDF congeners were generally not present or were present only as minor components (Rappe et al., 1975; Buser and Bosshardt, 1976; Buser, 1975; Rappe et al., 1982; Firestone et al., 1972).

Commercial polychlorinated biphenyl (PCB) mixtures, too, have been found to contain PCDFs in ppm amounts, whereas PCDDs have not been detected in these mixtures (Vos et al., 1970; Bowes et al., 1975b). PCB mixtures contain PCDFs having four to seven Cl atoms. The major isomers present have been identified, and the toxicities of some of these compounds (i.e., 2,3,7,8-TCDF and 2,3,4,7,8-PnCDF) are comparable to the toxicity of 2,3,7,8-TCDD. These two PCDF compounds represent more than 50% of the total PCDFs contained in some PCB mixtures (Rappe et al., 1982; Bowes et al., 1975a).

2,3,7,8-TCDD has also been identified in hexachlorophene, which is used as a bactericide. Hexachlorophene is prepared from 2,4,5-trichlorophenol and contains less than 15 µg/kg 2,3,7,8-TCDD (Esposito et al., 1980).

Burning

Complex mixtures of PCDDs and PCDFs have been found in the fly ash and flue gas emissions of municipal and industrial incinerators (Lustenhouwer et al., 1980; Olie et al., 1977; Buser and Bosshardt, 1970, 1978; Tiernan et al., 1983). Chlorophenols and chlorobenzenes are believed to be key intermediates in PCDD and PCDF formation from these incinerators; there is no evidence that PCBs also act as key intermediates (Tiernan et al., 1983). The levels of TCDDs and TCDFs in flue gas emissions of municipal incinerators can range from 0.1-2.5 $\mu g/m^3$; 2,3,7,8-TCDD and -TCDF are found as minor constituents (<5%) in both fly ash and flue gas. The type and amount of PCDD and PCDF emissions from industrial burning largely depend on the base material. However, in general, chlorophenols, -benzenes, -diphenyl ethers and -biphenyls will yield considerable quantities PCDDs and PCDFs if combusted at too low temperatures. This conversion occurs readily at combustion temperatures of several hundred degrees Celsius (Buser, 1978, 1979).

It has also been found that burning of lignin-like structures and vegetables can yield quantities of PCDDs and PCDFs in the $\mu g/g$ range (Olie et al., 1983; Liberti et al., 1983). The finding that burning of plant material can produce PCDDs and PCDFs, raises the question of the extent to which forest fires, for example, contribute to PCDD/PCDF formation and release into the atmosphere.

LEVELS OF PCDD AND PCDF FORMED

Chemical Production

Maximum production of 2,4,5-T was reached between 1960 and 1970, with a total of 106.3 million pounds (48.2 x 10^6 kg) produced. In the seventies, however, government restrictions led to decreased production, and in 1978 the total U.S. usage was estimated to be approximately 5 million pounds. By 1980, U.S. consumption was believed to be less than 2 million pounds (Esposito et al., 1980). The concentration of 2,3,7,8-TCDD in 2,4,5-T has been determined in several laboratories. Rappe reported concentrations from 0.05 to a maximum of 6.0 ppm for U.S. formulations of 2,4,5-T (Shepard, 1980). From concentrations of 2,3,7,8-TCDD found in Herbicide Orange (1:1 w/w 2,4-D and 2,4,5-T) before 1970, it was concluded that 2,4,5-T contained up to 100 ppm of 2,3,7,8-TCDD. If we assume that the upper 2,3,7,8-TCDD concentration limit was 100 ppm and the lower limit was 0.1 ppm, then the maximum amount of 2,3,7,8-TCDD produced from 1960-1970 was about 4.8 x 10^3 kg. There are no figures currently available on annual 2,3,7,8-TCDD production. However, when one considers the recent sharp reduction of 2,4,5-T production and that present formulations contain less than 0.1 ppm, the amounts of 2,3,7,8-TCDD released into the environment through use of 2,4,5-T are undoubtedly several orders of magnitude lower than in 1960-1970 (Esposito et al., 1980).

Although there are no accurate annual production figures for individual chlorophenol pesticides, the total production of all pesticides of this type was estimated to be 1.5 x 10^8 kg in 1980 (Rappe et al., 1982). Figures on one particular chlorophenol pesticide, pentachlorophenol (PCP), are available for the U.S. between 1972 and 1977. Average annual production during this period was about 2 x 10^7 kg. The PCDD and PCDF content of commericial PCP mixtures was measured to be in the range of 205-1070 ppm (Rappe et al., 1982). Using these figures and U.S. production estimates, it can be calculated that from 4 to 21 x 10^3 kg of PCDDs and PCDFs are produced annually in the U.S. during the PCP manufacture. Based on Canadian import statistics showing that the U.S. is the biggest producer of PCP, this value represents the majority of total world production of PCDDs and PCDFs from PCP manufacture (Jones, 1981). It should be noted that this total does not include PCDDs or PCDFs produced during the manufacture of lower chlorophenols. One of these lower chlorophenols, 2,3,4,6-tetrachlorophenol, deserves special attention because PCDD and PCDF levels·of 172 ppm were found in one sample

(Rappe et al., 1982). However, figures on current annual production of this chlorophenol are not available.

PCB production increased greatly at the end of the sixties, but by the end of the seventies, production decreased sharply due to environmental concerns. Although PCBs were manufactured in the U.S., Japan and Europe, it was estimated that the U.S. produced about half of the world total (Rappe and Buser, 1980). It was found in the 1970s that PCBs can be contaminated by PCDFs and the amount of these impurities that were produced can be estimated from sales figures. Table 1 shows the sales of three U.S. commerical PCB mixtures, Aroclors 1248, 1254 and 1260, from 1968-1975 and also shows the PCDF content of each (Rappe and Buser, 1980; Bowes et al., 1975a, 1975b). Using these figures, it can be estimated that a total of 84-94 kg of PCDFs was produced in the U.S. during this period. In particular, the most toxic 2,3,7,8-TCDF and 2,3,4,7,8, PnCDF isomers were produced in amounts of 8 and 14 kg, respectively. These totals are underestimates since they do not include the amounts of these isomers in Aroclor 1260. The Japanese commercial PCBs are known as Kaneclors and Kaneclors 300-600 were found to contain 1-18 ppm PCDFs (Rappe et al., 1983a). Measurements of French and German PCB mixtures revealed PCDF concentrations similar to those in the Aroclors and Kaneclors (Rappe and Buser, 1980).

TABLE 1.

	Arochlor Preparation Types		
	1248	1254	1260
1966-75 U.S. Sales	11.5×10^6 kg	34.3×10^6 kg	13.1×10^6 kg
PCDF Content	2.0 µg/g	1.5-1.7 µg/g	0.8-1.0 µg/g
2,3,7,8-TCDF Content	0.33 µg/g	0.11 µg/g	?
2,3,4,7,8-PnCDF Content	0.83 µg/g	0.12 µg/g	?
Estimated 2,3,7,8-TCDF Production	4 kg	4 kg	?
Estimated 2,3,4,7,8-PnCDF Production	10 kg	4 kg	?
Total Estimated PCDF Production	23 kg	51-58 kg	10-13 kg

The manufacture of commercial PCBs has been greatly reduced, and the amount of PCBs produced annually is now only a small fraction of the PCBs produced in the 1960s and 1970s. As a result, the greatest future risk from PCBs is the uncontrolled release of PCDFs into the environment due to the low-temperature burning of PCB-containing materials, such as transformers (Rappe et al., 1983a).

Incineration

The main source of PCDF/PCDD environmental contamination probably is municipal incineration. In the Netherlands, total PCDD/PCDF emissions via flue gas have been determined from regular emission measurements. It was estimated that 21.6 kg of PCDDs and 18.6 kg of PCDFs were emitted into the atmosphere annually, of which only a very small part, namely 24 grams, was 2,3,7,8-TCDD (unpublished results). Although the total amounts of PCDDs and PCDFs in fly ash were comparable to those in flue gas, the actual amount of fly ash produced is several orders of magnitude larger than the amount of flue gas produced. However, because fly ash is removed from the emitted gases by electrostatic precipitators, it is less likely to escape into the atmosphere.

ENVIRONMENTAL ROUTES OF HUMAN EXPOSURE

Presently, the most important means of human exposure to PCDDs and PCDFs are individual exposure in the workplace and general environmental exposure via incinerator emissions (Lustenhouwer et al., 1980; Rappe et al., 1982; Jones, 1981). Up to 400 pg/g of PCDDs and PCDFs have been detected in exposed workers (Rappe et al., 1982). Workers who handle 2,4,5-T, PCBs, and especially PCP, are most at risk, but municipal incinerator workers, too, can be contaminated by PCDDs and PCDFs through fly ash. However, human uptakes of PCDDs and PCDFs through occupational and general exposure are not yet accurately known (Reggiani, 1982; van den Berg et al., 1983). Another potential source of high levels of PCDDs and PCDFs is uncontrolled burning of PCP- and PCB-containing materials in the home. A less serious contamination source is waste water from wood treatment facilities. Direct human exposure from this source should be relatively low due to strong PCDD and PCDF adsorption to sediment. Although leachate from PCDD- and PCDF-containing waste dumps, such as fly ash dumps, is another source, levels should be very low because of this strong adsorption and the low solubility of these compounds (Shepard, 1980).

Both pesticide application and PCB use may lead to human exposure through contamination of food. In addition to the toxic PCDD isomers which arise in pesticides during manufacture, photochemical dechlorination of higher PCDDs and PCDFs may lead to more highly toxic, lower chlorinated isomers. However, these isomers, such as 2,3,7,8-TCDD, can be further reduced photochemically if a suitable solvent is present (Shepard, 1980). This situation seemed to exist in Seveso where measurements of 2,3,7,8-TCDD levels in plants from contaminated areas did not indicate appreciable accumulation of this compound. Even if the 2,3,7,8-TCDD is deposited on the soil, human exposure is limited by its low mobility in this medium. Studies in the U.S. showed that, even after several years, the highest concentrations were still in the top layers of soil (Shepard, 1980).

People can be exposed to PCBs through fish uptake and bioaccumulation of these compounds. In addition, PCDFs have also been shown in this type of biota and it appears that the levels of PCBs and PCDFs parallel one another (Rappe et al., 1981; Ryan et al., 1983). Human exposure to 2,3,7,8-TCDD can also occur by this route of exposure as evidenced by the findings of measureable levels in sediments and higher levels in fish (Shepard, 1980; Ryan et al., 1983). Indeed, although fish contain fewer PCDD/PCDF isomers than the sediments where the fish were caught, they retain the more toxic isomers (Stalling et al., 1983). Because of this, ingesting PCDDs and PCDFs from fish might be more hazardous than ingesting them from fly ash.

BIOACCUMULATION AND SELECTIVE RETENTION

One of the biggest problems in assessing risks from PCDDs and PCDFs in food is the selective retention by each organism of the different components of a PCDD/PCDF mixture as it moves through the food chain. It has been shown in rats, for example, that retention of PCDFs and PCDDs is strongly isomer dependent (Rappe et al., 1982; van den Berg et al., 1983). Recent studies have led to an understanding of the factors which influence retention. In PCDDs, it has been shown that the presence of two vincinal hydrogen atoms favors metabolism, while chlorine substitution on the lateral positions inhibits it (Tulp and Hutzinger, 1978). There is a large difference in liver retention of 2,3,7,8-TCDD in various mammalian species, indicating that the conversion of this compound to polar metabolites must be highly species-dependent. This also applies to PCDFs, although the retention of 2,3,7,8-TCDF is shorter in various species than its dioxin congener (Neal et al., 1982; Birnbaum et al., 1980,1981; Decad et al., 1981a, 1981b). This difference may be related to enzymatic attack on the oxygen bridge of 2,3,7,8-TCDD which was recently demonstrated in dogs and rats (Poiger and Buser, 1983). The PCDF molecule has a more strained oxygen bridge which could facilitate enzymatic attack, and thus decreased retention. Similarly, retention differences between 2,3,4,7,8-and 1,2,3,7,8-PnCDF suggest the possibility of enzymatic attack at the oxygen bridge (Kuroki et al., 1980; Yoshihara et al., 1981). The much higher retention time of the former is most likely due to the presence of a chlorine atom at the C4-position which could sterically hinder the attack. From these studies it appears that the stereochemical aspects which influence PCDF/PCDD metabolism are: 1. the presence of vincinal hydrogen atoms, 2. chlorine substitution on the lateral positions, and 3. chlorine substitution on the C4-position of the PCDF molecule.

Besides the stereochemical influence on PCDD/PCDF metabolism, molecular size may also play an important role in PCDD/PCDF retention and metabolism (Norback and Allen, 1975; Williams et al., 1972; Firestone et al., 1979). For example, ingested mixtures of hepta- and octa-chlorinated isomers were more poorly adsorbed than lower chlorinated isomers in rat intestines.

COMMON TOXIC EFFECTS OF PCDDs, PCDFs AND RELATED HYDROCARBONS

A number of recent reviews and comparative studies clearly indicate marked similarities in the toxic responses displayed by animals exposed to PCDDs (notably 2,3,7,8-TCDD), PCDFs, PCBs and PBBs. Although there are marked species, age and sex differences, common toxic responses to these halogenated aryl hydrocarbons include:

1. a wasting syndrome: a progressive weight loss which may not be related simply to decreased food consumption;
2. skin disorders: acne-type eruptions or chloracne, alopecia, edema, hyperkeratosis and blepharitis due to hypertrophy of the Meibomian glands;
3. lymphoid involution: thymic and splenic atrophy with (a) associated humoral and/or cell-mediated immunosuppression and/or (b) associated bone marrow and hematologic dyscrasias;
4. porphyria: disordered porphyrin metabolism of the cutanea tarda type;
5. endocrine and reproductive dysfunction: altered plasma levels of steroid and thyroid hormones with (a) menstrual irregularities, reduced conception rate, early abortion, excessive menstrual and postconceptional hemorrhage and anovulation in females and (b) testicular atrophy and decreased spermatogenesis in males;
6. teratogenesis: cleft palate and kidney malformations (e.g., renal agenesis);
7. carcinogenesis: e.g., hepatocarcinoma.

There is evidence to suggest that the same toxic syndrome described above is also caused by polychlorinated naphthalenes (Brinkman and Reymer, 1976) and polychlorinated azo- and azoxybenzenes (Taylor et al., 1977; Poland et al., 1976). However, relatively little is known about the biologic and toxic effects of the individual congeners comprising these classes of halogenated aryl hydrocarbons. It is also interesting to note that hexachlorobenzene, well known to cause porphyria (Ockner and Schmid, 1961; Cam and Nigogosyan, 1963; Lissner et al., 1975; Den Tonkelaar et al., 1978; Mendoza et al., 1979; Courtney, 1979), also causes reproductive disorders (Grant et al., 1974, 1977; Iatropoulos et al., 1976), cancer (Cabral et al., 1977, 1979), and both cleft palate and renal agenesis (Khera, 1974; Courtney et al., 1976). However, in contrast to other halogenated aryl hydrocarbons, hexachlorobenzene stimulates, rather than depresses, immunologic functions and increases spleen weight (Kimbrough and Linder, 1974; Kuiper-Goodman et al., 1977; Gralla et al., 1977; Koss et al., 1978; Hansen et al., 1979; Vos et al., 1979a 1979b).

Not all species are equally sensitive to the toxic effects of halogenated aryl hydrocarbons. The dose of TCDD lethal to 50% of exposed laboratory animals (LD_{50}) shows guinea pigs, chickens, mink and monkeys to be among the more sensitive species (LD_{50}=1-50 µg/kg), followed by rats and rabbits (LD_{50}=50-100 µg/kg) with the mouse being among the more resistant species (LD_{50}=100-200 µg/kg). Some species, such as the frog (Rana catesbeiana), appear totally resistant to the toxic effects of TCDD even at doses of 1 mg/kg (i.e., a dose 1,000 times the LD_{50} for guinea pigs) (Beatty et al., 1976).

The latent period between the time of exposure and time of death is also species specific and ranges from about one week (e.g., guinea pig) to one month (e.g., Rhesus monkey). Interestingly, this latent period cannot be shortened by increasing the dose to a "superlethal" level.

Species also differ qualitatively in their response to halogenated aryl hydrocarbons. For example, the edematous disorder, hydropericardium, is specific to chickens. Certain qualitative differences seem to reflect differences in the body distribution of halogenated aryl hydrocarbons. The relatively high levels of TCDD in the skin of the Rhesus monkey may account for the high sensitivity of this primate to TCDD's acneogenic effects. However, the observation that the guinea pig is resistant to the hepatotoxic effects of TCDD, despite the fact that most of the administered TCDD resides in the liver, indicates that factors besides pharmacodynamic differences are important in determining the qualitative responses to halogenated aryl hydrocarbons. For a given species, the female is often more susceptible than the male to the toxic (including carcinogenic) effects of halogenated aryl hydrocarbons. Moreover, susceptibility to toxicity usually decreases with age.

COMMON BIOLOGIC EFFECTS OF PCDDs, PCDFs AND RELATED HYDROCARBONS

One of the most sensitive and easily measured biochemical responses to halogenated hydrocarbons is the induction of hepatic microsomal, cytochrome P-450-dependent monooxygenases. Inducers of these drug-metabolizing enzymes have been divided into three main categories; phenobarbitone (PB)-type inducers of cytochrome P-450; 3-methylcholanthrene (MC)-type inducers of cytochrome P-448; and mixed (PB + MC)-type inducers. PCDFs and PCDDs, notably 2,3,7,8-TCDD, are inducers of cytochrome P-448-dependent monooxygenases [e.g., aryl hydrocarbon hydroxylase (AHH)] whereas commercial PCB mixtures (e.g., Arochlor 1254) and PBB mixtures (e.g., FireMaster FF-1) are potent mixed-type inducers of both cytochromes. The mixed-type induction characteristics of Aroclor and FireMaster are presumably due to the activities of their component halogenated biphenyls. It has been of particular interest to categorize inducers of these enzymes, because for several classses of halogenated hydrocarbons, there appears to be good correlation between the toxicity of a chemical and its ability to induce microsomal AHH activity (Poland and Knutson, 1982; Poland et al., 1979).

STRUCTURE-ACTIVITY RELATIONSHIPS OF PCDDs AND PCDFs

2,3,7,8-TCDD is the most acutely toxic, halogenated aromatic compound. This property, coupled with frequent human exposure to 2,3,7,8-TCDD resulting from industrial accidents, has resulted in considerable research on PCDD isomers and congeners. Poland and Glover (Poland and Glover, 1973) investigated the effects of structure on the activity of PCDDs on aryl hydrocarbon hydroxylase (AHH) (Table 2) and γ-aminolevulinic acid sythetase in chick embryo liver. They noted a "perfect correspondence between the whole animal toxicity data on the dibenzo-p-dioxin congeners and their ability to induce both enzymes". Moreover, a complementary structure-activity relationship was observed for the induction of AHH activity in rat hepatoma H-4-II-E cells in culture (Bradlaw and Casterline, 1979; Bradlaw et al., 1980).

TABLE 2. PCDDs: Effects of Structure on AHH Induction, Receptor Binding and Toxicity

PCDD Congener	Relative % Activity		LD_{50} Guinea Pig ($\mu g/kg$)
	Binding Affinity	AHH Induction	
2,3,7,8-TCDD	100	100	2
1,2,3,7,8,9-HCDD	20	22	60-100
1,3,7,8-TCDD	16	8	-
1,3,7-TCDD	14	0.06	-
2,8-DCDD	0	0	300,000
1,2,3,4,6,7,8,9-OCDD	0	0	-

Using radiolabelled 2,3,7,8-TCDD as a probe, Poland and co-workers (1979) also demonstrated high affinity binding of this compound to a cytosolic protein in rat and mouse liver with an equilibrium dissocciation constant K_D = 0.27 nm and a maximum binding capacity of 84 fmol/mg of cytosolic protein. Competitive binding experiments with 2,3,7,8-[^{3}H]TCDD and competing, unlabelled PCDD isomers and congeners showed that there was also a correlation between their activities as AHH inducers and their receptor protein binding affinities (Poland et al., 1979). These results thus suggest a structure-activity relationship for PCDDs as AHH inducers and as ligands for the receptor protein: (a) the most active congener 2,3,7,8-TCDD, contains only four lateral chlorine substituents; (b) further chloro substitution of the 2,3,7,8-tetrachloro nucleus gives less active (or inactive), more highly chlorinated congeners; and (c) removal of the lateral chloro substituents gives less active (or inactive), lower chlorinated PCDDs.

Further confirmation of the role of the receptor in mediating the toxic and biologic effects of PCDDs was obtained in studies on the effects of 2,3,7,8-TCDD on the genetically inbred C57BL/6J and DBA/2J strains of mice. The C57BL/6J mice were highly susceptible to the toxicity of 2,3,7,8-TCDD and the LD_{50} for the induction of AHH activity was about 1 nmol/kg, and 2,3,7,8-[^{3}H]TCDD specifically binds to a hepatic cytosolic receptor protein in these animals. In contrast, the DBA/2J strain of mice was relatively "nonresponsive" to 2,3,7,8-TCDD. Effects were observed only at much higher concentrations (> 10 times) than those required for comparable effects in the responsive C57BL/6J mice. Moreover, incubation of 2,3,7,8-[^{3}H]TCDD with hepatic cytosol from the DBA/2J mice indicated that only trace amounts of the receptor protein were present (Okey and Vella, 1982). These data and experiments with genetically inbred, responsive and nonresponsive mouse strains clearly support the segregation of the activity of 2,3,7,8-TCDD with the Ah locus.

The effects of structure on the biologic and toxic effects of PCDFs have not been extensively investigated due to difficulties in synthesis. However, it is apparent from several studies, that comparable, structure-activity correlations are observed for both PCDFs and PCDDs (Yoshihara et al., 1981; Poland and Knutson, 1982; Poland et al.,1979; Nagayama et al., 1983). The most active compounds are substituted in the lateral 2,3,7 and 8 positions. Furthermore, the addition of Cl substituents and the removal of lateral substituents tend to reduce activity. The following table (3) illustrates the structure-activity effect observed for PCDFs.

TABLE 3. PCDFs: Effects of Structure on AHH Induction Receptor Binding and Toxicity[a]

PCDF Congener	No. of Lateral Cl groups	Relative % Activity AHH[b] Induction	Relative % Activity Binding Affinity	Thymic Atrophy
2,3,7,8	4	20	35	+++
2,3,4,7,8	4	100	100	+++
1,2,3,7,8	4	25	20	++
1,2,3,4,7,8	4	7.0	8	++
2,3,6,8	3	<1.0	7	+
2,8	2	<0.1	<0.1	−

[a]   Yoshihara et al.; 1981, Nagayama et al.; 1983, Bandiera et al., unpublished
[b]   Estimated from preliminary data

These results and the structure-activity correlations observed for PCBs and PBBs support a common mechanism of action for the halogenated aryl hydrocarbons.

PCDDs, PCDFs AND RELATED COMPOUNDS: IN VITRO BIOASSAYS AS A METHOD FOR HAZARD ASSESSMENT

The induction of AHH activity by the toxic, halogenated aromatic compounds can be used as a short term in vitro test for this group of chemicals. The bioassay uses a rat hepatoma cell line which possesses low basal AHH activity and is highly inducible (Benedict et al., 1973; Owens and Nebert, 1975, 1976). The amount of AHH induction is determined by the fluorimetric assay of 3-hydroxybenzo[a]pyrene formation (Nebert and Gelboin, 1968) from benzo[a]pyrene (the substrate for the AHH enzyme assay) or by the fluorimetric determination of 7-ethoxyresorufin 0-deethylation (Pohl and Fouts, 1980). This bioassay has been used to assess the effects of structure on the activity of PCDD congeners as AHH inducers (Owens and Nebert, 1975). Moreover, there is an excellent correlation between relative potencies using the cell-culture induction assay and other assays for biologic and toxic potencies. The ED_{50} for AHH induction by 2,3,7,8-TCDD was 1.54 pmol/plate and comparable results have been obtained in Safe's laboratory. Moreover, the correlation between the activity of PCB congeners as AHH inducers in the rat and the hepatoma cell line and their potency in the cytosol receptor assay has been recently confirmed using this assay (Kimbrough et al., 1978). This test can also be used to evaluate the presence of other biologically active, halogenated aromatics (i.e., AHH inducers) in food extracts (Bradlaw and Casterline, 1979). For example, several gelatin samples have been shown to contain pentachlorophenol and related PCDD impurities including the 1,2,3,6,7,8- and 1,2,3,7,8,9-hexachloro- and 1,2,3,4,6,7,8-heptachlorodibenzo-p-dioxins which exhibit AHH activity. The results confirmed the correlation between the concentration of the "toxic dioxins" in the samples and their "bioassay TCDD equivalents" (Bradlaw and Casterline, 1979). The specific binding of AHH inducers such as 2,3,7,8-TCDD to a high-affinity, low capacity, cytosolic receptor protein can be readily utilized as a bioassay for this group of compounds. The binding of a specific ligand or mixture of ligands can be determined by measuring the dose-dependent displacement of 3[H]-2,3,7,8-TCDD previously bound to the protein (Okey et al. 1979; Sawyer et al., 1983). From these results the EC_{50} values for the competing ligands can be calculated. This bioassay has been used for the analysis of a fraction containing a complex mixture of PCDDs and PCDFs which had been obtained by extraction of fly ash from a municipal incinerator (Lustenhouwer et al., 1980; Olie et al.,

1977; Kooke et al., 1981; Hutzinger et al., 1980). A detailed GC and GC-MS analysis of this sample was not possible. However, isomer-specific analysis for 2,3,7,8-TCDD indicated a concentration of 3.9 ng/m^3 or a total of 11.7 ng of this compound in the total extract (from 3 m^3 of air). The total PCDD/PCDF fraction was dissolved in 0.50 ml DMSO, and the activity of this fraction in displacing the [^{3}H]-TCDD from the hepatic cytosol receptor was compared to the competitive displacement of the [^{3}H]-TCDD by unlabelled TCDD.

The receptor assay was previously used to determine the binding affinity of the PCDD/PCDF fraction obtained from a Netherlands municipal incinerator fly ash extract. The results showed that the 2,3,7,8-TCDD or "dioxin equivalents" present in the fraction was over forty times higher than the actual concentration of 2,3,7,8-TCDD (Table 4). This is consistent with the contribution of the other biologically active PCDDs and PCDFs in this fraction. The estimated EC$_{50}$ values for the half-maximal induction of AHH and EROD by the extracts was 1.04×10^4 and 6.18×10^3 mm^3 of gaseous material/plate. Based on the EC$_{50}$ values obtained for the fly ash extract and taking into account the dilution factors, the estimated "dioxin content" of the Netherlands fly ash extract was 99.2 and 302.5 ng based on the AHH and EROD assays respectively. This represents an enhancement factor of 8-26, which is comparable to, but less than, that observed using the receptor bioassay.

Using a similar approach, the (active) "dioxin content" of five North American fly ash samples were estimated using the receptor and induction assays (Table 5). Based on the levels of TCDD in the Amsterdam fly ash, the 2,3,7,8-TCDD concentration equivalents of each fly ash extract can be calculated for five samples. The results show that the estimated concentrations of "active" 2,3,7,8-TCDD-like PCDDs/PCDFs using the AHH and EROD assays were comparable and followed the sample order $1 \geq 4 \geq 5 \geq 2,3$. These data were also consistent with the order of potency in the receptor assay, except that sample no. 4 exhibited twice the activity of the next most potent fly ash sample.

TABLE 4. PCDDs in North American Fly Ash Samples (ng/g)

Sample	Cl$_4$DD	Cl$_5$DD	Cl$_6$DD	Cl$_7$DD	Cl$_8$DD	PCDDs
1	85	213	354	184	97	918
2[a]	-	-	-	-	-	-
3	2.7	6.6	11.6	5.7	3.5	30.1
4	12.9	37.5	75.6	41.9	35.2	203.1
5	2.4	7.9	9.7	9.1	2.1	31.2

a <0.5 ng/g

TABLE 5. Comparative Bioassay Analysis of Fly Ash Extracts

Estimated Dioxin Content (ng/g)

Sample	PCDDs (ng/g)	PCDFs (ng/g)	AHH (ng/g)	EROD (ng/g)	Receptor Assay (ng/g)
1	918	2363	3.93	4.55	32
2	<0.5	<0.5	-	-	-
3	30.1	68.3	-	-	3.5
4	203.1	91.3	3.93	4.55	65.0
5	31.2	31.2	1.45	2.25	11

It is evident that the correlation between AHH-induction potencies and receptor-binding activities, which has been observed for individual PCDDs and PCDFs, is observed with some mixtures of these compounds. These results support the utility of this type of in vitro bioassay as a preliminary screening method for potential hazard assessment. However, it is not known if the toxic or biologic effects of PCDD and PCDF mixtures are additive, synergistic or antagonistic. This will require model studies with individual compounds and reconstituted mixtures. A recent report by Rizzardini and coworkers (Rizzardini et al., 1983) indicates that coadministration of 2,3,7,8-TCDD and 2,3,7,8-TCDF to C57BL/6J mice results in antagonistic or protective effects related to the induction of microsomal cytochrome P-450 and 7-ethoxycoumarin 0-deethylase. In a comparable experiment, 2,3,7,8-TCDD alone (1.2 ug/kg) inhibited antibody production (80%), whereas 2,3,7,8-TCDF (10 ug/kg) was inactive. Coadministration of both toxicants resulted in only 50% inhibition of antibody production. These protective or antagonistic effects contrast to the reported synergistic effects of coadministraiton of toxic haloaromatics on cleft-palate formation (J. McKinney, unpublished results). The apparently conflicting data on the interactive effects of halogenated aromatics require further clarification, because human exposure represents mostly exposure to a complex mixture of chemicals rather than exposure to an individual toxicant.

ELECTRE: JUDGING THE TOXICOLOGICAL SIGNIFICANCE OF DIFFERENT PCDD/PCDF SOURCES

This section is a first attempt at relating potential PCDD/PCDF sources with their possible effect in a mathematical way by Electre. Because many required data are not yet available and value judgements are often impossible to make, this exercise must be considered only as a example. Therefore, THE RESULTS DO NOT CONSTITUTE A VALID RISK ASSESSMENT.

For the purpose of this exercise, nine different PCDD/PCDF sources are considered:

1. Municipal incineration
2. Incineration of chemical waste
3. PCDFs in PCB
4. Transformer fires
5. 2,4,5-Trichlorophenol
6. Tetrachlorophenol
7. Pentachlorophenol
8. 2,4,5-Trichlorophenoxyacetic acid
9. Industrial chlorine processes

All these different sources produce qualitatively and quantitatively different mixtures of PCDD and PCDF congeners and isomers. For the purpose of this evaluation, production and use of different chlorophenols and 2,4,5-T are different entries. Also considered as different categories are PCDFs produced in commercial PCB and PCDFs formed during transformer fires. On the other hand, potential PCDD/PCDF sources from all other industrial processes are collected in one class.

The processes and factors important in the eventual toxic effect of PCDD/PCDF produced by different sources are the following:

1. Production: Amount of total PCDD/PCDF produced irrespective of their toxicity (structure), bioavailability and propensity for release.
2. Release: Potential for release.
3. Bioavailability: Factors which influence the bioavailability, e.g., strong adsorption.
4. Distribution: Potential for environmental dispersion, e.g., particulate matter in flue gases versus fly ash in dump sites.
5. Population Size: Size and density of population which is located near the source.
6. Toxicity: Toxic potential of PCDD and PCDF isomers and congeners present, e.g., 2,3,7,8-TCDD vs. octaCDD.

Criteria for Judgement of Sources

As indicated above, different PCDDs/PCDFs coming from different sources cannot be compared directly. Not only is this true from a toxicological point of view but also when route of release, environmental distribution and biological availability are considered.

The problem of judging several PCDD/PCDF pollution sources using a number of unrelated criteria can be approached by applying multicriteria-analysis methodology. One such method, Electre, has been developed for multicriteria analysis in the economic sciences (Nijkamp, 1977). Recently Electre was suggested for evaluation of environmentally important hazardous substances (Opperhuizen and Hutzinger, 1982).

By using non-comparable criteria, Electre can be applied in selecting alternatives, namely sources in this case. During the Electre procedure, all alternatives are compared as pairs in all criteria. This results in dominance relationships among all alternatives, so that ranking of the alternatives can be achieved. Some of the most elegant aspects of Electre are: (1) all criteria are scored in their own dimensions, and (2) all criteria can be weighed, so that the relative importance of the different criteria can be expressed.

Because the data on PCDDs and PCDFs necessary for an evaluation of this kind are very limited, only relative values for each criterion are used. As shown in Table 6., these relative values range from I to IX where IX represents the most important source (e.g., the highest production level, most toxic product, release in most densely populated areas, etc.), conversely, I is the least important source.

TABLE 6. Relative Importance of PCDD/PCDF Sources

	Production	Release	Bioavail-ability	Distribution	Pop. Density	Toxicity	
	A	B	C	D	E	F	
I	9	6	4	5	9	6	
II	3	5	3	5	6	5	
III	3	3	9	9	2	7	
IV	1	4	6	3	5	8	
V	5	1	8	4	4	9	
VI	6	5	9	4	4	6	
VII	8	7	9	6	7	6	
VIII	2	9	9	6	2	9	
IX	7	8	7	8	3	5	
Weight Factor	1	3	3	2	3	5	Total 17

I	Incineration
II	Chemical Waste Burning
III	PCDFs in PCBs
IV	Transformer Fires
V	$2,4,5-,Cl_3$- Phenol
VI	Cl_4- Phenol
VII	Cl_5- Phenol
VIII	2,4,5-T
IX	Cl- Processes

Moreover, each criterion has the weight factor indicated at the bottom of Table 6. For example, the table shows that toxicity has the highest weight factor.

Applying the data of Table 6, two concordance indicators, namely C_{mn} and C_{nm}, can be formed for each pair of sources. The value of C_{mn} is the sum of the criteria weights for which source m is not worse than source n. Thus, for every criterion that contributes to C_{mn}, the value of the m-score in Table 6 is lower or equal to the n-score.

These concordance indicators are summarized in Table 7. High C_{mn} values indicate that m, based on weighted criteria, is not worse than n.

TABLE 7. Summary of Concordance Indicators (C_{mn})

m / n	I	II	III	IV	V	VI	VII	VIII	IX
I		17	8	9	9	14	9	4	9
II	2		7	9	8	8	0	4	9
III	10	11		6	8	10	10	9	10
IV	8	8	11		6	6	5	3	8
V	8	9	9	11		10	5	8	10
VI	8	13	10	10	12		8	7	11
VII	13	17	10	12	12	17		9	12
VIII	13	13	14	14	13	13	13		11
IX	8	8	7	9	9	6	5	6	

Example:
C_{mn}
$C_{12} = 2$
$C_{21} = 1+3+3+2+3+5 = 17$

For those criteria which do not contribute to the concordance indicator of m versus n (C_{mn}), a discordance value can be calculated (D_{mn}). This D_{mn} value of criterion i, for which the m value in Table 6 is higher than the n value, is calculated by multiplication of the differences between the m and the n value by the weight of the criteria. Thus, for every m-n combination, several $d_{m,n,i}$ values can arise. To simplify the Electre selection, only the maximum value of the $d_{m,n,i}$ is chosen. This is called the discordance indicator. These indicator values are summarized for all source pairs in Table 8.

TABLE 8. Summary of Discordance Indicators (D_{mn})

m \ n	I	II	III	IV	V	VI	VII	VIII	IX
I		-	15(C)	10(F)	15(F)	15(C)	15(C)	15(C+F)	9(D)
II	9(E)		15(C)	15(F)	20(F)	18(C)	18(C)	20(F)	12(C)
III	21(E)	12(E)		9(E)	10(F)	6(B+E)	15(E)	18(B)	15(B)
IV	12(E)	4(D)	12(D)		6(C)	9(C)	9(B+C)	15(B)	12(B)
V	15(B)	12(B)	10(D)	9(B)		12(B)	18(B)	24(B)	21(B)
VI	15(E)	6(E)	16(D)	10(F)	15(F)		9(C)	15(F)	9(B)
VII	8(E)	-	6(D)	10(F)	15(F)	-		15(F)	4(D)
VIII	21(E)	12(E)	6(D)	15(E)	6(E)	6(E)	15(E)		4(D)
IX	18(E)	9(E)	16(F)	15(F)	20(F)	6(C)	12(E)	20(F)	

( ) = Criterion involved

Selection and Ranking of All Sources

According to Tables 7 and 8, it is obvious that the high C_{mn} and low D_{mn} values indicate that the n-source is worse than the m-source. To facilitate the selection, a value for p can be used to restrict C_{mn} values, and a value q to restrict D_{mn} values. By a step-wise decrease of p and increase of q, the following dominance rules can be obtained (Table 9):

TABLE 9. Choice of p Values for Ranking Sources

If p Value Is:	13	10
Source #		
1 is not worse than ...	7,8	3
2 is not worse than ...	6,7,8	3,6
3 is not worse than ...	8	4,6
4 is not worse than ...	8	5,6
5 is not worse than ...	8	6
6 is not worse than ...	7,8	1,3,5
7 is not worse than ...	8	--
8 is not worse than ...	--	--
9 is not worse than ...	--	3,5,6

With a p value of 13, sources 7 and 8 are normally worse than all others. According to Table 7, it can be seen that 8 is worse than 7. According to Table 8, source 9 is much better than 7 and 8. Using a p value of 11 and excluding sources 7 and 8, it is not easy to decide between sources 3, 5 and 6 solely by applying C_{mn} values. Based on the D_{mn} values from Table 8, source 6 is the worst of the three, whereas no simple distinction can be obtained between 3 and 5. However, a dominance in Table 7 of source 3 over 5 ($C_{35}=9$ while $C_{53}=8$), leads to a rather arbitrary distinction between the two. In distinguishing between 1,2 and 9, use of Table 8 results in a rapid estimation of 1, because of the significantly higher values of D_{ln} over D_{nl}. Moreover, source 2 is preferred over source 9, because D_{29} is 9 and D_{92} is 12.

In summary, the sources can be hierarchically ranked according to decreasing importance:

1.	2,4,5-T
2.	Cl_5-phenol
3.	Cl_4-phenol
4.	Cl_3-phenol
5.	PCDF in PCBs
6.	Incineration
7.	Transformer fires
8.	Cl-processes
9.	Chemical waste burning

ACKNOWLEDGEMENT

The financial assistance of the National Institutes of Health (ES02937) to S. Safe is gratefully acknowledged.

REFERENCES

Bandiera, S., Sawyer, T., Mason, G. and Safe, S. Unpublished results.

Beatty, P.W., Holscher, M.A. and Neal, R.A. 1976. Toxicity of 2,3,7,8-tetrachlorodibenzo-p-dioxin in larval and adult forms of Rana catesbeiana. Bull. Environ. Contam. Toxicol. 5:578-581.

Benedict, W.F., Geilen, J.E., Owens, T.S., Niwa, A. and Nebert, D. 1973. Aryl hydrocarbon induction in mammalian liver cell culture IV: Stimulation of the enzyme activity in established cell lines derived from rat or mouse hepatoma and from normal rat liver. Biochem. Pharmacol. 22:2766-2769.

Birnbaum, L.S., Decad, G.M. and Matthews, H.B. 1980. Disposition and excretion of 2,3,7,8-tetrachlorodibenzofuran in the rat. Toxicol. Appl. Pharmacol. 55:342-352.

Birnbaum, L.S., Decad, G.M., Matthews, H.B. and McConey, E.E. 1981. Fate of 2,3,7,8-TCDF in the monkey. Toxicol. Appl. Pharmacol. 57:189-196.

Bowes, G.W., Mulvihill, M.J., de Camp, M.R. and Kende, A.S. 1975a. Chromatographic characteristics of authentic chlorinated dibenzofurans: Identification of two isomers in American and Japanese polychlorinated biphenyls. J. Agric. Food Chem. 23:1222-1223.

Bowes, G.W., Mulvihill, M.J., Simoneit, B.R.T., Burlingame, A.L. and Risebrough, R.W. 1975b. Identification of chlorinated dibenzofurans in American polychlorinated biphenyls. Nature 256:305-307.

Bradlaw, J.A. and Casterline, J.L. Jr. 1979. Induction of enzyme activity in cell culture: A rapid screen for detection of planar polychlorinated organic compounds. J. Assoc. Offic. Anal. Chem. 62:904-916.

Bradlaw, J.A., Garthoff, L.G., Hurley, N.E. and Firestone, D. 1980. Comparative induction of aryl hydrocarbon hydroxylase activity in vitro by analogues of dibenzo-p-dioxin. Food Cosmet. Toxicol. 18:627-635.

Brinkman, U.A.Th. and Reymer, H.G.M. 1976. Polychlorinated naphthalenes. J. Chromatog. 127:203-243.

Buser, H.R. 1975. Analysis of polychlorinated dibenzodioxin and dibenzofurans in chlorinated phenols by mass fragmentography. J. Chrom. 107:295-310.

Buser, H.R. 1978. Polychlorinated dibenzo-p-dioxins and dibenzofurans: Formation, occurrence and analysis of environmentally hazardous compounds. Thesis, University of Umea, Sweden.

Buser, H.R. 1979. Formation of polychlorinated dibenzofurans and dibenzo-p-dioxins from the pyrolysis of chlorobenzenes. Chemosphere 8:415-424.

Buser, H.R. and Bosshardt, H.P. 1970. Polychlorierte dibenzo-p-dioxine, dibenzofurane und benzole in der asche kommunaler und industrieller verbrennungsanlagen. Mitt. Geb. Lebensmittelunters. Hyg. 69:191-199.

Buser, H.R. and Bosshardt, H.P. 1974. Determination of 2,3,7,8-tetrachlorodibenzo-1,4-dioxin at parts per billion levels in technical grade 2,3,5-trichlorophenoxyacetic acid, in 2,4,5-T allylester and 2,4,5-T amine salt herbicide formations by quadruple mass fragmentography. J. Chrom. 90:71-77.

Buser, H.R. and Bosshardt, H.P. 1976. Determination of polychlorinated dibenzo-p-dioxins and dibenzofurans by combined gas chromatography-mass spectrometry. J. Assoc. Offic. Anal. Chem. 59:562-569.

Buser, H.R., Bosshardt, H.P., Rappe, C. and Lindahl, R. 1978. Identification of polychlorinated dibenzofuran isomers in fly ash and PCB pyrolyses. Chemosphere 5:419-429.

Buser, H.R., Bosshardt, M.P. and Rappe, C. 1978. Formation of polychlorinated dibenzofurans (PCDFs) from the pyrolysis of PCBs. Chemosphere 7:109-119.

Buser, H.R. and Rappe, C. 1979. Identification of polychlorinated dibenzofurans (PCDFs) retained in patients with Yusho. Chemosphere 8:157-174.

Buser, H.R., Rappe, C. and Gara, A. 1978. Polychlorinated dibenzofurans (PCDFs) found ing Yusho oil and in used Japanese PCBs. Chemosphere 7:439-449.

Cabral, J.R.P., Shubik, P., Mollner, T. and Raitano, F. 1977. Carcinogenic activity of hexachlorobenzene in hamsters. Nature 269:510-511.

Cabral, J.R.P, Mollner, T., Raitano, F. and Shubik, P. 1979. Carcinogenesis of hexachlorobenzene in mice. Int. J. Cancer 23:47.

Cam, C. and Nigogosyan, G. 1963. Acquired toxic porphyria cutanea tarda due to hexachlorobenzene. J. Amer. Med. Assoc. 183:88-92.

Chen, P.H., Gaw, J.M., Wong, C.K. and Chen, C.J. 1980. Levels and gas chromatographic patterns of polychlorinated biphenyls in the blood of patients after PCB poisoning in Taiwan. Bull. Environ. Contam. Toxicol. 25:325-329.

Courtney, K.D. 1979. Hexachlorobenzene (HCB): A review. Environ. Res. 20:225-266.

Courtney, K.D., Copeland, M.F. and Robbins, A. 1976. The effects of pentachloronitrobenzene, hexachlorobenzene and related compounds on fetal development. Toxicol. Appl. Pharmacol. 35:239-256.

Decad, G.M., Birnbaum, L.S. and Matthews, H.B. 1981a. Distribution and excretion of 2,3,7,8-TCDF in C57BL/6J and DBA/2J mice. Toxicol. Appl. Pharmacol. 59:564-573.

Decad, G.M., Birnbaum, L.S. and Matthews, H.B. 1981b. 2,3,7,8-TCDF tissue distribution and excretion in guinea pigs. Toxicol. Appl. Pharmacol. 57:231-240.

Den Tonkerlaar, E.M., Verschuuren, H.G., Bankovska, J., DeVries, T., Kroes, R. and Van Esch, G.J. 1978. Hexachlorobenzene toxicity in pigs. Toxicol. Appl. Pharmacol. 43:137-145.

Esposito, M.P., Tiernan, T.O. and Dryden, F.E. 1980. Dioxins. EPA-600/2-80-197.

Fara, G.M. 1983. The work of the International Steering Committee for the study of the Health effects of the Seveso accident: Its methodology, its issues and its conclusions. Chemosphere 12:785-790.

Firestone, D., Ress, J., Brown, N.L., Barron, R.P. and Damico, J. 1972. Determination of polychlorodibenzo-p-dioxins and related compounds in commercial chlorophenols. J. Assoc. Off. Anal. Chem. 55:85-92.

Firestone, D., Clower, M., Borsetti, A.P., Teske, R.H. and Long, P.F. 1979. Polychlorodibenzo-p-dioxin and pentachlorophenol residues in milk and blood of cows fed technical pentachlorophenol. J. Agric. Food Chem. 27:1171-1177.

Gizzi, F., Reginato, R., Benfenati, E. and Fanelli, R. 1982. Comparative induction of aryl hydrocarbon hydroxylase activity in vitro by analogues of dibenzo-p-dioxin. Chemosphere 11:577-583.

Gralla, E.J., Fleischman, R.W., Luthra, Y.K., Hagopian, M., Baker, J.R., Esber, H. and Marcus, W. 1977. Toxic effects of hexachlorobenzene after daily administration to beagle dogs for one year. Toxicol. Appl. Pharmacol. 40:227-239.

Grant, D.L., Iverson, F., Hatina, G.V. and Villeneuve, D.C. 1974. Effects of hexachlorobenzene on liver porphyrin levels and microsomal enzymes in the rat. Environ. Physiol. Biochem. 4:159-163.

Grant, D.L., Phillips, W.E.J. and Hatina, G.V. 1977. Effect of hexachlorobenzene on reproduction in the rat. Arch. Environ. Contam. Toxicol. 5:207-216.

Greenlee, W.F. and Poland, A. 1979. Nuclear uptake of 2,3,7,8-TCDD in C57BL/6J and DBA/2J mice. J. Biol. Chem. 254:9814-9821.

Hansen, L.G., Simon, J., Dorn, S.B. and Teske, R.H. 1979. Hexachlorobenzene distribution in tissues of swine. Toxicol. Appl. Pharmacol. 51:1-7.

Hardell, L. 1980. Relation of soft tissue sarcoma, malignant lymphoma and colon cancer to phenoxy acids, chlorophenols and other agents. Scand. J. Work and Environ. Health 7:119-130.

Heida, H. 1983. TCDD in bottom sediments and eel around a refuse dump near Amsterdam, Holland. Chemosphere 12:503-509.

Huckins, J.N, Stalling, D.L. and Smith, W.A. 1978. Foam-charcoal chromatography for analysis of polychlorinated dibenzodioxins in Herbicide Orange. J. Assoc. Off. Anal. Chem. 61:32-38.

Hutzinger, O., Olie, K., Lustenhouwer, J.W.A., Okey, A.B., Bandiera, S. and Safe, S. 1980. Polychlorinated dibenzo-p-dioxins (PCDD) and polychlorinated dibenzofurans (PCDF) in emission from urban incinerators, average and peak values. Chemosphere 10:19-25.

Iatropoulos, M.J., Hobson, W., Knauf, V. and Adams, H.P. 1976. Morphological effects of hexachlorobenzene toxicity in female rhesus monkeys. Toxicol. Appl. Pharmacol. 37:433-444.

Jones, P.A. 1981. Chlorinated phenols in the environment. E.P.S. Canada 3-EC-81-2.

Kashimoto, T., Miyata, H. and Kunita, N. 1981. The presence of polychlorinated quaterphenyls in the tissues of Yusho victims. Food Cosmet. Toxicol. 19:334-340.

Khera, K.S. 1974. Teratogenicity and dominant lethal studies on hexachlorobenzene in rats. Food Cosmet. Toxicol. 12:471-477.

Kimbrough, R.D. and Linder, R.E. 1974. The toxicity of technical hexachlorobenzene in the Sherman strain rat: A preliminary study. Res. Commun. Cheml. Pathol. Pharmacol. 8:653-664.

Kimbrough, R., Buckley, J., Fishbein, L., Flamm, G., Kaza, L., Marcus, W., Shibko, S.,and Teske, R. 1978. Animal Toxicology. Environ. Health Perspect. 24:173-184.

Kooke, R.M.M., Lustenhouwer, J.W.A., Olie, K. and Hutzinger, O. 1981. Extraction efficiencies of polychlorinated dibenzo-p-dioxins and polychlorinated dibenzofurans from fly ash. Anal. Chem. 53:461-463.

Koss, G., Seubert, S., Seubert, A., Koransky, W. and Ippen, H. 1978. Studies on the toxicology of hexachlorobenzene. III. Observations on a long-term experiment. Arch. Toxicol. 40:285-294.

Kuiper-Goodman, T., Grant, D.L., Moodie, C.A., Korstrud, G.O. and Munro, I.C. 1977. Subacute toxicity of hexachlorobenzene in the rat. Toxicol. Appl. Pharmacol. 40:529-549.

Kuroki, H., Masuda, Y., Yoshihara, S. and Yoshimura, H. 1980. Accumulation of polychlorinated dibenzofurans in the livers of monkeys and rats. Food Cosmet. Toxicol. 18:387-392.

Liberti, A., Goretti, G. and Russo, M.V. 1983. PCDD and PCDF formation in the combustion of vegetable wastes. Chemosphere 12:661-663.

Lissner, R., Goerz, G., Eichenauer, M.G. and Ippen, H. 1975. Hexachlorobenzene-induced porphyria in rats: Relationship between porphyrin excretion and induction of drug-metabolizing liver enzymes. Biochem. Pharmacol. 24:1729-1731.

Lustenhouwer, J.W.A., Olie, K. and Hutzinger, O. 1980. Chlorinated dibenzo-p-dioxins and related compounds in incinerator effluents. Chemosphere 9:501-522.

May, G. 1983. TCDD: A study of subjects 10 and 14 years after exposure. Chemosphere 12:771-778.

Mendoza, C.E., Shields, J.B. and Laver, G.W. 1979. Comparison of the porphyrinogenic activity of hexabromobenzene and hexachlorobenzene in primiparous Wistar rats. Bull. Environ. Contam. Toxicol. 21:358-364.

Miyata, H., Murakami, T. and Kashimoto, T. 1979. Investigation on organochlorinated compounds formed in Kanemi rice oil that caused the "Yusho". J. Food Hyg. Soc. Japan 20:1.

Nagayama, J., Kuroki, H., Masuda, Y. and Kuratsune, M. 1983. A comparative study of polychlorinated dibenzofurans, polychlorinated biphenyls and 2,3,7,8-TCDD on aryl hydrocarbon hydroxylase inducing potency in rats. Arch. Toxicol. 53:177-184.

Neal, R.A., Olson, J.R., Gasiewicz, T.A. and Geiger, L.E. 1982. The toxicokinetics of 2,3,7,8-tetrachlorodibenzo-p-dioxin in mammalian systems. Drug Metab. Rev. 13:355-385.

Nebert, D.W. and Gelboin, H.V. 1968. Substrate-inducible microsomal aryl hydrocarbon hydroxylase in mammalian cell culture. I. Assay and properties of induced enzyme. J. Biol. Chem. 243:6242-6249.

Nijkamp, P. 1977. Theory and application of environmental economics. North Holland Publishers, Amsterdam.

Nilsson, C.A., Norstrom, A., Andersson, K. and Rappe, C. 1978. Impurities in commercial products related to pentachlorophenol. In Pentachlorophenol: Chemistry, Pharmacology, and Environmental Toxicology, ed. K.R. Rao, pp. 313-323, Plenum Press, New York.

Norback, D.H. and Allen, J.R. 1975. Tissue distribution and excretion of octachlorodibenzo-p-dioxin in the rat. Toxicol. Pharmacol. 32: 330-338.

Norstrom, A., Rappe, C., Lindahl, R. and Buser, H.R. 1980. Analysis of some older Scandinavian formations of 2,4-dichlorophenoxy-acetic acid and 2,4,5-trichlorophenoxyacetic acid for contents of chlorinated dibenzo-p-dioxins and dibenzofurans. Scand. J. Work Environ. Health 5:375-378.

Norstrom, R.J., Hallett, D.J., Simon, M. and Mulvihill, M.J. 1982. Analysis of Great Lakes herring gull eggs for tetrachlorodibenzo-p-dioxins. In Chlorinated Dioxins and Related Compounds, eds. O. Hutzinger, R.W. Frei, E. Merian, F. Pocchiari, pp. 173-181,Pergamon Press, Oxford.

Ockner, R.K. and Schmid, R. 1961. Acquired porphyria in man and rat due to hexachlorobenzene intoxication. Nature 189:499.

Okey, A.B. and Vella, L.M. 1982. Binding of 3-methylcholanthrene and 2,3,7,8-tetrachlorodibenzo-p-dioxin to a common Ah-receptor site in mouse and rat hepatic cytosols. Eur. J. Biochem. 127:39-47.

Okey, A.B., Bondy, G.P., Mason, M.E., Kahl, G.F., Eisen, H.J., Guenthner, T.M. and Nebert, D.W. 1979. Regulatory gene product of the Ah locus. J. Biol. Chem. 254:11636-11648.

Olie, K., Vermeulen, P.L. and Hutzinger, O. 1977. PCDD and PCDF trace constituents of fly ash and flue gas of some municipal incinerators in the Netherlands. Chemosphere 6:454-459.

Olie, K., van den Berg, M. and Hutzinger, O. 1983. Formation and fate of PCDD and PCDF from combustion processes. Chemosphere 12:627-636.

Opperhuizen, A. and Hutzinger, O. 1982. Multi-criteria analysis and risk assessment. Chemosphere 11:675-678.

Owens, I.S. and Nebert, D.W. 1975. Aryl hydrocarbon hydroxylase induction in mammalian liver-derived cell cultures. Mol. Pharmacol. 11:94-104.

Owens, I.S. and Nebert, D.W. 1976. Aryl hydrocarbon hydroxylase induction in mammalian liver-derived cell cultures: Effects of various metabolic inhibitors on the enzyme activity in hepatoma cells. Biochem. Pharmacol. 25:805-813.

Pohl, R.J. and Fouts, J.R. 1980. A rapid method for assaying the metabolism of 7-ethoxyresorufin by microsomal subcellular fractions. Anal. Biochem. 107:150-155.

Poiger, H. and Buser, H.R. 1983. Structure elucidation of mammalian TCDD-metabolites. In Human and Environmental Risks of Chlorinated Dioxins and Related Compounds, eds. R.E. Tucker, A.L. Young and A.P. Gray, pp. 483-492, Plenum Press, New York.

Poland, A. and Glover, E. 1973. Chlorinated dibenzo-p-dioxins: Potent inducers of -aminolevulinic acid synthetase and aryl hydrocarbon hydroxylase. II. A study of the structure activity relationship. Mol. Pharmacol. 9:736-747.

Poland, A., Glover, E., Kende, A.S., DeKamp, M. and Giandomenico, C.M. 1976. 3,4,3',4'-tetrachloroazoxybenzene and azobenzene: Potent inducers of aryl hydrocarbon hydroxylase. Science 194:627-630.

Poland, A., Greenlee, W.F. and Kende, A.S. 1979. Studies on the mechanism of toxicity of the chlorinated dibenzo-p-dioxins and related compounds. Ann. N.Y. Acad. Sci.

320:214-230.

Poland, A. and Knutson, J.C. 1982. 2,3,7,8-TCDD and related halogenated aromatic hydrocarbons: Examination of the mechanisms of toxicity. Ann. Rev. Pharmacol. Toxicol. 22:517-554.

Rappe, C. and Buser, H.R. 1980. Chemical properties and analytical methods. In Halogenated Biphenyls, Terphenyls, Naphthalenes, Dibenzodioxins and Related Products, ed. R. Kimbrough, pp. 41-76, Elsevier, Amsterdam.

Rappe, C., Gara, A. and Buser, H.R. 1975. Identification of polychlorinated dibenzofurans (PCDFs) in commercial chlorophenol preparations. Chemosphere 7:981-991.

Rappe, C., Buser, H.R. and Bosshardt, H.P. 1978. Identification and quantification of polychlorinated dibenzo-p-dioxins (PCDDs) and dibenzofurans (PCDFs) in 2,4,5-T ester formulations and Herbicide Orange. Chemosphere 7:431-438.

Rappe, C., Buser, H.R. and Bosshardt, H.P. 1979. Dioxins, dibenzofurans, and other polyhalogenated aromatics: Production, use, formation and destruction. Ann. N.Y. Acad. Sci. 320:1-18.

Rappe, C., Buser, H.R., Stalling, D.L., Smith, L.M. and Dougherty, R.C. 1981. Identification of polychlorinated dibenzofurans in environmental samples. Nature 292:524-526.

Rappe, C., Nygren, M., Buser, H.R. and Kauppinen, T. 1982. Occupational exposure to polychlorinated dioxins and dibenzofurans. In Chlorinated Dioxins and Related Compounds, eds. O. Hutzinger, R.W. Frei, E. Merian, F. Pocchiari, pp. 495-513, Pergamon Press.

Rappe, C., Marklund, S., Berqvist, P.A. and Hansson, M. 1983a. Polychlorinated dibenzo-p-dioxins, dibenzofurans and other polynuclear aromatics formed during incineration and polychlorinated biphenyl fires. In Chlorinated Dioxins and Dibenzofurans in the Total Environment, eds. G. Choudhary, L.H. Keith and C. Rappe, pp. 99-124, Butterworth Publishers, Boston.

Rappe, C., Nygren, M., Buser, H., Masuda, Y., Kuroki, H. and Chen, P.H. 1983b. Identification of polychlorinated dioxins (PCDDs) and dibenzofurans (PCDFs) in human samples, occupational exposure and Yusho patients. In Human and Environmental Risks of Chlorinated Dioxins and Related Compounds, eds. R.E. Tucker, A.L. Young and A.P. Gray, pp. 241-253, Plenum Press, New York.

Reggiani, C. 1982. Toxicology of TCDD and related compounds: Observations in man. In Chlorinated Dioxins and Related Compounds, eds. O. Hutzinger, R.W. Frei, E.Merian and F. Pocchiari, pp. 463-493, Pergamon Press, Oxford.

Rizzardini, M., Romano, M., Tursi, F., Salmona, M., Vecchi, A., Sironi, M. Gizzi, F., Benfenati, E., Garattini, S. and Fanelli, R. 1983. Toxicological evaluation of urban waste incinerator emissions. Chemosphere 12:559-564.

Ryan, J.J., Lau, P.Y., Pilon, J.C. and Lewis, D. 1983. 2,3,7,8-Tetrachlorodibenzo-p-dioxin and 2,3,7,8-tetrachlorodibenzofuran residues in Great Lakes commercial and sport fish. In Chlorinated Dioxins and Dibenzofurans in the Total Environment, eds. G. Choudhary, L.H. Keith and C. Rappe, pp. 87-97, Butterworth Publishers, Boston.

Sawyer, T., Bandiera, S., Safe, S., Hutzinger, O. and Olie, K. 1983. Bioanalysis of polychlorinated dibenzofuran and dibenzo-p-dioxin mixtures in fly ash. Chemosphere

12:529-535.

Schecter, A. 1983. Contamination of an office building in Binghampton, N.Y. by PCBs, dioxins, furans and biphenylenes after an electrical panel and electrical transformer incident. Chemosphere 12:669-680.

Shepard, B.M. 1980. Review of literature on herbicides, including phenoxyherbicides and associated dioxins, Veterans Administration, VA 101 (93), p. 823, Washington, D.C.

Stalling, D.L., Smith, L.M., Petty, J.D., Hogan, J.W., Johnson, J.L., Rappe, C. and Buser, H.R. 1983. Residues of polychlorinated dibenzo-p-dioxins and dibenzofurans in Laurentian Great Lakes fish. In Human and Environmental Risks of Chlorinated Dioxins and Related Compounds, eds. R.E. Tucker, A.L. Young and A.P. Gray, pp. 221-240, Pergamon Press, Oxford.

Taylor, J.S., Wuthrich, R.C., Lloyd, K.M. and Poland, A. 1977. Chloracne from manufacture of a new pesticide. Arch. Dermatol. 113:616-619.

Tiernan, T.O., Taylor, M.L., Garrett, J.H., van Ness, G.F., Solch, J.G., Deis, D.A. and Wagel, D.J. 1983. Chlorodibenzodioxins, chlorodibenzofurans and related compounds in the effluents from combustion processes. Chemosphere 12:595-606.

Tulp, M.Th.M. and Hutzinger, O. 1978. Rat metabolism of polychlorinated dibenzo-p-dioxins. Chemosphere 7:761-768.

van den Berg, M., Olie, K. and Hutzinger, O. 1983. Uptake and selective retention in rats of orally administered chlorinated dioxins and dibenzofurans from fly ash and fly ash extract. Chemosphere 12:537-544.

Vos, J.G., Koeman, J.H., van der Maas, H.L., ten Oever de Brauw, M.C. and Vos, R.H. 1970. Identification and toxicological evaluation of chlorinated dibenzofuran and chlorinated naphthalenes in two commercial polychlorinated biphenyls. Food Cosmet. Toxicol. 8:625-633.

Vos, J.G., Van Logten, M.J., Kreeftenberg, J.G. and Kruizinga, W. 1979a. Hexachlorobenzene-induced stimulation of the humoral immune response in rats. Ann. N.Y. Acad. Sci. 320:535-550.

Vos, J.G., Van Logten, M.J., Kreeftenberg, J.G., Steerenberg, P.A. and Kruizinga, W. 1979b. Effect of HCB on the immune system of rats following combined pre- and postnatal exposure. Drug Chem. Toxicol. 2:61-76.

Williams, D.T., Cunningham, H.M. and Blanchfield, B.J. 1972. Distribution and excretion studies of octachlorodibenzo-p-dioxin in the rat. Bull. Environ. Contam. Toxicol. 7:57-62.

Yoshihara, S., Nagata, K., Yoshimura, H., Kuroki, H. and Masuda, Y. 1981. Inductive effect on hepatic enzymes and acute toxicity of individual polychlorinated dibenzofuran congeners in rats. Toxicol. Appl. Pharmacol. 59:580-588.

Young, A.L. and Shepard, B.L. 1983. A review of on-going epidemiological research in the U.S. on the phenoxy herbicides and chlorinated dioxin contaminants. Chemosphere 12:749-759.

Chapter 3

DIOXINS: SOME TECHNICAL POLICY ISSUES FOR THE U.S.

William W. Lowrance
Senior Fellow and Director
Life Sciences and Public Policy Program
The Rockefeller University

"Public policy" is a desired course of action--for the country, for the state, or for some group within society. What are the desired courses of action on dioxin? And what considerations should be weighed as we move toward setting policy? I would like to develop a portrait of where the issue stands and what problems we are trying to solve.

My first observation is that there are quite serious reasons for concern about dioxins. It is a very mysterious, potentially very toxic, family of compounds.

We can detect the dioxins more sensitively, using chemical-analytic methods, than any other compound on earth. I believe there is no other substance that we can reliably detect at the sensitivity we do dioxins. It is now possible to detect them down to parts-per-quadrillion. I remember when parts-per-million was a pretty big accomplishment. Parts-per-billion was a sufficient accomplishment to garner notices in Nature and Science. Then we got to parts-per-trillion. And now we are hearing about parts-per-quadrillion--extraordinary sensitivity. The analytic chemists have moved quickly and are saying that dioxins are there: in the environment; in fish; in our bodies.

But the big question is: So what? We really don't know. Facetiously I would suggest that we need to declare a moratorium on dioxin analytical chemistry for about ten years! The precision and accuracy of its findings are so many orders of magnitude ahead of the abilities of the health and environmental sciences to interpret them that the chemists could slow down and we wouldn't lose very much.

The compounds are widely diffused. There are tiny traces of them, perhaps not everywhere, but in many places. However, there are "hot spots" at old industrial sites, current industrial sites, and places where the materials have been used in the past. The dioxins are persistent. They tend to accumulate in the fatty tissues of living organisms, and move up the food chain.

The compounds are extraordinarily toxic to lower species; there is no contesting that. Yet the mystery is that human beings who have been exposed as a result of the accident at Seveso or other industrial situations are not clearly dying from that exposure.

Overall, we just don't know enough. Scientifically, we are in such an uncertain position that it is very difficult to know what policy to take. So our policy has to be one of strategic development. How are we going to tackle these things? We can't do everything at once. I will mention a couple of discrete problems.

First, the materials come from a lot of sources. Dr. Hutzinger made it very clear that dioxins have many origins. I see the dioxin problem as being, in part, like the asbestos problem in being a leftovers problem. I don't think we are likely ever again to have the national difficulty with these compounds that we've had in the past years. Nor do I think we are likely to generate similar compounds in the future without more concern and more control. And, like asbestos, we are going to have to clean the messes up. That already has cost our national treasury quite a lot, and it will cost a good bit more.

Second, we need to worry not only about TCDD, but about all of the dioxins and related compounds. That's a big challenge. How many of dioxin's relatives do we have to look at? Is it more efficient to try to look at the furans along with the dioxins, or to pursue them separately? I can't believe that we shouldn't be doing them all at one time. The difficulty is to put the furans, and the other related compounds, on the agenda for research without unduly alarming the public and causing another crisis of the sort we have had with the dioxins. Dioxins, to review for any who are not chemists, are a fairly large family of compounds. The ones we are talking about, the chlorinated dibenzodioxins, come in seventy-five varieties. TCDD, familiarly known that way because its full name is tetrachlorodibenzodioxin, is the one that people have been most concerned about. We have to keep pressing the issue of whether we want to know about just that particular variety, TCDD, or about all of the others. On most tests TCDD is one of the most toxic. TCDD is also one of the most prevalent in the environment, but there are other compounds out there that have been far less thoroughly studied. The dibenzofurans are close relatives and they come in even more isomers, more varieties, than the dioxins.

Now, those of you who are toxicologists start thinking: Goodness, we have now spent ten or fifteen years doing expensive detailed toxicology on TCDD--how are we ever going to do the next hundred of these compounds? They are difficult to study, and they are dangerous to study. How do we handle such possibly toxic materials in the middle of major medical centers or universities?

All around the country we have studied environmental samples, looking mainly for TCDD, but not for the other isomers, or looking at the dioxins, but not the furans. We need to be making decisions in central places like the U.S. Environmental Protection Agency, to decide what we are going to analyze for. Wouldn't there be efficiencies in doing them all at one time? Wouldn't there be efficiencies in synthesizing standard reference samples of furans and dioxins, maybe radioactively labeled, so that they can be studied analytically and toxicologically? Shouldn't we make a national investment in preparing a stockpile of materials whose identity we are absolutely certain of, that could be distributed to investigators who have need to use them? It wouldn't have to be very much material; to the analytical chemists, a stockpile is an amount you can hardly see.

A third set of considerations has to do with exposure. Our principal concern is whether we are exposed to these compounds. They cannot harm us unless they actually enter our bodies. In some ways this is a fairly simple question but it hasn't been pursued very well with dioxins and related materials.

In the last few months, we have seen the results of the first fat assays. The U.S. Veterans Administration took veterans' fat samples. The Canadian government looked at fat from cadavers of people in Ontario. The Swedes have studied fat from people living in forested areas and in cities in Sweden. All of these analyses are now being completed, and we are beginning to see a pattern in the controls as well as those who have had possible exposure as a result of their work or location. Something on the order of a part-per-trillion of dioxins is being found in the fat. It is beginning to appear that there is something like a part-per-trillion in human fat in many parts of the world. I would be surprised if it doesn't turn out to be ubiquitous in our tissues the way DDT is, although at much lower concentrations than DDT. (It is not clear that this DDT in our tissues does anything to us.) We need to know the background level, so when we are concerned about accidents, fires, and other such possible exposure situations, we can decide what is getting into people's bodies.

The route of exposure can be through drinking water, or through soil (either via dermal absorption or through breathing airborne soil). It can even be, in the case of children, from eating the soil. Nobody really knows how to estimate how many grams of soil children eat. At Times Beach, Missouri, part of the analytic problem has been to estimate how much dioxin the children have taken into their bodies by ingestion, inhalation, or skin contact with soil.

We need indicators of exposure. It may be that, in addition to analyzing for the chemical, we can use methods of the kind Dr. Hutzinger was describing and look at the induction of enzymes. Another possibility is that immunological assays would give some index to human exposure. I think it is crucial to develop better indices. One index that has been referred to repeatedly, but that I think is problematic, is that of chloracne. On occasion the statement has been made that if a person doesn't develop this skin condition, chloracne, and lacks other clinical symptoms, they are not likely to develop them; this assertion has not been fully tested. I have heard of cases in which clinicians believe that some of their patients have had other clinical signs but simply have not had chloracne. According to some dermatologists, chloracne itself is rather difficult to identify.

The possible modes of human toxicity are many. In animal studies, we know that dioxin exposure induces formation of hepatic and other enzymes, and development of chloracne-like symptoms in a number of species. Cancer can be induced by routine feeding. A variety of reproductive effects, especially birth defects and spontaneous abortions, are induced in animals. Immunological consequences also occur in animals. In people, the story is just not so clear. We are trying to learn from accidents and other unfortunate human exposures. Certainly we don't have the complete portfolio.

It is clear to me that we should not limit ourselves to the set of mechanisms mediated by the so-called "cytosolic receptor". For the moment, we should keep a lot of mechanistic possibilities open and investigate many different ones at the same time. The work on the P-450 system receptor system is elegant work, but I am not sure it can account for the effects that occur in the whole organism. We should keep a lot of approaches going until we learn more, and then go more deeply into one or two possibilities.

Do the dioxins cause cancer? Again, it's a very mixed review. I think it can now be said from the mouse assays done by Dr. Kociba and his colleagues at Dow, and by others at the National Cancer Institute and elsewhere, that dioxins, at some doses, are indeed carcinogenic to rodents.

Furthermore, the dioxins appear to be carcinogenic promoters; that is, they not only induce cancer themselves but they seem to have a potentiating effect. If administered to rodents in very, very low concentrations, low even compared to the ones it takes to induce cancer, somehow they potentiate the effects of benzpyrene and other chemicals that we know are carcinogenic for human beings. The fact that they are promoters in rodents, and perhaps in humans, raises a whole set of new policy questions. I don't think the country has dealt with the promoter question for any carcinogen. What should be done about a compound that potentiates the effects of other carcinogens? Should we treat it differently from the way we do other carcinogens? I have no answer, except to say that I think we should take a very cautious course. We don't have any scientific way at the moment of deciding how to treat them, other than by treating them as strong carcinogens. Maybe over time we will think of some other way. This is one of the features of dioxins that make them different from most compounds.

What is the prime type of cancer that dioxins are conjectured to cause in human beings? The principal kind suggested is soft-tissue sarcoma. Some of the reports are dubious.

That turns out to be a very "soft" category. A wide range of pathological conditions are covered by the rubric, "soft tissue sarcoma". Sarcomas are very abnormal growths. They can affect everything from the blood to the brain and a lot of other tissues. It is very difficult to identify them and count them for epidemiologic analyses. Sarcoma registries have now been set up in several states. They have been developed for the workplace by the National Institute for Occupational Safety and Health; that registry is now four or five years old. The International Agency for Research on Cancer is helping coordinate the development of sarcoma registries in different countries, and the National Cancer Institute is undertaking a new program to do very much the same thing. Those registries will help. But obviously it will take many years before enough legitimate soft tissue sarcoma cases can be confirmed, and can be traced back to look for associations that can indicate causes for those cancers.

What we need most of all is a sense of proportion. Several previous speakers said they aren't convinced that dioxins are the most toxic things around; certainly I am not. But we need to develop that sense of proportion. We need to compare the dioxins to other trace compounds in the environment. How bad are they compared to similar compounds and to less similar compounds? Can we compare them to other carcinogens? In this country we have worked on many dozens or hundreds, depending on how you look at it, of substances suspected of causing cancer. Since carcinogenicity is one of the prime problems associated with the dioxins, we need to compare their potency and exposure to other carcinogens. How much dioxin is there in different places? How serious a contributor is it to air pollution, water pollution, and food contamination? Only when we ask those questions can we get an estimate of the relative importance of dioxins. If we don't perform that exercise, if we don't develop that sense of proportion, we will likely go ahead and condemn more towns, buy more people out, spend an incredible amount of money, and devote a lot of major laboratory attention to the dioxin problem. Maybe we should. But I urge that we spend substantial effort right now trying to decide how big a problem it looks to be, so we can set priorities reasonably.

What are some of the remedies we need for the current emergencies? The states which have had the most trouble so far with dioxins are Missouri, New Jersey, Michigan, and New York, and a few others. Dioxins are not uniformly spread throughout the United States. We do need to handle the clear emergencies first, and move toward identifying other potentially hazardous sites.

Taking samples of dirt, water, and fish, and analyzing them for dioxins is very tedious and expensive. Analytical costs range in the thousands of dollars per sample. Sampling and analyzing one site is a research project in itself. We need to ensure that analytic techniques are of very high quality. Quite a few analyses in the past have been suspect. These compounds occur along with lots of other things that look like them chemically; they are very difficult to sort out. While it is boring to say "quality control, quality control", we have to keep saying it. Standardization of methods, cross-calibration, exchange of samples between laboratories, and development of internal standards (which are in short supply, and non-existent for some of the dioxins and furans) are needed.

Of course, we also need a wide range of health studies. I have mentioned some of the types that should be done: reproductive studies, cancer studies, immunological studies. Many of these are under way in a wide variety of institutions. They need to be continued for the long term, though, the way we are continuing to follow-through on the PBBs episode in Michigan.

Obviously we need methods for permanently destroying dioxins. These darn things are hard to get rid of. Not only are they persistent in the environment, they resist burning and they resist easy chemical destruction. Incineration, photolysis, and other such techniques theoretically are available. Some have been tested in the field. But routine disposal of these materials on a fairly large scale is quite a task. What, for example, is to be done with all the dirt dug up at Times Beach, Missouri? A half million truckloads or something like that is going to be stored temporarily until it is decided how to destroy the dioxins. That, of course, just displaces the problem to our descendents, and the problem is not going to be solved unless we commit money to simple things like how to burn it, or extract it and photolyze it.

Three time horizons can be envisioned. One is the short-term emergencies. Those now seem to be coming under control. The medium-term issues the Superfund can help take care of; a lot of clearly identified sites now are being cleaned up and plans are being made. The problem is that we probably could spend the entire Superfund cleaning up dioxin sites. Although that is not a bad objective, there are a lot of other toxic waste problems demanding solution. And there are other problems, having to do with air pollution, acid rain, and other hazards, that are probably affecting health at least as much as and probably more than the dioxins are; they deserve some of those scarce dollars. Then there are the long-term problems, of which I have mentioned some aspects. My urging is that we stay on the dioxin problem, learn from it, and not give it up in a couple of years when the main emergencies are cleaned up -- because surely, the dioxin issue is prototypical of a great many other risks.

Let me mention now a few things going on around the country. It is hard to keep up with all the action.

The U.S. Environmental Protection Agency has developed an overall guidance document, entitled <u>Dioxin Strategy</u>, which it released in November. This strategy involves characterizing sites into seven tiers: from the ones that are clearly identified as emergencies where there are dioxins and people could be exposed if they were not moved, on down to sites that are barely worth attention and need to be looked into. So it attempts to set priorities, proposes some analytic approaches, and promotes some techniques for cleaning up sites. The Toxic Substances Control Act gives EPA the authority to follow the movements of these materials; after they are cleaned up, or are being transported, they have to be followed and reported to EPA. Under the Clean Water Act they can be regulated, and although regulations haven't been promulgated yet, that is being discussed. The Superfund office, in the Office of Solid Waste and Emergency Response, has been charged with leading the agency's work on these matters. The regional offices obviously are hard at work, and there is some prospect that the regional offices are going to be brought into coordination with EPA headquarters; the regions have acted fairly independently so far. The EPA laboratory in Cincinnati has been developing an overall Health Effects Document.

The U.S. Centers for Disease Control have been deeply involved, particularly in health emergencies such as at Times Beach. One of the difficulties for the Administration is to sort out whether this is an environmental problem or a health problem, and therefore, whether responsibility belongs in EPA or in CDC, and if it continues to belong in both of them, how to coordinate those efforts. EPA simply doesn't have the health expertise that the CDC and others have, and CDC and others don't have the environmental expertise, staff, and resources. Obviously the problem concerns both kinds of agencies.

The U.S. Food and Drug Administration has been developing interim guidelines for exposure in food. As I understand it, those are not yet final and are subject to some debate.

NIOSH and NCI and others I have mentioned are working on the sarcoma registries.

The Veterans Administration and the Air Force have been studying military exposure to Agent Orange containing dioxins.

In Missouri, the Governor's Task Force sent its final report to Governor Bond in October. I found that a very interesting, solid report, and I urge its reading. I think it is important for states to take control of some aspects of these issues. It's a very localized problem.

Scientists in Missouri are now organized to contribute to research on the dioxin issue. The proposal in Missouri is centered mainly around the contaminated farms and Times Beach. The plan is to scrape the soil off the surface and deposit it in a very secure facility, a bunker like the one that was built for Seveso in Italy, including all appropriate environmental monitoring, while ultimate disposal is studied. I don't think this is just a postponement; it is an important step. Also, there are proposals to use the condemned town as a site for studying environmental decay of the materials.

New York State has, to its regret, had several episodes: a fire in a Binghamton state office building, Love Canal, and some toxic waste dumps. New York has been doing a lot of research on the dioxins.

Much industrial research is being conducted, of course. One of my regrets is that government has not yet learned how to fully tap the research going on in major chemical industries. Much of their information is becoming available, and I applaud the industries who are making it available voluntarily. We need to find ways to draw upon that expertise, making whatever arrangements need to be made so that industry can share scientific and health information openly, without penalty. None of those companies would have wished for their dioxin expertise, but now they have a lot to share.

As a social dispute, the dioxin affair has been an episode of very great uncertainly, fear, anger, and concern. The issue has a very complex social background--I think we probably wouldn't feel the same way about dioxins had they not been part of Agent Orange used in Vietnam. Those overtones exist, still. I have sat in Congressional hearings and listened to scientists trying to describe what the situation is. The testimony is often: "We don't know yet;" and "It will be twenty years before we do know" and so on. The Congress and the country don't know how to respond to that. Another characteristic is that a lot of lawyers have gotten involved. (It is more reasonable to try to call off the analytical chemists than to try to call off the lawyers.) A lot of major legal cases are proceeding right now. One of the things I think can be done is to "fill the middle" on disputes. Often we hear from the extremes: from those people who believe dioxin is the most poisonous thing on earth, and from those who say that it's no big deal and just causes a rash. Surely the truth is somewhere in the middle of those opinions. Scientists all along the spectrum need to get involved. Most scientists, unfortunately, prefer to stay in the laboratory, and not to get out in the middle of these controversies. I have been pleased that the American Chemical Society and medical and environmental groups have been convening conferences to try to develop a full picture.

Chapter 4

DIOXINS IN CANADA - DECIDING THE PUBLIC HEALTH RISK

A. B. Morrison
Health Protection Branch
Health and Welfare Canada

BACKGROUND

Public interest in Canada on dioxins parallels that in the United States, and reflects the extent to which Canadian public opinion is influenced by events in the U.S. and coverage of them in the American media. In the late 1950s, chick edema disease, resulting from dioxin contamination of fats used in formulating chicken feed, caused deaths of millions of chicken broilers in the U.S. Despite intensive research efforts, identification of the causative factor(s) did not occur until 1966, when it was shown that hexachlorinated dibenzo-p-dioxin displayed properties similar to material isolated from toxic fat and in addition produced chick edema disease in chickens (Firestone, 1973). By this time, attention had swung to the phenoxy herbicides 2,4-D and 2,4,5-T, which had been used as defoliants by U.S. troops in the Vietnam war. Public perception in both Canada and the U.S. of the morality of the war heightened concern over findings that 2,3,7,8-TCDD was present in significant amounts in specific defoliant mixtures such as Agent Orange. In 1981, researchers in Agriculture Canada reported the presence of dioxins in 2,4-D sold in Canada (Cochrane et al., 1981). Although the isomers found were not 2,3,7,8-TCDD, and are in fact, considered much less toxic than 2,3,7,8-TCDD, the problem of dioxins in 2,4-D continues to be of significant public concern in Canada to this day.

At about the same time, scientists in the Department of National Health and Welfare announced that dioxins had been found in the livers of chickens raised on litter composed of wood shavings contaminated with pentachlorophenol (Ryan and Pilon, 1982).

Recent Canadian Concerns

Several other widely publicized episodes, all occurring outside of Canada, served to heighten public concerns over dioxins in the last few years. The first involved the widely known survey of miscarriages in Alsea, Oregon, which implicated forest spraying with phenoxy herbicides. Although the survey has been discredited by many authoritative groups, and must be given little credence, it aroused intense public debate, and was widely used by anti-pesticide lobbyists and environmental groups as evidence of harm from forest spraying operations. Rational examination of the claims on the basis of their scientific merit was made more difficult by a U.S. decision in 1979 to discontinue use of 2,4,5-T in forest spraying operations. Four Canadian provinces (Ontario, British Columbia, New Brunswick and Saskatchewan), have discontinued use of 2,4,5-T for forest spraying purposes, and continued public controversy resulted in Quebec suspending spraying with 2,4,5-T for the 1983 season. A recent major court judgement in Nova Scotia has, perhaps, both reduced and heightened concerns about forest spraying operations (Nunn, 1983). The case involved a suit brought by 15 plaintiffs against Nova

Scotia Forest Industries, a large forest products company, with headquarters in Sweden. In a judgement which is certain to draw world-wide attention, Mr. Justice Nunn of the Nova Scotia Supreme Court touched repeatedly on the propriety of having scientific matters determined in a Court of law. "It hardly seems necessary", he said, "to state that a Court of law is not the forum for the determination of matters of science. Those are for science to determine, as facts, following the traditionally accepted methods of scientific inquiry. A substance neither does nor does not create a risk to health by Court decree, and it would be foolhardy for a Court to enter such an enquiry. If science itself is not certain, a Court cannot resolve the conflict, and make the thing certain." The judge continued along the same vein as follows:

"To some extent this case takes on the nature of an appeal from the decision of the regulatory agency and any such approach through the Courts ought to be discouraged in its infancy. Opponents to a particular chemical ought to direct their activities towards the regulatory agencies or, indeed, to government itself where broad areas of social policy are involved. It is not for the Court to become a regulatory agency of this type. It has neither the training nor the staff to perform this function."

In commenting on actions taken in other countries vis-a-vis using chemicals in forest spraying operations, Mr. Justice Nunn noted as follows: "I do not mention regulatory agencies of other countries but there are some countries, notably Sweden, where 2,4,5-T is either restricted or prohibited. However, I have no evidence before me indicating that any such restriction or prohibition is the result of a scientific enquiry. All seem to be political decisions made for whatever reason."

Pertinent portions of the conclusions reached by Mr. Justice Nunn include the following:

"....as a general point, ...I accept the evidence of the defendant's witnesses as representing the generally accepted view of responsible scientists, and also as indicative of the risks involved. Each of them categorically states that neither 2,4-D and 2,4,5-T in the concentration to be sprayed on Nova Scotia forests pose any health hazard whatsoever."

"Were I required to do so, and perhaps to allay public fears, I will add that the strongest evidence indicates that these substances sprayed in the Nova Scotia environment will not get into or travel through the rivers or streams, nor will they travel via groundwater to any lands of the plaintiffs who are adjacent to or near the sites to be sprayed.

Further, if any did the amount would be so insignificant that there would be no risk."

It goes without saying that this judgement will itself stimulate a great deal of controversy. In many respects, the issue is a political and social one, which transcends science, and evokes deeply emotional responses on both sides.

A second incident which aroused fears in Canada about public health effects of dioxins was the celebrated industrial accident at Seveso, Italy, involving 2,4,5-trichlorophenol production. Considerable areas of the surrounding town and nearby countryside were contaminated with dioxins, and many domestic animals died. This episode received widespread publicity in the press, which portrayed it as the release of a deadly poisonous cloud of "the most toxic chemical made by man", with long-term effects on public health. Perhaps fortunately, 2,4,5-trichlorophenol, which has consistently been identified as the major international manufacturing and waste disposal problem in the dioxin field, has never been produced in Canada.

Closer to home, Canadians have been deeply concerned about the Love Canal and Hyde Park waste disposal sites in Niagara Falls, New York. Although controversy about the extent and nature of health problems related to the chemicals disposed of at these sites still remains, they have focused the public's attention on chemical dumps in general.

Problems of contamination of Lake Ontario from the U.S. dump sites were heightened in 1980 by the reported presence of 2,3,7,8-TCDD in Lake Ontario herring gull eggs (Norstrom et al., 1982). This followed demonstrations by the New York State Department of Health of measurable amounts of 2,3,7,8-TCDD in fish from Lake Ontario (New York State Department of Health, 1979). Subsequent refinements in analytical techniques by workers at the Health Protection Branch and elsewhere have shown that 2,3,7,8-TCDD can be measured with confidence in fish at parts per trillion (ppt) levels (Ryan, et al., 1983b). Extensive analyses of fish from the Great Lakes by Canadian and U.S. scientists have shown that traces of TCDD are confined mainly to fish from Lake Ontario, with the highest levels for commercial fish in carp, catfish and eels (Ryan et al., 1983a).

Since dioxins have very low water solubilities, but much higher affinity for fats and proteins, they tend to bioaccumulate and are more readily detected in biological samples than in water. Although there have been reports of dioxins in raw water from the Great Lakes, there have been none to date of dioxins in Canadian drinking water, at the current limit of detection in the parts per quadrillion range. The ever increasing sensitivity of analytical methodology suggests, however, that dioxins may eventually be detected in drinking water.

Health Protection Branch scientists recently found that each of 22 human adipose tissue samples analyzed contained measurable amounts of 2,3,7,8-TCDD (Department of National Health and Welfare, 1983). Twenty-one of the samples contained an average of 10 ppt; one sample contained 130 ppt. Although the samples came from hospitalized patients in Kingston and Ottawa, nothing is known about the personal histories or dietary habits of the people involved. No significant difference was noted between the levels in residents from each location, nor were male-female differences apparent. The dioxin levels found in the samples did not correlate with the levels of other contaminants detected in the same samples.

All tissue donors died of natural causes, and most were well advanced in age. Causes of death were typical of those seen in a random population sample (heart disease, accidents, etc.). No link to the known effects of dioxin poisoning was apparent or expected, with such minute levels. The significance of exposure to these low levels of dioxin is not clearly understood at this time.

It is now well established that incineration, particularly of municipal garbage and chlorinated industrial waste, produces trace quantities of dioxins emitted as gases or adsorbed on particulate matter, if the combustion temperature is not high enough. Most are the higher chlorinated dioxins, and less than 1% is 2,3,7,8-TCDD. Large amounts of municipal and industrial garbage are incinerated in Canada, and the amount is expected to increase in the future, as the availability of suitable landfill sites decreases, and energy reclamation programs become more extensive. Although the significance of combustion as a source of dioxins is not yet fully known, the "trace chemistries of fire" hypothesis put forward by researchers of Dow Chemical, (Dow Chemical Co., 1978), seems in general to be supported by available evidence. Thus, forest fires, which are not uncommon in Canada, may represent a significant natural source of the higher chlorinated dioxins.

Amounts of Dioxins in the Canadian Environment

Preliminary attempts have been made to determine the probable quantities of dioxins entering the Canadian environment each year (Interdepartmental Committee, 1983). The major sources include chemicals containing dioxins, waste dumps, and combustion. Available estimates may be summarized as follows. All data must be considered extremely tentative. Furthermore, the fate of released dioxins, including pathways through the environment and chemical transformations, is largely unknown.

Chemicals containing dioxins. It is estimated that approximately 140 grams of dioxins originating as contaminants of 2,4-D are released into the environment each year, assuming a use pattern of 4,500 tonnes and 3 dioxins present at a maximum of 10 ppb.

From 2,4,5-T, it is estimated that only 5 mg of 2,3,7,8-TCDD is released annually, assuming a use pattern of 500 kg.

From chlorinated phenols used in the wood preserving industry, perhaps as much as 1,500 kg of dioxins are released, much of which is hepta and hexachlorodibenzo-p-dioxins. Much of the total would remain in treated wood and not be released, unless the wood is burned.

No data are yet available for other chemicals, including Hexachlorophene, Triclosan, Dicamba and MCPA.

Contamination of phenoxyherbicides and pharmaceutical products does not rank as a significant source of contamination of the general environment, but may be highly significant for individuals in particular circumstances. Workers in industries that manufacture or use materials containing dioxins are potentially at elevated risk relative to the general population from exposure to dioxins in these chemicals. High risk occupational groups involved include:

1. workers involved in treatment of wood products with chlorinated phenols, or who make extensive use of treated wood products;
2. workers who manufacture chlorinated phenols or phenoxyherbicides; (Of the dioxin-containing chemicals, only 2,4,5-T, 2,4-D, tetrachlorophenol and pentachlorophenol are known to have been manufactured in Canada, and none is being manufactured at present.)
3. pesticide applicators.

Waste dumps. Dioxins in landfills may originate from industrial organic wastes, from disposal of fly ash from incinerators, and possibly from transformer oils and dielectrics.

As indicated previously, Canadian concerns focus on dumps in or near Niagara Falls, New York. The amount of 2,3,7,8-TCDD contained in the Niagara waste dumps is estimated at 45 kg in the Love Canal site and 2.23 tonnes in the Hyde Park site. The S-area and 102nd Street dumps are reported to contain equivalent quantities of 2,4,5-trichlorophenol wastes, of unknown TCDD content. Investigations are also underway at landfills near Elmira, Ontario, where 2,4,5-T and 2,4-D were produced in the past, and where dioxins were found in groundwater of one of several test wells at the site. Other current potential problem areas include the St. Clair River, Saginaw Bay in Lake Huron, and the Detroit River. The potential for movement of dioxins primarily through groundwater with subsequent contamination beyond the dump area is substantial.

Combustion. From municipal incinerators, it is estimated that 1-50 kg of dioxins may be present on emitted fly ash. Perhaps 100 times this amount are precipitated and usually deposited in landfills. Municipal and industrial incinerators probably account for the largest source of dioxin input into the Canadian environment. Emitted fly ash, distributed over urban areas around an incinerator, contaminates air, soil and sediments. A much more serious potential problem arises from precipitated fly ash deposited in landfills. Inadequate data are available on dioxins in incinerator flue gases.

The data base for other sources of dioxin arising from combustion is fragmentary at best. Forest fires have perhaps the greatest potential as natural sources of dioxins. There is a special need for additional data on burning of chlorophenol-treated wastes.

ASSESSMENT OF RISK

Risk embodies two concepts - the magnitude of the harm and the probability of its occurrence (Royal Society of Canada, 1982). The management of risk involves a series of stages:

1. identification of adverse effects associated with exposure;
2. quantification of the risk involved;
3. evaluation of the risk, usually in comparison with others, in terms of relative costs and benefits;
4. development and implementation of strategies to minimize or control the risk.

In December 1981, the National Research Council of Canada published a report entitled "Polychlorinated dibenzo-p-dioxins: Criteria for their effects on man and his environment" (NRC, 1981). This report reviewed and assessed the scientific knowledge of sources, amounts, pathways, persistence and fate of dioxins in the environment, and evaluated available data on toxicity. At approximately the same time, the Federal Ministers of the Environment and National Health and Welfare established an Expert Advisory Committee on Dioxins under the Environmental Contaminants Act. This Committee, the so called Willes Committee, was charged, inter alia, with evaluating the toxicity of dioxins and the risks they represent to humans and non-human species. The Committee's report was made public in mid-December 1983. The Committee concluded that "regardless of arguments about the significance of species differences in sensitivity, the validity of risk assessments, and other uncertainties which may take years to resolve, it is quite clear that dioxins are very unpleasant things to have in our environment, and the less we have of them the better. It is, in fact, imperative to reduce dioxin exposure to the absolute possible minimum." The Committee's detailed recommendations on quantitative aspects of the risk associated with dioxins are presented in its report, to which readers are referred. In brief, they do not differ substantially from those of other groups which have examined the toxicity of dioxins and the risks they represent to human health.

Problems in Risk Assessment

Problems of assessing health risks from dioxins reflect generic constraints faced by governments in making decisions on safety of chemicals. These constraints include the following:

1. The scientific data upon which regulatory decisions are based is almost always less complete and incontrovertible than regulators would prefer. Even the best studies suggest avenues and possibilities for future work, and there is no perfect study which answers all questions and provides unequivocal proof leading to a perfect solution. Deficiencies in the data base inevitably lead to differing interpretations about their significance with proponents of one side or the other arguing that the data support their already-arrived-at position. The regulatory agency is caught in the middle, between those who criticize it for being slow in acting to protect the public, and others, who stand to lose economically if action is taken, who complain that the agency should not have acted at all.
2. Available scientific data is almost invariably derived from high dose studies in experimental animals. Estimation of low levels of risk for human populations by extrapolation of this animal data requires expert judgement and is fraught with uncertainty and lack of precision. The toxicity of dioxins in animal species, including man, depends on numerous factors including the level, duration and route of exposure, the genetic makeup of the individual, susceptibility (encompassing factors such as repair mechanisms and immunological status), biotransformation and exposure to other chemicals. These factors vary between individuals in a

population. At best, therefore, prediction of effects involves estimation of the range in response to dioxins in the population. Basic differences between humans and laboratory animals in anatomy, physiology, biochemistry and genetics can be substantial, and significantly influence the conclusions reached on the nature and extent of the risk involved. Even the choice of animal species can be significant: there can be as much as 5,000 fold difference in oral LD50 for the 2,3,7,8-TCDD isomer in the guinea pig and the hamster (Kociba and Schwetz, 1982). Data from humans would, of course, be preferred for assessment of health effects of dioxins. Although some data on acute exposure in human populations are available, they are so fragmentary and of such controversial quality as to be of essentially little value in making public health decisions about management of these chemicals.

3. The media, and even some scientists, often fail to differentiate between the various congeners of dioxin. Hazard clearly depends on which congener is described, but dioxin is often vilified in the press as "the most toxic chemical made by man......" In fact, what is usually being referred to is the 2,3,7,8-TCDD isomer. The toxicities of the other congeners are less well understood, but marked differences are apparent (Kociba and Schwetz, 1982).

4. There are definite limitations to our systems for reporting adverse effects in human subjects from chemicals, and the cause and effect linkage may be extremely difficult to construct given the limitations of the analytical tools at our disposal. Effects of chronic low-level exposure in subjects receiving a number of chemical entities, which may or may not interact with each other, are especially difficult to assess.

5. The analytical chemists have outstripped the biologists. As a result, we now can measure fractions of a part per trillion of dioxins with precision and accuracy, but we have very little idea about the biological significance, if any, of the analytical results. Furthermore, there seems to be no practical end in sight to the ability of the chemists to measure fewer and fewer molecules of dioxins.

6. Sensational news stories originating in the U.S. are widely reported in the Canadian media and many members of the Canadian public almost automatically assume they are applicable to Canada. Furthermore, regulatory proposals in the U.S., which may antedate regulatory decisions by as much as several years, and may bear little resemblance to action finally taken by American authorities, often are treated as de facto decisions by Canadians. To cap it all off, the inferiority complex under which Canadians labor in respect of their dealings with the U.S. results oftentimes in more credence being given by Canadians to official U.S. statements than to those from the Canadian government. Living next to a giant is not easy!

THE FEDERAL APPROACH TO MANAGEMENT OF DIOXINS

Federal management of the dioxin problem in Canada must be seen as part of an integrated response to management of chemicals in general. It is based upon recognition of the fact that chemical contamination of the environment is but a symptom of a more pervasive problem - the past, current and potential future mismanagement of chemicals. Better management of chemicals by our society depends upon recognition and understanding by the public of a number of factors, including the following: the benefits and risks of using chemicals; choices available, including alternative chemicals; the responsibility of various sectors of society; economic costs of regulation on the domestic industry and on trade with other countries; impact of regulation on international relations; impact on future regulatory policy; ability to enforce the law; tradeoffs with other programs; the feasibility and cost of educating users and handlers of chemicals; the limitations of the science base underlying decisions. Effective management deals not only with necessary remedial action, but is prevention oriented, and able to learn from the mistakes of the past, to ensure they don't occur in the future.

In May 1981 the Federal Cabinet expressed concerns regarding the extent and effectiveness of activities related to toxic chemicals within the Federal government as a whole. It called for a review to develop an integrated overall management approach and mechanisms to ensure that the total governmental effort on toxic chemicals is molded into a coherent whole. As a result, an Interdepartmental Committee on Toxic Chemicals was set up at senior official level, to provide direction and develop an overall policy framework for Cabinet approval.

The Federal approach to dioxins, developed by the Interdepartmental Committee on Toxic Chemicals has four major components:

1. to reduce environmental contamination of dioxins from dioxin-containing chemicals by proper management of their life-cycles, including practices in the past for disposing of industrial wastes;
2. to reduce environmental contamination of dioxins from combustion, by suitable control techniques;
3. to carry out necessary research and monitoring activities to ensure that actions taken result in declining levels of dioxins in various environmental compartments;
4. to provide management and communications strategies needed to fulfill leadership roles.

In pragmatic terms, this approach is based on the premise that, although there is much which still needs to be learned about dioxins, sufficient information currently exists to initiate vigorous activities to control major known sources of dioxins in Canada. At the same time, it is recognized that additional investigations are needed to identify new areas requiring control or remedial activities, to improve our ability to assess effects on health and environmental quality, and to improve the effectiveness of current control procedures.

Potential release pathways for dioxins during the "life-cycle" of dioxin-containing chemicals have been identified. They include the following:

1. manufacturing and formulation;
2. sites for disposal of manufacturing wastes;
3. importation;
4. transportation and storage;
5. registration and use.

This approach, which attempts to consider key control points in the overall life-cycle of dioxin-containing chemicals, is proving to be very useful in identification of major problem areas, and development of necessary control procedures. An example will illustrate: Pentachlorophenol, used for wood treatment and preservation, was manufactured in the past, utilizing a closed system, at two Canadian locations. There is no current Canadian manufacturing going on. No industrial accidents during manufacturing are known to have occurred. Disposal of still bottom wastes was by deep-well injection. Current importation amounts to about 2,500 tonnes annually; formulation into final product occurs at point of use. Accidents at point of use have been recorded and a storage tank fire occurred in 1982. Contamination of boxcars during transportation, with further contamination of subsequent material carried in the boxcars is known to have occurred. For example, in an episode several years ago, a boxcar containing pentachlorophenol was inadequately cleaned. Oats which were subsequently carried in the car involved were contaminated with pentachlorophenol residues. Dairy cattle many hundreds of miles away from the initial point of contamination were given feed containing the contaminated oats: residues of hexa - and octachlorodibenzodioxins were found at ppb levels in milk and cheese. The food products involved were not allowed to be sold and the milk from the dairy cows in question was monitored until free of dioxin residues.

Points where pentachlorophenol can enter the environment are obvious from the above description, as are procedures needed to control potential problems, and prevent problems from occurring in the future.

FEDERAL GOVERNMENT ACTIONS TO CONTROL DIOXINS

Manufacture

At the present time, no dioxin-containing chemicals are manufactured in Canada although 2,4,5-T, 2,4-D, tetrachlorophenol and pentachlorophenol are known to have been manufactured in Canada in the past. There is no evidence 2,4,5-trichlorophenol has ever been manufactured in Canada, but Federal agencies are actively investigating this matter with the chemical industry. Authority to impose controls on the use of chemicals and to require companies to disclose information concerning uses of commercial chemicals is provided by the Environmental Contaminants Act, administered jointly by Environment Canada and National Health and Welfare.

Disposal of Wastes

Plants which manufactured 2,4-D, 2,4,5-T, tetrachlorophenol and pentachlorophenol in the past were permitted to use deep-well injection for disposal of manufacturing waste. Provincial agencies are re-examining each site to ensure that problems are not occurring. In a joint venture between the Federal government and most of the provinces, investigations are underway to ensure that wastes associated with dioxin-containing chemicals were not disposed of in either currently active or abandoned waste dumps.

The disposal of dioxin-containing chemicals in U.S. dumps poses a problem for Canada in the Niagara River area. The Federal Department of the Environment has recently identified the Niagara River area as the major source of lower Great Lakes contamination. Cooperative efforts between the Federal and Ontario governments and counterpart U.S. agencies are continuing to ensure adequate containment of the wastes, but progress is slow.

Monitoring of Foods

Monitoring of fish from the Great Lakes, and of drinking water is being carried out, to detect increased contamination should such occur in the future. Since 1980, a regulation under the Food and Drugs Act has prohibited the sale of foods containing chlorinated dibenzo-p-dioxins. In 1982, an exemption was granted whereby fish containing 20 ppt or less of 2,3,7,8-TCDD may be sold. The 20 ppt level provides a safety margin of approximately 2,000, for a person ingesting 16 grams of fish daily (the national average) based on rat reproduction and carcinogenicity studies.

Transportation

The Transportation of Dangerous Goods Act, administered by Transport Canada, is intended to ensure that adequate safety standards are established for packaging, handling and transporting dangerous goods. Dioxin-containing chemicals are listed under the Act as acutely toxic or environmentally hazardous substances. Provision is also made to provide documentation for waste materials intended to be discarded. The waste manifest ensures that the indicated type and quantity of waste shipped actually arrives at its intended destination and that the recipient is authorized to receive the wastes in question.

Registration

The Pest Control Products Act, administered by Agriculture Canada, regulates pesticide use. Regulations have been promulgated under the Act to limit the levels of dioxin in 2,4-D and 2,4,5-T. The dioxin content of 2,4-D may not be higher than 10 ppb of any congener; that of 2,4,5-T may not exceed 100 ppb of 2,3,7,8-TCDD. These regulations have resulted in nearly 100 fold reduction in the contribution made by these herbicides to dioxin contamination of the environment. Tetrachlorophenol and pentachlorophenol are registered pesticides; regulations on dioxin content are under consideration. In cooperation with the forest products industry, labor groups and Provincial governments, the Federal government has initiated the development of Codes of Good Practice intended to ensure that these chemicals are handled more safely. Many agricultural uses of pentachlorophenol have been discontinued, as has its use in the leather and textiles industries. Monitoring of imported textiles and leather goods is underway. Educational programs are being utilized to alert farmers and the lumber industry to potential problems related to use of pentachlorophenol-treated wood shavings as bedding or litter for farm animals.

Combustion

National criteria for dioxin emissions in air have not yet been developed under the Clean Air Act, although authority to do so exists therein. The Province of Ontario, however, has been very active in this area, in examining various aspects of incinerator design and operating conditions and in monitoring municipal incinerators in various cities. Ontario has developed a provisional maximum guideline for ambient air, 30 pg of 2,3,7,8-TCDD per cubic metre. At the point of impingement of the plume from a single point source at ground level, the maximum concentration should not exceed 450 pg of 2,3,7,8-TCDD per cubic meter on an annual basis.

I trust the foregoing provides a summary of the current status of concerns about dioxins in Canada, and of actions underway to address those concerns. Dioxins will undoubtedly remain of great concern to the public, health professionals and governments during the rest of this decade. Public policy on their management must be based on the advisability of reducing exposure to them to the absolute minimum practically attainable. But we must regain and retain a sense of proportion about how important dioxins really are in the overall scheme of management of toxic chemicals.

REFERENCES

Cochrane, W.P., Singh, J., Miles, W. and Wakeford, B. 1981. Determination of chlorinated dibenzo-p-dioxin contaminants in 2,4-D products by gas chromatography-mass spectrometric techniques, J. Chromatography 217:289-299.

Department of National Health and Welfare. July 15, 1983 News Release.

Dow Chemical Company. 1978. The trace chemistries of fire: A source of and routes for entry of chlorinated dioxins into the environment. Dow Chemical Co., Midland, Michigan, 46 pp. plus appendices.

Firestone, D. 1973. Etiology of chick edema disease. Env. Health Perspectives 5:59-66.

Interdepartmental Committee on Toxic Chemicals, Government of Canada, 1983 Unpublished Data.

Kociba, R.J. and Schwetz, B.A. 1982. A review of the toxicity of 2,3,7,8-tetrachlorodibenzo-p-dioxin (TCDD) with a comparison to the toxicity of other chlorinated dioxin isomers. Assoc. Food and Drug Officials Quarterly Bull. 46:168-188.

NRC. 1981. Polychlorinated dibenzo-p-dioxins: Criteria for their effects on man and his environment. Associate committee on scientific criteria for environmental quality. National Research Council of Canada, Draft Publication NRCC No. 18574.
New York State Department of Health. April 24, 1979 News Release.

Norstrom, R.J, Hallett, D.J., Simon, M. and Mulvihill, M.J. 1982. Analysis of Great Lakes herring gull eggs for tetrachlorodibenzo-p-dioxins. In Chlorinated Dioxins and Related Compounds: Impact on the Environment, ed. O. Hutzinger, R.W. Frei, E. Merian and F. Pocchiari, pp. 173-181, Pergamon Press, New York.

Nunn, D.M. 1983. Decision in the case of Victoria Palmer et al. versus Nova Scotia Industries, rendered by Mr. Justice D. Merlin Nunn, Supreme Court of Nova Scotia, Trial Division, Halifax N.S., September 15, 1983.

Royal Society of Canada. 1982. A Symposium on the Assessment and Perception of Risk to Human Health in Canada, ed. J.T. Rogers and D.V. Bates, pp.3-22, Ottawa.

Ryan, J.J and Pilon, J.C. 1982.   Chlorinated - dibenzodioxins and - dibenzofurans in chicken litter and livers arising from pentachloro-phenol contamination of wood shavings. In Chlorinated Dioxins and Related Compounds: Impact on the Environment, ed. O. Hutzinger, R.W. Frei, E. Merian and F. Pocchiari, pp. 183-189, Pergamon Press, New York.

Ryan, J.J., Lau, P.-Y., Pilon, J.C. and Lewis, D. 1983a.   2,3,7,8-Tetrachlorodibenzo-p-dioxin and 2,3,7,8-tetrachlorodibenzofuran residues in Great Lakes commercial and sport fish.   In Chlorinated Dioxins and Dibenzofurans in the Total Environment, ed. G. Choudhary, L.H. Keith and C. Rappe, pp. 87-97, Butterworth, Boston.

Ryan, J.J., Pilon, J.C., Conacher, H.B.S. and Firestone, D. 1983b.   Interlaboratory study on determination of 2,3,7,8-tetrachlorodibenzo-p-dioxin in fish.   J. Assoc. Off. Anal. Chem. 66:700-707.

Chapter 5

PANEL DISCUSSION – SECTION 1

CYNAR:	I'm going to address questions to two people; to Dr. Hutzinger and Dr. Morrison. To Dr. Hutzinger: What is the final disposal method for dioxin at this time? If it is incineration, how is it done and by what method of incineration and at what temperatures? And to Dr. Morrison: How can dioxins be eliminated from fly ash? Is dioxin only distributed in fly ash? If fly ash is not released into the environment, does that mean that dioxins are not released? In other words, can they be released in the flue gases themselves? Also to Dr. Morrison: You mentioned there are high risk occupational groups in Canada, but you did not mention incineration workers as being one of them. Why not?
LEADER:	Dr. Morrison, would you like to respond to a couple of those?
MORRISON:	Well, the first series of questions dealt with dioxins in fly ash versus dioxins in flue gases. There's clearly some in both but we don't have enough quantitative data on flue gases. We do have some on fly ash, both that which is released up the stack and that which is precipitated and disposed of in landfills. It's clear that some also is emitted in flue gases and we need to do a lot more work on the quantification of that. We also need to do a great deal more work on the way those concentrations and the relative proportions are influenced by incinerator design, incinerator operation, and so on. Insofar as whether or not incinerator workers are at risk, I don't think anybody knows. I suppose if they hung their noses over the top of the stack they'd probably be at great risk, but they might be at risk from other things before the dioxins would get them.
CYNAR:	What temperatures are the municipal incinerators operated at in Canada?
MORRISON:	I suppose they are the same temperatures as in the U.S. but I don't have the slightest idea what they are. They're hot, I can assure you that.
LEADER:	Dr. Hutzinger, would you like to respond?
HUTZINGER:	Yes. There is no set, final method of disposal for dioxins and furans. It is assumed that incineration is the most effective method if the temperature is high enough and the residence time of the gases is long enough. As in a chemical waste incinerator,

it's considered to produce 99.999% destruction.

CYNAR: Can you comment on a temperature?

HUTZINGER: I'm not a technologist but the various operators in the Netherlands have told me it's between 800 and 1100 degrees; 800 being the limit of stench. If it goes below 800, the stuff that is emitted is foul smelling. If it goes above 1100, the slag becomes liquid and you have problems with the incineration bed. It's apparently very hard to determine the exact temperature in the whole combustion chamber. It's not that easy.

SCHMIDT: In Michigan, the State Department of Public Health has advised that no fish should be eaten from the Tittabawassee and Saginaw Rivers downstream from Dow Chemical company in Midland due to 2,3,7,8-TCDD. My question is: Are there any other bodies of water anywhere in the world where similar public health advisories exist due to dioxins or furans in the fish?

LEADER: Dr. Lowrance, would you like to respond to that?

LOWRANCE: I don't know. Does anyone here know of any other cases of that kind? In Canada perhaps?

MORRISON: As a general, cautionary statement, we have suggested that a steady diet of fish from the Great Lakes Basin, especially from the lower Great Lakes, would probably not be tremendously advisable, but you have to be reasonably pragmatically sensible about the whole thing. A single meal is not likely to be a problem. Someone who eats that fish day in and day out, especially if they are pregnant, might have some difficulty. So we have tried to be reasonably cautious and pragmatic without trying to establish hard and fast legal-type restrictions. We've said that the occasional meal was probably not a difficulty. However, you might want to think about the consistent consumption of fish from the lower Great Lakes.

SCHMIDT: Does that suggest that we have a unique situation in this state?

MORRISON: Maybe you just have a unique state health department.

HUMPHREY: With respect to Wayne's question, the state of New York, I believe, has made equally stringent statements with respect to fish, and in fact, they have taken a rather unique approach to all contaminants in fish. If I'm not incorrect, their position is that all fish taken from waters bordering or in the state of New York are assumed to be contaminated and therefore should not be eaten except for those sites where systematic tests have shown that the water and the fish are clean. I don't think the Tittabawassee River watershed is the only place in the country although it definitely represents an area of concern.

HILKER: I am with the New York Department of Health and I had to respond to the comment about the Michigan Health Department. I'm not a regulator. I'm a scientist. I work in the labs, but I am aware that there are restrictions on the taking of fish from Lake Ontario which borders on New York State and also from the Hudson River which flows down from upstate towards New York

City.

LOWRANCE:	But not necessarily because of the dioxins themselves. Is that correct?

HILKER: As I understand it, it is not entirely due to dioxins. Of course you are probably aware that there is a great problem with PCBs, particularly in the Hudson River. If you want further information, I'm sure the Health Department would be able to supply quite extensive booklets on those places and those species of fish which are restricted within the state.

LIEBENSTEIN: First of all, Wisconsin has closed a section of the Wisconsin River to commercial fishing for carp only. It's about a 27 mile reach and it has a 20,000 acre flowage. The levels of the carp were between 60 and 75 parts per trillion and there were about 50 to 100,000 pounds of these fish, most of which were shipped to the state of New York. Secondly, I have a question for Dr. Morrison. Is Canada considering a tolerance level or an action level for 2,3,7,8-TCDF?

MORRISON: Right now we're not. I'm very reluctant to get myself tied down to specific legal limits in an area where the science base is shifting so quickly that we'll just get ourselves into a mess. I want to be as flexible as I can possibly be. I wish I didn't have to have a legal limit on TCDD in fish because that will have to be changed without question, as we get more data. I'm reluctant to extend these legal limits the slightest bit until we have a far better science base than we have now.

MILLNER: First, I'd like to answer a question and then ask a question of the panel. In the Spring River in Missouri there is a ban limiting fish consumption to two fish per week. That's a ban by the state of Missouri. My question is: What are the background levels of TCDD in soils and what is a reasonable and achievable clean-up level?

HUTZINGER: I think the first question should be answered by Ron Hites, who's been doing a lot of analysis.

CZUCZWA: It is in the low part per trillion range or not detected in soils.

LOWRANCE: Where is that?

CZUCZWA: In remote locations. I will present some data this afternoon.

CULLUM: Dr. Lowrance, you mentioned that dioxins may be tumor promoters and also discussed the correlation of cancer with cigarette smoking. Do you have any rough numbers of how many more deaths per thousand might occur after exposure -- long term or short term?

LOWRANCE: I don't think we have the information to begin to answer that question. I wish we did and I think that's an exercise we need to move toward.   My own intuitive perception is that it's an extraordinarily lower potential for an average exposure, let's say for a smoker, compared to average intake of dioxins from the environment. You have to adjust it. You just can't look at gram of material versus gram of material.

CULLUM: Do you think it's a tumor promoter? Does it increase the overall background tumor incidence?

LOWRANCE: It's possible that it could, and that's one of the reasons promoters are very special and worth being concerned about. On the other hand, there's an incredibly small amount in the environment. We haven't, in the United States, done the same kind of mass totaling that Dr. Morrison reviewed for us in Canada. However, that was a fairly small amount of material spread over Canada. Also, although it is a promoter in experimental animals, it's a complicated story. For example, some mice don't respond the same way others do.

LEADER: I just heard the Surgeon General say a couple of weeks ago that 55 million people in the United States smoke 30 or more cigarettes per day. I would just consider the relative weights of these exposures.

STALLING: I'd like to ask Otto Hutzinger to elaborate briefly on the information he provided from Steve Safe's enzyme induction studies relating the TCDD concentration to the other active compounds. Second, I'd like to ask the two gentlemen about policy formulation, issues, thoughts, perspectives on the furan versus dioxin question. If we look at the toxicological dose response, it seems that we're in an insane situation focusing solely on this 2,3,7,8-TCDD when the environmental perspective so clearly calls for a much broader policy. I'd like your comments on that.

HUTZINGER: Let me talk about the receptor binding assay because I know a little bit more about that. It seems that most toxic effects are mediated by this receptor binding, so the receptor binding should be a good indication of the expression of toxic effects. If you do this assay you get all 2,3,7,8-type compounds which bind to this receptor and presumably which are toxic. You can analyze for 35 dioxins and 75 furans, and even if you can identity each and every one of them you still don't know the toxic action because not enough of the compound is available to do toxicity testing. If you do collective receptor binding you presumably get some overall idea of the presence of the toxic isomers and congeners in both series of compounds.

LEADER: The other question about the relationship of furans and dioxins.

LOWRANCE: I feel strongly that we ought to be looking, Dave, at the furans and other materials as seems appropriate and not waste any time getting to this work. It's been moving fairly slowly in the United States in response to a few emergencies but nothing serious yet. There is a lot of interest among scientists.

MORRISON: I think that's right. There's no question that we have to consider the furans and dioxins together. How to do that, how to introduce that concept to the public is extremely difficult without losing all credibility in the process. The public has been so frightened by the dioxin issue that it is hard to say that not only are there those terrible things but there's a whole class of other terrible things and you're not just going to be killed ten times, you're going to be killed fifty times. The opposite side is that people become so cynical about yet another episode that you lose all credibility. So you have to tread your way through the middle and introduce the complexity of the problem without making people even more hysterical or cynical that they don't believe anything that you say. It's a very, very hard thing for public policy to try to do.

LOWRANCE: Let me just add that in many cases part of the concern over the dibenzofurans is arising through the PCBs concern. It now appears that a lot, and maybe most, of the toxic action of PCB materials can be attributed to impurities or minor components such as the dibenzofurans. This is changing the way we think about PCBs and is getting the furans on the docket.

GANNON: For the last several years I've been working on a research project trying to turn coal waste, both scrubber sludge and fly ash, into a resource, by mixing these substances with cement and making concrete blocks for use in construction both in terrestrial and aquatic situations. Our bioassays in the laboratory showed that at least heavy metals were sequestered and stabilized in this cement matrix. My question to Dr. Hutzinger is: What might the situation be for the stability of dioxin-type compounds in this matrix?

HUTZINGER: I can't really say for sure, but my personal opinion is that these dioxins will not be released in the cement. We've done some artificial rain experiments where we put fly ash in a big column and watered it down for weeks on end. We could not detect any dioxin or furans in the effluent.

GANNON: The work is progressing quite well in the marine situation and these are being used in artificial reef pilot projects in Long Island Sound now and we're doing comparable work in fresh water. Since we're only looking at heavy metals, I was concerned about other contaminants.

AUDIENCE MEMBERS CONTRIBUTING TO THE PANEL DISCUSSION: David Cynar, Resource Recovery, Warren Waste to Energy Associates, 30100 Van Dyke, Warren, MI 48093; Wayne Schmidt, Michigan Conservation Clubs, 2101 Wood Street, Lansing, MI 48912; David Hilker, New York State Department of Health, Albany, NY 12201; Lee Liebenstein, Wisconsin Department of Natural Resources, Box 7921, Madison, WI 53707; Glenn Millner, Ecology Environment Co., P.O. Box D, Buffalo, NY 14225; and Malford E. Cullum, Food Science and Human Nutrition, Michigan State University, East Lansing, MI 48824.

Section 2
Analysis and Monitoring

Chapter 6

ANALYTICAL METHODOLOGY FOR THE DETERMINATION OF PCDDs IN ENVIRONMENTAL SAMPLES: AN OVERVIEW AND CRITIQUE

W.B. Crummett, T.J. Nestrick and L.L. Lamparski
Analytical Laboratories
Dow Chemical U.S.A.

The analytical process for the determination of chlorinated dioxins in environmental samples is positively awesome in sensitivity, selectivity, and scope (Crummett, 1982, 1983). Data can now be generated having any desired degree of certainty down to sub parts per trillion levels (Table A).

The limit of detection has gone from parts per billion in 1970 to parts per quadrillion in 1983 causing analytical chemists as well as editors to talk about the "vanishing zero" (Zweig, 1978), the "shrinking zero", or the "receding zero". The trend is inexorable and must be dealt with realistically.

TABLE A. Detection Limits the Determination of 2,3,7,8-TCDD in Environmental Samples

Year	Detection Limit Picograms/Gram
1965	1,000,000
1970	50,000
1975	10
1980	0.2
1983	0.01

Likewise the specificity of the methodology has improved from 20 isomers being included in the chromatographic peak used to measure 2,3,7,8-TCDD to only one of all the 22 TCDD isomers in 1979 (Table B) (Nestrick et al., 1980).

TABLE B. Specificity of Analytical Method for 2,3,7,8-TCDD in Environmental Samples

Year	Number of Possible Isomers In Peak
1966	20
1973	17
1977	11
1979	1

Although methodology is now available which is capable of determining the 22 isomers of tetra (Nestrick et al., 1980) and the 10 isomers of hexa (Lamparski and Nestrick, 1981) individually, this is only occasionally applied. Thus, data taken by different laboratories are rarely directly comparable. When the methodology became isomer-specific, the possibility of false positive results due to interferences was practically eliminated. However, this has not been well documented.

Meanwhile the methodology was applied to a wide variety of environmental samples with some apparent success. These include plant tissues, animal tissues, plant products, animal products, chemical products, combustion products, waste materials, air, water and soil (Tiernan, 1983).

The rigor required to assure the quality of data varies with the many factors which govern the separation and measurement processes. Although these factors often do not need to be optimized, they must be understood, controlled and monitored in order to provide results of known quality (Crummett, 1979; ACS CEI, 1980; Crummett and Taylor, 1982). This was emphasized in 1981 by a National Research Council of Canada (McLeod, 1981) panel which wrote a comprehensive review of PCDD analysis with emphasis on limitations.

The choice of methodology depends on the matrix to be analyzed, and the sensitivity, specificity and the degree of certainty required in the data. Special newly developed techniques (Crummett et al., 1983) which make quality assurance on individual samples possible include: (1) the use of labeled isotopes as internal standards, (2) special performance chromatographic systems designed and monitored to remove interferences and separate isomers, (3) rigorous criteria for recovery data, and (4) rigorous criteria for detection and determination of the compound of interest.

Various analytical systems have been previously classified (Crummett, 1982, 1983; Mahle and Shadoff, 1982; Tiernan, 1983) according to the degree of resolution achieved in each of three stages: (1) sample preparation, (2) sample introduction into the mass spectrometer, and (3) mass spectrometry.

Sample preparation consists of (1) initial sample treatment, (2) liquid-liquid partition, (3) column chromatography, and (4) high pressure liquid chromatography. These are used in numerous combinations to isolate the PCDDs from most of the interfering substances. References to the early work have been given in a previous report (Crummett, 1982). Some recent publications which are representative of state-of-the-art technology and present details of the techniques are given in the following table (1):

TABLE 1. Analytical System -- Stage I: Extraction-Cleanup Techniques

INITIAL SAMPLE TREATMENT	RECENT REFERENCES
Dissolution	Cochrane et al.(1981)
Digestion	
In Base	Jensen et al.(1981)
In Acid	Langhorst & Shadoff (1980)
	Zabik & Zabik (1980)
Direct Extraction	Cochrane et al. (1981)
	Harless et al. (1980)

LIQUID-LIQUID PARTITION	
Against Conc. H2SO4	Jensen et al. (1981)
Against Aqueous Base	Pfeiffer et al. (1978)

COLUMN CHROMATOGRAPHY	
Alumina	Cochrane et al. (1981)
Silica Gel	Cochrane et al. (1981)
Florisil	Ryan & Pilon (1980)
Ion Exchange Resin	Blaser et al. (1976)
Charcoal	Huckins et al. (1978)
Gel Permeation	Dougherty et al. (1980)
Reagent Modified Silica	Lamparski & Nestrick (1980)
MgO/Celite 545	O'Keefe et al. (1983)

HIGH PERFORMANCE LIQUID CHROMATOGRAPHY	
Normal Phase	Lamparski & Nestrick (1980)
	Langhorst & Shadoff (1980)
Reversed Phase	O'Keefe et al. (1983)
Reversed + Normal Phase	Lamparski & Nestrick (1980)
	Langhorst & Shadoff (1980)

The power of high performance liquid chromatography to separate isomers has been demonstrated by the separation of all 22 isomers of T_4CDD (Nestrick et al., 1979) and the 10 isomers of H_6CDD (Lamparski and Nestrick, 1981) using reversed phase and normal phase HPLC consecutively. Although collaborative studies using these techniques have not yet been done, several laboratories (Nieman et al., 1983; Smith et al., 1982; Tosine et al, 1982) have reported success using these and similar approaches.

Very few direct comparisons of the efficiencies of the various extraction-cleanup procedures have yet been done. One of the most informative has been that by U.S. Food and Drug Administration (FDA) scientists (Brumley et al., 1981) who examined six extracts of fish samples (3 spiked and 3 unspiked) prepared by each of six different laboratories using procedures in use at that time in their respective laboratories. Under the GC/MS conditions used by the FDA, the procedures of Lamparski et al., (1979) and Huckins et al., (1978) were the most effective.

SAMPLE INTRODUCTION

Introduction of the sample into the mass spectrometer is accomplished by either (1) a direct probe, (2) packed column gas chromatography, (3) capillary column gas chromatography, or (4) a second mass spectrometer. The various types of these techniques are summarized in the following tables.

As can be easily seen from Table 2, there are many ways whereby samples can be introduced into the mass spectrometer. Although no direct comparison of these various methods has been made, many investigators have become strong advocates of the latest technology, which is capillary column gas chromatography. The main advantage of these columns is their capacity to separate isomers. For example, Buser and Rappe (1980) demonstrated that 2,3,7,8-TCDD could be separated from all of its 21 isomers by use of a Silar 10C capillary column using OV-17 and OV-101 capillaries for confirmation. Harless et al., (1980,1982) emphasize "the total enhancement of the high resolution mass spectrometry detection techniques" produced by the use of capillary columns.

TABLE 2. Analytical System -- Stage II: Mass Spectrometer Sample Introduction

TECHNIQUE	SELECTED RECENT REFERENCES
Direct Probe	Baughman & Meselson (1973)
Packed Column GC	
OV-1	Fanelli et al. (1980)
OV-101	Phillipson & Puma (1980)
OV-3	Lamparski et al. (1978)
OV-7	Erk et al. (1979)
OV-17	Liberti et al. (1981)
OV-105	Lamparski et al. (1978)
OV-210	Hass et al. (1978)
OV-225	Chae et al. (1977)
OV-17/Poly S-179	Chess & Gross (1980)
	Lamparski & Nestrick (1981)
SE-30	Cochrane et al. (1981)
XE-60	Mieure et al. (1977)
Carbowax 20M	Eiceman et al. (1980)
SP-2100	Phillipson & Puma (1980)
Dexil 300	Van Ness et al. (1980)
Capillary Column GC	
OV-17 WCOT	Liberti et al. (1981)
OV-61 WCOT	Buser (1975)
OV-101 WCOT	Cavallaro et al. (1982)
OV-17/Poly S-179	Nestrick et al. (1980)
Silar 10C	Buser & Rappe (1980)
SE-30 WCOT	Harless et al. (1980)
SE-54	Cochrane et al. (1981)
SP-2100	Mitchum et al. (1980)
Methyl Silicone WCOT	Norstrom et al. (1982)

* Tables 2,4,5,6,7,8,9,10, and 11 are reprinted with permission from Chemosphere 12, W.B. Crummett, Status of Analytical Systems for the Determination of PCDDs and PCDFs, 1983, p.429, Pergamon Press Ltd.

MEASUREMENT BY MASS SPECTROMETRY

Mass spectrometry in the electron impact mode was first used for the identification of PCDDs by Ress et al., (1970). Since then it has had extensive development. As shown in the table below (3), at least a dozen models operating at low resolution ($M/\Delta M < 3000$) have been used to both identify and determine PCDDs after separation by Stages I and II.

TABLE 3. Stage III: Mass Spectrometry (Low Resolution Electron Impact) M/ΔM<2000

MS Model	T_4CDD Limit of Detection pg	M/ΔM	Reference
LKB-9000	6	600	Crummett & Stehl (1973)
	5-10	400	Hummel (1977)
	2-10	400	Shadoff & Hummel (1978)
	50	---	Adamoli et al. (1978)
LKB-9000S	20	---	di Domenico et al. (1979)
LKB-2091	250	400	Fanelli et al. (1980)
Finnigan 3000	50	Unit	Adamoli et al. (1978)
Finnigan 3200	20	Unit	di Domenico et al. (1979)
	40-80	Unit	Cavallaro et al. (1982)
Finnigan 4000	1-20	Unit	Buser & Rappe (1983)
Finnigan 4023	1-2	Unit	Tosine et al. (1982)
HP-5984A	20	Unit	di Domenico et al. (1979)
-5992A	40-60	Unit	Lamparksi & Nestrick (1980)
-5992	5-10	Unit	Norstrom et al. (1982)
-5985B	3	Unit	Norstrom & Simon (1983)
Extra-Nuc.	1000	Unit	Tiernan et al. (1981)
Kratos 30	5	1000	Langhorst & Shadoff (1980)
Kratos 80	0.5-2	1000	Nestrick & Lamparski (1982)
Varian - 311A	10	1000	Ryan & Pilon (1980)

Very little work has been done at medium resolution (M/ΔM = 2500 to 9000) as shown in Table 4, although this approach would be expected to have some advantage in sensitivity over that of the same instrument operated at higher resolution.

TABLE 4. Stage III: Mass Spectrometry -- Medium Resolution Electron Impact

MS Model	T_4CDD Limit of Detection pg	M/ΔM	Reference
Kratos-30	5-10	3000	Hummel (1977)
Kratos-50	50	2000	Chess & Gross (1980)

Although high resolution mass spectrometry (M/ΔM > 9000) was used as early as 1973 (Baughman and Meselson, 1973), it has only recently been emphasized by some mass spectroscopists (Harless et al., 1980). Some of the experience with this approach is summarized below (Table 5):

TABLE 5. Stage III: Mass Spectrometry -- High Resolution Electron Impact

MS Model	T_4CDD Limit of Detection pg	$M/\Delta M$	Reference
Varian 311A	5-10	9000	Harless et al. (1980)
AEI MS-9	5	10000	Baughman & Meselson (1973)
Kratos MS-30	100	12000	Tiernan et al. (1981)
Kratos MS-30	2-10	9000	Shadoff & Hummel (1978)
Kratos MS-50	1-10	10000	Smith et al. (1982)

Chemical ionization mass spectrometry has been under investigation as a possible detector and monitor for PCDDs. The quantitative results of this work are summarized in the following table (6):

TABLE 6. Stage III: Mass Spectrometry -- Chemical Ionization

MS Model	T_4CDD Limit of Detection pg	$M/\Delta M$	Reference
Finnigan 3300	50-500	Unit	Hass et al. (1978)
Extra-Nuc.	10-30	Unit	Mitchum et al. (1980)
			Cairns et al. (1980)

More recently (Tou et al., 1982) MS/MS has been used as a detector. Using a Finnigan triple stage quadrupole mass spectrometer, the limit of detection for 2,7-DCDD and 1,3,7-T_3CDD was found to be about 10 picograms.

It is evident from the tables that the limit of detection for T_4CDD is very much the same on high resolution instruments as on low resolution ones. The advantage of high resolution lies in its ability to separate interfering ions in the mass spectrometer.

Criteria for the confirmation of the homologue and specific isomer are essential to any analysis. Harless et al., (1980) have proposed the following:

HARLESS CRITERIA FOR HOMOLOGUE AND SPECIFIC ISOMER CONFIRMATION

1. Correct HRGC-HRMS retention time for 2,3,7,8-T_4CDD.

2. Correct HRGC-HRMS multiple ion response for $^{37}Cl_4$-T_4CDD and T_4CDD masses (simultaneous response for elemental composition of m/z 320, m/z 322, m/z 328).

3. Correct chlorine isotope ratio for the molecular ions (m/z 320 and m/z 322).

4. Correct responses for the co-injection of sample fortified with $^{37}Cl_4$-T_4CDD and T_4CDD standard.

5. Response of the m/z 320 and m/z 322 must be greater than 2.5 times the noise level.

SUPPLEMENTAL CRITERIA PROPOSED BY HARLESS

1. COCl loss indicative of T_4CDD structure, and
2. HRGC-HRMS peak matching analysis of m/z 320 and m/z 322 in real time to confirm the T_4CDD elemental composition.

These criteria are useful and are accepted by almost all analytical scientists whenever capillary gas chromatography (HRGC) is used. However, the limit of detection in criterion 5 would be better defined as 3 times the noise level (ACS CEI, 1980). The supplemental criteria provide confirmation but usually cannot be applied at concentration levels near the limit of detection where such information is most needed.

THE ANALYTICAL PROCESS

The three stages of the analytical process may be categorized according to resolving power: low (L), medium (M), and high (H). The categories of sample preparation are described as follows (Table 7):

TABLE 7. Stage I -- Sample Preparation

Resolving Power	Description
L	Chemical Treatment and/or Extraction No Chromatography
M	L + Column Chromatography
H	M + High Pressure Liquid Chromatography

The sample introduction into the mass spectrometer may be described as follows (Table 8):

TABLE 8. Stage II -- MS Sample Introduction

Resolving Power	Decription
L	Direct Probe (No Gas Chromatography)
M	Packed Column GC
H	Capillary Column GC

Likewise, the operation of the mass spectrometer may be assigned rankings as follows (Table 9):

TABLE 9. Stage III -- Mass Spectrometry (MS)

Resolving Power	Description
L	Low Resolution (M/ΔM 2500)
M	Medium Resolution (M/ΔM = 2500 to 9000)
H	High Resolution (M/ΔM 9000)

Obviously, these can be put together in all possible combinations to create various methods. Thus, methods could be developed which could be described by each of these acronyms (Table 10).

TABLE 10. Possible Analytical Methods For The Determination of PCDDs and PCDFs

LLL	MLL	HLL
LLM	MLM	HLM
LLH	MLH*	HLH
LML	MML*	HML*
LMM	MMM	HMM
LMH	MMH*	HMH
LHL	MHL	HHL*
LHM	MHM	HHM
LHH	MHH*	HHH*

At least seven of these (marked with asterisks) have been used recently to determine dioxins in environmental samples. Some of the studies are summarized in Table 11 along with the limits of detection and estimated ability to resolve TCDD isomers.

TABLE 11. Performance of PCDD Analytical Methods on Environmental Samples

Analytical System	Limit of Detection ppt	Number of T$_4$CDD Isomers Separated	Sample Matrix	Reference
MLH	0.2-3	0	Human milk	Meselson & O'Keefe (1977)
MMH	0.1-6	4-12	Human milk	Gross (1980)
MMH	3-6	4-12	Human milk	Tiernan et al. (1981)
MMH	1-6	15-22	Human milk	Shadoff et al. (1977)
HML	0.5-1	15-22	Human milk	Loomis et al. (1980)
MMH	2-4	4-12	Human adipose tissue	Gross (1980)
MHH	3-5	15-22	Human adipose tissue	Gross (1980)
MML	1	4-12	Bovine milk	Mahle et al. (1977)
MML	2-10	4-12	Bovine tissues	Jensen et al. (1981)
MML	10	4-12	Fish	Fukuhara et al. (1975)
MML	3-5	4-12	Gull eggs	Norstrom et al. (1982)
HML	4-20	15-22	Fish	Lamparski et al. (1979)
HHL	0.6-2	22	Flyash	Nestrick & Lamparski (1982)
HHL	1-2	22	Fish	Tosine et al. (1982)
MHH	4-13	15-22	Fish	Harless & Lewis (1982)
HHH	1-5	22	Fish	Smith et al. (1982)

In most of these studies the specificity of the method for 2,3,7,8-TCDD is the most important consideration and several of these methods are specific for this isomer.

Even though each step in the methodology just described is well understood, results generated by its use need to be carefully interpreted and documented if they are to be compared with other similar data. This is made clear by the ACS guidleines and reaffirmed at the IUPAC Conference in Helsinki (Crummett and Taylor, 1982). A Canadian panel (McLeod, 1981) applied the ACS guidelines to rate publications and found only two that came close to meeting the guidelines.

TABLE 12. Observed Concentration in Parts per Trillion

CDD Isomers	1933 Milorganite	1981 Milorganite	1982 Milorganite
2378-TCDD	2.2 (0.8)[a]	11	16
1469-TCDD	nd (0.6)[b]	nd (0.7)	nd (0.7)
1269-TCDD	nd (0.6)	nd (0.7)	nd (0.7)
1267-TCDD	nd (0.6)	nd (0.7)	nd (0.7)
1289-TCDD	nd (0.6)	nd (0.7)	nd (0.7)
1369-TCDD	1.4 (0.4)	1.4 (0.6)	3.4 (0.7)
1247+1248-TCDDs	4.8	1.4 (0.6)	3.2 (0.7)
1278-TCDD	1.4 (0.4)	2.2 (0.6)	3.0 (0.7)
1268-TCDD	1.4 (0.4)	1.1 (0.6)	2.4 (0.7)
1237+1238-TCDDs	2.2 (0.4)	93	140
1279-TCDD	1.6 (0.4)	1.4 (0.6)	3.4 (0.7)
1478-TCDD	0.8 (0.4)	0.8 (0.6)	2.0 (0.7)
1236-TCDD	nd (0.4)	nd (0.6)	nd (0.7)
1239-TCDD	nd (0.4)	nd (0.6)	nd (0.7)
1246+1249-TCDDs	nd (0.9)	nd (0.7)	nd (0.8)
1368-TCDD	7.2	9.2	15
1379-TCDD	3.5 (0.6)	6.0	12
1378-TCDD	5.5 (0.6)	10	22
1234-TCDD	1.8 (0.6)	nd (0.6)	nd (1.1)
Total TCDDs	33.8	137.5	222.4

[a] Value in parentheses is limit of detection, defined as 2.5 x (peak to valley) noise in an adjacent region of the mass chromatogram. If the limit of detection is less than 10% of the observed signal, it is not reported.
[b] nd = not detected at specified limit of detection.

(Reproduced with permission from Lamparski et al., 1984.)

From the studies already done it is obvious that analytical systems can be designed to address any reasonable question about the nature and concentration of chlorinated dioxins in the environment. Isomer specific determination of 2,3,7,8-TCDD can be done with detection limits from 1-10 parts per trillion in particulate matter and animal tissue and to 1 part per quadrillion in water. 2,3,7,8-TCDD can also be determined non-isomer specifically as one of a number of TCDD isomers. Other isomer groups (penta-, hexa-, hepta, and octa-) can also be handled in the same way. Any particular isomer group can thus be extensively examined or totally ignored.

Until now the emphasis has been on 2,3,7,8-TCDD. However, there is a growing tendency for scientists to emphasize the need for more complete data. The reason for this becomes very clear from an examination of a few such data sets. Tables 12, 13 and 14 show the results of analyses which are isomer-specific for tetra-, hexa-, hepta-, and octa-isomers on Milorganite* samples taken in the years 1933, 1981 and 1982 (Lamparski et al., 1984). The concentration of the hexa-, hepta- and octa-isomers remained constant in all three samples. However, there was a significant change in the concentration of a few of the tetra-isomers. This suggests that it may be of interest to examine these more closely. A simple way to do this is to calculate the percent each TCDD isomer is of the total TCDD isomers. Such results are given in Table 15.

---

*Milorganite: TM for dried municipal sewage sludge from Milwaukee, Wisconsin.

TABLE 13. Observed Hexa-CDD Concentrations in Milwaukee Milorganite Samples

CDD Isomers	Observed Concentration in Parts per Trillion		
	1933 Milorganite	1981 Milorganite	1982 Milorganite
124679+124689-HCDDs	350	340	420
123468-HCDD	72	72 (18)	100
123679+123689-HCDDs	650	710	620
123469-HCDD	nd (32)	nd (18)	nd (14)
123478-HCDD	22 (3.0)	nd (18)	15 (5.7)
123678-HCDD	280	220	200
123467+123789-HCDDs	83	70 (18)	73
Total HCDDs	1457	1412	1428

(Reproduced with permission from Lamparski et al., 1984.)

TABLE 14. Observed Hepta- and Octa-CDD Concentrations in Milwaukee Milorganite Samples

CDD Isomers	1933 Milorganite	1981 Milorganite	1982 Milorganite
1234679-H7CDD	5000	4600	4000
1234678-H7CDD	4700	4800	3600
Total H7CDD	9700	9400	7600
OCDD	59000	50000	60000

(Reproduced with permission from Lamparski et al., 1984.)

TABLE 15. TCDD Isomer Pattern in Milwaukee Milorganite Samples

	Percent of Total TCDD		
TCDD ISOMER	1933	1981	1982
2378	6.5	8.0	7.2
1247+1248	14.2	1.0	1.4
1278	4.1	1.6	1.3
1268	4.1	0.8	1.1
1237+1238	6.5	67.6	62.9
1279	4.7	1.0	1.5
1478	2.3	0.6	0.9
1368	21.3	6.7	6.7
1379	10.4	4.4	5.4
1378	16.3	7.3	9.9

These data suggest that the isomer pattern may be related to the source. Table 16 shows the TCDD isomer pattern in particulate matter from wood combustion (Nestrick and Lamparski, 1982). Only those samples which showed dioxin isomer signals greater than 10 times noise are selected because the certainty of the data must be quite high for this purpose. A flat distribution of TCDD isomers is observed.

TABLE 16. TCDD Isomer Pattern in Particulates From Wood Combustion

TCDD Isomer	Percent of Total TCDD						
	NH*		OR		MN		MI
	Oak	Oak	Fir	Fir	Birch	Oak	Oak
2378	2.0	4.2	3.5	4.2	2.9	6.4	3.3
1247+1248	9.7	9.1	8.9	12.5	10.2	10.2	7.7
1278	5.9	5.2	6.4	7.4	6.8	7.0	4.7
1268	6.5	5.6	8.0	8.3	8.1	7.9	4.4
1237+1238	11.0	9.9	7.6	14.6	13.1	10.5	6.4
1279	4.9	8.4	10.1	10.2	8.9	9.5	5.7
1478	1.3	3.3	6.0	1.8	3.1	3.2	1.8
1368	10.7	5.2	4.5	5.1	8.9	3.0	18.8
1379	12.5	4.8	4.9	4.2	7.0	4.1	12.8
1378	7.9	8.4	6.0	9.8	6.0	11.1	11.1

(*state of sample origin)

Table 17 shows the TCDD isomer pattern in soil and dust from four different United States cities. There is some variation in the 2378-TCDD isomer percentage. Otherwise the patterns are very nearly alike.

TABLE 17. TCDD Isomer Pattern In Dust & Soil From Four U.S. Cities

TCDD Isomer	Percent of Total TCDD			
	City 1	City 2	City 3	City 4
2378	4.4	3.9	8.9	22.1
1247+1248	6.6	6.7	5.7	3.8
1278	3.4	5.6	3.1	1.7
1268	4.2	5.3	3.9	1.9
1237+1238	9.0	10.8	7.5	5.3
1279	3.2	3.7	3.1	2.2
1478	0.1	0.9	1.4	0.7
1368	32.6	23.0	27.7	32.9
1379	13.2	12.8	15.9	14.4
1378	7.6	6.6	6.2	5.5

For comparison purposes typical TCDD isomer patterns from four different type samples are shown in Table 18. The three sources, sludge, wood smoke, and municipal incinerators do not completely account for all of the isomers observed in the cities. Nor can the dioxin content of commercial products alone account for the isomer pattern of City 3.

TABLE 18. Comparison Of TCDD Isomer Patterns

TCDD Isomer	Range in the Percent of Total TCDD			
	Sludge 1982	Wood Combustion Particulates MN	City 3	Municipal Incinerator[30]
2378	7.2	6.4	8.9	3.8
1247+1248	1.4	10.2	5.7	10.7
1278	1.3	7.0	3.1	4.4
1268	1.1	7.9	3.9	6.2
1237-1238	62.9	10.5	7.5	12.7
1279	1.5	9.5	3.1	4.5
1478	0.9	3.2	1.4	1.8
1368	6.7	3.0	27.7	15.0
1379	5.4	4.1	15.9	12.3
1378	9.9	11.1	6.2	9.5

In a similar manner the HCDD isomer patterns can be examined. A summary of such an examination is shown in Table 19. Although in this case the observed pattern of the sources suggests that the three sources could account for the pattern observed in City 3, we know from the TCDD isomer pattern that it cannot.

TABLE 19. Comparison Of HCDD Isomer Patterns

HCDD Isomer	Percent of Total HCDD			
	Sludge 1982	Wood Combustion Particulates MN	City 3	Incinerator Composite
124679+124689	29.4	15.3	20.4	14.1
123468	7.0	6.1	19.4	26.2
12379+123689	43.4	56.7	35.2	29.6
123469	0.0	0.0	0.0	3.5
123478+123678	15.1	12.3	14.8	14.4
123467+123789	5.1	9.6	10.2	12.3

Some investigators use isomer group ratios as patterns to relate dioxin findings to their source. If we do that for the analyses just reported, Table 20 results. From these patterns the sludge and city samples appear to contain dioxins from pentachlorophenol. However, isomer specific patterns already examined do not support that conclusion.

TABLE 20. Isomer Group Pattern Comparison

Isomer Group	Percent of Total Dioxins			
	Sludge 1982	Wood Combustion Particulates MN	City 3	Incinerator
TCDD	0.3	5.2; 3.3	0.3	12.7
H_6CDD	2.1	18.3;64.6	3.7	35.8
H_7CDD	11.0	43.8;28.7	17.0	28.6
OCDD	86.6	32.6; 3.4	79.9	22.6

Recently, some investigators (Buser and Rappe, 1983) recommended analyzing for the 2378-substituted polychlorinated dibenzo-p-dioxins (PCDDs) specifically because of their perceived higher toxicities and to use them as indicators of sources. If we examine the same samples for these congeners, Table 21 results.

TABLE 21. Comparison Of 2378 Substituted PCDDs Patterns

PCDD Congener	Percent of Total			
	Sludge 1982	Wood Combustion Particulates MN	City 3	Incinerator Fly Ash
2378 TCDD	0.3	0.2	0.6	0.8
12378 P$_5$ CDD	--	--	--	--
123478+123678 HCDD	0.3	9.6	0.5	8.0
123789 HCDD+ 123467 HCDD	0.1	7.5	0.3	7.3
1234679 H$_7$CDD	5.9	24.0	8.3	21.8
1234678 H$_7$CDD	5.3	22.8	10.1	22.9
OCDD	88.1	46.7	80.2	39.3

Some of these patterns are probably very meaningful but the meaning is not obvious. Much more data will need to be acquired from a complete set of source samples before the patterns can be unambiguously interpreted. In the meantime, it is premature to associate sources with isomer patterns and any such association must be viewed as speculative.

To acquire data necessary to elucidate the meaning of isomer patterns requires the very finest in analytical methodology. Although this methodology has already been described, it deserves further consideration here. The ACS guidelines define the analytical process as consisting of the plan model, sampling, measurement, the data set, confirmation and documentation. The following discussion, however, is limited to the measurement process and to the determination of the 22 tetrachlorodibenzo-p-dioxins (TCDDs) in particular (Crummett et al., 1983).

METHODOLOGY REQUIRED FOR DETERMINING ISOMER DISTRIBUTION PATTERNS (AS APPLIED TO WOOD COMBUSTION PARTICULATES)

Bulk Matrix Removal Steps

The chlorinated dioxins are removed from particulate matter by Soxhlet extraction using benzene as a solvent. A representative aliquot of the sample, ground and homogenized, is added to a Soxhlet extractor together with the internal standard, [^{13}C]-2,3,7,8-TCDD, over a bed of glass wool on silica. The resulting solution is subjected to three column clean-up steps to remove interfering substances present in large quantities.

The benzene extract is passed through a column consisting of layers of silica, cesium-silica, basic alumina and silica. This treatment removes acidic species, polar compounds, and compounds of low solubility.

The effluent from the first column is concentrated by atmospheric pressure distillation and diluted four fold with hexane. It is then passed through a second column consisting of layers of silica, 22 percent sulfuric acid on silica, 44 percent sulfuric acid on silica, silica, aqueous sodium hydroxide on silica, and silica. This column removes basic species, many polynuclear aromatic compounds, terpenes, and easily oxidizable compounds.

The 1:3 benzene:hexane solution from the second column is concentrated as before and further diluted with hexane to obtain a 1:16 benzene:hexane solution. This solution is passed through a third column consisting of layers of silica, 44 percent concentrated sulfuric acid on silica, silica, aqueous sodium hydroxide on silica, and silica. This column eliminates less easily oxidizable materials and any traces of materials which may have escaped the second column.

Specific Chemicals Removal Steps

Effluent from the third column is evaporated to dryness and the residue dissolved in hexane. The hexane solution is passed through a fourth column consisting of 10 percent silver nitrate on silica. This column removes aliphatic halides, sulfur compounds, and any residual polar species.

Effluent from the fourth column is passed into a flash chromatographic column packed with basic alumina. A wash with hexane removes hydrocarbons, chlorobenzenes, and certain other low polarity compounds. A wash with 50 percent carbon tetrachloride removes aliphatic substituted aromatics, polychlorinated biphenyls, some polyhalogenated napthalenes, and pesticides. A final elution with 50 percent methylene chloride in hexane removes the chlorinated dioxins and dibenzofurans.

The residue from this elution is dissolved in hexane. It still contains polyolefins and some residual oxidizable materials at very low levels. These are removed by a fifth column packed with aqueous potassium permanganate and sodium hydroxide on silica.

These separations have required the use of 66 pieces of glassware, each of which must be cleaned twice with a thoroughness which will not permit contamination by even 1 picogram of the dioxin to be determined. At this point the residue represents about 1 part per million parts of starting sample. To determine dioxins at the 1 part per trillion level, 1 part must be isolated from another million parts.

Chlorinated Dioxin Fractionation

Reversed phase, high performance, liquid chromatography (HPLC) on Zorbax ODS with methanol eluent removes chemically similar species and separates CDDs by degree of chlorination thus giving partial separation of CDD isomers. Six fractions of CDDs are collected. In order of elution these are: (1) a TCDD isomer fraction containing the 1469-, 1269-, 1267-, and 1289- isomers; (2) a TCDD isomer fraction containing the 2378-, 1369-, 1247-, 1248-, 1278-, 1268-, 1237-, 1238-, 1279-, 1246-, 1478-, 1236-, 1239-, and 1249-isomers; (3) a TCDD isomer fraction containing the 1368-, 1379-, 1378-, and 1234-isomers; (4) a hexachlorodibenzodioxin (HCDD) fraction containing all 10 HCDD isomers; (5) a fraction containing both hepta (H_7CDD) isomers; and (6) a fraction containing the octachlorodibenzodioxin (OCDD).

Each of the first four fractions can be further separated by normal phase HPLC on silica. The second fraction is thus separated into four new fractions, the first of which contains only 2,3,7,8-TCDD and the fourth only 1249-TCDD. The second fraction contains 1369-, 1247-, 1248-, 1278-, 1268-, 1237-, 1238-, and 1279-TCDD. The third fraction contains 1246-, 1478-, 1236-, and 1239-TCDD. The second and third fractions are now of a composition which can be analyzed for specific isomers by high resolution gas chromatography-low resolution mass spectrometry.

Gas Chromatography-Mass Spectrometry

Specific isomers in the HPLC fractions are separated and measured by high resolution mass spectrometry using the following conditions.

HRGC-LRMS Instrumental Conditions
Kratos MS·80 (slightly modified) and Carlo Erba 4160 GC
0.32 mm ID x 30 M J & W fused silica: DB-5 (0.25 m)
2 l split injection: Injector @ 300°C
He Carrier: 33 cm/sec. linear velocity
Open-split interface: all fused silica construction
Interface @ 270°C. Reentrant @ 270°C
Combination Source: EI Mode//300°C// 2 x 10^{-6} Torr
TCDDs Column Temperature: 210°C isothermal
TCDD Ions: Internal standard m/z 335.930
          Native TCDDs m/z 319.896 & 321.893

Examination of the four fractions from the HPLC separation of the TCDD isomers by this system reveals only one peak in the first fraction due to the 2,3,7,8 isomer; 6 peaks in the second fraction, 4 being completely free of other isomers while the pairs 1247-and 1248-as well as 1237- and 1238- are not resolved; 4 peaks in the third fraction with all isomers resolved; and 1 peak in the fourth fraction being due to 1249-TCDD alone.

The other fractions from the reversed phase HPLC separation can also be taken through the system. Thus, the 22 isomers of TCDD are separated.

TCDD Identification Criteria

Criteria used to identify TCDDs with a very high degree of certainty (95 percent) are:
1. Correct reversed phase HPLC retention window.
2. Correct silica HPLC retention window.
3. Correct high resolution GC retention time.
4. Correct chlorine isotope ratio at m/z 320 and 322.
5. Response exceeds limit of detection. (3x peak to valley noise in mass chromatography).
6. ^{13}C·2,3,7,8·TCDD internal standard recovery is between 50 to 125%.
7. High resolution mass spectrometry confirmation (when necessary).

The Data Set

The data set consists of (a) field samples, (b) field blanks, (c) spiked field blanks, and (d) reagent blanks. The field blanks are selected from the field samples - those that showed "not detectable" quantities of 21 of the 22 isomers of TCDD from the analysis. They are spiked with all 22 analytical standards of the 22 natural isomers of TCDD at two concentration levels and analyzed to obtain recovery data.

Qualitative Confirmation of Validated Measurements

Confirmation that each of the TCDD isomers identified was in fact a TCDD isomer is made by high resolution gas chromatography-high resolution mass spectrometry at a mass resolution of ca. 9000. However, this may not be necessary as the low resolution (ca. 1000) mass chromatograms at m/z 322, m/z 320, and m/z 336 are free of extraneous peaks, even when the TCDD signals are very close to the limit of detection.

Analytical Standards

A major limitation to attempting the analysis just described is the unavailability of analytical standards. Only a few are available in pure form. Even when available and added to a matrix their recovery cannot be assured to be equivalent to the recovery of the same compounds which have been naturally incurred. To help resolve this situation, Nestrick et al. (1983) have proposed using National Bureau of Standards SRMs #1648 and #1649 to demonstrate ability to remove and measure the dioxins present in dust and soil. The analyses are given in Tables 22, 23 and 24. The samples should also be analyzed for the penta isomers as at least one of these has been found in eggs of the Great Blue Heron (Norstrom and Simon, 1983), fish and herring gulls (Buser and Rappe, 1983) as well as in fly ash from municipal incinerators.

TABLE 22. TCDD Content Of National Bureau Of Standards SRMs #1648 and 1649

	Concentration (Parts Per Trillion = pg/g)	
TCDDs	SRM #1648: St. Louis, MO	SRM #1649: Washington, DC
2378-TCDD	47	6.7 (1.1)
1469-TCDD	3.9 (1.0)	2.2 (0.7)
1269-TCDD	9.6 (1.0)	3.8 (0.7)
1267-TCDD	5.5 (1.0)	1.8 (0.7)
1289-TCDD	6.5 (1.0)	2.5 (0.7)
1369-TCDD	21	8.8
1247 + 1248-TCDDs	30	11
1278-TCDD	17	9.5
1268-TCDD	21	9.0
1237 + 1238-TCDDs	40	18
1279-TCDD	16	6.4
1246-TCDD	7.6	3.2 (0.7)
1478-TCDD	7.6	1.6 (0.7)
1236-TCDD	7.5	3.2 (0.7)
1239-TCDD	6.4 (0.7)	3.8 (0.7)
1249-TCDD	7.4	2.3 (0.6)
1368-TCDD	150	39
1379-TCDD	84	22
1378-TCDD	33	11
1234-TCDD	12 (1.7)	3.8 (0.7)
Total TCDDs	533	170
^{13}C-2378-TCDD Recovery	89%	69%

TABLE 23. TCDF & HCDD Content of NBS SRMs

TCDF	Concentration (Parts Per Trillion = pg/g)	
	SRM #1648: St. Louis, MO	SRM#1649: Washington, DC
2378-TCDF	380	102
^{13}C-2378-TCDF Recovery	85%	98%

HCDDs	Concentration (Parts Per Billion = ng/g)	
124679 + 124689-HCDDs	1.2	0.87
123468-HCDD	1.2	0.75
123679 + 123689-HCDDs	2.4	1.6
123469-HCDD	0.09 (0.05)	0.18 (0.04)
123478 + 123678-HCDDs	1.4	0.50
123467 + 123789-HCDDs	0.68	0.48
Total HCDDs	7.0	4.4

TABLE 24. H$_7$CDD & OCDD Content of NBS SRMs

H$_7$CDDs	Concentration (Parts Per Billion = ng/g)	
	SRM #1648: St. Louis, MO	SRM #1649: Washington, DC
1234679-H$_7$CDD	14.9	18.1
1234678-H$_7$CDD	17.2	18.4
	32.1	36.5
OCDD	Concentration (Parts Per Billion = ng/g)	
OCDD	149	173

We conclude that enough is known to allow the analytical chemist to take appropriate samples, store and transport them properly, pretreat them for analysis, identify the dioxins and measure them, interpret the data properly, and document the results appropriately.

Enough is also known to appropriately select the liquid chromatographic, gas chromatographic and mass spectrometric techniques to achieve any analysis desired. We can design methods which are custom made to find or not to find, to identify or not to identify, to emphasize or ignore any single PCDD congener, PCDD isomer group, or any combination thereof.

To select the appropriate methodology requires a knowledge of why the analysis is being done. Most of the work to date appears to have been attempting to prove that 2,3,7,8-TCDD is present in the environment. This only requires methodology capable of the isomer specific determination of 2,3,7,8-TCDD. Increasingly, however, scientists are attempting to relate dioxin data to the dioxin sources. Although insufficient data are available to make such correlations, it appears that methodology must be used which can determine many of the dioxins isomer-specifically. Isomer group determinations give only partial information and can be misleading.

Isomer-specific analysis for the TCDD, HCDD, H7CDD, and OCDD isomers has been done. This requires the most sophisticated methodology and the cost is very great, as much as $3000 per sample. Because of this, as well as limitations on trained personnel and equipment, samples for this analysis should be carefully selected. Analytical screening procedures may be useful as an aid in this selection. A number of biological screens have been proposed. These include radio immunoassay (McKinney et al., 1982), aryl hydrocarbon hydroxylase-(AHH)-induction assay (Bradlaw and Casterline, 1979; Sawyer et al., 1983), cytosil receptor assay (Hutzinger et al., 1981), and keratinization (Knutson and Poland, 1980). Unfortunately, these have not been sufficiently developed and the MS/MS system using "flash" chromatography coupled to tandem mass spectrometry (Sakuma et al., 1983) may be the preferred screening method.

Much data will need to be acquired before the analytical results can be reliably related to the dioxin source. Once this relationship has been established taking into account transformations of isomer ratios which can occur in the environment, the methodology may possibly be further optimized and greatly simplified. Until this is done, however, methodology yielding complete identification and measurement of many isomers is necessary. Let us hope we have the courage to promote its use, awesome though it is.

REFERENCES

Adamoli, P., Angeli, E., Bandi, G., Bertolotti, A., Bianchi, E., Bonifort, L., Camoni, I., Cattabeni, F., Colli, G., Colombo, C., Corradi, C., De Angelis, L., De Felice, G., di Domenico, A., Di Muccio, A., Elli, G., Fanelli, R., Fittipaldi, A., Frigero, A., Galli, G., Grassi, P., Gualdi, R., Invernizzi, G., Jemma, A., Luciano, L., Manaro, L., Marinella, A., Merli, F., Nicosia, S., Rizzelo, F., Rossi, C., Rossi, G., Salvatore, G., Sampolo, A., Schmidt, F., Taggi, G., Tebaldi, E., Zaino, E. and Zapponi, G. 1978. Analysis of 2,3,7,8-tetrachlorodibenzo-para-dioxin in the Seveso area. In Chlorinated Phenoxy Acids and Their Dioxins, ed. C. Ramel. Ecol. Bull. 27:31-38.

ACS Committee on Environmental Improvement. 1980. Data acquisition and data quality evaluation in environmental chemistry. Anal. Chem. 52:2242-2249.

Baughman, R. and Meselson, M. 1973. An analytical method for detecting TCDD (Dioxin): Levels of TCDD in samples from Vietnam. Environ. Health Persp. 5:27-35.

Blaser, W. W., Bredeweg, R.A., Shadoff, L.A. and Stehl, R.H. 1976. Determination of chlorinated dibenzo-p-dioxins in pentachlorophenol by gas chromatography/mass spectrometry. Anal. Chem. 48:984-986.

Bradlaw, J.A. and Casterline, J.L. 1979. Induction of enzyme activity in cell culture: A rapid screen for detection of planar polychlorinated organic compounds. J. Assoc. Off. Anal. Chem. 62:904-916.

Brumley, W.C., Roach, J.A.G., Sphon, J.A., Dreifuss, P.A., Andrzejewski, D., Neiman, R.A. and Firestone, D. 1981. Low-resolution multiple ion detection gas chromatographic-mass spectrometric comparison of six extraction cleanup methods for determining 2,3,7,8-tetrachlorodibenzo-p-dioxin in fish. J. Agri. Food Chem. 29:1040-1046.

Buser, H.R. 1975. Analysis of polychlorinated dibenzo-p-dioxins and dibenzofurans in chlorinated phenols by mass fragmentography. J. Chromatogr. 107:295-310.

Buser, H.R. and Rappe, C. 1980. High-resolution gas chromatography of the 22 tetrachlorodibenzo-p-dioxin isomers. Anal. Chem. 52:2257-2262.

Buser, H.R. and Rappe, C. 1983. Isomer-specific separation of 2,3,7,8-substituted polychlorinated dibenzo-p-dioxins (PCDDs) by high resolution gas chromatography/mass spectrometry. Private communication.

Cairns, T., Fishbein, L. and Mitchum, R.K. 1980. Review of the dioxin problem. Mass spectrometric analyses of the tetrachlorodioxins in environmental samples. Biomed. Mass Spectrom. 7:484-492.

Cavallaro, A., Bandi, G., Invernizzi, G., Luciani, L., Mongini, E. and Gorni, G. 1982. Negative ion chemical ionization MS as a structure tool in the determination of small amounts of PCDD and PCDF. In Chlorinated Dioxins and Related Compounds: Impact on the Environment, ed. O. Hutzinger, R.W. Frei, E. Merian and F. Pocchiari, pp.55-65, Pergamon Press, Oxford.

Chae, K., Cho, L.K. and McKinney, J.D. 1977. Synthesis of 1-amino-3,7,8-trichlorodibenzo-p-dioxin and 1-amino-2,3,7,8-tetrachlorodibenzo-p-dioxin as haptenic compounds. J. Agri. Food Chem. 25:1207-1209.

Chess, E. K. and Gross, M.L. 1980. Determination of tetrachlorodioxins by mass spectrometric metastable decomposition monitoring. Anal. Chem. 52:2057-2061.

Cochrane, W.P., Singh, J., Miles, W. and Wakeford, B. 1981. Determination of chlorinated dibenzo-p-dioxin contaminants in 2,4-D products by gas chromatography/mass spectrometric techniques. J. Chromatogr. 217:289-299.

Crummett, W.B. 1979. Fundamental problems related to validation of analytical data elaborated on the example of TCDD. Toxic. Environ. Chem. Rev. 3:61-71.

Crummett, W.B. 1982. Analytical methodology for the determination of PCDDs and PCDFs in products and environmental samples: An overview and critique. In Human and Environmental Risks of Chlorinated Dioxins and Related Compounds, ed. R.E. Tucker, A.L. Young and A. P. Gray, pp.45-63, Plenum Press, New York.

Crummett, W.B. 1983. Status of analytical systems for the determination of PCDDs and PCDFs. Chemosphere 12:429-446.

Crummett, W.B. and Stehl, R.H. 1973. Determination of chlorinated dibenzo-p-dioxins and dibenzofurans in various materials. Environ. Health Persp. 5:15-25.

Crummett, W.B. and Taylor, J.K. 1982. Guidelines for data acquisition and data quality evaluation in environmental chemistry. In IUPAC Collaborative Interlaboratory Studies in Chemical Analysis, ed. H. Egan and T.S. West, pp. 63-65, Pergamon Press, Oxford and New York.

Crummett, W. B., Nestrick, T. J. and Lamparski, L.L. 1983. Advanced/good analytical techniques elaborated on the detection of polychlorinated dibenzodioxins in environmental samples. In Pesticide Chemistry: Human Welfare and the Environment, Vol. 4, ed. J. Miyamoto, P.C. Kearney, R. Greenhalgh and N. Drescher, pp. 61-66,, Pergamon Press, Oxford.

Crummett, W.B., Stehl, R.H., Hummel, R.A. and Shadoff, L.A. 1979. A search for chlorinated dioxins in the environment. CIPAC Proceedings Symposium Papers, ed. W.R. Bontoyan, pp. 91-107, CIPAC Proceedings Symposium Series 1, CIPAC Publication, Hertfordshire, England.

di Domenico, A., Merli, F., Boniforti, L., Camoni, I., DiMuccio, A., Taggi, F., Vergori, L., Colli, G., Elli, G., Gorni, A., Grassi, P., Invernizzi, G., Jemma, A. Luciani, L., Cattabeni, F., DeAngelis, L., Galli, G., Chiabrando, C. and Fanelli, R. 1979. Analytical techniques for 2,3,7,8-tetrachlorodibenzo-p-dioxin detection in environmental samples after the industrial accident at Seveso. Anal. Chem. 51:735-740.

Dougherty, R.C., Whitaker, M.J., Smith, L.M., Stalling, D.L. and Kuehl, D.W. 1980. Negative chemical ionization studies of human and food chain contamination with xenobiotic chemicals. Environ. Health Persp. 36:103-108.

Eiceman, G.A., Viau, A.C. and Karasek, F.W. 1980. Ultrasonic extraction of polychlorinated dibenzo-p-dioxins and other organic compounds from fly ash from municipal incinerators. Anal. Chem. 52:1492-1496.

Erk, S., Taylor, M.L. and Tiernan, T.O. 1979. Determination of 2,3,7,8-tetrachlorodibenzo-p-dioxin residues on metal surfaces. Chemosphere 8:7-14.

Fanelli, R., Castelli, M.G., Martelli, G.P., Noseda, A. and Garrattini, S. 1980. Presence of 2,3,7,8-tetrachlorodibenzo-p-dioxin in wildlife living near Seveso, Italy: A preliminary study. Bull. Environ. Contam. Toxicol. 24:460-462.

Fukuhara, K., Takeda, M., Uchiyama, M. and Tanabe, H. 1975. Analytical method for 2,3,7,8-tetrachlorodibenzo-p-dioxin in sec. foods. Eisei Kagaku 21:318-325.

Gross, M.L. 1980. Direct testimony of Dr. Michael L. Gross before the Administrator, United States Environmental Protection Agency, EPA Exhibit No. 223. FIFRA Docket Nos. 415 et al.

Harless, R.W. and Lewis, R.G. 1982. Quantitative determination of 2,3,7,8-tetrachlorodibenzo-p-dioxin residues by gas chromatography/mass spectrometry. In Chlorinated Dioxins and Related Compounds: Impact on the Environment, ed. O Hutzinger, R.W. Frei, E. Merian and F. Pocchiari, pp.25-35, Pergamon Press, Oxford.

Harless, R.L., Oswald, E.O., Wilkinson, M.K., Dupuy, A.E., Jr., McDaniel, D.D., and Han Tai. 1980. Sample preparation and gas chromatography/mass spectrometry determination of 2,3,7,8-tetrachlorodibenzo-p-dioxin. Anal. Chem. 52:1239-1245.

Harless, R.L., Oswald, E.O., Lewis, R.G., Dupuy, A.E., McDaniel, D.D. and Han Tai. 1982. Determination of 2,3,7,8-tetrachlorodibenzo-p-dioxin in fresh water fish. Chemosphere 11:193-198.

Hass, J.R., Friesen, M.D., Harvan, D.J. and Parker, C.E. 1978. Determination of polychlorinated dibenzo-p-dioxins in biological samples by negative chemical ionization mass spectrometry. Anal. Chem. 50:1474-1479.

Huckins, J.N., Stalling, D.L. and Smith, W.A. 1978. Foam charcoal chromatography for analysis of polychlorinated dibenzodioxins in Herbicide Orange. J. Assoc. Off. Anal. Chem. 61:32-38.

Hummel, R.A. 1977. Clean-up techniques for the determination of parts per trillion of 2,3,7,8-tetrachlorodibenzo-p-dioxin (TCDD). J. Agric. Food Chem. 25:1049-1053.

Hutzinger, O., Olie, K., Lustenhouwer, J.W.A., Okey, A.B., Bandiera, S. and Safe, S. 1981. Polychlorinated dibenzo-p-dioxins and dibenzofurans: A bioanalytical approach. Chemosphere 10:19-25.

Jensen, D.J., Hummel, R.A., Mahle, N.H., Kocher, C.W. and Higgins, H.S. 1981. A residue study on beef cattle consuming 2,3,7,8-tetrachlorodibenzo-p-dioxin. J. Agric. Food Chem. 29:265-268.

Knutson, J.C. and Poland, A. 1980. Keratization of mouse teratoma cell XB produced by 2,3,7,8-tetrachlorodibenzo-p-dioxin: An in-vitro model of toxicity. Cell 22:27-36.

Lamparski, L.L. and Nestrick, T.J. 1980. Determination of tetra-, hexa-, hepta-, and octachlorodibenzo-p-dioxin isomers in particulate samples at parts per trillion levels. Anal. Chem. 52:2045-2054.

Lamparski, L.L. and Nestrick, T.J. 1981. Synthesis and identification of the 10 hexachlorodibenzo-p-dioxin isomers by high performance liquid and packed column gas chromatography. Chemosphere 10:3-18.

Lamparski, L.L. Mahle, N.H. and Shadoff, L.A. 1978. Determination of pentachlorophenol, hexachlorodibenzo-p-dioxin, and octachlorodibenzo-p-dioxin in bovine milk. J. Agri. Food Chem. 26:1113-1116.

Lamparski, L.L., Nestrick, T.J. and Stehl, R.H. 1979. Determination of part-per-trillion concentrations of 2,3,7,8-tetrachlorodibenzo-p-dioxin in fish. Anal. Chem. 51:1453-1458.

Lamparski, L.L., Nestrick, T.J. and Stenger, V.A. 1984. Presence of dioxins in a sealed 1933 sample of dried municipal sewage sludge. Chemosphere, in press.

Langhorst, M.L. and Shadoff, L.A. 1980. Determination of parts-per-trillion concentrations of tetra-, hexa-, hepta- and octa-chlorodibenzo-p-dioxins in human milk samples. Anal. Chem. 52:2037-2044.

Liberti, A., Brocco, D., Cecinato, A. and Possanzini, M. 1981. Determination of polychlorinated dibenzo-p-dioxins and dibenzofurans in the emission from urban incinerators. Mikrochim. Acta Wein 1:271-280.

Loomis, T.A., Shadoff, L.A. and Langhorst, M.L. 1980. Chlorinated dioxins in human milk and their toxicological significance. Submited for publication, Fund. Appl. Toxicol.

Mahle, N.H. and Shadoff, L.A. 1982. The mass spectrometry of chlorinated dibenzo-p-dioxins. Biomed. Mass Spectrom. 9:45-60.

Mahle, N.H., Higgins, H.S. and Getzendaner, M.E. 1977. Search for the presence of 2,3,7,8-tetrachlorodibenzo-p-dioxin in bovine milk. Bull. Environ. Contam. Tox. 18:123-130.

McKinney, J., Albro, P., Luster, M., Corbett, B., Schroeder, J. and Lawson, L. 1982.

Development and reliability of a radioimmunoassay for 2,3,7,8-tetrachlorodibenzo-p-dioxins. In Chlorinated Dioxins and Related Compounds: Impact on the Environment, ed. O. Hutzinger, R. W. Frei, E. Merian and F. Pocchiari, pp. 67-75, Pergamon Press, Oxford, England.

McLeod, H. (Chairman), Panel of Associate Committee on Scientific Criteria for Environmental Quality. 1981. Polychlorinated dibenzo-p-dioxins: Limitations to the current analytical techniques. National Research Council of Canada, NRCC No. 18576.

Meselson, M. and O'Keefe, P.W. 1977. Human milk monitoring: Preliminary results for twenty-one samples: 12/15/76. Letter to Congressman Jim Weaver.

Mieure, J.P., Hicks, O., Kaley, R.G. and Michael, P.R. 1977. Determination of trace amounts of chlorodibenzo-p-dioxins and chlorodibenzofurans in technical grade pentachlorophenol. J. Chromatogr. Sci. 15:275-277.

Mitchum, R.K., Moler, G.F. and Korfmacher, W.A. 1980. Combined capillary gas chromatography/atmospheric pressure negative chemical ionization/mass spectrometry for the determination of 2,3,7,8-tetrachlorodibenzo-p-dioxin in tissue. Anal. Chem. 52:2278-2282.

National Research Council of Canada. 1981. Polychlorinated dibenzo-p-dioxins. NRCC No. 18574. Publications, NRCC/CNRC, Ottawa, Canada K1A OR6.

Nestrick, T.J. and Lamparski, L.L. 1982. Isomer-specific determination of chlorinated dioxins for assessment of formation and potential environmental emission from wood combustion. Anal. Chem. 54:2292-2299.

Nestrick, T.J., Lamparski, L.L. and Stehl, R.H. 1979. Synthesis and identification of the 22 tetrachlorodibenzo-p-dioxin isomers by high performance liquid chromatography and gas chromatography. Anal. Chem. 51:2273-2281.

Nestrick, T.J., Lamparski, L.L. and Townsend, D.I. 1980. Identification of tetrachlorodibenzo-p-dioxin isomers at the 1-ng level by photolytic degradation and pattern recognition techniques. Anal. Chem. 52:1865-1874.

Nestrick, T.J., Lamparski, L.L. and Crummett, W.B. 1983. Proposed Adoption of National Bureau of Standards SRMS #1648 and #1649 As "Reference Particulate Matrices" for Analytical Methodology Quality Assurance in CDDs/CDFs Determination. Presented before the 186th National American Chemical Society meeting, August 29, 1983.

Nieman, R., Brumley, W., Firestone, D. and Sphan, J. 1983. Analysis of fish for 2,3,7,8-tetrachloro-dibenzo-p-dioxin by electron capture capillary gas chromatography. Anal. Chem. 55:1497-1504.

Norstrom, R.J. and Simon, M. 1983. Preliminary appraisal of tetra- to octachlorodibenzodioxin contamination in eggs of various species of wildlife in Canada. In Pesticide Chemistry: Human Welfare and the Environment, Vol. 4, ed. J. Miyamoto, P.C. Kearney, R. Greenhalgh and N. Drescher, pp. 165-170, Pergamon Press, Oxford.

Norstrom, R.J., Hallet, D.J., Simon, M. and Mulvihill, M.J. 1982. Analysis of Great Lakes herring gull eggs for the tetrachlorodibenzo-p-dioxins. In Chlorinated Dioxins and Related Compounds: Impact on the Environment, ed. O. Hutzinger, R.W. Frei, E. Merian and F. Pocchiari, pp. 173-181, Pergamon Press, Oxford.

O'Keefe, P., Meyer, C., Hilker, D., Aldons, K., Jelue-Tyror, B., Dillon, K. and Donelly, R. 1983. Analysis of 2,3,7,8-tetrachlorodibenzo-p-dioxin in Great Lakes fish.

Chemosphere, 12:325-332.

Oswald, E.O. 1978. Summary of results for analyses of samples of fish from Michigan-EPA Region V-for 2,3,7,8-tetrachlorodibenzo-paradioxin (TCDD). 20 December letter to Mr. Karl E. Bremmer, Toxic Substances Coordinator, U.S. EPA, Chicago, Illinois 60604.

Pfeiffer, C.D., Nestrick, T.J. and Kocher, C.W. 1978. Determination of chlorinated dioxins in purified pentachlorophenol by liquid chromatography. Anal. Chem. 50:800-804.

Phillipson, D.W. and Puma, B.J. 1980. Identification of chlorinated methoxybiphenyls as contaminants in fish and as potential interferences in the determination of chlorinated dibenzo-p-dioxins. Anal. Chem. 52:2328-2332.

Ress, J., Higginbottom, G.R. and Firestone, D. 1970. J. Assoc. Off. Anal. Chem. 53:628-634.

Ryan, J.J. and Pilon, J.C. 1980. High performance liquid chromatography in the analysis of chlorinated dibenzodioxins and dibenzofurans in chicken liver and wood shaving samples. J. Chromatogr. 197:171-180.

Sakuma, T., Gurprasad, N., Tanner, S.D., Ngo, A., Davidson, W.R., McLeod, H.A. and Lau, B. 1983. The Application of "Flash" Chromatography-Tandem Mass Spectrometry Analysis of Complex Samples for Chlorinated Dioxins and Dibenzofurans. Presented at the 186th National American Chemical Society Meeting, August 27, 1983.

Sawyer, T., Bandiera, S., Safe, S., Hutzinger, O. and Olie, K. 1983. Bioanalysis of polychlorinated dibenzofuran and dibenzo-p-dioxin mixtures in fly ash. Chemosphere 12:529-535.

Shadoff, L.A. and Hummel, R.A. 1978. Determination of 2,3,7,8-tetrachlorodibenzo-p-dioxin in biological extracts by gas chromatography mass spectrometry. Biomed. Mass Spectrom. 5:7-13.

Shadoff, L.A., Hummel, R.A., Lamparski, L.L. and Davidson, J.H. 1977. A search for 2,3,7,8-tetrachlorodibenzo-p-dioxin (TCDD) in an environment exposed annually to 2,4,5-trichlorophenoxy-acetic acid ester (2,4,5-T) herbicides. Bull. Environ. Contam. Toxicol. 18:4778-485.

Smith, R.M., Hilker, D.R., O'Keefe, P.W., Aldons, K.M., Meyer, C.M., Kumar, S.N. and Jelus-Tyror, B.M. 1982. Determination of tetrachlorodibenzo-p-dioxins and tetrachlorodibenzofurans in environmental samples by high performance liquid chromatography, capillary gas chromatography and high resolution mass spectrometry. In Human and Environmental Risks of Chlorinated Dioxins and Related Compounds, ed. R.E. Tucker, A.L. Young and A.P. Gray, pp. 73-94, Plenum Press, New York.

Tiernan, T.O. 1983. Analytical chemistry of polychlorinated dibenzo-p-dioxins and dibenzofurans: A review of the current status. In Chlorinated Dioxins and Dibenzofurans in the Total Environment, ed., G. Choudhary, Keith, L.H. and C. Rappe, pp. 211-237, Butterworth Publishers, Boston.

Tiernan, T.O., Taylor, M.L., Solch, J.G., Van Ness, G.F. and Garrett, J.H. 1981. Quantitation of parts-per-trillion levels of 2,3,7,8-tetrachlorodibenzo-p-dioxin in EPA-furnished extracts of biological materials. Final report. Cooperative Agreement No. CR8068646-01. Josephine Huang, EPA Project Officer, Office of Research and Development, Washington, D.C. 20460.

Tosine, H., Smillie, D. and Rees, G.A.V. 1982. Comparative monitoring and analytical methodology for polychlorinated dibenzo-p-dioxins in fish. In Human and Environmental Risks of Chlorinated Dioxins and Related Compounds, ed., R.E. Tucker, A.L. Young, A.P. Gray, pp. 127-139, Plenum Press.

Tou, J.C., Zakett, D. and Caldecourt, V. 1982. Applications of MS/MS to chemical problems. In Tandem Mass Spectrometry (MS/MS), ed., F.W. McLafferty. To be published by John Wiley and Sons, New York.

Van Ness, G.F., Solch, J.G., Taylor, M.L. and Tiernan, T.O. 1980. Tetrachlorodibenzo-p-dioxins in chemical wastes, aqueous effluents, and soils. Chemosphere 9:553-563.

Zabik, M.E. and Zabik, M.J. 1980. Dioxin levels in raw and cooked liver, loin steaks, round, and patties from beef fed technical grade pentachlorophenol. Bull. Environ. Contam. Toxicol. 24:344-349.

Zweig, G. 1978. The vanishing zero: Ten years later. J. Assoc. Off. Anal. Chem. 61:229-248.

Chapter 7

DIOXINS AND DIBENZOFURANS IN AIR, SOIL AND WATER

Jean M. Czuczwa and Ronald A. Hites
School of Public and Environmental Affairs and Department of Chemistry
Indiana University

INTRODUCTION

Polychlorinated dibenzodioxins (PCDD) and dibenzofurans (PCDF) are generated by combustion sources (Olie et al., 1982; Bumb et al., 1980), and the effluents from these sources, carrying particulates containing PCDD and PCDF, enter the atmosphere. The particulates will sooner or later leave the atmosphere, depositing the PCDD and PCDF on soil or in water. Thus, combustion may be an important source of PCDD and PCDF found in the environment. This paper is a review of combustion-generated dioxins and furans and their fate in air, soil, and the aquatic environment.

We begin this review by characterizing the dioxin and furan congener profiles produced in combustion sources including municipal waste incineration, chemical waste incineration, coal burning and wood burning. We will then predict the most important combustion sources of dioxins and furans. We will also calculate an "average combustion" congener profile and use this to compare the PCDD and PCDF generated in combustion sources to those found in environmental samples. Air and soil samples will be discussed to show that combustion is a source of dioxins and furans found in the environment, and that PCDD and PCDF are dispersed by airborne transport through the atmosphere.

The analysis of sediments is the main focus of our work. Surficial sediments from locations in the Great Lakes and Lake Zurich will be used to show that atmospheric transport is the major mechanism bringing dioxins and furans to remote locations. Dated sediment cores yield information on the historical input of dioxins and furans to the environment. We find a post-1940 increase in sedimentary PCDD and PCDF which is related to the production and subsequent incineration of chlorinated aromatic chemicals.

It is useful to briefly explain how we generated the figures in this paper. We used published work which reported quantitative data for dioxins and furans. In each figure, the data are presented as total concentration for each congener class (tetra- to octachlorofurans, then dioxins). If a congener class was not measured, it is not labeled on the lower axis. When a number of observations were reported by an investigator, the arithmetic average is presented; when a range was given (particularly Bumb et al., 1980) the geometric average of the high and low values was calculated. In all cases, the concentration given on the figure is that of octachlorodioxin. Finally, only work from the refereed literature was used.

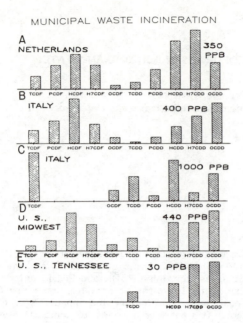

Figure 1. Dioxin and furan congener profiles found on fly ash from municipal incinerators. Reported concentrations are for octachlorodioxin in all cases. (Adapted from the following: A, Olie et al., 1982, Table 7; B, Liberti et al., 1982, Table II, Liberti and Brocco, 1982, Table II; C, Cavallaro et al.,1982; D, Czuczwa and Hites, 1984; E, Bumb et al., 1980.)

AIR

Combustion Effluents Released to Air

Municipal waste incineration. Measurements now exist of dioxins and furans in particulate matter from several combustion sources. Figure 1 contains a summary of analyses of effluents of municipal waste incinerators. No consistent trends in the congener profiles are observed. It is apparent that these sources are highly variable. Octachlorodioxin (OCDD) concentrations averaged as high as 1000 ppb (Cavallaro et al., 1982). Since typically 2% of the particles formed in municipal incinerators are released to the atmosphere (Lustenhouwer et al., 1980) and since incineration is currently used to dispose of 10% of all solid wastes, combustion of municipal wastes may be an important source of dioxins and furans in the environment.

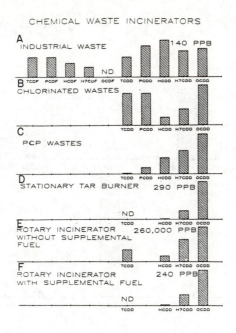

Figure 2. Dioxin and furan congener profiles found on fly ash from chemical waste incineration. (Adapted from: A, Buser and Bosshardt, 1978; B, C, Tiernan et al, 1983; D-F, Bumb et al., 1980.)

Chemical waste incineration. Analyses of effluents from the incineration of chemical wastes are shown in Figure 2. Variation in the congener profiles is again seen. The OCDD concentration ranged from 140 to 260,000 ppb, significantly higher than municipal waste incineration. The effect of combustion conditions on the formation of PCDD and PCDF is clearly seen (Figure 2E and 2F) in a rotary incinerator operated with and without supplemental fuel (Bumb et al., 1980).

The importance of elevated temperatures for the destruction of PCDD and PCDF has only recently been appreciated. Incinerators which were not operated under the most stringent conditions could have released large amounts of PCDD and PCDF to the environment. Thus, we conclude that chemical waste incineration is an important source of dioxins and furans.

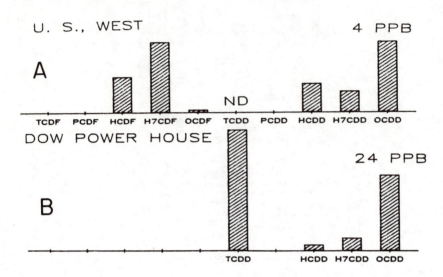

Figure 3. Dioxin and furan congener profiles found on fly ash from coal burning. (Adapted from A, Czuczwa and Hites, 1984; B, Bumb et al., 1980.)

Coal burning. Coal fly ash is another possible source of combustion-generated dioxins and furans (see Figure 3). The analysis of two coal fly ash samples from a western coal-fired power plant (Figure 3A), analyzed by our laboratory, showed a predominance of OCDD. The average concentration of OCDD was 4-24 ppb, and is low in comparison to municipal incinerator fly ash.

Wood burning. Some studies of the combustion of wood and pentachlorophenol (PCP) treated wood are shown in Figure 4. Particulates from residential wood burning units (Nestrick and Lamparski, 1983) contain low levels of dioxins, primarily the hexa-, hepta- and octachlorinated isomers, while the combustion of PCP treated wood produced higher concentrations of dioxins. Again, significant variation is noted.

Average combustion congener profiles. In Figure 5, we show the calculated average congener profiles for each type of combustion. It is interesting to note the relative amounts of dioxins and furans produced in each type of combustion. The combustion of chemical wastes and municipal wastes (which may contain synthetic chemicals) produce the greatest amount of PCDD and PCDF, while the combustion of wood and coal produced smaller amounts. Thus, we conclude that chemical and municipal waste incineration are the major combustion sources of dioxins and furans. Combustion of coal and wood (presumably including natural combustion such as forest fires) is a minor source of PCDD and PCDF. We will test these conclusions below.

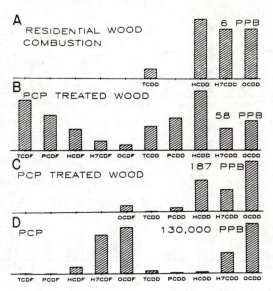

Figure 4. Dioxin and furan congener profiles found on fly ash from wood and PCP treated wood burning. (Adapted from: A, Nestrick and Lamparski, 1983; B, Olie et al., 1983; C, Chui et al., 1983; D, Buser and Bosshardt, 1976.)

From Figure 5 it is obvious that there is great variability in combustion congener profiles. In fact, when we calculated an "average" combustion profile (Figure 5, bottom), we see no specific congener classes are preferred. All classes are present in about equal amounts with the exception of OCDF, which is consistently low. In addition, combustion samples characteristically contain many isomers within each congener class. How do these trends compare to those found in environmental samples?

Air Particulates

Analyses of air particulates are shown in Figure 6. We see that dioxins and furans are associated with air particulates. One notes that environmental samples are enriched in OCDD compared to combustion source samples. The most abundant furans are the heptachlorofurans (H7CDF). The highest level of OCDD (2000 ppb) is found in Midland, Michigan (Bumb et al., 1980), which suggests that combustion of chemical wastes is an important local source of PCDD and PCDF.

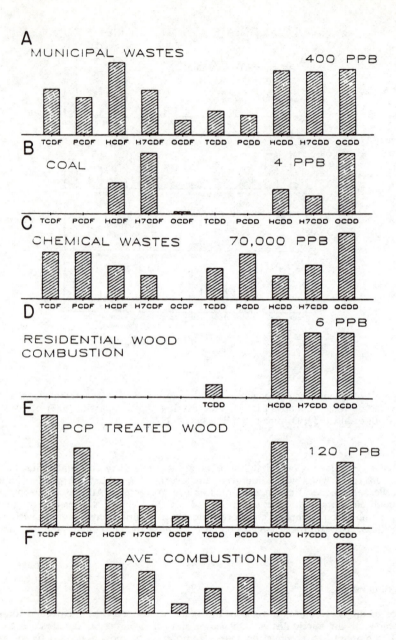

Figure 5. Average dioxin and furan congener profiles from various combustion processes. Averaged from the information in Figures 1-4.

AIR PARTICULATES

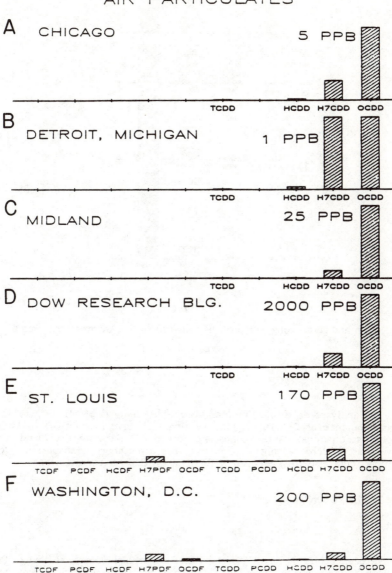

Figure 6. Dioxin and furan congener profiles found in air particulate samples. (Adapted from: A-D, Bumb et al., 1980; E-F, this work.)

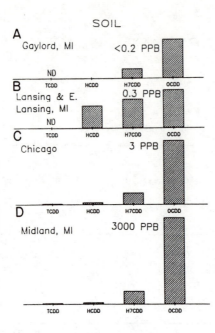

Figure 7. Dioxin and furan congener profiles found in soil. (Adapted from Bumb et al., 1980.)

SOIL

As seen in the analyses of air particulates above, the analysis of soil (Figure 7) also shows a predominance of OCDD. Again, we find high levels of OCDD in Midland, Michigan close to chemical waste combustion sources. Dioxins are also found in rural locations such as Gaylord, Michigan suggesting that atmospheric transport may carry combustion particulates (with their load of PCDD and PCDF) to remote areas.

THE AQUATIC ENVIRONMENT

Water

No data have been published on PCDD and PCDF in natural waters. Although PCDD and PCDF were found in Great Lakes fish (Stalling et al., 1983), we lack information on the concentration and congener profiles of PCDD and PCDF in water itself. There is an obvious need for research in this area.

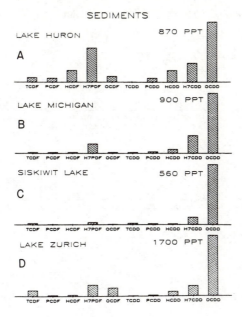

Figure 8. Dioxin and furan congener profiles found in surficial lake sediments (ppt).

Aquatic Sediments

Surficial sediments.   Sediments are the ultimate sink of many anthropogenic compounds. We report in Figure 8 the analysis of surficial sediments from the Great Lakes, Siskiwit Lake and Lake Zurich for PCDD and PCDF. The coordinates for these sample sites are reported below. Analytical methods are described in Czuczwa and Hites (1984). Dioxin and furan congener profiles are similar in all sediments and are similar to those in the air and soil samples reported above. OCDD predominates, with lesser amounts of H7CDF and H7CDD. The average concentrations of OCDD found in Lake Huron (870 ppt) and Lake Michigan (900 ppt) are equal, suggesting that atmospheric transport is the common source of dioxins and furans to both areas.

ENVIRONMENTAL SAMPLES

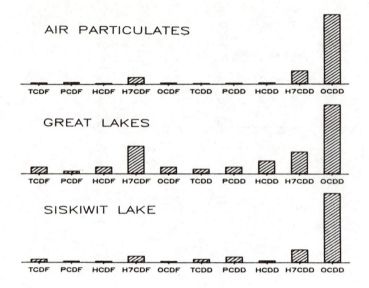

AIR PARTICULATES

TCDF PCDF HCDF H7CDF OCDF TCDD PCDD HCDD H7CDD OCDD

GREAT LAKES

TCDF PCDF HCDF H7CDF OCDF TCDD PCDD HCDD H7CDD OCDD

SISKIWIT LAKE

TCDF PCDF HCDF H7CDF OCDF TCDD PCDD HCDD H7CDD OCDD

Figure 9. Comparison of dioxin and furan congener profiles in various environmental samples.

The Siskiwit Lake sediment provides useful support for this hypothesis. Siskiwit Lake is a lake on Isle Royale, a wilderness island in Lake Superior. There is no flow of water from Lake Superior to Siskiwit Lake, so the only mechanism by which dioxins and furans can reach this area is by atmospheric transport. As seen in Figure 8, dioxins and furans were found in sediments from Siskiwit Lake in amounts similar to those found in Lake Huron and Lake Michigan. This suggests that atmospheric transport of combustion particulates was the major source of dioxins and furans found in these locations of the Great Lakes.

To investigate whether this phenomenon is global, we analyzed sediment from Lake Zurich (Figure 8, bottom). We again found many isomers of dioxins and furans and a predominance of OCDD, H7CDD, and H7CDF. The OCDD concentration (1700 ppt) is higher than that found in the Great Lakes, perhaps indicative of the more extensive use of combustion for waste disposal in Europe.

If we compare results from analyses of several of the environmental samples (Figure 9) we note some similarities. The dioxin and furan congener profiles in sediments are similar to those found in air particulates, indicating that the atmosphere is a source of dioxins to soils and sediments. The similarity is remarkable between the air particulates and the sediment from Siskiwit Lake where atmospheric transport could be the only source of PCDD and PCDF.

We do not yet understand why we find enrichment in OCDD in environmental samples relative to combustion sources. OCDD may be more stable than other PCDD and PCDF. Further study is needed in this area.

Historical record of dioxins and furans in sediment cores. We believe that dioxins and furans emitted on particulates from combustion sources travel through the atmosphere to remote locations where they are deposited in sediments. Sediments, sampled in such a way that the historical input of materials is preserved, can be analyzed for dioxins and furans. Thus, analyses of dated sediment cores provide us with the relative historical emission rates of PCDD and PCDF. Since combustion practices have changed with time, we should see similar changes in the dioxins and furans found in sediment cores.

We can use historical emission rates to address three questions about combustion-generated dioxins and furans. First, Bumb et al., (1980) use data on emissions from a variety of combustion sources to suggest that dioxins and furans have been formed since the advent of fire. Is there any evidence for this in the sediment record? Second, is coal a major source of PCDD and PCDF? Coal combustion has been extensive since 1900. If this source is significant it should be apparent in sediment core studies. Third, can we find any evidence to suggest that PCDD and PCDF are formed in significant amounts only when combustion fuels contain chlorinated precursor compounds present in chemical and municipal wastes?

In Figure 10A to C, we show the analyses of sediment cores from 3 locations in Lake Huron (Core 1, 43° 30'N, 81° 55'W; Core 3, 43° 50'N, 82° 0'W; Core 4, 44° 0'N, 82°, 10'W). We show the most abundant species, OCDD, H7CDD, H7CDF and OCDF. The concentrations are plotted against the average year of deposition. The congener ratios remain relatively constant with depth suggesting that these compounds are stable after burial. In all cases, we see significant increases in PCDD and PCDF after the 1940's. The small background amounts of dioxins, (predominantly OCDD) reported before 1940 are not significantly greater than our laboratory background; and therefore, they may not be indicative of inputs due to natural or coal combustion sources.

In Figure 10D, we find the same trend for a location from northern Lake Michigan (43° 43'N, 86° 38'W). Again, significant amounts of dioxins and furans occur after 1940. We have not yet determined sedimentation rates for the Siskiwit Lake core (48° 02'N, 88° 48'W). However, based on previous work, we estimate a sedimentation rate of 0.1 cm/yr, and use this to calculate depositional ages. Therefore, the results from this core (see Figure 10E) must be considered prelimininary, but it is apparent that PCDD and PCDF increased with time.

The core from Lake Zurich, shown in Figure 10F, had yearly carbonate laminae or varves (Kelts and Hsu, 1978). The dating of this sediment core is, therefore, done in a straightforward manner by counting yearly lamina. Mixing effects between layers are minimal. Thus, this core is ideal for studying the historical input of dioxins and furans. We again see an increase in PCDD and PCDF after 1940. Congener ratios are again constant with depth.

Figure 11, bottom, shows the historical trends for the cores from the Great Lakes, Siskiwit Lake and Lake Zurich. The agreement is remarkable despite the uncertainties inherent in environmental measurements. If we compare these trends with that for the use of coal (shown in Figure 11, top) we would have expected dioxins and furans to increase around 1900. Thus, coal is clearly not a major source of PCDD and PCDF found in these sediments.

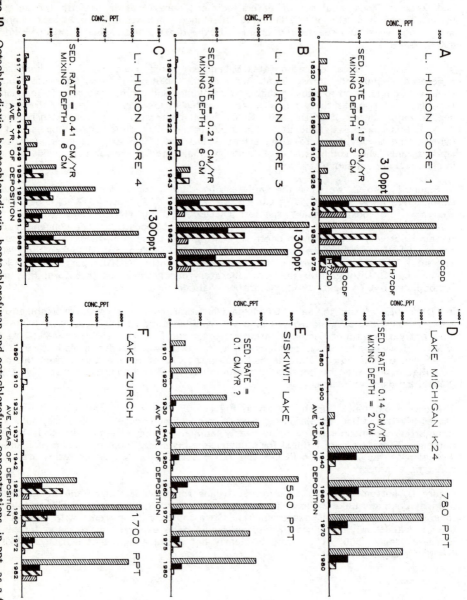

Figure 10. Octachlorodioxin, heptachlorodioxin, heptachlorofuran and octachlorofuran concentrations, in ppt, as a function of average year of deposition in several sediment cores. A–C, Lake Huron Sediment cores; D, Lake Michigan sediment core; E, Siskiwit Lake sediment core (depositional ages preliminary); F, Lake Zurich sediment core. Concentration given is OCDD.

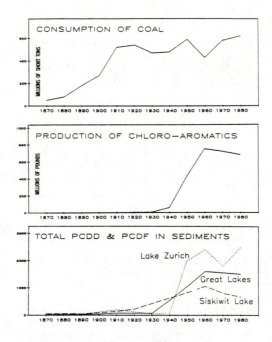

Figure 11. U.S. consumption of coal (top) and production of synthetic chlorinated organics (taken from Czuczwa and Hites, 1984) compared to the total PCDD and PCDF in sediment cores from the Great Lakes, Siskiwit Lake and Lake Zurich (bottom).

Records for the production of chlorinated aromatics are shown in Figure 11, middle. Production has increased steadily since 1940, and this trend agrees well with the dioxin and furan profiles for the sediment cores. Some portion of the chemical wastes produced in the synthesis of chloro-aromatics are incinerated. As we noted above, the emission of dioxins and furans from such incineration is one source of PCDD and PCDF. Chlorinated aromatic compounds produced by the chemical industry are used in a variety of products, some of which enter solid wastes, with a portion eventually being disposed of by incineration. This is a second source of airborne PCDD and PCDF.

Thus, we believe that the observed historical increase in PCDD and PCDF found in the sedimentary record is the result of the combustion of chlorinated compounds present in combustion fuels. We see no evidence of inputs from coal or natural combustion sources. The high levels of dioxins and furans presently accumulating in the sedimentary environment are not due to the advent of fire, but are indirectly due to the chemical industry.

ACKNOWLEDGEMENTS

We are grateful to B.J. Kimble for the fly ash samples, to D.N. Edgington, S.J. Eisenreich, B.D. McVeety, P.A. Meyers, F. Niessen, and J.A. Robbins for the various sediment samples, and to S.L. Sikes for clerical support. This work was supported by the U.S. Department of Energy (Grant No. 80EV-10449).

REFERENCES

Bumb, R.R., Crummett, W.B., Cutie, S.S., Gledhill, J.R., Hummel, R.H., Kagel, R.O., Lamparski, L.L., Luoma, E.V., Miller, D.L., Nestrick, T.J., Shadoff, L.A., Stehl, R.H. and Woods, J.W. 1980. Trace chemistries of fire: A source of chlorinated dioxins. Science 210:385-390.

Buser, H.R. and Bosshardt, H.P. 1976. Determination of polychlorinated dibenzo-p-dioxins and dibenzofurans by combined gas chromatography-mass spectrometry. J. Assoc. Offic. Anal. Chem. 59:562-569.

Buser, H.R. and Bosshardt, H.P. 1978. Polychlorinated dibenzo-p-dioxins, dibenzofurans and benzenes in ash from municipal and industrial incinerators. Mitt. Gebiete Lebensm. Hyg. 69:191-199.

Cavallaro, A., Bandi, G., Invernizzi, G., Luciani, L., Mongini, E. and Gorni, G. 1982. Negative ion chemical ionization MS as a structure tool in the determination of small amounts of PCDD and PCDF. In Chlorinated Dioxins and Related Compounds: Impact on the Environment, ed. O. Hutzinger, R.W. Frei, E. Merian and F. Pocchiari, pp. 55-65. Pergamon Press, Oxford.

Chui, C., Thomas, R.S., Lockwood, J., Li, K., Halman, R. and Lao, R.C. 1983. Polychlorinated hydrocarbons from power plants, wood burning and municipal incinerators. Chemosphere 12:607-616.

Czuczwa, J.M. and Hites, R.A. 1984. Environmental fate of combustion-generated polychlorinated dioxins and furans. Environ. Sci. Technol. (in press).

Kelts, K. and Hsu, K.J. 1978. Freshwater carbonate sedimentation. In Lakes: Chemistry, Geology, Physics, ed. A. Lerman, pp. 295-323. Springer-Verlag, New York.

Liberti, A. and Brocco, D. 1982. Formation of polychlorodibenzodioxins and polychlorodibenzofurans in urban incinerator emissions. In Chlorinated Dioxins and Related Compounds: Impact on the Environment, ed. O. Hutzinger, R.W. Frei, E. Merian and F. Pocchiari, pp. 245-251. Pergamon Press, Oxford.

Liberti, A., Brocco, D., Cerinato, A. and Natalucci, A. 1982. Sampling and determination of polychlorodibenzo-p-dioxins, dibenzofurans and their precursors in the incineration process of urban wastes. In Analytical Techniques in Environmental Chemistry 2, Volume 7, ed. J. Albaiges, pp. 281-286. Pergamon Press, Oxford.

Lustenhouwer, J.W.A., Olie, K. and Hutzinger, O. 1980. Chlorinated dibenzo-p-dioxins and related compounds in incinerator effluents. Chemosphere 9:501-522.

Nestrick, T.J. and Lamparski, L.L. 1983. Assessment of chlorinated dibenzo-p-dioxin formation and potential emission to the environment from wood combustion. Chemosphere 12:617-626.

Olie, K., Lustenhouwer, J.W.A. and Hutzinger, O. 1982. Polychlorinated dibenzo-p-dioxins and related compounds in incinerator effluents. In Chlorinated Dioxins and Related Compounds: Impact on the Environment, ed. O. Hutzinger, R.W. Frei, E. Merian and F. Pocchiari, pp. 227-243. Pergamon Press, Oxford.

Olie, K.M, Berg, M. and Hutzinger, O. 1983. Formation and fate of PCDD and PCDF from combustion processes. Chemosphere 12:627-636.

Stalling, D.L., Smith, L.M., Petty, J.D., Hogan, J.W., Johnson, J.L., Rappe, C. and Buser, H.R. 1983. Residues of polychlorinated dibenzo-p-dioxins and dibenzofurans in Laurentian Great Lakes fish. In Human and Environmental Risks of Chlorinated Dioxins and Related Compounds, ed. O. Hutzinger, A.L. Young and A.P. Gray, pp. 221-240. Plenum Press, New York.

Tiernan, T.O., Taylor, M.L. , Garrett, J.H., VanNess, G.F., Solch, J.G., Deis, D.A. and Wagel, D.J. 1983. Chlorodibenzodioxins, chlorodibenzofurans and related products in the effluents from combustion processes. Chemosphere 12:595-606.

Chapter 8

DIOXINS AND FURANS IN THE ENVIRONMENT: A PROBLEM FOR CHEMOMETRICS

D.L. Stalling, J.D. Petty and L.M. Smith
Columbia National Fisheries Research Laboratory
U.S. Fish and Wildlife Service
Route 1, Columbia, Missouri

W. J. Dunn III
University of Illinois Medical Center - Chicago

INTRODUCTION

It is difficult to assess the extent and biological impact of contamination on the global ecosystem from polychlorinated dibenzo-p-dioxins (PCDDs) and dibenzofurans (PCDFs) because measurement of the residues of these chemicals at low part-per-trillion concentrations is uncertain (National Research Council Canada, 1981a) and the toxicological responses to both acute and chronic exposures are species dependent (Decad et al., 1982). Although the distribution and effects of 2,3,7,8-tetrachlorodibenzo-p-dioxin (TCDD) have been the subject of many scientific investigations, books, reviews and news media reports, few chronic toxicity data for humans or aquatic organisms are available (Honchar and Halperin, 1981; Tognoni and Bonaceorsi, 1982; Environmental Protection Agency, 1983a; Helder, 1980; Helder, 1981). However, TCDD in combination with phenoxyacid herbicides and certain chlorophenols is now considered to be a probable human carcinogen (Environmental Protection Agency, 1983b). Moreover, an increased incidence of soft-tissue sarcomas has been reported in workers exposed to chlorinated phenoxyacid herbicides or certain chlorophenols (Hardell et al., 1981). The phenoxy herbicides and chlorophenols have been shown to contain both PCDD and PCDF as impurities and are now considered to be a source of these environmental contaminants. Another major source of these materials is the conversion of PCBs to PCDFs by pyrolytic processes (Hutzinger et al., 1982; Olie et al., 1977; Ahling et al., 1977; Buser et al., 1978). Concern about PCDDs and PCDFs is focused on the isomers with 2,3,7,8-chlorine substitution since these have been shown to be the most toxic and physiologically active in laboratory studies (Goldstein, 1980; Poland et al., 1983).

Our knowledge of environmental contamination with PCDDs and PCDFs has been generally limited to studies of their occurrence in soil (Kleopfer et al., 1983; Thibodeaux, 1983), sediments (Stalling et al., 1983a; Czuczwa and Hites, 1983), combustion particulates (Rappe et al., 1983; Taylor et al., 1983), fish (Stalling et al., 1983a; Harless et al., 1983; Ryan et al., 1983), and birds (Norstrom et al., 1982). Present evidence suggests that most of the PCDD contamination stems from improper chlorophenol waste disposal (Harless et al., 1982), from accidents in transportation, from the manufacture of chlorinated phenols (National Research Council Canada, 1981b; Esposito et al., 1980a) or from products based on 2,4,5-trichlorophenol, such as hexachlorophene (Esposito et al., 1980b) and 2,4,5-trichlorophenoxyacid herbicides (2,4,5-T, Herbicide Orange) (Esposito et al., 1980a). In addition, industrial accidents involving 2,4,5-trichlorophenol have led to exposures of humans to TCDD as well as environmental contamination (Reggiani, 1983). The major dietary source of TCDD in humans appears to be fish (Environmental Protection Agency, 1983). While PCDDs arise principally from dimerization of chlorophenols, PCDFs are primarily produced from pyrolysis of PCBs (Rappe et al.,

1983). PCDFs have been implicated in the TCDD-like symptoms in humans exposed to PCB contaminated rice oil in Japan (Yusho Disease) (Kuratsune, 1980) and Taiwan (Chen et al., 1981).

Although toxicological profiles of aquatic organisms are limited, it has been determined that short-term exposure of fish fry to low part-per-trillion concentrations of TCDD decreases growth and survival, and increases mortality (Helder, 1980; Helder, 1981). An outdoor pool study, indicated that a major portion of the TCDD bioconcentrates in aquatic plants and at the hydrosoil-water interface, and that TCDD's half-life is greater than one year (Matsumura et al., 1983). Studies in model ecosystems and pools suggest a TCCD bioconcentration factor of 4,000 to 25,000 in aquatic organisms (Isensee and Jones, 1975; Isensee, 1978; Yockim et al., 1978). Other studies show that the bioconcentration of PCDFs (contaminants produced by pyrolysis of PCBs) in natural waters is on the same order as that of the PCBs (Stalling et al., 1983a). No steady state bioconcentration factor has been determined for TCDD but its bioconcentration potential has been estimated by liquid-liquid chromatography analysis (Vieth et al., 1979) to exceed 100,000 (Environmental Protection Agency, 1983a).

The discovery of PCDF and PCDD residues in fish and sediments from some rivers and lakes provided impetus for increased environmental and toxicological studies on aquatic systems. Determinations of sources, transport, fate, and bioaccumulation of these materials are the key elements in assessing their environmental impact. In part I of this paper we will summarize the results of some of our analyses for PCDFs and PCDDs in environmental samples. In part II, we will discuss the application of chemometric methods to the study of multi-component residues and how this approach can enhance our comprehension of large amounts of data.

Because there are 75 PCDDs and 135 PCDFs, including 22 TCDDs and 38 TCDFs, comprehensive residue analyses for each class of compounds are not routinely performed. However, the 2,3,7,8-chlorine substituted dibenzo-p-dioxin can be separated from the other dioxin isomers (Buser and Rappe, 1984) and progress is being made in the synthesis, separation, and quantitation of 2,3,7,8-chlorine substituted dibenzofuran (Mazer et al., 1983; Bell, 1983).

Analyses of PCDD and PCDF residues create large data sets that are difficult to interpret. Isomer compositions may vary widely due to environmental factors such as contamination sources or incineration conditions. In addition, isomer distributions of PCDDs and PCDFs in sediments appear to differ markedly from those measured in the surrounding biota (Stalling et al., 1983a; Czeczwa and Hites, 1983). The factors controlling such isomer distributions are largely unknown. Thus, the contamination profiles of PCDFs and PCDDs associated with PCBs, chlorophenols, and combustion inputs into the aquatic ecosystem are not well characterized. Chemometric methods (Kowalski, 1980) can greatly improve the ability of investigators to define and understand such complex problems.

In part II, we will focus on the application of one chemometric technique, SIMCA (Soft Independent Modeling of Class Analogy), to quality control and characterization of complex mixtures of PCDFs, PCDDs, and PCBs. Chemometrics is a relatively new branch of science concerned with the development of novel mathematical and statistical methods and their application to chemical problems (Kowalski, 1980). Pattern recognition techniques based on approaches such as SIMCA, MACUP (Wold, 1982) and ARTHUR (Kowalski, 1973) are especially relevant tools to apply to characterization of PCDF and PCDD data being generated. Applications of SIMCA to gas chromatographic isomer specific PCB analyses have demonstrated the utility of these chemometric approaches (Stalling et al., 1983b; Dunn et al., 1984).

The power of principal components modeling (Wold et al., 1983) in describing multivariate data associated with residue analysis for PCBs, PCDFs, and PCDDs lies in the ability of SIMCA to present these data graphically, as well as in statistical terms. Sample data are treated as points in higher dimensional space and projections of these data are made in two or three dimensional space in a way that preserves most of the existing relations among samples and between variables (Wold and Sjostrom, 1977). This feature is especially helpful in visualizing data of more than three dimensions. In addition, it allows assignment of an unknown sample to a given type or class by comparison with the class model of related samples.

RESIDUES OF PCDFs AND PCDDs IN AQUATIC ECOSYSTEMS

The impetus for our survey of PCDD and PCDF residues in fish was the discovery that pyrolysis of Aroclors 1254 and 1260 produces PCDF congeners, including the 2,3,7,8-chlorine substituted form (Rappe and Buser, 1980). Because no previous data existed on the isomer distribution of PCDDs or PCDFs in fish or other aquatic organisms, we undertook an assessment of the environmental distribution of these chemicals (Stalling et al., 1983a). This effort was a preliminary step toward assessing the impact of these contaminants on Great Lakes fish. We also sought to correlate the concentrations of PCDFs with the levels of PCBs known to be present in Great Lakes fish (Schmitt et al., 1981). A longer term goal was to develop analytical methods for isomer specific analyses of PCBs, PCDDs, and PCDFs in fish. These data may provide a basis for evaluating the impacts of environmental contaminants on the various Great Lakes fish stocks and aid in assessing contaminant related problems.

Analytical methods were developed that enabled isomer specific analysis for the TCDDs as well as the enrichment of PCDDs and PCDFs having four or more chlorines (Rappe et al., 1983; Stalling et al., 1983a). Multiple adsorption chromatography modules based on use of carbon (Smith, 1981; Stalling et al., 1981a), alkali metal silicates (Stalling et al., 1981b), and sulfuric acid impregnated silica gel were integrated to provide adequate removal of co-extractives and known interferences such as PCBs, phenoxyphenols, and related compounds (Smith and Johnson, 1983).

The analysis of a snapping turtle from the Hudson River established the previously unknown presence of the more toxic 2,3,7,8-chlorine substituted PCDF in aquatic organisms (Rappe et al, 1981). This sample contained ca. 3 ug/kg of total PCDFs. Residues of PCDDs and PCDFs were then measured in many samples of Great Lakes fish (Stalling et al., 1983a) at sampling sites shown in Figure 1. The results for 2,3,7,8-TCDF, -TCDD and the total concentrations of PCDDs and PCDFs are summarized in Figure 2.

Seemingly greater contamination of fish with PCDDs and PCDFs existed at sites associated with large-scale production of chemicals or with hazardous waste disposal (e.g., Tittabawassee River and Love Canal; sampling sites 8-11 and 16, 17 in Figure 1). These data also demonstrated that PCDF residues exceeded those of the PCDDs at all locations. No samples were found that did not contain PCDFs in measurable concentrations. Detection levels for TCDD and TCDF by electron impact low resolution mass spectrometry were on the order of $1-3 \times 10^{-12}$ g/g whole fish (sample size of 10-50 g). Selected data for individual isomers detected in analyses of common carp (Cyprinus carpio) and herring gulls (Larus argeutatus) are summarized in Tables 1 and 2.

These analyses identified the major PCDD and PCDF isomers as those having 2,3,7,8-chlorine substitution. In all samples, 2,3,7,8-TCDD was the predominant or exclusive TCDD isomer observed. The residues in many samples had PCDF isomer distributions similar to those in human liver samples from Yusho patients (Rappe and Buser, 1980) and seal and turtle fat (Rappe et al., 1981).

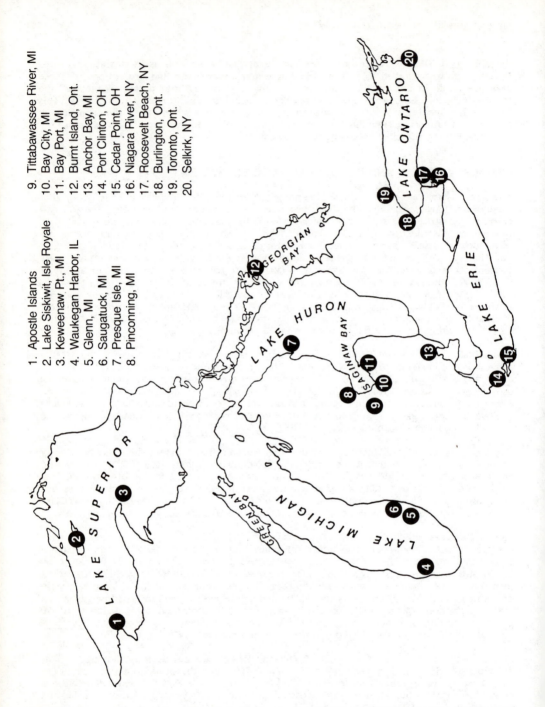

1. Apostle Islands
2. Lake Siskiwit, Isle Royale
3. Keweenaw Pt., MI
4. Waukegan Harbor, IL
5. Glenn, MI
6. Saugatuck, MI
7. Presque Isle, MI
8. Pinconning, MI

9. Tittabawassee River, MI
10. Bay City, MI
11. Bay Port, MI
12. Burnt Island, Ont.
13. Anchor Bay, MI
14. Port Clinton, OH
15. Cedar Point, OH
16. Niagara River, NY
17. Roosevelt Beach, NY
18. Burlington, Ont.
19. Toronto, Ont.
20. Selkirk, NY

FIGURE 1. Great Lakes Sampling Sites in Survey for PCDDs and PCDFs in Fish (1980-1982).

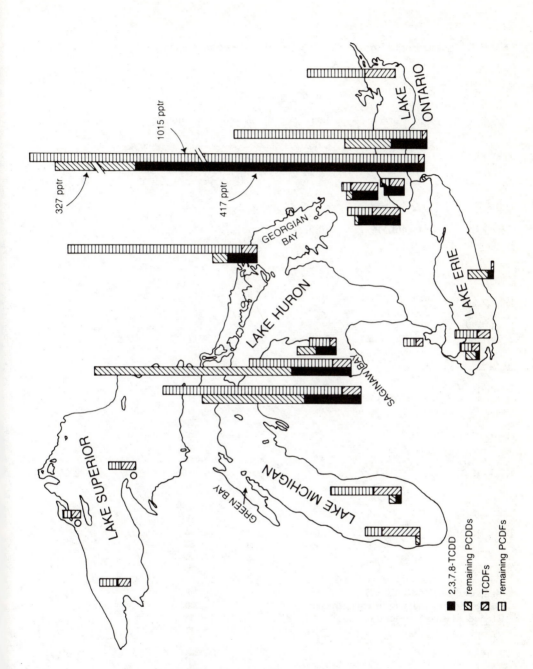

FIGURE 2. Residues of PCDDs and PCDFs in Whole Fish from the Great Lakes and Tributaries.

TABLE 1. Dibenzofuran Isomer Residues (pg/g) in Composite Samples Analyzed

	Sample and Site				
Isomer[1]	Herring gull No. 1 Lake Huron	Herring gull No. 2 Lake Huron	Common Carp Lake Huron	Common Carp Lake Erie	Grass Carp[3] Lab Control
Tetra-Cl					
2,3,7,8-	4(0.5)[2]	2(0.5)	11	11	1.5
2,3,6,7-			2(0.5)	3(0.5)	
Penta-Cl					
1,2,4,7,8-/ 1,3,4,7,8-	<2	<2	2(2)	3	2
1,2,3,7,8-	<2	<2	5	1	1
2,3,4,7,8-	16(2)	20(2)	11	4(1)	1(1)
Hexa-Cl					
1,2,3,4,7,8/ 1,2,3,6,7,8-	7(3)	4(2)	5(2)	2(2)	
Other					2(1)
Hepta-Cl					
1,2,3,4,6,7,8-	<4	<4	3(3)	<4	
1,2,3,4,6,8,9-					2(1)
Octa-Cl	<8	<8	<4	<8	<3
Total PCDFs	27	26	41	24	10

[1] Measured by GC–NI–CI–MS
[2] Detection limit shown in parentheses
[3] Ctenopharyngodonn idella

TABLE 2. Dibenzo-p-dioxin Residues (pg/g) in Composite Samples Analyzed

	Sample and Site				
Isomer[1]	Herring gull No.1 Lake Huron	Herring gull No.2 Lake Huron	Common Carp Lake Huron	Common Carp Lake Erie	Grass Carp Lab Control
Tetra-Cl					
2,3,7,8-	165(0.5)[2]	75(1)	28	3	0.5
1,3,6,8-			0.8(0.5)		
Other				2(1)	
Penta-Cl					
1,2,3,7,8-	20(2)	18(2)	11(1)	2(1)	<2
Hexa-Cl					
1,2,3,4,7,8-	11(2)	17(2)	5(2)	3(2)	<3
Hepta-Cl					
1,2,3,4,6,7,8-	<4	<4	3(3)	5(5)	<2
Octa-Cl	<4	<4	3(3)	5(5)	5(3)
Total PCDD	196	110	52	17	6

[1] Measured by GC-EI-MS
[2] Detection limit shown in parentheses

Fish from Lake Superior and Siskiwit Lake did not contain measurable levels of TCDD or other PCDDs (Stalling et al, 1983a). Fish and herring gulls from Saginaw Bay and fish from Lake Huron contained high concentrations of 2,3,7,8-TCDD and more complex mixtures of other PCDD congeners (Stalling et al., 1983a). These isomer specific analyses confirm that tetrachlorodioxin residues in the aquatic ecosystems examined were composed predominantly of the 2,3,7,8-TCDD isomer (Stalling et al., 1983a; Rappe et al., 1981; Mitchum et al., 1982).

The ratio of PCDFs to PCBs in seven samples ranged from 2.2 to 12.1 x 10^{-6} (Stalling et al., 1983a). These values were remarkably consistent among samples from the same general location. Because PCDFs may be present at about 10 ug/g PCB and the residues include many isomers in addition to the 2,3,7,8-chlorine substituted ones found predominantly in the fish and herring gull samples, the ratio determined in the environmental samples suggests an increase in the 2,3,7,8-chlorine substituted isomers relative to that expected. This increase could result from thermal conversion of PCBs to PCDFs or from a somewhat larger bioconcentration factor for PCDFs than for PCBs, or both.

Additional analyses of fish and sediments from the Housatonic River at Woods Pond, MA, revealed that, although PCB residues in fish and sediments were similar, residues of PCDFs in the sediment differed in composition from those in silt (Stalling et al., 1983a; Petty et al., 1983). PCDFs in the sediment were largely hepta- and octa-chlorodibenzofurans whereas the fish contained predominantly 2,3,7,8-TCDF and 2,3,4,7,8-pentachlorodibenzofuran. Similarly, for PCDD residues, octachlorodibenzo-p-dioxin (octa-CDD) was the dominant isomer in sediments and 2,3,7,8-TCDD was the only isomer detected in fish.

CHEMOMETRICS IN PCB, PCDD AND PCDF ANALYSIS

As the data base for PCDDs and PCDFs in the environment broadens, difficulties arise in comparing the composition and distribution of these materials in a variety of samples. The complexity of the PCDD and PCDF residues in fly ash and other combustion-related materials poses an even greater challenge to understanding the factors which influence the composition of the residue and identifying the sources of the residues. It is in maintaining rugged quality control for isomer specific analyses and in evaluating data from a broad spectrum of analyses that chemometric methods can lead to improved understanding of the occurrence of these materials in the environment.

Application of multivariate statistical methods to the study of such problems has been referred to as chemometrics (Kowalski, 1980). SIMCA, a pattern recognition technique based on principal components (Wold, 1982), was selected for application to the problems of establishing similarities among sample residue profiles.

Capillary gas chromatographic analyses of complex mixtures of substances such as PCBs, PCDDs, and PCDFs produce large quantities of complex data. Difficulties in evaluating the results from such analyses of environmental samples prompted us to search for an improved method for characterizing and comparing information. This is especially important when there are large numbers of samples to be analyzed. When capillary gas chromatographic data are examined visually (chart paper or tabular data), it is difficult to detect minor (or perhaps major) differences due to sample location or to various physiochemical processes. A limited discussion of the principles and application of SIMCA, a principal components method, in the analysis of multi-constituent residues will be provided before it is applied to our data.

General Discussion of SIMCA

Consider a series of gas chromatograms obtained on a large number of samples ($\underline{N}$). These samples can all contain the same number of constituents ($\underline{P}$) — in the present examples 69 PCB isomers or 45 Cl_4- and Cl_5-PCDFs. Such data can be tabulated in matrix form as in Figure 3. Each row of the matrix is a chromatogram with the elements of the matrix, x_{ki}, representing the concentration of peak $\underline{i}$ in sample $\underline{k}$.

First consider the hypothetical case where there is no variation in composition of the samples, either in relation to the relative concentrations of constituents or in the absolute concentrations of isomers. If the $\underline{N}$ samples were projected into $\underline{P}$ space, due to the prior requirements of identity, they would appear as a tight cluster (Figure 4). In this example, variation would be due to measurement error.

Each sample can be modeled by Equation (1)

$$x_{ki} = m_i + e_{ki} \tag{1}$$

where m_i is the mean concentration of each peak in the matrix and e_{ki} represents the error of measurement and the error associated with the mathematical modeling of the data array (model error).

Peak Number

Sample number	1	2	3	.	.	i	.	P
1						.		
2						.		
3						.		
.						.		
$\underline{k}$	.	.	.	.	.	x_{ki}		
.								
$\underline{N}$								

FIGURE 3. Matrix Representation of Sample Analysis for $\underline{P}$ Peaks and $\underline{N}$ Samples (Chromatography Data Matrix).

We now redefine our requirement for identity and allow the samples to be _similar_. This is analogous to having a group of N samples of the same species, type of Aroclor, or mixture of Aroclors. Such data can be shown to be modeled by Equation (2):

$$x_{ki} = m_i + \sum_{a=1}^{A} t_{ka} b_{ai} + e_{ki} \tag{2}$$

in which A-product terms have been added to Equation (1) to account for the variation in the data (Wold et al., 1983). This is a principal components model in which b_{ai} is the loading of peak i (Beta$_i$) in term a, and t_{ka} is the score of object k in term a; b is a peak specific term and t is an object or sample specific term. The variation about the mean, m_i, can be random or systematic. Random variation can be due to measurement error; this type of variation can be used for quality assurance of the data. If the measured variation is systematic, it can be the result of class-specific internal variation, which can be used in classification or correlation studies.

Figure 4 illustrates the cases in which the data are represented by a point ($A=0$), line ($A=1$) or plane ($A=2$). A is the number of product terms in Equation (2). Samples clustered around a point could represent replicate analyses of a single sample in which there is no variation other than measurement error and the product term in Equation 2 is 0. When the product term A has the value 1 or 2, the data vary about the mean, m_i, and the position of each object on the line or plane is given by the peak coordinates. An example of data that could be represented by a line in the projections are those from an analysis of a range of concentrations of a single Aroclor ($A=1$). Data that could be represented in a plane might result from the analysis of the fractional composition of two (or more) Aroclor mixtures ($A=2$). In Figure 4, q designates the class number of these hypothetical samples.

One can use principal components plots to visualize higher dimensional data. Their use is equivalent to projecting the higher dimensional data onto a two-dimensional plane. Such plots are helpful in interpreting chromatographic or other scientific data composed of many measurements (peaks or dimensions).

If it is known from the history of the samples illustrated in Figure 3 that they represent q-distinctly different groups or classes, a classification problem can be formulated. These classes may represent samples from different locations, different species, different kinds of pollution or from living organism with varying degrees of exposures to chemical mixtures.

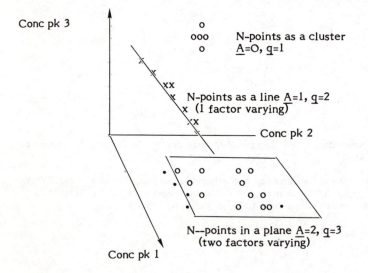

FIGURE 4. Clustering of Three Classes of Samples. Samples that are identical ($A=0$, $q=1$) or have one factor ($A=1$, $q=2$) or two factors that vary ($A=2$, $q=3$). Class number = q, and A = number of product terms in Equation (2).

Using SIMCA, one can derive Q-disjoint principal components models for distinct classes. This derivation is given in Equation (3) and a hypothetical set of data representing three classes ($q=3$) of data of increasing complexity is shown in Figure 4.

$$x_{ki}{}^q = m_i{}^q + \sum_{a=1}^{A} t_{ka}{}^q \, b_{ai}{}^q + e_{ki}{}^q \tag{3}$$

From the $e_{ki}{}^q$-values in Equation (3), a standard deviation for each object can be calculated and from these a residual standard deviation for each class (q) can be obtained. Twice the residual standard deviation around the line or above and below the plane for a class defines a volume in P-space where classes have a high probability of occurrence. Classification of an unknown can be based on its projection into P-space and determination of its position. It may be within or outside of the boundaries of the defined classes. This method has a number of other features (Wold and Sjostrom, 1977); we present only a limited discussion here. Application of principal components analysis and the closely related factor analysis, to scientific data has been well reviewed (Wold, 1982; and Wold et al., 1983).

To obtain a visual representation of the data for the class or classes being examined, one can project the data onto a two-dimensional plane. The best plane in mapping is that described by the first two principal components. Usually the class separations are readily visualized. By examining the clusters of samples in the graphical projections, the analyst can gain insight into sample outliers (from the principal components plot), and information about relationships among variables in the samples in that data set (from the variable plots of the sample loading terms -- b_{ai}). Samples that differ from the main cluster of samples can be readily detected. Three-dimensional plots derived from the first, second, and third components can sometimes clarify additional relations among samples.

The comparability of samples can be evaluated using geometrical constructs based on the standard deviations of the variables modeled by SIMCA. By enclosing classes in volume elements in descriptor space, the SIMCA method provides information about the existence of similarities among the members of the defined classes. Relationships among samples, when visualized in this way, increase one's ability to formulate questions or hypotheses about the data. The selection of variables on the basis of their modeling power can also provide clues as to how samples within a class are similar, because the derived class model allows comparisons of the internal variation of these variables.

SIMCA can also be applied to the problem of correlating measurable effect variables with the compositions of the classified samples. In correlation analyses one may wish to determine how certain sample variables, such as sediment composition, organic content, and lipid concentration, influence the composition of measured residues or concentrations of PCBs, PCDDs, or PCDFs.

This determination cannot be made by using multiple regression techniques because there are too many independent variables, x_{ki}, relative to dependent variables, y_{kj}. In SIMCA, the partial least squares method is used. This method was proposed by Wold (1975) and was discussed further by Wold (1982).

Application of partial least squares to problems in the analysis of PCDFs, PCDDs and PCBs, although relevant to the problems faced in environmental studies of PCDFs and PCDDs, is beyound the scope of this paper. This topic is discussed by S. Wold (1975; 1982), Dunn et al. (1984) and Stalling et al. (1983b).

SIMCA software is available in two interactive forms, both developed by Wold (1982): (1) a Fortran version which runs on Control Data Corporation (CDC) machines, and (2) a SIMCA-3B version executing from compiled Basic programs. SIMCA-3B pattern recognition programs for CPM (Digital Research, Pacific Grove, CA) and MS-DOS (Microsoft Corporation, Bellevue, WA) on 8088 or 8086 based microcomputers are available from Principal Data Components, 2505 Shepard Blvd., Columbia, MO 65201.

The Fortran version is useful for analysis of very large data sets, e.g., 400 x 70 matrices. SIMCA-3B is menu driven and applicable to intermediate sized data sets. The CPM version is limited to 50 samples and 50 variables, whereas the MS-DOS version can evaluate ca. 100 samples by 100 variables. The SIMCA-3B version includes the PLS-2 program developed by Wold (1982).

Applications of SIMCA to Chromatography Data

A typical gas chromatogram of a PCB mixture is given in Figure 5. The chromatogram represents a 1:1:1:1 mixture of Aroclors 1242, 1248, 1254, and 1260. It contains more than 100 component peaks, of which 69 were used in the SIMCA analysis (Stalling et al., 1983b and Dunn et al., 1984). In the discussion that follows, the SIMCA method is applied to quality assurance in PCB analyses, including classification of different Aroclor types, and the data resulting from the analysis of nine samples for 45 Cl_4 and Cl_5 PCDF isomers are examined. These nine samples were related to PCB fires or potential pyrolysis of PCBs (Petty et al., 1983).

The PCB data represent concentrations of 69 individual isomers determined by gas chromatographic analysis of Aroclors 1242, 1248, 1254 and 1260 (Stalling et al., 1983b); Figure 5. As in most such problems, some form of pretreatment of the data is warranted. In all examples discussed in this report, the data have been normalized to relative concentration (or peak height) by dividing the individual response by the total sum of the responses or concentration determined for the sample.

Quality Assurance

Principal components analysis can be used to detect analytical problems such as sample variations due to instrument error, noise, or missed peaks. Application of SIMCA to this kind of problem is illustrated by an examination of replicate PCB analyses by capillary chromatography (Figure 6). These data represent replicate assays of a 1:1:1:1 mixture of Aroclors. Fitting the data for the four samples to a two component model (A2 and plotting the first two principal components score values, t_i; Theta 1 vs Theta 2, Equation 3) shows that samples 19 and 20 are very different from samples 17 and 18 (Figure 7).

The plot of the loadings for each chromatographic peak (Beta 1 and Beta 2, Equation 3) reveals information about the sources of the variance in the four samples (Figure 8). Information in Table 3 confirms these findings, and it is clear that the variability is largely the result of the failure to detect two peaks (peak 1 [variable 5], peak 4 [variable 8]). Also, peak 63 (variable 67) in sample 20 indicates a concentration which is 9% greater than the average concentration measured in all samples.

The data show that peak 1 is zero in samples 19 and 20, that peak 5 is zero in sample 19, and that there is about 12% variation in peak 63 in samples 19 and 20. Only a careful examination of the data plot for each analysis reveals these deviations in the chromatograms. These results illustrate the utility of principal components analysis for checking the internal consistency of complex chromatograms.

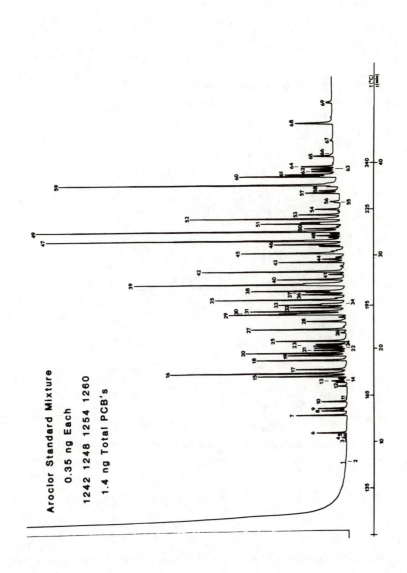

FIGURE 5. Capillary Gas Chromatogram of 1:1:1:1 Aroclor 1242: 1248: 1254: 1260. (C$_{87}$ 0.25 mm x 100 M glass capillary column).

Aroclor Standard Mixture

0.35 ng Each

1242 1248 1254 1260

1.4 ng Total PCB's

NORMALIZED COMPOSITION HISTOGRAMS OF 4 REPLICATE ANALYSES

(TRS3/6/82)

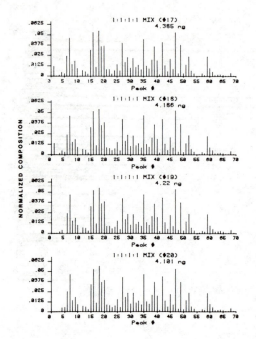

FIGURE 6. Fractional Composition Histograms from Four Replicate Analyses of Aroclor Mixture.

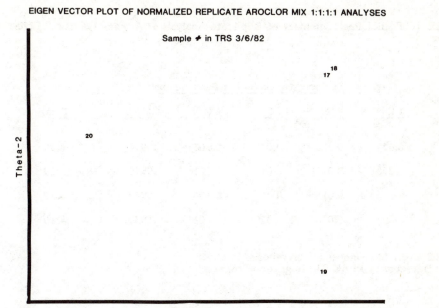

FIGURE 7. Principal Components Plot Derived from Fractional Composition Replicate Aroclor Analysis (Figure 2).

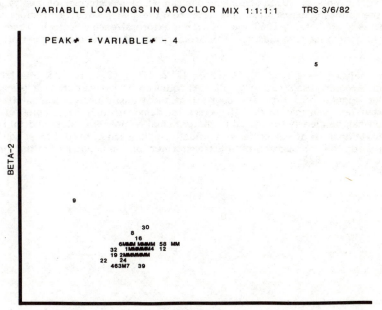

FIGURE 8. Plot of Variable Loadings (Betas) in Aroclor Mixture.

TABLE 3. Partial Peak Summary of Replicate Analysis of Aroclor 1242:1248:1250:1260 Mixture

| Sample No. | Concentration (ng) of Peak Number | | | | | Total |
	1 (5)[1]	4 (8)	5 (9)	6 (10)	63 (67)	
17	0.054	0.020	0.014	0.106	.0933	4.38
18	0.058	0.020	0.014	0.101	.0956	4.19
19	0[2]	0.016	0[2]	0.104	.0929	4.22
20	0[2]	0.020	0.020	0.101	.1030	4.10

[1] SIMCA Variable Number in parenthesis
[2] Not Detected by PEAK-11 Integration Program

Classification

To illustrate the use of SIMCA in classification problems, we applied the method to the analysis of 23 PCB samples -- 20 standards and one sample of transformer oil analyzed in triplicate. In the following example, sample data from the analysis of five Aroclors were used (Aroclors 1242, 1248, 1254, 1260 and a 1:1:1:1 mixture of each Aroclor). Together, these sample data comprise five classes. The Aroclor content of the transformer oil was unknown.

Four replicate analyses were made of Aroclors 1242, 1248, 1254, 1260, and a 1:1:1:1 mixture of each Aroclor. Application of SIMCA, followed by generation of a principal components plot (Figure 9) of the data, shows that the transformer oil was similar to Aroclor 1260, but not identical to it. These results demonstrate that samples of the various Aroclors can be clearly separated in the principal components plots and that the results of replicate analysis are essentially identical. Application of partial least squares to the estimation of the composition of the transformer oil was made by Stalling et al. (1983b) and Dunn et al. (1984).

Application of SIMCA to PCDF and PCDD Analyses

We have begun to apply SIMCA to the analysis of samples containing complex PCDF and PCDD residues. Data from the analysis of PCDFs (Cl$_4$ and Cl$_5$ isomers) by capillary gas chromatography/electron-impact low resolution mass spectrometry were obtained from Dr. Christoffer Rappe, University of Umea, Umea, Sweden (Rappe et al., 1983). A brief description of the samples and their origin is presented in Table 4. The identities assigned to the isomers in the ion chromatograms are given in Table 5. Peak heights of the various Cl$_4$ and Cl$_5$ isomers were measured in the ion chromatograms and a data matrix was prepared. The peak heights were totaled and each peak height was expressed as percent of total peak height. These data are summarized in Table 6. There were 405 individual measurements in the nine samples .

A two component principal components model was applied to the nine samples. A plot of the first and second component theta values for each sample is presented in Figure 9. This plot shows that none of the samples were identical to the standard mixture (sample 9). Samples 2, 6, 7 and 8 are similar with respect to their first principal component and samples 1, 3, 4, and 6 are similar with respect to the second principal component. The loading plot (Beta 1 vs Beta 2) indicates that there are several groups of peaks that show similar variation (Figure 10).

A more detailed examination of these samples should reveal which peaks are responsible for the major differences between samples. The concentration of peak 11 varies from 2.3% in sample 5 (locomotive) to 8.1% in sample 1 (soot from a Binghamton State Office Building fire). These two samples are most dissimilar with respect to their first principal component values. Samples 2 and 5 differ most from sample 8 with respect to peak 5. Among the samples, peak 5 is lowest -- 0.22% -- in sample 8 vs 5.72% in sample 2 and 7.18% in sample 5. Additional differences in sample composition are readily apparent from the compositions of peaks having similar loading values (Beta 1 and Beta 2) in Figure 10, i.e., peaks .9, 15,, .11, 17, 33,, and .40, 21, 45, 14, 19,. As the size of the data set examined increases, the utility of this approach becomes more important as relations of sample similarity are quantitated in the sample Theta values. Correlations of these values with environmental factors may be attempted, i.e., correlations of changes in Theta values with distance from sources, temperature of incineration, or chemical reaction conditions. Results from these correlations are likely to provide information on factors affecting the composition or amount of contaminants. This, in turn, can contribute to a broader understanding of the problem being studied.

Quality control among various laboratories or individuals can readily be assessed by examining multiple analyses of the same sample mixture of PCDDs or PCDFs. The principal components plots, when used in this manner, can reveal which variables are most subject to interferences or losses and which analysts, instruments, or cleanup procedures yield the most consistent results.

TABLE 4. SIMCA Number, Site

No.	Site	Origin
1	Binghamton, NY	Transformer fire, state office building
2	Stockholm, Sweden	Capacitor accident
3	Surahammar, Sweden	PCB fire
4	Hallstahammar, Sweden	Capacitor accident
5	(Not provided)	Locomotive
6	Canada	Municipal waste incineration
7	Eksjo, Sweden	Municipal waste incineration
8	Denmark	Hazardous waste incineration
9	Umea, Sweden	Laboratory standard solution

[1] Data supplied by Dr. Christoffer Rappe, University of Umea, Umea, Sweden. Refer to Rappe et al., 1983 for further discussion of the samples.

TABLE 5. Isomer Structure Assigned to C_{14} and C_{15} Dibenzofurans Separated by HighResolution Gas Chromatography/Mass Spectrometry

Isomer Assignment[1]

	Tetrachloro-		Pentachloro-
1	1,3,6,8-	23	1,3,4,6,8-
2	1,3,7,9- + 1,3,7,8-	24	1,2,4,6,8-
3	1,3,4,7	25	2,3,4,7,9-
4	1,4,6,8-	26	1,3,4,7,8-
5	1,3,6,7- + 1,2,4,7-	27	1,3,4,7,9- + 1,2,3,6,8-
6	1,3,4,8-	28	1,2,4,7,8-
7	1,3,4,6- + 1,2,4,8-	29	1,2,4,7,9- + 1,3,4,6,7-
8	1,2,3,7- + 1,2,6,8- +	30	1,2,4,6,7-
	1,4,7,8- + 1,3,6,9-	31	2,3,4,6,9- + 1,2,3,4,7-
		32	1,3,4,6,9-
9	2,3,4,9- + 1,2,3,4-	33	1,2,3,4,8- + 1,2,3,7,8-
10	1,2,3,8- + 2,4,6,8-	34	1,2,3,4,6-
	1,3,6,7- + 1,2,3,6-	35	1,2,3,7,9-
11	1,2,7,8-	36	1,2,3,6,7-
12	1,2,6,7- + 1,2,7,9-	37	2,3,4,6,8- + 1,2,4,6,9-
13	2,3,6,8-	38	1,3,4,8,9-
14	2,4,6,7-	39	1,2,3,6,9-
15	1,2,3,9- + 1,2,6,9-	40	2,3,4,8,9-
16	1,2,6,9-	41	1,2,3,4,9-
17	2,3,7,8-	42	1,2,4,8,9-
18	2,3,4,8-	43	2,3,4,7,8-
19	2,3,4,6-	44	1,2,3,8,9-
20	2,3,6,7-	45	2,3,4,6,7-
21	3,4,6,7-		
22	1,2,8,9-		

[1] Isomer assignments and ion intensity data supplied by Dr. Christoffer Rappe, University of Umea, Umea, Sweden.

TABLE 6. Tetrachloro -and Pentachloro-dibenzofuran Residues Detected in Samples from PCB Fires or Pyrolysis (Table 4) Electron Impact Mass Spectrometry. Data represent ion intensities expressed as percentage of total ion intensity of tetra-(variables 1-22) and penta-chloro-(variables 23-45) isomers. Refer to Table 5 for isomer assignments.

1 Binghamton State Office Building

0	3.17003	1.26801	.3458	.63401
2.01729	1.38329	5.9366	0	3.63112
8.06916	3.22767	1.38329	1.0951	1.0951
2.36311	9.16427	0	0	8.81844
1.78674	6.34006	.34582	0	.57637
2.30548	5.4755	2.47839	3.1124	1.0951
1.49856	.74928	9.10663	0	0
2.24784	1.78674	1.15274	.9222	.34588
0	1.15274	2.59366	1.5562	1.84438

2 Stockholm Capacitor Explosion

1.03605	6.25777	3.06672	.95317	5.71902
1.6759	2.32076	5.5947	0	5.47037
4.72441	3.68835	2.48653	1.0775	2.11355
.58019	3.27393	1.98923	0	3.31538
1.16038	1.65769	0	.82884	.66387
3.4397	4.35143	1.65769	1.65769	2.48653
6.21633	0	3.56403	1.16038	0
1.24327	2.81807	.66308	1.78201	2.11355
0	0	4.39287	0	3.10816

3 Surahammar, PCB Fire

0	1.4821	0	0	1.15274
1.15274	2.0585	4.2816	1.31741	2.75834
3.78757	2.2643	2.59366	2.1408	1.31741
0	6.1754	2.05846	1.89378	6.0107
2.63483	.7822	.61754	1.48209	1.02923
0	5.7670	5.51667	3.95224	3.91107
3.49938	.6587	4.73446	1.85261	0
2.34664	3.2524	1.02923	0	2.34664
.411692	.8234	6.17538	0	4.73446

4 Hallstahammar, Capacitor Explosion

.795455	1.81818	0	0	0
.852273	1.53409	3.23864	0	7.67045
8.52273	3.86364	0	1.81818	1.98864
2.27273	6.64773	0	0	5.68182
1.30682	.79546	0	0	0
0	1.47727	6.76136	3.06818	3.01136
3.125	0	8.52273	0	0
2.32955	5.90909	0	0	3.52273
1.76136	0	7.95455	.79546	2.95455

5 Residues on Locomotive

.92873	1.23839	1.54799	1.9195	7,18266
.557276	3.03406	3.34365	5.69659	3.34365
2.35294	1.85759	2.8483	2.16718	9.28793
0	1.9195	2.78638	1.42415	2.78638
1.36223	.30960	0	.99071	3.90093
0	1.85759	4.14861	1.30031	3.40557
9.34985	0	2.97214	1.11455	0
.928793	3.46749	0	0	.2477
.371517	1.17647	3.71517	.309598	2.8486

6 Canadian Municipal Waste Incinerator

3.18231	1.99569	0	1.26753	2.18447
1.48328	2.53506	3.93743	3.07443	4.04531
2.96656	2.93959	3.452	3.263221	2.64293
0	2.21143	2.69687	2.31931	3.29018
1.8069	0.35060	2.21143	2.85868	1.726
0.62028	4.04531	2.50809	3.23625	2.42718
0.62028	0.59331	3.66775	1.53722	0
2.07659	2.99353	0.566343	0	3.8835
1.34844	0.431500	3.69471	0.35059	3.91046

7 Eksjo Municipal Waste Incinerator

0.150432	4.06168	0	0.564122	1.05303
0.714554	1.20346	3.19669	4.21211	5.64122
2.63257	2.40692	3.57277	4.51297	4.32493
0.526514	2.10605	2.82061	3.87364	4.66341
4.13689	0.37608	0.225649	0.188041	0.48891
0	2.36931	2.2941	2.85822	2.10605
3.08387	0	4.24972	1.61715	0
2.55735	3.15908	0.977811	0	4.47537
1.05303	0	5.64122	0.639338	5.26514

8 Denmark Hazardous Waste Incineration

0.530504	2.29885	0.309461	0.30946	0.22104
1.06101	0.928382	0	0	3.31565
3.80195	3.75774	4.02299	6.67551	6.23342
0.486295	2.65252	4.42087	6.05659	6.05659
4.95137	0.66313	0.530504	0.75155	1.19363
0	2.69673	1.76835	2.25464	1.90097
2.25464	0	3.18302	1.5473	0
2.21043	3.18302	0.707339	0.442087	4.02299
0.66313	0.618921	4.19982	0.442087	6.67551

9 Umea, Standard Mixture of PCDFs and PCDDs

1.64788	3.81613	1.56114	2.13935	2.60191
1.30095	2.80428	0	4.19196	2.42845
4.36542	1.79243	2.71755	1.82134	1.56114
1.64688	1.4455	1.90807	1.41659	1.61897
1.85025	2.22608	1.73461	2.48627	2.51518
1.93698	2.13935	3.58485	0.72275	4.39433
2.19717	3.64267	2.08153	3.20902	1.06967
1.61897	2.02371	3.03556	3.67158	1.90807
1.61897	1.85025	1.87916	2.11044	1.7057

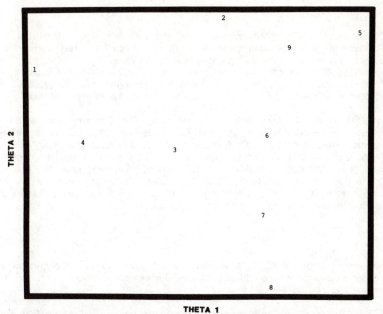

FIGURE 9. Principal Components Plot of Samples Containing Cl4 and Cl5-PCDFs Associated with PCB Pyrolysis or Fires. Each sample was analyzed for 45 components.

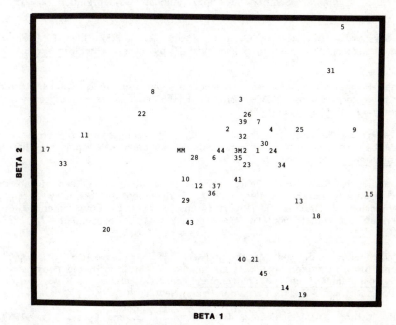

FIGURE 10. Plot of Loading Values for Nine Samples Analyzed for Cl4 and Cl5-PCDF Components.

SUMMARY

Residues of PCDDs and PCDFs exist in many of the nation's fish. Defining the composition and extent of this contamination will require extensive analytical effort. Methods are available for separation and quantitation of PCDFs and PCDDs, but they must be further developed to enable quantitation of the 2,3,7,8-substituted isomers of both groups of contaminants. Although the present methods can be applied to characterize environmental residues, their performance must be carefully evaluated.

The increasing availability of 8- and 16 bit microcomputers makes the application of advanced chemometric techniques an effective and powerful tool. With these resources, chemists and environmental scientists can deal more effectively with the complex data being generated and thus, better elucidate important factors such as quality control, sample origin, and physiochemical impacts. Application of chemometrics can provide increased use of data that, in the case of PCDDs, PCDFs, and PCBs, are costly to obtain. These data are important in defining the scope of dioxin and furan pollution and in formulating plans to minimize adverse environmental impacts.

REFERENCES

Ahling, B., Lindskog, A., Jansson, B. and Sundstrom, G. 1977. Formation of polychlorinated dibenzo-p-dioxins and dibenzofurans during combustion of a 2,4,5-T formulation. Chemosphere 8:461-468.

Bell, R.A. 1983. The synthesis and characterization of isomers of polychlorinated dibenzofurans, tetra- through octa. Paper no. 7, Environmental Chemistry Section, Proceedings of Symposium on Dioxins and Dibenzofurans in the Total Environment, 186th National American Chemical Society Meeting, August 28-September 2, 1983, Washington, D.C.

Buser, H.-R., Bosshardt, H.P., Rappe, C. and Lindahl, R. 1978. Identification of polychlorinated dibenzofuran isomers in fly ash and PCB pyrolyses. Chemosphere 6:419-429.

Buser, H.-R. and Rappe, C. 1984. Isomer-specific separation of 2,3,7,8-substituted polychlorinated dibenzo-p-dioxins (PCDDs) using high-resolution gas chromatography and mass spectrometry. Anal. Chem. In press.

Chen, P.H., Chang, K.T. and Lu, Y.D. 1981. Polychlorinated biphenyls and polychlorinated dibenzofurans in the toxic rice-bran oil that caused PCB poisoning in Tai Chung. Bull. Environ. Contam. Toxicol. 26:489-495.

Czuczwa, J.M. and Hites, R.A. 1983. Sources and fates of dioxins and dibenzofurans as told to us by sediment cores. Paper no. 27, Environmental Chemistry Section, Proceedings Symposium on Dioxins and Dibenzofurans in the Total Environment, 186th National American Chemical Society Meeting, August 28-September 2, 1983, Washington, D.C.

Decad, G.M., Birnbaum, L.S. and Mathews, H.B. 1982. Disposition of 2,3,7,8-tetrachlorodibenzofuran in guinea pigs, rats and monkeys. In Chlorinated Dioxins and Related Compounds: Impact on the Environment, eds. O. Hutzinger, R.W. Frei, E. Merian and F. Pocchiari, pp. 307-315, Pergamon Press, New York.

Dunn, W.J., III, Stalling, D.L., Schwartz, T.R., Hogan, J.W. and Petty, J.D. 1984. Classification and quantitation of PCBs in environmental samples using SIMCA pattern recognition. Anal. Chem. In press.

Environmental Protection Agency. 1983a. Health Assessment Document for Dioxins, in review, Environmental Protection Agency, Office of Research and Development, Criteria and Assessment Office, Cincinnati, OH.

Environmental Protection Agency, press statement, July 29, 1983b. Peer Review Panel, Workshop on Dioxins, organized by Environmental Protection Agency, 26 West St. Clair St., Cincinnati, OH 45268.

Esposito, M.P., Tiernan, T.O. and Dryden, F.E. 1980a. In Dioxins, EPA-600/2-80-197, pp. 89-93, United Stated Environmental Protection Agency, Cincinnati, OH.

Esposito, M.P., Tiernan, T.O. and Dryden, F.E. 1980b. In Dioxins, EPA-600/2-80-197, pp. 106-108, United States Environmental Protection Agency, Cincinnati, OH.

Esposito, M.P., Tiernan, T.O. and Dryden, F.E. 1980c. In Dioxins, EPA-600/2-80-197, pp. 98-106, United States Environmental Protection Agency, Cincinnati, OH.

Goldstein, J.A. 1980. Structure-activity relationships for the biochemical effects and the relationship to toxicity. In Halogenated Biphenyls, Terphenyls, Naphthalenes, Dibenzodioxins and Related Products, ed. R.D. Kimbrough, pp. 151-190, Elsevier/North Holland Biomedical Press, Amsterdam.

Hardell, L., Eriksson, M., Lenner, P. and Lundgren, E. 1981. Malignant lymphoma and exposure to chemicals, especially organic solvents, chlorophenols, and phenoxy acids: A case-control study. Br. J. Cancer 43:169-176.

Harless, R.L., Osward, E.O., Lewis, R.G., Dupuy, A.E., Jr., McDaniel, D.D. and Tai, H. 1982. Determination of 2,3,7,8-tetrachlorodibenzo-p-dioxin in fresh water fish. Chemosphere 2:193-198.

Harless, R.L., Lewis, R.G., Dupuy, A.E. and McDaniel, D.D. 1983. Analysis of 2,3,7,8-tetrachlorodibenzo-p-dioxin residues in environmental samples. In Human and Environmental Risks of Chlorinated Dioxin and Related Compounds, eds. R.E. Tucker, A.L. Young and A.P. Gray, pp. 161-171, Plenum Press, New York.

Helder, T. 1980. Effects of 2,3,7,8-tetrachloro-p-dioxin (TCDD) on early life stages of the pike (Esox lucius L.). Sci. Total Environ. 14:255-264.

Helder, T. 1981. Effects of 2,3,7,8-tetrachlorodibenzo-p-dioxin (TCDD) on early life stages of the rainbow trout (Salmo gairdneri, Richardson). Toxicol. 19:101-112.

Honchar, P.A. and Halperin, W.E. 1981. 2,4,5-T, trichlorophenol, and soft tissue sarcoma. Lancet I(8214):268-269.

Hutzinger, O., Frei, R.W., Merian, E. and Pocchiari, F. (eds.). 1982. Chlorinated Dioxins and Related Compounds: Impact on the Environment, 658 pp., Pergamon Press, Oxford.

Isensee, A.R. 1978. Bioaccumulation of 2,3,7,8-tetrachlorodibenzo-p-dioxin. Ecol. Bull. 27:255-262.

Isensee, A.R. and Jones, G.E. 1975. Distribution of 2,3,7,8-tetrachloro-p-dioxin (TCDD) in aquatic model ecosystems. Environ. Sci. Technol. 9:668-672.

Kleopfer, R.D., Bann, W.W., Yue, K.T. and Harris, D.J. 1983. Occurrence of tetrachlorodibenzo-p-dioxin in environmental samples from southwest Missouri. In Chlorinated Dioxins and Dibenzofurans in the Total Environment, eds. G. Choudhary, L.H. Keith and C. Rappe, pp. 193-207, Butterworth Publishers, Boston.

Kowalski, B.R.   1973.   Pattern recognition II.   Linear and nonlinear methods for displaying chemical data. J. Amer. Chem. Soc. 95:686-693.

Kowalski, B.R. 1980. Chemometrics. Anal. Chem. 52:112R-122R.

Kuratsune, M.   1980.   Yusho.   In Halogenated Biphenyls, Terphenyls, Naphthalenes, Dibenzodioxins and Related Products, ed. R.D. Kimbrough, pp. 287-302, Elsevier/North Holland Biomedical Press, Amsterdam.

Matsumura, F., Quensen, J. and Tsushimoto, G. 1983. Microbial degradation of TCDD in a model ecosystem.   In Human and Environmental Risks of Chlorinated Dioxin and Related Compounds, eds. R.E. Tucker, A.L. Young and A.P. Gray, pp. 191-219, Plenum Press, New York.

Mazer, T., Heilman, F.D., Noble, R.W. and J.J. Brooks. 1983. Synthesis of the 38 tetrachlorodibenzofuran isomers and identification by capillary column gas chromatography/mass spectrometry. Anal. Chem. 55:104-110.

Mitchum, R.K., Korfmacher, W.A., Moler, G.F. and Stalling, D.L. 1982. Capillary gas chromatography/atmospheric pressure negative chemical ionization mass spectrometry of the 22 tetrachloro-dibenzo-p-dioxins. Anal. Chem. 54:719-722.

National Research Council Canada.   1981a.   Polychlorinated dibenzo-p-dioxins: Limitations to the current analytical techniques. National Research Council of Canada, (NRCC No. 18576).

National Research Council Canada. 1981b.   Chlorinated Phenols: Criteria for Environmental Quality (NRCC NO. 18578).

Norstrom, R.J., Hallet, D.J., Simon, M. and Mulvihill, M.J.   1982.   Analysis of Great Lakes herring gull eggs for tetrachlorodibenzo-p-dioxins.   In Chlorinated Dioxins and Related Compounds: Impacts on the Environment, eds. O. Hutzinger, R.W. Frei, E. Merian and F. Pocchiari, pp. 173-181, Pergamon Press, Oxford.

Olie, K., Vermeullen, P.L. and Hutzinger, O.   1977.   Chlorinated-p-dioxins and the chlorobenzofurans are trace components of fly ash and flue gas from and municipal incinerators in the Netherlands. Chemosphere 6:455-459.

Petty, J.D., Smith, L.M., Bergqvist, P.-A., Johnson, J.L., Stalling, D.L. and Rappe, C. 1983.   Composition of polychlorinated dibenzofuran and dibenzo-p-dioxin residues in sediments of the Hudson and Housatonic rivers.   In Chlorinated Dioxins and Dibenzofurans in the Total Environment, eds. G. Choudhary, L.H. Keith and C. Rappe, pp. 203-208, Butterworth Publishers, Boston.

Poland, A., Knutson, J. and Glover, E.   1983.   A consideration of the mechanism of action of 2,3,7,8-tetrachlorodibenzo-p-dioxin and related halogenated aromatic hydrocarbons. In Human and Environmental Risks of Chlorinated Dioxins and Related Compounds, eds. R.E. Tucker, A.L. Young and A.P. Gray, pp. 539-559, Plenum Press, New York.

Rappe, C. and Buser, H.-R.   1980.   Chemical properties and analytical methods.   In Halogenated Biphenyls, Terphenyls, Naphthalenes, Dibenzodioxins and Related Products, ed. R.D. Kimbrough, pp. 47-76, Elsevier/North Holland Biomedical Press, New York.

Rappe, C., Buser, H.-R., Stalling, D.L., Smith, L.M. and Dougherty, R.C.   1981. Identification of polychlorinated dibenzofurans in environmental samples.   Nature 29:524-526.

Rappe, C. Marklund, S. Bergqvist, P.-A. and Hansson, M. 1983. Polychlorinated dibenzo-p-dioxins, dibenzofurans and other polychlorinated aromatics formed during incineration and polychlorinated biphenyl fires. In Chlorinated Dioxins and Dibenzofurans in the Total Environment, eds. G. Choudhary, L.H. Keith and C. Rappe, pp. 99-124, Butterworth Publishers, Boston.

Reggiani, T. 1983. A mortality study of workers employed at the Monsanto Company plant in Nitro, West Virginia. In Human and Environmental Risks of Chlorinated Dioxin and Related Compounds, eds. R.E. Tucker, A. L. Young and A.P. Gray, pp. 575-591, Plenum Press, Amsterdam.

Ryan, J.J., Lau, P.-Y., Pilon, J.C. and Lewis, D. 1983. 2,3,7,8-Tetrachlorodibenzo-p-dioxin and 2,3,7,8-tetrachlorodibenzofuran residues in Great Lakes fish. In Chlorinated Dioxins and Dibenzofurans in the Total Environment, eds. G. Choudhary, L.H. Keith and C. Rappe, pp. 87-97, Butterworth Publishers, Boston.

Schmitt, C., Ludke, J.L. and Walsh, D.F. 1981. Organochlorine residues in fish: National Pesticide Monitoring Program, 1970-1974. Pest. Monitoring J. 14:136-281.

Smith, L.M. 1981. Carbon dispersed in glass fibers as an adsorbent for contaminant enrichent and fractionation. Anal. Chem. 53:2152-2154.

Smith, L.M. and Johnson, J.L. 1983. Evaluation of interferences from seven series of polychlorinated aromatic compounds in an analytical method for polychlorinated dibenzofurans and dibenzo-p-dioxins. In Dioxins and Dibenzofurans in the Total Environment, eds. G. Choudhary, L.H. Keith and C. Rappe, pp. 321-332, Butterworth Publishers, Boston.

Stalling, D.L., Petty, J.D., Smith, L.M. and Dubay, G.R. 1981a. Contaminant enrichment modules and approaches to automation of sample extract cleanup. In Environmental Health Chemistry, ed. J.D. McKinney, pp. 177-193, Ann Arbor Science Publishers, Ann Arbor, MI.

Stalling, D.L., Petty, J.D. and Smith, L.M. 1981b. Chromatographic enrichment of acidic compounds from organic solvents using alkali metalsilicates. J. Chrom. Sci. 19:16-26.

Stalling, D.L., Smith, L.M., Petty, J.D., Hogan, J.W., Johnson, J.L., Rappe, C. and Buser, H.-R. 1983a. Residues of polychlorinated dibenzo-p-dioxins and dibenzofurans in Laurentian Great Lakes fish. In Human and Environmental Risks of Chlorinated Dioxin and Related Compounds, eds. R.E. Tucker, A.L. Young and A.P. Gray, pp. 221-240, Plenum Press, New York.

Stalling, D.L., Dunn, W.J., III, Schwartz, T.R., Hogan, J.W., Petty, J.D., Johansson, E., Wold, S. 1983b. Application of SIMCA, a principal components method, in isomer specific analysis of PCBs. In Proceedings of Symposium on The Role of Chemometrics in Pesticide/Environmental Residue Analytical Determinations, 185th American Chemical Society, March 20-25, 1983, Seattle, WA (to be published by American Chemical Symposium Series, Kurtz, D.A., in press).

Taylor, M.L., Tiernan, T.O., Garrett, J.H., VanNess, G.F. and Solch, J.G. 1983. Assessment of incineration processes as sources of supertoxic chlorinated hydrocarbons: Concentrations of polychlorinated dibenzo-p-dioxins/dibenzofurans and possible precoursor compounds in incinerator effluents. In Chlorinated Dioxins and Dibenzofurans in the Total Environment, eds. G. Choudhary, L.H. Keith and C. Rappe, pp. 125-164, Butterworth Publisher, Boston.

Thibodeaux, L.J. 1983. Offsite transport of 2,3,7,8-tetrachlorodibenzo-p-dioxin from a production disposal facility. In <u>Chlorinated Dioxins and Dibenzofurans in the Total Environment</u>, eds. G. Choudhary, L.H. Keith and C. Rappe, pp. 75-86, Butterworth Publishers, Boston.

Tognoni, G. and Bonaceorsi, A. 1982. Epidemiological problems with 2,3,7,8-tetrachlorodibenzo-p-dioxin (TCDD): A critical review. <u>Drug Metab. Rev.</u> 13:447-469.

Vieth, G.D., Defoe, D.L. and Bergstedt, B.V. 1979. Measuring and estimating the bioconcentration factor of chemicals in fish. <u>J. Fish. Res. Board Can.</u> 36:1040-1048.

Wold, H. 1975. Soft modeling by latent variables: The nonlinear iterative partial least squares approach. In <u>Perspective in Probability and Statistics: Papers in Honor of M.S. Bartlett</u>, ed. J. Gani, pp. 117-142, Academic Press, London.

Wold, S. 1982. The analysis of multivariate chemical data using SIMCA and MACUP. <u>Kemia-Kemi</u> 9:401-405.

Wold, S. and Sjostrom, M. 1977. SIMCA: A method for analyzing chemical data in terms of similarity and analogy. In <u>Chemometrics: Theory and Application</u>, ACS Symposium Series No. 52, p. 243, American Chemical Society, Washington, D.C.

Wold, S. Albano, C., Dunn, W.D., III, Esbensen, E., Helberg, S., Johansson, E. and Sjostrom, M. 1983. Pattern recognition: Finding and using regularities in multivariate data. In <u>Food Research and Data Analysis</u>, eds. H. Martens and H. Russwurm, Jr., pp. 147-188, Applied Science Publishers, New York.

Yockim, R.S., Isensee, A.R. and Jones, G.E. 1978. Distribution and toxicity of TCDD and 2,4,5-T in an aquatic model ecosystem. <u>Chemosphere</u> 7:215-220.

Chapter 9

PANEL DISCUSSION – SECTION 2

YOUNG: Dave, I was fascinated with your fish data and would just like to ask: Is there a chance to look at archive samples of fish? Have you thought about it? Have you looked into it?

STALLING: I've thought about it and it's strictly fund-limited, manpower limited and instrument-limited.

YOUNG: Well, I think some of us ought to be able to come up with something to have you take a look at some fish.

STALLING: There are some samples from the National Pesticide Monitoring Program that do go back over time. And to some extent, the archive isn't in the best of shape but it has improved since we took over the management of it.

RODGERS: I want to ask the speakers to address the issue of what Dr. Stalling referred to as disproportionality. This has to do with the octa, hexa, hepta ratios from the physical samples compared to the biological samples in the fish and how that might occur; whether they are selectively forcing these samples within their bodies or if there's a metabolic explanation or if there is some other hypothesis.

CZUCZWA: The reason you find a lot of the less chlorinated isomers in the water and the more chlorinated isomers in sediment samples may be related to the relative water solubilities which decrease as you increase the number of chlorines on these compounds. Another reason you may not find some of the more chlorinated species in fish is that these compounds are so insoluble that they are also insoluble in lipid material and may just not bioaccumulate to any degree.

STALLING: I would amplify on that a bit. I think we have to look at the whole process on a modeling basis and here I'm not talking about the kind of modeling you referred to here previously. But I believe that you could think about this process involving two or three stage inputs. It may be that the environmental loading of the microparticulates from combustion sources will strongly favor the higher chlorinated dioxins and dibenzofurans. Thus, you may have relatively inert and unavailable particulate fractionation in sediments. I have seen no particle size distribution analysis in sediments to date. To my knowledge, it has never been attempted. We have no information in the literature on the dibenzofuran or dioxin distribution among particle sizes in sediments. Another thing is that all of the 2,3,7,8 substituted isomers appear to be very slowly metabolized. The fish residues from the woodpond study could be overlaid on the liver studies from the Yusho exposure. Biologically, these materials are very, very persistent and it may relate to some of the binding possibilities in the organisms as well. I have recently come to the opinion that we have multiple types of inputs into the environment and they may be more strongly segregated than in the case of PCBs. I did not mention that in the case of the woodpond analysis the PCB in fish and sediment could be overlaid on each other. When you move a million times away from the PCB levels, there could be some adsorption factors playing important roles; that has to be studied. It's simply not, in my opinion, known.

NICOLL:

I'd like to know, in your analyses and comparisons of the various dioxins and the incinerator processes, what technologies were studied and at what temperatures and what kind of combustion areas were used?

CZUCZWA:

What do you mean by combustion areas?

NICOLL:

Well, you can combust in a semi-suspension. You can combust in a batchload, use secondary burning, fluidized bed, etc. and, of course, at varying temperatures and with varying retention times.

CZUCZWA:

I don't really have information on the various types of combustion systems and the combustion conditions for many of those samples. There seems to be quite a bit of variation even in one specific incinerator depending on what day you take these samples.

RICE:

I have heard a lot of talk about particulate dioxins and dibenzofurans. My particular work involves the gaseous phase distribution versus particulates in air and I wonder what anyone might know about the various distribution ratios of particulates to gases in air of these compounds.

CZUCZWA:

I don't know of any studies looking particularly at vapor phase versus particulate phase. Just going by the evidence of the ultimate fate of these compounds; i.e., that they end up in sediments, there seems to be suggestion that it's strongly adsorbed on particles. In a lot of model aquatic ecosystems the studies are on only the 2,3,7,8 isomer and the TCDD that's recovered tends to be bound to the sediments. However, there are losses from the system and some of them may be from volatilization. I don't think it's really been studied thoroughly but there is that possibility.

STALLING:

The first thing that I want to say is that I'm not an expert in this area so I can at least speculate with some impunity. In Science about a year or two ago, there was a very detailed study on the morphology of particulates, and there was some work going on at the Oak Ridge National Laboratories in which they were looking at the desorption kinetics of organics from various particulates. What I'm leading to is that one of the techniques that might be applied in characterizing these emissions is Magic Angle ^{13}C

NMR characterization. What I believe is at the root of the disparity of results is that in some of the particulates you have very carbon-rich particles. However, the carbon content in these emissions can vary tremendously from essentially inorganic rocks to very carbon-rich particles. I believe we can model what's going on by looking at the aromatic content of these particulates and there are some very detailed publications by J. Chafter at Monsanto who has applied Magic Angle spinning to the characterization of the aromatic properties. There may be other publications but we should look at the aromatic carbon content in relationship to the dioxin and dibenzofuran isomer distribution and I predict that the higher the organic carbon fraction, the more highly enriched with the octa furan or dioxin the residue profile should be. The other simple thing to do is frontal analysis chromatography by putting these particulates in a chromatography column and using a gradient elution between hexane and, say xylene or toluene, and then analyzing the materials as they elute to give you a desorption profile of these materials.

ZABIK: Any other questions? If not, we thank you for attending.

AUDIENCE MEMBERS CONTRIBUTING TO THE PANEL DISCUSSION: Arthur Nicoll, Energy Alpha Recovery, Inc., 30100 VanDyke, Suite 325, Warren, MI 48093; and Clifford Rice, University of Michigan, 3116 First Building, Ann Arbor, MI 48109.

Section 3
Dynamics of Dioxins
in the Environment

Chapter 10

ORIGINS OF POLYCHLORODIBENZO-P-DIOXINS (PCDD) AND POLYCHLORODIBENZOFURANS (PCDF) IN THE ENVIRONMENT

N.C.A. Weerasinghe and M.L. Gross
Department of Chemistry
University of Nebraska

INTRODUCTION

Contamination of the environment by polychlorinated dibenzo-p-dioxins (PCDDs) originates from three major sources: the use of certain herbicides, chemical waste and incineration. In addition, all forms of fire are also thought to be sources of PCDDs (Bumb et al., 1980; Czuczwa and Hites, 1984; Esposito et al., 1980). Polychlorinated dibenzofurans (PCDF), currently known to be more widespread than PCDD, enter the environment from two main sources: as a contaminant in PCB and as a byproduct of incineration. The dibenzofurans are also known to be formed in accidental PCB fires and possibly in all types of combustion.

Herbicides containing esters of 2,4,5-trichlorophenoxyacetic acid (2,4,5-T) have been used in a variety of ways in both the United States and abroad. These phenoxy herbicides are still being used on rice and sugar grown in certain parts of the USA. The trichlorophenoxy herbicides contain trace amounts of tetrachlorodibenzo-p-dioxins (TCDDs) as impurities resulting during the synthesis of precursors (Crummett and Stehl, 1973). The manufacture and use of herbicides and related chemicals and the disposal of production waste products have led to most instances of environmental contamination, particularly those involving the highly toxic 2,3,7,8-tetrachlorodibenzo-p-dioxin.

In this review, an attempt has been made to provide some perspective of the various sources of PCDD and PCDF in the environment. Much of the research cited herein has been conducted at the University of Nebraska-Lincoln with several collaborators, and the review should not be considered an exhaustive survey.

NORMAL USE OF HERBICIDES

Several studies have been conducted in order to evaluate the bioaccumulation, bioconcentration and biomagnification of 2,3,7,8-TCDD, as a result of the normal use of the phenoxy herbicides.

TCDD in Deer Tissue

The uptake of 2,3,7,8-TCDD in deer tissue as a result of an aerial application of 2,4,5-T on the Blodgett National Forest of California was recently studied (Harless et al., 1983). Twelve deer were placed in an enclosure within the forest, and 2,4,5-T containing <0.1 ppm of 2,3,7,8-TCDD was applied (3 lb/acre) to an eight acre plot. Deer were sacrificed at intervals during the course of the study, and the distribution of 2,3,7,8-TCDD in muscle, adipose tissue, liver and bone marrow was determined in two laboratories (University of Nebraska and EPA, Research Triangle Park) by using gas chromatography/high resolution mass spectrometry (GC/HRMS). Extremely low concentrations of 2,3,7,8-TCDD ("not detected" to 27 ppt) were found in the samples. There was no 2,3,7,8-TCDD detected in the bone marrow, and the highest concentration detected was 27 ppt in the muscle. However, the frequency of confirmed detections was highest for samples taken from deer who resided in the sprayed area for four weeks (see Table 1). Five out of the nine samples were found to contain TCDD, whereas no other confirmed detections were made except for one muscle sample taken from a deer that was sacrificed after two weeks. A confirmed detection refers to a sample which was found to contain TCDD in both laboratories.

TABLE 1

Sample	Muscle	Adipose	Liver
Control	0/2*	0/2	0/2
48 hrs	0/3	0/2	0/3
2 weeks	1/3	0/3	0/3
4 weeks	2/3	1/3	2/3

* Number of confirmed positives/number of samples

The conclusions that can be drawn from this study are that the 2,3,7,8-TCDD concentrations in the exposed tissue were distributed about an average which increased with the time of exposure. Although we cannot be sure of the average, it is clear that the average did increase as evidenced by the increasing number of detections for deer who resided longer in the sprayed area. Thus, the bioavailability of 2,3,7,8-TCDD after normal aerial application was evident for a long time.

TCDD in Other Animal Tissue

In this study (Ryan et al., 1974), cattle, sheep and goats were allowed to graze on land treated with 2,4,5-T which contained 40 ppb of 2,3,7,8-TCDD. The liver and the adipose tissues of the exposed animals were analyzed for the possible bioaccumulation of 2,3,7,8-TCDD. There were several positive samples with levels of 2,3,7,8-TCDD in the range of 6-41 ppt in the fat while the liver concentrations were 1-5 ppt.

In the same study (Ryan et al., 1974), four different calves were fed 2,4,5-T (100-1800 ppm) containing 0.5 ppm of 2,3,7,8-TCDD for 28 days. The 2,3,7,8-TCDD was found predominantly in the adipose tissue, and as expected, the levels were higher at the higher intakes of 2,4,5-T.

However, no 2,3,7,8-TCDD was found in fat from beef cattle fed with Ronnel insecticide at a detection limit of 5 to 10 ppt (Shadoff et al., 1977). The results were interpreted to indicate that there is no bioaccumulation of 2,3,7,8-TCDD at that level of administration of the insecticide.

It has been also reported (Kocher et al., 1978) that specimens of tissue taken from steers which had grazed on rangeland treated with 2,4,5-T had no noticeable levels of 2,3,7,8-TCDD, except for 3-4 ppt that showed up in some fat samples obtained from steers confined to an area which had been sprayed in its entirety with 2,4,5-T.

TCDD in Human Milk

An alleged high frequency of miscarriages among pregnant mothers who lived in the vicinity of Oregon forests which had been sprayed with 2,4,5-T was postulated to be due to 2,3,7,8-TCDD. In order to determine whether there was a correlation of miscarriages and exposure to TCDD, milk from mothers residing in forested areas of northern California, Oregon and Washington states were analyzed for 2,3,7,8-TCDD residues (Gross, 1980). The control subjects were taken from Los Angeles and Alaska where 2,4,5-T exposure was not likely. One hundred and three human milk samples were analyzed, and no 2,3,7,8-TCDD was detected with a detection limit averaging about 1 ppt.

TCDD in Environmental Samples From Herbicide-treated Areas

In order to evaluate the residue levels of 2,3,7,8-TCDD in the environment and in biota as a result of aerial application of the herbicide 2,4,5-T in Oregon forests, samples of several different matrices from the environment and biota were analyzed. This study was carried out jointly by the University of Nebraska and the U.S. Environmental Protection Agency (U.S. EPA), and replicate samples of a number of extracts were analyzed at both laboratories (Gross, 1980).

The study was divided into two phases. In phase I, water and sediment samples collected from the area were analyzed for 2,3,7,8-TCDD by GC/HRMS. Fourteen surface water samples were analyzed, and none were found to contain 2,3,7,8-TCDD at an average detection limit of ten parts-per-quadrillion. Sediment samples were taken from ten sites which also had been sampled for water. No TCDD was detected in seven of the samples. Two samples showed low levels (2 ppt or less) which could not be confirmed in later analyses. A detectable level (3-20 ppt) of TCDD was found in one sample by both laboratories.

In phase II of this study, sampling was extended to drinking water filters, animal tissue, and whole animals (mice, shrew, birds and newts). No TCDD was detected in any samples except for a level of 3 ppt that was found in a sample of products of conception and one newt on the first round of analysis. These detections could not be confirmed. Some confusion arose about this phase of the study in the popular press in the fall of 1983, and it was alleged that a significant fraction of sludge samples from this area contained high levels of TCDD. The confusion was due to an error in sample labeling in a final report, and it was later determined that the sludge was not taken from the Oregon region.

TCDD in Sugar

2,4,5-T and Silvex are two herbicides commonly used on sugar cane. We were called upon by the Baltimore Sun Newspaper to address the problem of the possible residues of 2,3,7,8-TCDD that could be carried over to the refining process of sugar. Samples of sugar at four different stages of refinement were collected from a sugar mill in Liberia parish, Louisiana, and analyzed for 2,3,7,8-TCDD using packed column GC/HRMS. No 2,3,7,8-TCDD was detected in any of the samples at an average detection limit of 1 ppt (Weerasinghe et al., 1983).

Plant uptake of 2,3,7,8-TCDD has been studied and found to be rather insignificant or highly unlikely (Leng, 1972; Isensee and Jones, 1971; Nash and Beall, 1980; Jensen et al., 1983). For example, the dissipation of TCDD on grass grown in a microecosystem was reported to be complete within 3.9-7.1 days (Nash and Beall, 1980). Under field conditions, TCDD applied to leaves seems to dissipate rapidly in the first few weeks (half life = 52 days) (Jensen et al., 1983). The dissipation may be partially due to photolysis. The absence of TCDD residues in sugar may be ascribed to the lack of uptake by the sugar cane plant, to photodegradation on the leaf surface, or loss of the TCDD in the sugar manufacturing process. However, the number of samples analyzed was limited, and conclusions drawn at this point should be considered tentative.

TCDD in Soil

Accumulation of 2,3,7,8-TCDD in soil after normal application of 2,4,5-T herbicide was investigated (Gross, 1978). Sixteen soil samples were collected at different intervals after normal application (3-10 lb/acre) of the herbicide. Among the 16 samples collected, 12 samples were found to contain TCDD in the range 8-40 ppt with an average detection limit of 6 ppt. Thus, after normal spraying, detectable levels of TCDD can be found in a high percentage of the samples. Nevertheless, the levels found seemed to bear no relation to the sampling time, perhaps because the duration of the study was short (72 days) or because of carry over from previous spray applications.

It is now clear that low levels of 2,3,7,8-TCDD can be detected in some environmental and biological samples after normal application of 2,4,5-T herbicide. A question which remains is how much of the TCDD is available to the biota and how much of it dissipates throughout the environment. The environmental transformation of a pollutant can occur by photolysis, hydrolysis and volatilization. The major route of environmental transformation for TCDD appear to be photolysis. Reductive dechlorination in the presence of hydrogen donors appears to be the major pathway of photodegradation (Esposito et al., 1980).

In a preliminary study of TCDD dissipation in the environment, it was reported (Kearney et al., 1972) that the time required to remove 50% of TCDD applied to soil appeared to be greater than one year, and for sediments the respective time was ca. 2 years under controlled conditions (Ward and Matsumara, 1978). The persistence of 2,3,7,8-TCDD in water is reported to be longer than in sediments (Ward and Matsumura, 1978).

Biotransformation of TCDD may occur but to a very small extent and, thus, has not been considered a significant step in the removal of TCDD. Microbial transformation of TCDD in 100 different strains of microbes was tested (Matsumara and Benezet, 1973). It was observed that only a few strains had the ability to degrade TCDD. The residue levels of TCDD in soil and sediments provide confirmation for this observation (Young et al., 1978).

Bioaccumulation of TCDD in aquatic animals is evident, but it has been argued that there is no significant biomagnification within a food chain (Isensee and Jones, 1975). However, in controlled studies, an accumulation factor of 2-2.6 x 10^4 was observed in snails, fish and daphnids exposed to 2,3,7,8-TCDD for 3-6 days. The studies have been conducted in a model ecosystem over a limited period of time. Thus, extrapolation of the results to the environment may be doubtful.

There is insufficient evidence to indicate any bioconcentration of TCDD in aquatic animals after normal application of TCDD. This may be because it is difficult to disseminate the residues from normal application into the aquatic environment because of photodegradation and adherence to soil.

The discussion thus far has been confined to 2,3,7,8-TCDD. Phenoxy herbicides containing 2,4,5-T have been reported to also contain 2,7-di, penta, hexa, hepta and octochlorodibenzo-p-dioxins to a lesser extent than 2,3,7,8-TCDD (Veterans Administration, 1981). In addition to 2,4,5-T, chlorophenols, especially pentachlorophenol, a heavily used antimicrobial agent, is known to contain both PCDD and PCDF as byproducts of synthesis (U.S. EPA, 1978; Rappe and Buser, 1980). Because approximately 44 million pounds of pentachlorophenol are used every year in the USA, the normal use of this material is potentially a more serious problem than the use of 2,4,5-T and other herbicides.

EXCESSIVE USE OF HERBICIDES

The exposure of veterans who served in Vietnam to herbicides containing 2,4,5-T (Agent Orange) and the follow-up studies that are now underway to determine the effects of long term exposure to TCDD in rhesus monkeys will now be discussed. The defoliation program in Vietnam is considered an example of the excessive use of herbicides.

TCDD in Tissue of Vietnam Veterans

Nearly 12 million gallons of the Agent Orange (a mixture of 2,4,5-T and 2,4-D) were used in Vietnam between 1962-1970. It was estimated that 2,4,5-T produced during the period contained maximum TCDD concentrations of 15-47 ppm. A joint study was undertaken by the University of Nebraska and the U.S. Veterans Administration to monitor the adipose tissue of some veterans who served in Vietnam (Gross et al., 1984).

The strategy was to analyze adipose tissue from 20 veterans who claimed to be exposed to Agent Orange. Ten persons who were not in Vietnam, but underwent treatment at VA hospitals, were taken as controls. The abdominal adipose tissues were analyzed using GC/HRMS. Ten of the 20 tissue samples analyzed were found to have measurable levels of TCDD.

On the basis of the veterans description of exposure, three were classified as heavily exposed to Agent Orange. Among these three, two had the highest levels (25-99 ppt) of TCDD in the fat. Of the veterans with light exposure (total number of five), three had low levels (5-7 ppt) of TCDD. Among the others (total number of twelve), five had low levels (3-13 ppt) of TCDD.

Confirmation of these results was sought via an interlaboratory study involving two U.S. EPA laboratories with considerable expertise in tissue analysis. The tissue containing up to 99 ppt of TCDD was found to have 173 ppt by the EPA workers, and that containing 35 ppt was reanalyzed and found to have 86 ppt. Tissue from the third heavily exposed veteran, which was found to contain a non detectable level of TCDD in the first round of analyses, now had 20 ppt of TCDD. The analysis at the University of Nebraska has poor recovery of the internal standard (20%), and therefore, it is suspect.

Thus, it appears that the veterans who were heavily exposed to Agent Orange carry low levels of TCDD in their body fat ten years after exposure. It is significant that two and possibly three of the three most heavily exposed men had the highest levels of TCDD in their body fat. It is unlikely that the exposure could have occurred as a matter of chance or from unrelated exposure in the USA. More studies are advocated to establish higher confidence in these conclusions. One pertinent investigation would involve a determination of the persistence of 2,3,7,8-TCDD in primates. The observations on veterans' tissues point to a long half-life.

Persistence of 2,3,7,8-TCDD in Primate Tissue

Human birth defects were thought to be associated with the use of defoliant herbicides in Vietnam and the Oregon forests (Smith, 1979). Birth defects and miscarriages have been reported in rhesus monkeys exposed to 2,3,7,8-TCDD under laboratory conditions (Barsotti et al., 1979; Schantz et al., 1979). In the early studies of TCDD exposure in the rhesus monkey, it was reported that at an accumulated dose of 1 µg/kg, abortions occurred with minimal toxicity (McNulty, 1980) to the mother, and at 5 µg/kg, delayed maternal death was observed. At a dose level of 0.01-0.02 µg/kg/day, reduction of fertility occurred (Allen et al., 1977).

The first estimate of the persistence of 2,3,7,8-TCDD in primate tissue was made as part of a preliminary study involving acute exposure of a single rhesus monkey. After administration of a single dose of 1 µg/kg/body weight (McNulty et al., 1982), it was determined that the TCDD had a half-life of approximately one year in fat.

Bowman and coworkers (unpublished results) at the Primate Center of the University of Wisconsin have embarked on a study to determine the effect of 2,3,7,8-TCDD on the nervous system, reproduction, offspring development and body clearance. In a preliminary investigation, the persistence of TCDD after chronic exposure at 25 ppt over a period of 4 years was studied. After 4 years of exposure the monkeys were taken off the TCDD diet and biopsied for subcutaneous and mesenteric fat. The fat biopsy was also repeated after six months. The GC/HRMS analysis of the tissue samples indicated easily detectable levels of TCDD in the tissues (600-1000 ppt). The apparent half-life in the mesenteric fat (determined from only two data points) was approximately 13 months which agrees with the previous observation (McNulty et al., 1982).

Estimate of Veterans Exposure to Agent Orange

The conclusion that the so-called "heavily exposed" veterans absorbed 2,3,7,8-TCDD in Vietnam has been criticized because the extent of exposure would have been too large and the concentration in fat tissue at the time of departure from Vietnam would have been unacceptably high. Knowing the half-life, it is now possible to estimate the daily exposure to Agent Orange over one year that is required to give a level of 100 ppt in fat ten years later and to judge whether that exposure is reasonable. The level ten years earlier, immediately following exposure and assuming a half-life of one year, would have been 100 ppb in fat. If a typical veteran has 15 kg of fat in his body and the distribution of TCDD is uniform, then a daily exposure to approximately 2-4 g of Agent Orange (which contains 2ppm of TCDD) for one year would have been sufficient. If the half-life is two years, then the concentration in fat would have been only 3.2 ppb and the amount of Agent Orange ingested would have been ca. one drop per day for one year. A two year half-life may not be unreasonable as the half-life in primates may be underestimated. Moreover, these daily exposure estimates are based on the assumption that the decay of TCDD does not show a rapid initial fall off followed by a slower rate; i.e., we have assumed that the decay is noncomposite.

TCDD in Monkey Offspring

As part of the study at the University of Nebraska, the effect of TCDD on the progeny of the exposed monkeys was studied (Bowman et al., unpublished results). Eight mothers were fed 5 ppt of TCDD in their diet (daily intake of 200 g of food in the diet) for 8 months and breeding commenced at the eighth month. Seven of the eight conceived, resulting in five viable vaginal births, one by Cesarean section, and one periparturitional death. The mothers were allowed to nurse the offspring (total of six) for a period of four months. After an adaptation and stabilization period of one month, the offspring were biopsied via laparotomy for mesenteric fat. GC/HRMS analysis of the samples indicated levels of TCDD between 270-860 ppt in four of the six samples. The high levels are expected because the transferred TCDD is now distributed in a smaller content of fat compared to that of the mother. Nursing infant monkeys have been found to bioconcentrate PCB up to levels of 3.5-7 times higher than the corresponding values in mothers fat (Barsotti, 1980; Bailey et al., 1980). Thus, the TCDD transfer could have also occurred as a result of nursing, but placental transfer cannot be ruled out. The study indicates the accumulation of TCDD at that level of exposure and also biomagnification in the progeny. Health effects are still under investigation.

CHEMICAL WASTE

Evidence of environmental contamination by TCDD from improper storage, effluent discharge and non-specified use of phenoxy herbicide waste has been reported. The following discussion is confined to a few joint studies carried out between the University of Nebraska, U.S. EPA, Air Force and Syntex Agribusiness, Inc., on the possible accumulation of TCDD in the environment and in biota. The TCDD originates from point sources of contamination, usually chemical waste.

Love Canal

Love Canal, excavated in 1894 with the idea of joining the upper and the lower Niagara River, was a dumping ground for municipal and chemical waste from 1940-1953. It is believed that approximately 200 tons of 2,4,5-trichlorophenol waste was disposed of in the canal by Hooker Chemicals and Plastics Corporation. Evidence of contamination of the Love Canal area due to the movement of waste chemicals was sought in a recent study (U.S. EPA, 1982). Very high levels of TCDD were detected in sediments collected from some sumps and storm sewers. The levels detected were in the range of 670-9570 ppb in sump sediments. Some storm sewer sediments had levels as high as 672 ppb. An independent study reported a range of 0.9-312 ppb of TCDD in these storm sewer sediments (Smith et al., 1983). The possibility of leakage of chemicals into the sewers through faulty pipes and from runoff has been suggested to explain the high concentrations of TCDD in storm sewers. Moderately high levels were also detected in the river sediments; however, the ground water had no detectable levels as expected from the low water solubility of TCDD.

Verona, Missouri

Another incident of possible environmental contamination from a landfill occurred at a trichlorophenol plant in Verona, Missouri. Fish collected at different sites downstream from the source had measurable levels of TCDD. The highest level detected was 50 ppt in a sample collected near the source (see Table 2). As expected, the levels were lower in fish taken from sites more removed from the source.

TABLE 2. TCDD in Fish from Verona (ppt)

Sample ID	Conc. (dl)	'Isomers'*	2,3,7,8-TCDD
Site - 1	120 (10)	4	50
Site - 2	60 (13)	3	40
Site - 3	30 (12)	2	20
Site - 4	20 (8)	2	17
Site - 5	15 (12)	1	15
Site - 6	15 (7)	1	15
Site - 7	6 (5)	1	6
Site - 8	5 (5)	1	5
Site - 9	ND (16)		
Site - 10	ND (8)		

*   Identities of the other 'isomers' were not known

Gulfport, Mississippi

During the period of 1968-1977, 15,000 drums of Agent Orange were stored in the Gulfport, Mississippi, area by the Air Force.   The University of Nebraska, in collaboration with the Air Force, undertook to investigate the possibility that leakage from the drums was accompanied by movement of TCDD into the environment and biota (Gross, 1980).   Soils taken from the sites of possible spills had a mean TCDD concentration of 240 ppb. Several samples of biota in the vicinity were subjected to analysis by GC/HRMS (see Tables 3 and 4). The samples included crayfish, mosquito fish, frogs and turtles. It was evident that the levels of TCDD decreased with increasing distance from the source.   These and other results of analysis of biota near a contamination source are in accord with a hypothesis that TCDD can move in the environment.

TABLE 3. Gulfport, Mississippi Study (1976)

Site	Distance	Levels (ppt)
I	Imm. area	140-3500
I	Imm. area	1,600-7,200
II	3,000 ft.	200-2,200
III	7,000	45
IV	9,000	20
V	12,000	ND

TABLE 4. Gulfport, Mississippi Study (1979)

Site	Distance	Matrix	Levels (ppt)
II	3,000 ft.	Fish	175
III	7,000	Fish	88
III	7,000	Turtle (fat)	ND
IV	9,000	Fish	31
V	12,000	Fish	20

TCDD in Dairy Products

The contamination of Times Beach, in Missouri, was due to the application of 2,4,5-trichlorophenol waste oils for dust control in horse arenas and on roads.   As a consequence of the contamination, it was necessary to determine the possible bioaccumulation of 2,3,7,8-TCDD in the cows grazing in the proximal areas.   Several varieties of dairy products from Kraft, Inc. were analyzed at the University of Nebraska to determine whether toxic residues were accumulating in milk. No TCDD was found in fifteen samples at detection limits of 3 ppt or lower.

COMBUSTION

Disposal by combustion has been a method of solid waste disposal for over a century and is now known to be a major source of PCDD and PCDF. In addition to municipal waste incinerators, coal and fossil fuel plants, chemical waste burners, fireplaces, and wood stoves are other common combustion sources. Gasoline and diesel powered combustion engines, charcoal grills and cigarette smoke also have been postulated to be possible sources of PCDD and PCDF (Dow Chemical, 1978).

Municipal Solid Waste Incinerators

Municipal incinerators are probably the most significant combustion sources of PCDD and PCDF. The entry of PCDD and PCDF into the environment from municipal solid waste (MSW) can occur in three possible ways: from emissions which consist of fly ash and flue gases, from discharge of scrubber water, and from the bottom ash used in land reclamation. Fly ash makes up 4-10% (by weight) and flue gases 20% (by weight) of the total emissions. The fly ash produced during combustion has a particle size range from less than 30 µm to 850 µm. The emissions are controlled by using venturi scrubbers, electrostatic precipitators, cyclones, etc. Despite the use of these particulate emission control devices, 1-5% of the particulate emissions still escape the stack, and the majority of these are in the respirable range. PCDD and PCDF are known (Karasek et al., 1981) to concentrate predominantly on smaller particles (ca. 30 µm). The first reports of the identification of PCDD and PCDF in fly ash came from Europe (Olie et al., 1977; Buser et al., 1978). Later, these were confirmed in several studies in the USA (ASME, 1980), Canada (Eiceman et al., 1979) and Italy (Cavallaro et al., 1982) where PCDD and PCDF were found in the emissions of other municipal incinerators.

We emphasize that there are several types of incinerators. The older ones are generally small, batch-fed, and hand-stoked, with less efficient combustion and emission control. The newer incinerators are larger, continuous-fed and mechanically-stoked. The most modern incinerators are either fluidized-bed suspension burning systems or involve high temperature slagging processes.

The extent of PCDD and PCDF emissions from an incinerator depends on two basic factors: (a) the efficiency of destruction and (b) the efficiency of emission control. For 99.95% efficient destruction of PCDD, the combustion temperature should be 1177°C with a residence time of the combustibles ca. 1.3-1.5 sec in the combustion zone (U.S. EPA, 1981). However, due to inhomogeneity of the waste burned and the variation of the fuel characteristics, consistent temperatures in this range may not be obtained. Achievement of higher temperatures with proper design of the combustion chamber and use of supplemental fuel may be possible, but the limitations are the resistence of the refractory tiles to the high temperatures (>1200°C) and the desire to avoid production of large quantities of NO_x at high temperatures. Certain states have regulations bearing on the latter.

In this section, an attempt has been made to evaluate, based on the available literature, the formation and emissions of PCDD and PCDF from municipal incinerators. However, it should be pointed out that, in most instances, the literature may not be adequate to make assessments. Therefore, certain assumptions have been made so that results can be presented in a coherent fashion.

PCDD and PCDF levels in fly ash from several different incinerators are given in Tables 5 and 6. The levels specified as g/24 h are the total collectible levels on fly ash over a period of 24 h of operation. The levels were estimated by assuming that an average incinerator burns two metric tons of garbage per hour and that each metric ton burned produces 30 kg of fly ash. However, the amount burned could vary depending on the size of the incinerator and, therefore, the daily output of fly ash can vary accordingly. At the highest efficiency of available electrostatic precipitators, at least 1-2% of the fly ash would still escape into the environment. Therefore, the amount of ash emitted is considerably smaller than that found in the stack.

TABLE 5. Dioxins in Fly Ash from Incinerators (g/24h)

Sample ID	TCDD	PCDD	HCDD	H7CDD	OCDD
Italian	ND-3	.003-4	.001-150	.0004-55	.006-5
U.S.	.5		.8	1.2	1.8
U.S.	.6-12				
Netherlands	2-5	10-15	20-25	20-30	5-15
European	.12-7	.5-30	20-70	4-55	6-15

TABLE 6. Furans in Fly Ash from Incinerators (g/24h)

Sample ID	TCDF	PCDF	HCDF	H7CDF	OCDF
Italian	.03-.4				.0001-.9
U.S.	.7-9				
U.S.	3				
European	.06	.24	1.8	2.4	.6
European	.8	2.5	6.5	5.3	1.2
European	6.6	12	21	11	1.2
European	13	30	52	24	1.5

There is considerable variation among the various congeners of PCDD and PCDF on different days of sampling. This variation could be the result of changes in the waste and fuel characteristics, the amount of air, and the temperature of combustion. Excess water in the fuel causes the temperature of the combustion zone to decrease to ca. 500-600°C, thereby making the conditions more favorable for formation of PCDD and PCDF.

Levels of PCDD and PCDF in flue gases were found to be higher than in fly ash (see Tables 7 and 8) (Cavallaro et al., 1982; Teller and Lauber, 1983). The levels expressed as g/24 h, were calculated based on the assumption that the stack gas flow is 500 m^3/min. However, this rate could vary by a factor of 2 or 3. The amount listed (g/24 h) is an estimate of the actual amount emitted into the environment. It is evident that the amounts of TCDD and TCDF emitted could be as high as 0.14 and 1.2 g/24 h, respectively.

Most modern incinerators are designed to destroy combustibles more efficiently. Fluidized-bed incinerators fall into this category. Up to this date, there is only one report of the emission of PCDD and PCDF from this type of incinerator. Rappe et al., (1982) found that there was no significant change in the amount of PCDF formed compared to other incinerators investigated; however, the PCDD concentrations were reduced to a considerable extent (see Tables 7 and 8). More studies are necessary to determine more conclusively the efficiency of this type of incinerator.

TABLE 7. Dioxins in Flue Gas from Incinerators (g/24h)

Sample ID	TCDD	PCDD	HCDD	H7CDD	OCDD
Italian	.0007-.14	.002-.2	.14-27	.004-1	.005-6
U.S.	.002				
U.S.	.02				
Swedish*	.02	ND	ND	.03	.02
Swedish	.07	.12	.13	.09	.1
Netherland	.07	.6	.98	.98	.22

TABLE 8. Furans in Flue Gas from Incinerators (g/24h)

Sample ID	TCDF	PCDF	HCDF	H7CDF	OCDF
Italian	.14-1.2				.07-5
U.S.	.014-.021				
Swedish*	.04	.07	.08	.03	.01
Swedish	.07	.07	.05	.03	ND
Netherlands	.33	.70	1.2	8.1	.1

* Fluidized-bed incinerator

Other Combustion Sources of PCDD and PCDF

Besides municipal incinerators, several other sources of combustion contribute to environmental input of PCDD and PCDF. Among these, wood burning, accidental fires at industrial facilities and haphazard combustion of industrial waste produce significant amounts of both PCDD and PCDF that enter the environment.

Wood combustion. Wood combustion has been reported to be another source of PCDD and PCDF. A majority of scrap wood is impregnated with chlorophenols and chlorophenates, and, thus, burning of this type of wood and related wood products will produce PCDD and PCDF (Crosby et al., 1973; Rappe et al., 1978).

Combustion of non-treated wood is also thought to produce PCDD (Dow Chemical, 1978). In a recent survey of the formation of PCDDs in residential wood combustion, particulates from several facilities in different regions of the USA were analyzed. The PCDDs were found at parts-per-billion levels (Nestrick and Lamparski, 1982). The highest level (7.8 ppb) was in a facility with a masonry type of chimney burning birch and oak wood under low air restriction. However, there is significant variation of the concentrations of all PCDDs (a range of 0.002-2.5 ppb was found for TCDD) in the particulates collected from similar facilities burning red oak. The authors attributed this to possible fuel contamination and sampling difficulties (Nestrick and Lamparski, 1982).

Even though there is some evidence for the formation of PCDD and, more probably PCDF, in residential wood burning facilities, more studies are needed to provide concrete evidence. The wide variation found in data collected thus far may be largely accounted for by variable amounts of chlorinated synthetics combusted along with the wood. The amounts of PCDD and PCDF emitted in natural or pristine wood burning may be very small.

Accidental fires and haphazard burning. An accidental fire in an office building in Binghamton, New York, ruptured a transformer resulting in the release of soot throughout the building. The transformer contained a dielectric fluid which consisted of Aroclor 1254 and chlorobenzenes. Rappe et al. (1982) analyzed the soot and detected total concentrations of 20 and 2160 ppm of PCDD and PCDF, respectively. The toxic isomers, 2,3,7,8-TCDD and 1,2,3,7,8-pentaCDD were the predominant PCDD isomers. It is believed that chlorobenzenes are precursors for PCDD. The most toxic 2,3,7,8-TCDF, 1,2,3,7,8-, and 2,3,4,7,8-pentaCDF isomers were found to be the major PCDF constituents of the soot. Two composite soot samples from the same site were analyzed in an independent study (Smith et al., 1982) and were found to contain average PCDD and PCDF concentrations of 3 and 200 ppm, respectively.

It has been reported that pyrolysis conversion yields of PCDF from commercial PCB is in the range of 3-25% (Buser et al., 1979). From the results of a different study, it was estimated that the concentration of PCDF increased by a factor of 1500 as a result of the fire (Stalling et al., 1981). Thus, it is clear that accidental fires can produce high levels of PCDD and PCDF if the necessary precursors are present in the burning material. Besides the Binghampton fire, several other incidents of PCDF contamination from PCB fires have been reported (Rappe et al., 1982).

An example of haphazard fire is the incineration of wire scrap to recover metals (Hryhorczuk et al., 1981). An outbreak of illnesses among humans and horses living within a 1.3 km of a wire reclamation facility prompted a study to determine whether there was a possible correlation of health effects with the emissions. The incinerator was burning scrap wire, cables and X-ray paper in order to recover metals. One sample each of furnace ash and fly ash was found to contain 58 and 410 ppt of TCDD, respectively. The TCDF concentrations detected in the respective samples were 730 and 11,600 ppt. The source of these toxic materials may be polyvinyl chloride, a common wire insulation material.

Combustion Sources That Produce Minimal PCDD and PCDF

Some combustion sources are known to produce minimal or not detectable levels of PCDD and PCDF. Examples are coal and oil fired power plants and modern incinerators which burn waste efficiently. Burning of waste in rotary kiln type incinerators and at sea burning of chemical waste are examples of the latter.

Coal fired power plants. Use of coal as an energy source ranges from small residential furnaces to large industrial power plants. Fossil fuel powerhouses were reported (Dow Chemical, 1978) to be a source of both air and waterborne particulates containing TCDD and TCDF. However, fly ash collected downstream from an electrostatic precipitator located in the smoke stack of a large modern power plant was analyzed by Kimble and Gross (1980) and contained no TCDD isomers at a concentration of 1 ppt. The power plant was burning low-sulfur, high-ash coal. The chlorine content of the coal burned was ca. 50 ppm which is low compared to some coals which contain chlorine at levels as high as 3500 ppm.

An additional ten samples from other fossil power plants were analyzed subsequently, and no TCDD was detected (detection limits of 2-12 ppt) in eight samples. Two samples had low levels (2-12 ppt) of TCDD. The method did not distinguish 2,3,7,8-TCDD from the other isomers. Power plants are examples of efficient combustion, and the TCDD is not stable at temperatures found in those facilities.

Junk and Ford (1980) reviewed the emission characteristics of some combustion sources burning coal and coal with refuse. The presence of TCDD in fly ash and in emissions from such combustion sources could not be documented.

Rotary kiln. Two studies were focused on the formation and the efficiency of destruction of PCDD and PCDF in kiln type incinerators (Dow Chemical, 1978; Rappe et al., 1982). No TCDD was detected (detection limits of 2-8 ppb) in the Dow Chemical rotary kiln incinerator operated with supplemental fuel. However, hexa-, hepta- and octa-CDD were present in the emissions. The incinerator characteristics were not given by the authors. However, the authors found no PCDD or PCDF in the emissions of a cement kiln burning PCB. Approximately 4 m^3 of PCBs were burned at a feeding rate of 50 kg/h during the study. A "wet" oven operating condition of 1200-1300°C was used, and the high temperatures were probably responsible for the destruction of PCDD and PCDF.

Incineration at sea. At sea incineration on board the M/T Vulcanus has been found to be a cost effective and efficient method of destruction of raw chemical waste (Clausen et al., 1977). In a recent study (Ackerman et al., 1983) approximately 3500 metric tons of raw chemical waste consisting of PCBs (20-30% by weight), chlorobenzene, and pump oils, were burned at an average incineration temperature of 1303°C and a residence time of 1.3 sec for the combustibles in the combustion zone. The temperature was measured at the wall of the combustion chamber and the actual temperature of the flame was believed to be at least 250°C in excess of that of the wall.

The raw chemical waste was analyzed for TCDD and TCDF prior to burning, and no TCDD was detected at detection limits ranging from 2-4 ppb, but approximately 10-40 ppb of TCDF was found. There was no TCDD detected in the emissions (detection limits of <0.2 ng/m^3) indicating that no detectable levels of TCDD were formed during the incineration. The TCDF levels detected in the emissions were rather low (<0.3 ng/m^3), and, based on the results, the destruction efficiency for TCDF was found to be in excess of 99.9%. Therefore, it is evident that PCDD and PCDF emissions will be not detectable or very small in high temperature incineration irrespective of the nature of the fuel.

In summary, combustion can be a significant source of PCDD and PCDF in the environment. The PCDD and PCDF concentrations vary with fuel and combustion characteristics such that levels ranging from "not detected" to 10 g/24 h of PCDF can be emitted in the flue gases. Energy-efficient, modern incinerators are designed for highly efficient combustion, and they are equipped to control emissions by entrapment. However, most municipal incinerators are not efficient, operate with 60-150% excess air and, under these conditions, the fine particulate emission is approximately 0.1-0.3 g/dscf. In order to meet certain guidelines set for the maximum allowable ground level concentration (annual average of 30 pg/m^3 for PCDD and 1500 pg/m^3 for PCDF, Ministry of Environment, Ontario, Canada), it was suggested (Teller and Lauber, 1983) that the emission level must be reduced to 0.006 g/dscf. The reduction of the flue gas

TABLE 9. Emissions from Three Typical Municipal Incinerators

Type of Refuse	System Temperature (°F)			Particulates g/scf	Stack Conc. pg/m³		Emissions µg/ton of refuse		Max. Ground Level Conc. TCDD, g/m³
	Primary	Secondary	Stack		TCDD	TCDF	TCDD	TCDF	
A-1	1599	1605	375	0.218	8,400		110		1.94×10^{-12}
A-1	870	875	375	0.218	1,400	17,000	38	180	2.34×10^{-13}
A-2	1322	1834	409	0.199	1,100	14,000	15	94	3.03×10^{-13}
A-2	716	1001	409	0.199	1,300	8,300	16	160	3.35×10^{-13}
B	996	1494	427	0.669	4,400	47,700	51	540	3.89×10^{-13}
B	1193	1578	434	0.669	3,800	4,500	44	50	3.25×10^{-13}
B	1173	1557	439	0.669	2,500	10,900	34	180	2.07×10^{-13}
C-1			306	0.005	30,000	312,000	330	3400	3.47×10^{-12}
C-2				0.006	29,500	247,000	630	5300	3.44×10^{-12}

A-1   As received refuse, 25 tons per day
A-2   Trommeled refuse, 25 tons per day
B   As received refuse + waste oil – 40–50 tons per day
C-1   Densified refuse derived fuel – 50–70 tons per day
C-2   Coal. 30–35 tons per day
-     Stack flow rate was considered to be 360 DSCM/M for these calculations.

temperature in the emission control system to 100°C (usually 220°C) and efficient entrapment of particulates may help to meet the above requirements (Teller and Lauber, 1983).

Particulate emissions with relation to incinerator conditions from three typical incinerators have been compared (see Table 9). The study was conducted by the Systech Corporation, Xenia, Ohio, and the analyses were done at the University of Nebraska. It is evident that the incinerators operated under the reported conditions did emit TCDD and TCDF. However, the U.S. EPA concluded that the levels of TCDD were insufficient to cause human health effects to persons residing in the surrounding environment. Nevertheless, since it was a preliminary study, the health effect conclusions should be regarded as tentative.

TETRACHLORODIBENZOFURANS IN THE ENVIRONMENT

As indicated earlier, combustion and PCB are the two main sources of TCDF in the environment. PCB preparations are now known to contain trace levels of TCDF (Rappe et al., 1982). For instance, Aroclor 1242 was reported to contain 150 ppb of PCDF, of which at most 43% was found to be the most toxic 2,3,7,8-TCDF (Albro and Parker, 1979). Aroclor 1260, which is widely used in North America, was found to contain 0.2 ppm of TCDF (Bowes et al., 1975). However, Aroclor 1016, a replacement for 1242 which was introduced in the early '70s, had no TCDF at a detection limit of 0.001 ppm. It is well established that PCBs are ubiquitous in the environment. Thus, TCDF should occur more commonly in the environment than TCDD. Some of the environmental input of TCDF from PCB and from combustion may accumulate in fish. Therefore, the concentrations of TCDF in fish may serve as an indicator for bioaccumulation of PCDF.

TCDF in Fish

In several studies conducted by Stalling et al., it was reported that TCDF was found in fish in the range of 5-100 ppt (Stalling et al., 1981). 2,3,7,8-TCDF was one of the isomers present. A possible correlation between PCB and PCDF in fish was suggested by Dougherty et al. (1980). The change of PCB/PCDF ratios in fish might indicate the age of PCBs in the environment or the extent of PCDF input from emissions. In their studies, Stalling et al. reported PCB/PCDF ratios in the range of $0.08-0.44 \times 10^6$, which is somewhat lower than the respective ratios from Aroclor $(0.7-3.2 \times 10^6)$. Thus, either preferential transformation of PCB or additional input of PCDF from combustion sources is evident.

SUMMARY

In this review, we have identified and discussed the impact of three sources of PCDD and PCDF. These materials occur as by-products in the manufacture of certain commercial chemicals such as herbicides and chlorinated fluids such as PCBs. The normal use of herbicides is not a major environmental source of TCDD. There is, however, growing evidence that normal use does lead to modest accumulation in living systems which come in direct contact with and derive their food from exposed areas. On the other hand, bioaccumulation in humans residing near herbicide treated sites or in plants does not seem to be important.

The defoliation in Vietnam in the late 1960s is an example of excessive herbicide use. Some evidence now exists that humans who were "heavily exposed" by direct contact with Agent Orange carried TCDD in their adipose tissue ten years after exposure. The long term health effects are not known, although studies of persistence of 2,3,7,8-TCDD in other primates point to a long half life.

The disposal of chemical waste by burial has been a more significant assault on the environment than the use of herbicides. High levels of 2,3,7,8-TCDD in environmental and biological samples taken in the vicinity of point sources of contamination indicate some movement of TCDD in the environment.

The third source of PCDD and PCDF is combustion. The extent of emission of these toxic substances range from "not detected" in the combustion of natural fuel such as coal and certain types of wood to levels of g/day in older design waste incinerators. It is clear that high emissions can be avoided, even in combustion sources which burn chlorinated chemical waste, if the combustion is properly controlled.

Unlike 2,3,7,8-TCDD, which has not been commonly found in the environment and in living systems, 2,3,7,8-TCDF and other isomers are much more ubiquitous. This may be a consequence of the improper disposal of PCBs which contain low levels of PCDF.

REFERENCES

Ackerman, D.G., Mcgaughey, J.F., Wagoner, D.E. and Jackson, M.D. 1983. At-sea Incineration of PCB-containing Wastes Onboard the M/T Vulcanus. U.S. EPA, Research Triangle Park, NC, EPA-600/7-83-024. April, 1983.

Albro, P.W. and Parker, C.E. 1979. Comparison of the compositions of Aroclor 1242 and Aroclor 1016. J. Chromat. 169:161-166.

Allen, J.R., Barsotti, D.A. and Van Miller, J.P. 1977. Reproductive dysfunction in nonhuman primates exposed to dioxins. Toxicol. Appl. Pharmacol. 41:177 (abstract).

ASME research communication on Industrial and Municipal Wastes, Study on State of the Art of Dioxins from Combustion Sources, 1980.

Bailey, J., Knaff, V., Mueller W. and Hobson, W. 1980. Transfer of hexachlorobenzene and polychlorinated biphenyl to nursing infant rhesus monkeys: Enhanced toxicity. Environ. Toxicol. 21:190-196.

Barsotti, D.A. 1980. Gross, clinical and reproductive effects of PCBs in rhesus monkey. Ph.D. dissertation, University of Wisconsin.

Barsotti, D.A., Abrahamson, L.J. and Allen, J.R. 1979. Hormonal alterations in female rhesus monkeys fed a diet containing TCDD. Bull. Environ. Contam. Toxicol. 21:463-469.

Bowes, G.W., Mulvihill, M.J., Simoneit, B.R.T., Burlingame, A.L. and Risebrough, R.W. 1975. Identification of chlorinated dibenzofurans in American polychlorinated biphenyls. Nature 256:305-307.

Bowman, R.E. and co-workers. Unpublished results.

Bumb, R.R., Crummett, W.B., Cutie, S.S., Gledhill, J.R., Hummel, R.H., Kagel, R.O., Lamparski, L.L., Luoma, E.V., Miller, D.L., Nestrick, T.J., Shadoff, L.A., Stehl, R.H., Woods, J.S. 1980. The trace chemistries of fire: A source of chlorinated dioxins. Science 210:385-390.

Buser, H.R. and Rappe, C. 1979. Formation of polychlorinated dibenzofurans (PCDFs) from the pyrolysis of individual PCB isomers. Chemosphere 8:157-174.

Buser, H.R., Bosshardt, H.P., Rappe, C. and Lindehl, R. 1978. Identification of PCDF isomers in fly ash and PCB isomers. Chemosphere 7:419-429.

Cavallaro, A., Luciani, L., Ceroni, G., Rocchi, I., Invernizzi, G. and Gorni, A. 1982. Summary of results of PCDD analyses from incinerator effluents. Chemosphere 11:859-868.

Clausen, J.F., Fisher, H.J., Johnson, R.J., Moon, E.L., Tobias, R.F. and Zee, C.A. 1977. At-sea Incineration of Organochlorine Wastes Onboard the M/T Vulcanus. U.S. EPA, Research Triangle Park, NC, EPA 600/2-77-196 (NTIS PB 272-110/AS). September, 1977.

Crosby, D.G., Moilanen, K.W. and Wong, A.S. 1973. Environmental generation and degradation of dibenzodioxins and dibenzofurans. Environ. Health Perspect. 5:259-265.

Crummett, W.B. and Stehl, R.H. 1973. Determination of chlorinated dibenzo-p-dioxins and dibenzofurans in various materials. Environ. Health Perspect. 5:15-25.

Czuczwa, J. and Hites, R. 1984. This volume.

Dougherty, R.C., Whitaker, M.J., Smith, L.M., Stalling, D.L. and Kuehl, D.W. 1980. Negative chemical ionization studies of human and food chain contamination with xenobiotic chemicals. Environ. Health Perspect. 36:103-117.

The chlorinated dioxin task force, Michigan Division of the Dow Chemical, Midland, Michigan. 1978. The trace chemistries of fire: A source of and routes for the entry of chlorinated dioxins into the environment. (Also see ref. 1).

Eiceman, G.A., R.E. Clement and Karasek, F.W. 1979. Analysis of trace organic compounds in fly ash from municipal incinerators. Anal. Chem. 51:2243.

Esposito, M.H., Tiernan, T.O. and Dryden, F.E. 1980. Dioxins. U.S. EPA, Industrial Environmental Research Laboratory, Office of Research and Development, U.S. EPA, Cincinnati, OH.

Gross, M.L. 1978. Final report: Analysis of selected environmental samples for TCDD by GLC/MS techniques. EPA contract no. 68-01-4305.

Gross, M.L. 1980. Testimony in re: The Dow Chemical Co., et. al., FIFRA Docket No. 415, et. al., U.S. EPA Exhibit No. 223, pp. 27-29, EPA, Hearing Clerk's Office, 401 N. Street, S.W., Washington, DC, 20460.

Gross, M.L., Lay, J.O., Lyon, P.A., Lippstreu, D., Kangas, N., Harless, R.L., Taylor, S.E. and Dupuy, A.E., Jr. 1984. 2,3,7,8-Tetrachlorodibenzo-p-dioxin levels in adipose tissue of Vietnam veterans. Environ. Research 33:261-268.

Harless, R.L., Lewis, R.G., Dupuy, A.E. and McDaniel, D.D. 1983. Analyses for 2,3,7,8-tetrachlorodibenzo-p-dioxin residues in environmental samples. In Human and Environmental Risks of Chlorinated Dioxins and Related Compounds, eds. R.E. Tucker, A.L. Young and A.P. Gray, pp. 161-171, Plenum Press, New York.

Hryhorczuk, D.O., Withrow, W.A., Hesse, C.S. and Beasley, V.R. 1981. A wire reclamation incinerator as a source of environmental contamination with tetrachlorodibenzo-p-dioxins and tetrachlorodibenzofurans. Arch. Environ. Health 36:228.

Isensee, A.R. and Jones, G.E. 1971. Absorption and translocation of root and foliage applied 2,4-dichlorophenol, 2,7-dichlorodibenzo-p-dioxin and 2,3,7,8-dichlorodibenzo-p-dioxin. J. Agric. Food Chem. 19:1210-1214.

Isensee, A.R. and Jones, G.E. 1975. Distribution of 2,3,7,8-tetrachlorodibenzo-p-dioxin (TCDD) in aquatic model ecosystems. Environ. Sci. Technol. 9:668-672.

Jensen, D.J., Getzendaner, M.E., Hummel, R.A. and Turley, J. 1983. Residue studies for (2,4,5-trichlorophenoxy) acetic acid and 2,3,7,8-tetrachlorodibenzo-p-dioxin in grass and rice. Agric. Food Chem. 31:118-122.

Junk, G.A. and Ford, C.S. 1980. A review of organic emissions from selected combustion processes. Chemosphere 9:187-230.

Karasek, F.W., Clement, R.E. and Vian, A.C. 1981. Distribution of PCDDs and other toxic compounds generated on fly ash particulates in municipal incinerators. J. Chromat. 239:173-180.

Kearney, P.C., Woolson, E.A. and Ellington, C.P., Jr. 1972. Persistence and metabolism of chlorodioxins in soil. Environ. Sci Technol. 6:1017-1019.

Kimble, B.J. and Gross, M.L. 1980. Tetrachlorodibenzo-p-dioxin quantitation in stack-collected coal fly ash. Science 207:59-61.

Kocher, G.W., Mahle, N.H., Hummel, R.A., Shadoff, L.A. and Getzendaner, M.E. 1978. A search for 2,3,7,8-tetrachlordibenzo-p-dioxin in beef fat. Environ. Contam. Toxicol. 19:229-236.

Leng, M.L. 1972. Residues in milk and meat and safety to livestock from the use of phenoxy herbicides in pasture and rangeland. Down Earth 28:12-20.

Matsumara, F. and Benezet, H.J. 1973. Studies on the bioaccumulation and microbial degradation of 2,3,7,8-tetrachloro-p-dioxin. Environ. Health Perspect. 5:253-258.

McNulty, W.P. 1980. 2,3,7,8-TCDD: Abortions in rhesus macaques. Unpublished data submitted to U.S. EPA.

McNulty, W.P., Neilson-Smith, K.A., Lay, J.O., Jr., Lippstreu, D., Kangas, N., Lyon, P.A. and Gross, M.L. 1982. Persistence of TCDD in monkey adipose tissue. Fd. Chem. Toxicol. 20:985-987.

Nash, R.G. and Beall, M.L., Jr. 1980. Distribution of Silvex, 2,4-D and TCDD applied to turf in chambers and field plots. J. Agric. Food Chem. 28:614-623.

Nestrick, T.J. and Lamparski, L.L. 1982. Isomer-specific determination of chlorinated dioxins for assessment of formation and potential environmental emission from wood combustion. Anal. Chem. 54:2292-2299.

Olie, K., Vermeulen, P.L. and Hutzinger, O. 1977. Chlorodibenzo-p-dioxins and chlorodibenzofurans are trace components of fly ash and flue gas of some municipal incinerators in the Netherlands. Chemosphere 6: 455-459.

Rappe, C. and Buser, H.R. 1980. Occupational exposure to polychlorinated dioxins and dibenzofurans. In Chemical Hazards in the Workplace: Measurement and Control, ed. G. Choudhary, pp. 319-342, ACS Symposium Series, No. 149.

Rappe, C., Marklund, S., Buser, H.R. and Bosshardt, H.P. 1978. Formation of polychlorinated dibenzo-p-dioxins (PCDDs) and dibenzofurans (PCDFs) by burning chlorophenolics. Chemosphere 3:269-281.

Rappe, C., Marklund, S., Bergqvist, P.A. and Hansson, M. 1981. Department of Organic Chemistry, University of Umea, Umea, Sweden. Unpublished report.

Rappe, C., Marklund, S., Bergqvist, P.A. and Hansson, M. 1982. Polychlorinated dioxins (PCDDs), dibenzofurans (PCDFs) and other polynuclear aromatics (PCPnAs) formed during PCB fires. Chemica Scripta 20:56-61.

Ryan, J.F., Biros, F.J. and Harless, R.L. 1974. Proceedings of the 22nd Annual Conference on Mass Spectrometry and Allied Topics, Philadelphia, PA, May 1974.

Schantz, S.L., Barsotti, D.A. and Allen, J.R. 1979. Toxicological effects produced in nonhuman primates chronically exposed to fifty parts per trillion 2,3,7,8-tetrachlorodibenzo-p-dioxin (TCDD). Toxicol. Appl. Pharmacol. 48:A180 (abstract).

Shadoff, L.A., Hummel, R.A., Jensen, D.J. and Mahle, N.H. 1977. The gas chromatographic-mass spectrometric determination of 2,3,7,8-tetrachlorodibenzo-p-dioxin in fat from cattle fed Ronnel insecticide. Anali di chimica., 67:583-592.

Smith, J. 1979. EPA halts most uses of herbicide 2,4,5-T. Science 203:1090.

Smith, R.M., O'Keefe, P.W., Hilker, D.R., Jelus-Tyror, B.L. and Aldous, K.M. 1982. Analysis for 2,3,7,8-tetrachlorodibenzofuran and 2,3,7,8-tetrachlorodibenzo-p-dioxin in a soot sample from a transformer explosion in Binghamton, New York. Chemosphere 11:715-720.

Smith, R.M., O'Keefe, P.W. Aldous, K.M., Hilker, D.R. and O'Brien, J.R. 1983. 2,3,7,8-Tetrachlorodibenzo-p-dioxin in sediment samples from Love Canal storm sewers and creeks. Environ. Sci. Technol. 17:6-10.

Stalling, D.L., Smith, L.M., Petty, J.D., Hogan, J.W., Johnson, J.L., Rappe, C. and Buser, H.R. 1981. Presented at the 2nd International Conference on TCDD and Related Compounds, Washington, D.C., October, 1981.

Teller, A.J. and Lauber, J.D. 1983. 76th Annual Meeting and Exhibition of Air Pollution Control Association, Atlanta, GA, June 19-24, 1983.

U.S. EPA report on "The Ad Hoc Study Group of Chlorophenol Contaminants". EPA/SAB/78/001, 1978.

U.S. EPA, Region VI. 1981. Incineration of PCB, Summary of Approval for Research, Deer Park, Texas, February 6, 1981.

U.S. EPA Environmental Monitoring at Love Canal. 1982. A report of the Office of Monitoring Systems and Quality Assurance, ORD, U.S. EPA, Washington, D.C. 20460.

Veterans Administration, Review of Literature on Herbicides Including Phenoxy Herbicides and Associated Dioxins. Vol. I, Veterans Administration, No. V101 (93) P-823. 1981.

Ward, C.T. and Matsumara, F. 1978. Fate of 2,3,7,8-tetrachlorodibenzo-p-dioxin (TCDD) in a model aquatic environment. Arch. Environ. Contam. Toxicol. 7:349-357.

Weerasinghe, N.C.A., Meehan, J.L., Gross, M.L. and Gaines, J. 1983. Analysis of sugar for tetrachlorodibenzo-p-dioxin. J. Agric. Food Chem. 31:1377-1378.

Young, A.L., Calgani, J.A., Thalken, C.E. and Tremblay, J.W. 1978. The Toxicology, Environmental Fate, and Human Risk of Herbicide Orange and Associated Dioxins. USAF Occupational and Environmental Health Laboratory report no. USAF DEHL-78-92, 262 pp.

Chapter 11

FATE OF TCDD IN FIELD ECOSYSTEMS - ASSESSMENT AND SIGNIFICANCE FOR HUMAN EXPOSURES

Alvin L. Young*
Agent Orange Projects Office (10A7C)
Veterans Administration

Lorris G. Cockerham
Armed Forces Radiobiology Research Institute

INTRODUCTION

The toxin 2,3,7,8-tetrachlorodibenzo-p-dioxin (TCDD) is known to occur as both a contaminant of products made from trichlorophenol (Young, et al., 1978) and as a by-product from low temperature incineration of wastes containing chlorinated precursors (Esposito et al., 1980). The magnitude of environmental contamination by the 2,3,7,8-TCDD isomer is currently the subject of intense debate (Young, 1980). Although a number of TCDD sources have been identified, environmental monitoring programs for TCDD have generally been unsuccessful in documenting contamination (Esposito et al., 1980). However, with continued development of sophisticated instrumentation (Gas Chromatography-Mass Spectrometry, GC-MS) for detecting TCDD in picogram (1×10^{-12}g) quantities and with renewed interest in monitoring improper disposal of hazardous wastes, additional data on the distribution of TCDD in the environment may soon be forthcoming. In the interim, two environmental studies have been conducted on the fate and persistence of TCDD in natural ecosystems. Fanelli et al., 1980, and di Domenico et al., 1981, have continued to document the fate of TCDD near Seveso, Italy, following an industrial accident in 1976 that resulted in the contamination of over one square kilometer (km^2) of land in an industrial-agrarian community. The second, a long-term study, is of a unique military test site in Northwest Florida that received massive quantitites of the herbicides 2,4,5-trichlorophenoxyacetic acid (2,4,5-T) and 2,4-dichlorophenoxyacetic acid (2,4-D) in the course of developing defoliation spray equipment for use in the Vietnam Conflict, 1962-1970. Data from this study were initially released in 1974 (Young), 1975 (Young et al.) and updated in 1979 (Young et al.), 1982 (Cockerham and Young) and 1983 (Thalken and Young; Young; Young and Cockerham and Cockerham and Young). The purpose of the present report is to review the data obtained in human monitoring studies and compare these to data obtained from ecological studies of the fate of TCDD.

*New Address: Senior Policy Analyst for Life Sciences, Office of Science and Technology Policy, Executive Office of the President, Washington, D.C. 20506

HUMAN DATA

Accidental Exposure

Confirmation that TCDD accumulates in human tissues was provided by Facchetti et al., in 1981. This was the first case of human exposure to TCDD in which an analysis was made of cadaveric tissue to detect and study the distribution of dioxin. The subject of the study was a 55-year old woman who had died from a pancreatic adenocarcinoma 7 months after the ICMESA accident in Seveso in July, 1976. Although the cancer was not a result of the exposure to TCDD, the woman was significantly exposed to the toxic cloud. During the passage of the toxic cloud, the woman was eating a meal in her home with doors and windows open. In the four days after the event, the woman consumed vegetables from the garden attached to her home. Animals reared by the woman's family in an area adjacent to the home began to die about 15 days after the event. The woman was evacuated from her home and the associated area after 16 days. Subsequent tests for TCDD indicated that the subject had lived in a sector of Zone A which had a mean soil concentration of 185 $\mu g/m^2$. On the basis of the circumstances, it was presumed that the woman absorbed toxic substances contained in the cloud by inhalation, ingestion and contact. Although she did not develop toxic symptoms from the exposure, two young nephews living with her at the time of the accident developed serious chloracne. The results (means of three independent determinations) for the GC-MS analysis for TCDD in selected human tissues are shown in Table 1.

TABLE 1. Tissue Concentrations, Parts-per-Trillion, of 2,3,7,8-Tetrachlorodibenzo-p-dioxin in the Organs of a Woman Who Died of Cancer Seven Months After Exposure, Seveso, Italy[a]

Sample	2,3,7,8-TCDD/wet tissue (ppt)
Fat	1840[b]
Pancreas	1040[bc]
Liver	150[bc]
Thyroid	85[c]
Brain	60[b]
Lung	60[b]
Kidney	40[b]
Blood	6[c]

[a] Data from Facchetti et al., 1981
[b] Values obtained at a resolution of 2,500
[c] Values obtained at a resolution of 10,000

As noted, TCDD was present in all of the tissues analyzed. On the basis of the concentrations observed it was possible to distinguish four groups of tissues: adipose tissue and pancreas tissue with levels between 1,000 and 2,000 ppt; liver tissue with levels between 100 and 200 ppt; other tissues (thyroid, brain, lungs, kidneys) with levels between 10 and 100 ppt; and blood with levels less than 10 ppt. The levels in the pancreas may have been abnormally high due to presence of the cancerous cells.

The data suggest that blood levels are one-tenth the level of TCDD in liver tissue and one one-hundredth the level in adipose tissue. Reggiani (1981) estimated that the TCDD body burden in the above subject at the time of death was 40 µg. Because human milk has a high fat content, and TCDD is fat soluble, Reggiani (1981) also reported TCDD levels in human milk from mothers exposed to TCDD while living in Zones A and B of Seveso at the time of and immediately after the release of the toxic cloud. These data are shown in Table 2. These data are similar to the 1976 data shown in Table 2 from Baughman (1976) on levels of TCDD in mother's milk collected in 1970 from Vietnamese women living in areas sprayed with Agent Orange.

TABLE 2. TCDD Levels, Parts-per-Trillion, in Human Milk from Breast-feeding Mothers Exposed to TCDD in Seveso, Italy and South Vietnam

Sample Location	TCDD Level (Whole Milk Basis) (ppt)	Reference
Seveso (Zone A and B)	2.3 - 28.0	Reggiani, 1981
South Vietnam (Area Sprayed with Agent Orange)	40 - 50	Baughman, 1976

Environmental Exposure

The Environmental Protection Agency has analyzed human adipose tissue for TCDD. In 1981, Kutz reported on six specimens of human adipose tissue collected from residents of an urban Ohio county to serve as control specimens for analytical studies done in the EPA Dioxin Monitoring Program. These specimens were excised during post-mortem examinations from individuals with no recorded or known exposure to 2,4,5-T or silvex. Subsequently, they were analyzed in duplicate following the EPA Dioxin Monitoring Program protocol. Instrumental determinations were conducted at two independent laboratories.

The results, shown in Table 3, demonstrated that all specimens contained residues of TCDD. Levels ranged between 5 and 12 ppt, with a detection limit below 5 ppt. Kutz emphasized that all studies conducted to date, including this one, have been accomplished utilizing small sample sizes and deliberate specimen selection criteria. Consequently, these few data cannot be construed as being representative of the general population.

Recently, the Canadian scientists Ryan and Williams (1983) released data on the analysis of human fat tissue from the residents of the Great Lakes Area for TCDD residues. The fat samples (10 to 20 g) were obtained from deceased elderly hopital patients from the communities of Kingston and Ottawa, Ontario. The results obtained by the Ryan and Williams blind study are also shown in Table 3. Levels of TCDD were found in 22 of 23 samples analyzed. Values ranged from 4.1 to 130 ppt. Excluding the one outlying high sample, average values found were 10.7 + 5.4 (n=21) with the highest value being 21.8 ppt. Grouping of the 22 samples with regard to origin showed that the 12 Kingston samples had an average of 12.4 + 5.8 ppt (n=12) and the Ottawa samples 8.6 + 4.4 ppt (n=9) but the difference was only significant at about the $P = 0.1$ level. Ryan and Williams concluded from these data that human fat tissues from older patients in the Great Lakes area appear to have low but measurable amounts of TCDD.

The issue of Agent Orange and the Vietnam veteran prompted a study of TCDD in human adipose tissue collected from U.S. Vietnam-Era veterans. This study, reported by Hobson, et al., in 1983, was initiated in 1979 with the selection of two groups of adult males: 1) twenty-one Vietnam veterans, all but two of whom claimed health problems related to Agent Orange exposure, and who volunteered for the fat biopsy; and 2) twelve veterans with no service in Vietnam. Ten of the latter group had no known exposure to any herbicides, were undergoing elective abdominal surgery and volunteered to serve as controls. The other two individuals were active duty U.S. Air Force officers with known heavy and relatively recent exposure in connection with herbicide disposal operations. Each of the volunteers had a medical history, physical examination and routine clinical chemistry. The details of military service in Vietnam from the volunteer's report and his service record were examined to evaluate his potential exposure to herbicides. From the dates, location and nature of service, a rough estimate of the likelihood of exposure to TCDD was made without knowledge of the assay results.

The results of this study are also shown in Table 3. Fourteen of the 21 Vietnam veterans had levels of TCDD in their adipose tissue at or above the detection limit. Three of these men had detectable material that could not be validated as TCDD or the measured value was only questionably above the detection limit. Six Vietnam veterans had TCDD in amounts from 5 to 7 ppt. Three Vietnam veterans had TCDD in amounts from 9 to 13 ppt. One veteran had 63 and 99 ppt, and another had 23 and 35 ppt.

Of the 12 individuals who had never served in Vietnam, five had TCDD identified in their fat (4,6,7,7 and 14 ppt). Six had values low enough to be considered equivocal or the detected material was not validated as TCDD. The remaining veteran had no detectable TCDD. In the two Air Force officers with known heaviest exposure, measured TCDD was never more than 3 ppt above the limit of detection.

Among the 21 Vietnam veterans, there was no uniformity of symptoms, either immediately after exposure, at the time of biopsy, or during the intervening period. No one symptom or group of symptoms was common to veterans with detectible TCDD in their fat. The presence of TCDD did not mean ill health, nor did its absence indicate good health. No detailed statistical analysis of this small pilot series was attempted.

Hobson et al., (1983) concluded that the results of the very complex and technically difficult analysis indicated that very low levels of tetrachlorodibenzo-p-dioxins, believed to be TCDD, could be detected in human adipose tissue in the range 3-99 ppt. The levels, however, did not correlate with health status. The study results did indicate that the assay method was feasible, but would serve no clinically or administratively useful purpose until additional data are available on background levels in the general United States population.

The available data on TCDD residues in human tissue suggest that TCDD can be distributed throughout body tissues following accidental exposures. In such situations, a major site for storage of TCDD in the human body is in the adipose tissue. However, significant levels of residue (albeit, much lower than in adipose tissue) may be found in the liver and human milk. The monitoring of persons not involved in episodic events involving TCDD, suggest that adult human adipose tissue may have a "background" level of TCDD that may reflect a generalized contamination of our environment. This "background" level may be very low (approximately 10 ppt) and detectible only through the use of sophisticated analytical methods.

TABLE 3. Levels of 2,3,7,8-TCDD, Parts-per-Trillion, in Human Adipose Tissue[a]

Source	Total Number of Samples	Number Positive[a]	Range	Mean ± SD[b]	Reference
EPA Monitoring Program, in Ohio	6	6	5-12		Kutz, 1981
Great Lakes Area, Canada	23	22	4.1-21.8, 130	10.7±5.4 (n=21)	Ryan and Williams, 1983
			Kingston	12.4±5.8 (12)	
			Ottawa	8.6±4.4 (9)	
United States Veterans Administration	33	25	3-29, 99	7.7±5.5 (24)	Hobson et al., 1983
			Vietnam Experience	8.3±6.9 (13)	
			No Vietnam Experience	5.7±3.1 (11)	
Total	62	53	3-130	10 ppt	

a Detection limits defined in text
b Excluding outlying high samples

ANIMAL DATA

Laboratory Exposure Studies

The toxicology of TCDD has been thoroughly studied in the laboratory. Particular emphasis has been placed on the cellular distribution of TCDD in an attempt to understand more about its pharmacokinetics and to identify a target site for its toxicity. Gasiewicz et al., in 1983, concluded that the liver and the fat contained most of the body burden of the toxin, accounting for 50 and 10 times more ^{14}C activity, respectively, than any other tissues examined. Moreover, the rate of TCDD accumulation in the body, following single and repeated exposure, was largely accounted for by the rate of accumulation in liver and fat.

In 1976, Rose et al. found that in rats, TCDD approached steady-state concentrations in the body within 13 weeks, and the rate constant defining the approach to steady-state concentrations was independent of the dosage of TCDD over the dose range of 0.01 - 1.0 μg of TCDD/kg/day.

In 1978, Kociba et al. confirmed the conclusions of Rose et al. with an analysis of liver and fat tissues in rats exposed to TCDD in a two-year chronic toxicity and oncogenicity study. The data on the steady-state tissue concentrations of TCDD are shown in Table 4. The ingestion of 0.001 μg TCDD/kg/day (22 ppt in the diet) was considered by the authors to represent a no-effect level.

TABLE 4. Comparison of Levels of TCDD in Diet, Liver, and Fat of Rats Fed the Compound for Two Years[a]

Dose μgTCDD/kg/day	PPT TCDD in Diet 2 Years	PPT in Tissues at 2 Years	
		Liver	Fat
0.001	22	540	540
0.01	210	5,100	1,700
0.1	2,200	24,000	8,100

[a] Kociba et al., 1978

The above data suggest that in the monitoring for TCDD in animals, the major tissues that should be collected and analyzed are the liver and adipose tissues. Steady-state concentrations in these tissues should be reached after 90 days in animals exposed to a contaminated field site.

Accidental and Environmental Exposures

Seveso, Italy TCDD episode. The toxicity of the dioxin and associated materials in the cloud that contaminated the 1,800 ha area of Seveso, Italy has been documented by Wipf and Schmit, 1983. These data are shown in Table 5. The large number of animals that died in 1978 were either poisoned or slaughtered in order to prevent movement of these animals outside of the containment area. This action was taken as part of the initiation of the decontamination program.

TABLE 5. The Impact of the TCDD-Laden Toxic Cloud on Animals in Zones A and B, Seveso, Italy[a]

	Deaths 1976	Slaughtered 1978
Small Animals	3,281	77,078
Cattle	6	298
Horses/Donkeys	2	47
Swine	3	227
Sheep/Goats	1	66

[a] Data from Wipf and Schmid, 1983.

Fanelli et al., 1980, described the extensive sampling of wildlife in Zone A, Seveso, Italy, following the contamination of the area with TCDD, in July 1976. As noted in Table 6, high concentrations of TCDD had accumulated in most of the species sampled. Fanelli et al. concluded that the Seveso Accident represented a unique opportunity to investigate the effects and behavior of TCDD in wildlife. Furthermore, they recognized that TCDD could easily be spread to uncontaminated places by mobile animals which might have accumulated TCDD through the food chain. Indeed, as noted above, animals were slaughtered to prevent this from happening.

TABLE 6. The Concentration of TCDD, Parts-per-Trillion, in Wildlife Sampled in 1977 in the Contaminated Zones at Seveso, Italy[a]

Animal	Tissue	Mean TCDD Level
Field Mouse	Whole body	4,500
Rabbit	Liver	7,700
Toad	Whole body	200
Snake	Liver	2,700
	Fat	16,000
Earthworm	Whole body	12,000

[a] Data from Fanelli et al., 1980.

The observations on the wildlife at Seveso were limited to the few years immediately after the TCDD episode. In 1978, the Seveso Authority instituted a major clean-up of Zone A. With the destruction of the homes in 1980-81 and the removal of all contaminated material and soil in 1982 and 1983, the possibility of conducting any meaningful long-term studies is very small.

To date there have been no formal wildlife studies conducted at any of the contaminated sites at Love Canal or in Missouri (including Times Beach). Thus, the only site where long-term formal studies of wildlife continually exposed to TCDD have been conducted is the military test site on Eglin Air Force Base, Florida.

Test Area C-52, Eglin AFB, Florida Studies. The Eglin Reservation in Northwest Florida has served various military uses, one of them being the development and testing of aerial dissemination equipment in support of military defoliation operations in Southeast Asia. It was necessary for this equipment to be tested under controlled situations that would simulate actual use conditions as closely as possible. For this purpose, an elaborate testing installation, designed to measure deposition parameters, was established on the Eglin Reservation with direct aerial application restricted to an area of approximately 3 km^2 within Test Area C-52A in the southeastern part of the reservation. Massive quantities of herbicides, used in the testing of aerial defoliation spray equipment from 1962 through 1970, were released and fell within the instrumented test area. The uniqueness of the area prompted the United States Air Force to set aside the area in 1970 for research investigations. Numerous ecological surveys have been conducted since 1970. As a result, the ecosystem of this unique site has been well studied and documented.

1. Herbicide application. Although the total area for testing aerial dissemination equipment was approximately 3 km^2, the area was divided into four separate testing grids. The primary area was located in the southern portion of the testing area and consisted of a 37 ha instrumented grid. This was the first sampling grid and was in operation in June 1962. It consisted of four intersecting straight lines (flight paths) arranged in a circular pattern, each path at a 45° angle to those adjacent to it. Although this grid was discontinued after 2 years, it received the most intense testing. From 1962 to 1964, this grid (Grid I) received 39,550 kg 2,4-D and 39,550 kg of 2,4,5-T as the Herbicide Purple formulation (50 percent n-butyl 2,4-D, 30 percent n-butyl 2,4,5-T and 20 percent iso-butyl 2,4,5-T). Two other testing grids, Grid II and Grid IV, were sprayed with Herbicide Orange (50 percent n-butyl 2,4-D and 50 percent n-butyl 2,4,5-T). Grid II had an area of 37 ha and was located immediately north of Grid I. Grid II received 15,890 kg 2,4-D and 15,890 kg 2,4,5-T from 1964 through 1966. Grid IV was the largest and final grid established on Test Area C-52A. It was approximately 97 ha and received 20,000 kg 2,4-D and 17,570 kg 2,4,5-T from 1968 through 1970. Grid III was an experimental circular grid that received 1,300 kg 2,4-D from 1966 through 1970. Thus, for the four spray equipment calibration grids, a total of approximately 73,000 kg 2,4,5-T and 77,000 kg 2,4-D were aerially disseminated during the period 1962-1970. These data are summarized in Table 7.

2. Analysis of soil samples. Despite excellent records as to the number of missions and quantity of herbicide per mission, there was no way to determine the exact quantity of herbicide deposited at any point on the instrumented grids. The first residue studies of Test Area C-52A involved analyses of soils for phenoxy herbicides by both chemical and bioassay techniques. These studies showed that residues of the phenoxy herbicides rapidly disappeared. However, problems were encountered in these residue studies because of the heterogeneity of the test grids. Not only were there small geologic differences (soil types, contours, organic matter and pH), and differences in vegetation density and locations of water, but most important the herbicides had been sprayed on specific test arrays (i.e., along dictated flight paths) over a span of 8 years.

TABLE 7. Approximate Amount of 2,4,5-T and 2,4-D and Estimated Amount of TCDD Applied to Test Area C-52A, Eglin AFB Reservation, Florida, 1962-1970

Test Grid	Grid Area (ha)	2,4,5-T[a] (kg)	2,4-D[a] (kg)	TCDD[b] (kg)
I	37	39,550 (1962-1964)[c]	39,500 (1962-1964)	2.613
II	37	15,890 (1964-1966)	15,890 (1964-1966)	0.078
III	37	-	1,300 (1966-1970)	-
IV	97	17,570 (1968-1970)	20,000 (1968-1970)	0.087
Total	208	73,010	76,740	2.778

[a] Amount of 2,4,5-T and 2,4-D calculated on weight of active ingredient in the military Herbicides Orange and Purple.
[b] Amount of TCDD calculated from data on mean concentration of TCDD in the formulation of Herbicides Purple and Orange, i.e., 32.8 ppm TCDD in Purple and 1.98 ppm TCDD in Orange.
[c] Years when the specific grid received the herbicide contaminated with TCDD.

TABLE 8. Concentration of TCDD in a Soil Profile from Grid I, Test Area C-52A, Eglin AFB, Florida[a,b]

Soil Depth (cm)	TCDD (Parts-per-Trillion)
0.0 - 2.5	150
2.5 - 5.0	160
5.0 - 10	700
10 - 15	44
15 - 90	ND[c]

[a] Source: Young, et al., 1975.
[b] Grid I received on the average 1,069 kg/ha of 2,4,5-T Herbicide during 1962-1964. The soil samples were collected and analyzed in 1974.
[c] None detected; minimum detection limit < 10 ppt.

With the development of analytical methods capable of detecting TCDD in part per trillion concentrations, analyses of Grid I soils in 1973 confirmed the presence of TCDD. Consequently, a variety of sampling and residue monitoring studies for TCDD were conducted on the test area (Young, 1983). Because of the long-term nature of these studies, it has been necessary for more than one laboratory to provide analytical services. The reported TCDD analyses were obtained through Air Force contracts for analytical services from five different laboratories. The methods for analyses have been previously described (Shadoff and Hummel, 1978).

The analytical results of a 1974 sample from Grid I suggested that most of the TCDD would be found in the top 15 cm of soil (see Table 8). From June 1974 through April 1978, soil samples were collected in an attempt to define the magnitude of TCDD concentration remaining on the three grids that received 2,4,5-T herbicide. These data are shown in Table 9. The aerial application of herbicides on a test grid was neither uniform nor random but rather along discrete sampling arrays arranged to measure particle size and deposition. Moreover, since the flights also occurred either in-wind or cross-wind, and the testing of the aerial dissemination equipment for Grid I extended from June 1962 through July 1964, tremendous variations in residue levels would be predicted (note the range of soil TCDD levels for Grid I in Table 9).

TABLE 9. Concentrations of TCDD, Parts-per-Trillion, in Test Grid Soils, Test Area C-52A, Eglin AFB, Florida[a]

Grid	Number of Samples[b]	Range	Median	Mean
I	22	<10 – 1,500	110	325
II	6	<10 – 470	30	115
IV	26	<10 – 150	20	30

[a] Source: Young et al., 1979.
[b] 0 -15 cm increment, collected during the period June 1974 through April 1978.

Data from 1 m^2 plots sampled in August 1974 and again in January 1978 are presented in Table 10. Although the data from analysis of the samples are consistent in showing a downward trend, the magnitude of decrease between samples is inconsistent. This suggests that factors other than actual disappearance of TCDD may be involved. Indeed, samples collected in August 1974 were analyzed by one laboratory (in 1974) while the samples collected in January 1978 were analyzed by a different laboratory (in 1978). Although presumably the method was similar, the rather large variability suggests that the extraction of TCDD from soil (soil contaminated at least 14 years prior to extraction and analysis) and its subsequent analysis (via high resolution mass spectrometry) are no easy tasks.

TABLE 10. Disappearance of TCDD from Soils of Grid I, Parts-per-Trillion, Test Area C-52A, Eglin AFB, Florida[a]

Plot Number[b]	August 1974	January 1978
1	1,500	420
2	610	300
3	1,200	580
4	270	100
5	440	400
Mean	805±525	360±175

[a] Source: Young et al., 1979.
[b] Five subsamples from each 1-m^2 plot composited (1-10 cm depth).

3. Animal studies. Studies of the animals of Test Area C-52A began in 1970. However, detailed investigations of key species (e.g., the beachmouse, Peromyscus polionotus and the six-lined racerunner, Cnemidophorus sexlineatus) did not begin until 1973. Key species have been repeatedly studied in subsequent years (1974, 1975 and 1978). The birds were studied in 1974 and 1975. Insect studies were conducted in 1970, 1971 and 1973, while aquatic communities were examined in 1970 and again in 1973 and 1974. Lists of species and descriptions of habitats were recorded and TCDD residue analyses were conducted throughout all years of study.

Probably, the most startling observation about Test Area C-52A, is that biological organisms are abundant. The composition of species is diverse and the distribution extensive. In February 1969, a "list of species" for the test grids was initiated. Whenever a species was observed on or associated with the grids, that species was recorded. More than 340 species of organisms were observed and identified on or associated with the test area. The sheer number of species testifies to the extensiveness of the ecological studies that have been conducted on this unique area. Today, over 300 biological samples (plants and animas) have been analyzed for TCDD. TCDD residues have now been found in a wide spectrum of animals collected from the test area. Approximately one-third of the species examined for TCDD residues have been positive. Tables 11, 12, 13, 14 and 15 provide data on those species (mammals, birds, insects, reptiles, amphibians and fish respectively) found to have detectable levels of TCDD.

TABLE 11. TCDD Residues, Parts-per-Trillion, in Mammals Collected on Test Area C-52A, Eglin AFB, Florida[a]

| Species | Tissue | TCDD Residue Analysis (ppt) | |
		Concentration	Detection Limit
Deer	Fat	ND[b]	4
	Liver	ND	5
	Kidney	ND	4
Opossum	Fat	ND	10
	Liver	ND	10
Rabbit	Liver	ND	8
	Pelt	ND	2
Cotton Rat	Liver	10 - 210	
Beachmouse	Liver	300 - 2,900	
	Pelt	130 - 200	

[a] Source: Young and Cockerham, 1983.
[b] ND = Not Detected.

TABLE 12. TCDD Residues, Parts-per-Trillion, in Avian Species Collected on Test Area C-52A, Eglin AFB, Florida[a]

| Dominant Species | No. Samples[ab] | TCDD Residue Analysis (ppt) | | Mean |
		Organ	Range	
Southern Meadowlark	3	Liver	100-1,200	440
	1	Stomach		10
Mourning Dove	2	Liver		50
	1	Stomach		10
Savannah Sparrow	1	Liver		69
	1	Stomach		84

[a] Composites from at least 6 birds.
[b] Source: Young and Cockerham, 1983.

TABLE 13. TCDD Residues, Parts-per-Trillion, in Insects Collected on Test Area C-52A, Eglin AFB, Florida[a]

Family	TCDD Residue Analysis (ppt)
Grasshoppers	ND (3)[b]
Crickets	18-26
Composite of Soil and Plant-Borne Insects	40
Burrows Spiders	115
Insect Grubs (Coleoptera)	238

[a] Source: Young and Cockerham, 1983.
[b] ( ) Detection limit.

TABLE 14. TCDD Residues, Parts-per-Trillion, in Reptiles and Amphibians Collected on Test Area C-52A, Eglin, AFB, Florida[a]

Species	Tissue	TCDD Residue Analysis (ppt) Concentration	Detection Limit
Six-lined Racerunner	Viscera	360	50
	Trunk	370-430	40
Snake	Whole body	420	-
Southern Toad	Whole body	1,360	90
Eastern Coach-whip Snake	Muscle	ND[b]	14
	Fat	148	64
	Skin	20	20
Pine Snake (Immature)	Whole body	ND	70

[a] Source: Young and Cockerham, 1983.
[b] ND = Not Detected.

TABLE 15. TCDD Residue, Parts-per-Trillion, in Aquatic Species Collected from the Drainage Systems of Test Area C-52A, Eglin AFB, Florida[a]

Species	Tissue	TCDD Residue Analysis (ppt) Concentration
Mosquito Fish	Whole body	12
Sailfish Shiner	Whole body	12
Spotted Sunfish	Skin	4
	Gonads	18
	Muscle	4
	Gut	85

a   Source: Young and Cockerham, 1983.

Why are the above species contaminated with TCDD while other species found on the same test area are not? Examination of the species by ecological niche suggests that the commonality is a close relationship to the soil. For example, the beachmouse and hispid cotton rat dig burrows. The cotton rat digs burrows near the water and in areas of high vegetation density, e.g., the centers of the old flight paths. The deer, opossum and rabbit do not burrow, but rather nest/rest upon the vegetation. The crickets, ground spiders and soil-borne insect grubs were significantly contaminated; the grasshoppers were not. The Southern Toad lives in abandoned rodent burrows. The Spotted Sunfish is a bottom feeder and its visceral mass is comprised largely of silt and detritus.

In general, the levels of TCDD in the organisms appeared to be close to the mean levels of TCDD found in the soils. The exceptions to this observation are the beachmouse, toad and the Southern Meadowlark. Studies on the mice and meadowlarks revealed a similar behavior - they both are fastidious groomers/preeners. In the case of the beachmouse, the animal burrows in contaminated soil and during the evenings enters and leaves the burrow frequently. Each time the animal goes into or out of the burrow, it passes through the 15 cm zone of TCDD-contaminated soil. In the burrow the animal grooms the contaminated particles from the pelt. The TCDD accumulates in the liver.

The meadowlark kicks-up top soil and "dusts" its feathers. Preening results in the ingestion of the soil. It should, however, be noted that the meadowlark also ingests soil-borne insects. These insects probably have a significant amount of TCDD on them due to the adherence of contaminated soil particles. Thus, the role of the insect in contaminating the bird is not clear. The Southern Toad ingests primarily soil-borne insects and here too, the role of contaminated soil particles on the insect versus ingested TCDD within the insect is not clear.

It is clear from the Eglin studies that accumulation of TCDD occurs in animals. The magnitude of those levels apparently depends upon the levels of TCDD in the soil. Only two species have been adequately studied to address body-burden levels of TCDD. Samples of the six-lined racerunner have been collected and analyzed for three consecutive years. The samples have been consistent for all three years, i.e., levels of 360, 370 and 430 ppt TCDD. The levels in the visceral mass and the trunk are the same, suggesting the levels are at equilibrium. If the median (not mean) soil level for TCDD is used (because of distribution - the racerunner has an extensive range within its habitat), a concentration factor of 4 exists (110 ppt in soil vs. 400 ppt as body burden).

TCDD analyses have been conducted on components of the beachmouse and its habitat. The present analytical capability permits an analysis of a single liver sample. The significance of this capability can be seen in Table 16. The mound soil is that soil removed during the course of digging the burrow. If it represents mean exposure, then the concentration factor for animals from site 0-4 is between 6 and 7 for females (500 divided by 75 = 6.67) and 18 to 19 for males (1400 divided by 75 = 18.67). The concentration factors for site 0-7 is between 6 and 7 for females (1900 divided by 285 = 6.67) and approximately 9 for males (2600 divided by 285 = 9.12). It is assumed in these studies that body burden levels of TCDD are equivalent to liver levels of TCDD. The concentration factors are lower for the females because these females were either pregnant or were nursing pups and, as noted in Table 16, the fetuses or pups were contaminated from placental transport or from TCDD in the milk.

TABLE 16. TCDD Residue, Parts-per-Trillion, in Soil and Beachmice from Selected Sites on Grid I, Test Area C-52A, Eglin AFB, Florida, April 1978[a]

Grid Location

Component	Site 0-4			Site 0-7		
Soil	0-5 cm	=	150	0-5 cm	=	510
	5-10 cm	=	155	5-10 cm	=	520
	10-15 cm	=	440	10-15 cm	=	440
	Mound Soil[b]	=	75	Mound Soil	=	285
Beachmice						
Burrow 1.	Female: Liver	=	500	Female: Liver	=	1,900
	Pelt	=	110	Pelt	=	160
	Pups: Liver	=	500	Fetuses: Whole body	=	150
	Pelt	=	150	Male: Liver	=	2,600
	Fetuses:			Pelt	=	150
	Whole body	=	40			
Burrow 2.	Female: Liver	=	490			
	Pelt	=	140			
	Fetuses:					
	Whole body	=	90			
	Composite Males:					
	Liver	=	1,400			
	Pelt	=	160			

[a] Source: Thalken and Young, 1983.
[b] Soil removed by the mouse from the burrow.

How long does it take beachmice to accumulate these levels of TCDD, assuming no previous exposure? In 1974, beachmice were obtained from the control site at Eglin and raised in an animal colony in the laboratory. In October 1975, these "tagged" animals were transported to Grid I and released. Three months later, a small number of these animals were captured. At the time of recapture, animals indigenous (native) to the site were also captured. The results indicated that the liver and pelt concentrations of TCDD of both tagged and native beachmice were the same. These data thus suggested that body burden levels of TCDD were reached within about 3 months at this site.

4. Beachmouse data: In 1973, when the data on TCDD in the Eglin test site soil first became available, an extensive research effort was initiated on the beachmouse, the most common mammalian species reported on Test Area C-52A. Subsequent studies were conducted in 1974, 1975 and 1978. Residue levels in the liver and on the pelts of these animals have already been given. The approach taken was to collect beachmice from the test grid and a control site and compare them for as many parameters as possible. In those females that were pregnant, the fetuses were also critically examined.

All animals were prepared for examination using a cervical dislocation procedure to accomplish humane euthanasia. Euthanatized animals were photographed, weighed, measured and systematically examined for developmental defects such as cleft palate, cleft lip, polydactyly and microphthalmia. All internal organs were examined for gross lesions and individually weighed. Representative sections of each tissue were placed in neutral 10 percent buffered formalin and processed for microscopic study by the Veterinary Pathology Division, Armed Forces Institute of Pathology, Washington, D.C. 20305. All remaining tissues from mice captured in the test and control areas were pooled according to sex and maturity, placed in glass jars, frozen and retained for TCDD analysis.

Histopathological examinations were performed on 255 adult or fetal beachmice from the test area and a control area. Examinations were performed on the heart, lungs, trachea, salivary glands, thymus, liver, kidneys, stomach, pancreas, adrenals, large and small intestine, spleen, genital organs, bone, bone marrow, skin and brain. Initially, the tissues were examined on a blind basis. All microscopic changes were recorded including those interpreted as minor or insignificant. The tissues were then re-examined on a control versus test basis, which demonstrated that the test and control mice could not be distinguished histopathologically.

Body and organ weight comparisons have been made for the pregnant beachmice and the mature male beachmice. These were the two largest segments of the population that were captured. A two-factor (treatment and year) disproportional analysis of covariance of organ weights revealed that liver weights for pregnant females were significantly greater (P <.01) in test area beachmice and this difference was consistent over the years of observation. The lack of other adverse effects from TCDD in mice from Grid I may indicate the presence of some mechanism for physiological adaptation. Indeed, the increase in liver weight may reflect an increase in enzymatic activity associated with low level exposure to TCDD. An ultrastructural study of liver tissue from the test and control site females and males showed no morphologic differences (Cockerham and Young, 1982).

The mean number of fetuses per observed pregnancy was 3.1 and 3.4 for the test area and a control area, respectively. A single female beachmouse is capable of producing litters every 26 days. At this frequency, the animals collected in 1978 may have been at least 50 generations removed from the population studied in 1973.

It is apparent that the studies at Eglin AFB have provided a unique opportunity to evaluate the environmental fate and ecological impact of TCDD. The soil serves as the reservoir for TCDD and the major source of contamination for those animals containing residue. Although TCDD persists in the soil, the Eglin data suggests that the bulk of TCDD disseminated in herbicide onto the test area disappeared immediately after application (probably via photodegradation, see Young, 1983), and thus failed to accumulate to levels that would have been acutely toxic.

COMPARISONS BETWEEN HUMAN AND ANIMAL MONITORING STUDIES

The animal studies suggest that the major site for accumulation of TCDD following an acute exposure is the liver and fat. Indeed, the single study (Facchetti et al., 1981) that has been conducted on distribution in human organs after an acute exposure tend to support these data. Likewise, the levels of TCDD in these organs are obviously associated with acute exposure because they are so high. The levels of TCDD in the mice and other mammals at Seveso suggest that the TCDD associated with the cloud was readily "bioavailable" to the wildlife and to the humans living in the contaminated area.

The wildlife studies at Seveso and Eglin have similarities and differences. The time periods between the entrance of TCDD into the ecosystem and the sampling of the animals are vastly different. Most Seveso studies were conducted within the first two years after contamination occurred, while the first Eglin sampling of wildlife for TCDD was not done for more than 10 years after the last application of herbicide (Grid I). The bioavailability of the TCDD changes over time. At Eglin, not only were the residues within the soil but they were probably more tightly bound to soil particles, thus limiting the magnitude of exposure to certain species, e.g., the rabbits.

One other observation can be made; the levels of TCDD in such species as the snakes at Eglin suggest the food chain plays a role as a source of human contamination. The level measured in the snake adipose tissue (149 ppt, Table 14) is not that different than the levels of TCDD recorded as "outlyers" in the human adipose study by Ryan and Williams (130 ppt) or Hobson et al. (99 ppt). Stalling et al., 1983, has confirmed the presence of TCDD in fish of the Great Lakes. An individual who has a high dietary intake of contaminated fish may reflect that contamination by "higher than background" levels of TCDD in the adipose tissue.

The challenges that now confront scientists are to determine if the human has a "background" level of TCDD in the adipose; and, if so, the sources of the TCDD, the significance of TCDD "outlyer" levels that occur in some individuals, and the toxicological implications of long-term, low-level exposure to TCDD to human and animal populations. To this end, the toxicological data obtained on the beachmouse at Eglin AFB, Florida, are encouraging in that long-term, low level exposure to TCDD under field conditions has had minimal effects upon the health and reproduction of this species.

REFERENCES

Baughman, R.W. 1976. Tetrachlorodibenzo-p-dioxins in the environment. High resolution mass spectrometry at the picogram levels. Diss. Abstr. Int. 36 (7):3380B.

Cockerham, L.G. and Young, A.L. 1982. The absence of hepatic cellular anomalies in TCDD-exposed beachmice - A field study. Environ. Toxicol. Chem. 1:299-308.

Cockerham, L.G. and Young, A. L. 1983. Ultrastructural comparison of liver tissues from field and laboratory TCDD-exposed beachmice. Environ. Sci. Res. 26:373-389.

di Domenico, A., Viviano, G. and Zapponi, G. 1981. Environmental persistence of 2,3,7,8-TCDD at Seveso. In Chlorinated Dioxins and Related Compounds: Impact on the Environment, ed. O. Hutzinger, R.W. Frei, E. Merian and F. Pocchiari, pp 105-114, Pergamon Press, Oxford.

Esposito, M.P., Tiernan, T.O. and Dryden, F.E. 1980. Dioxins, Environmental Protection Technology Series, Document EPA/600/2-80-197. Available from the National Technical Information Service, Springfield, Virginia.

Facchetti, S., Fornari, A. and Montagna, M. 1981. Distribution of 2,3,7,8-tetrachlorodibenzo-p-dioxin in the tissues of a person exposed to the toxic cloud at Seveso. Forsensic and Environmental Application 1:1405-1414.

Fanelli, R., Castelli, M.G., Martelli, G.P., Noseda, A. and Garattini, S. 1980. Presence of 2,3,7,8-tetrachlorodibenzo-p-dioxin in wildlife living near Seveso, Italy: A preliminary study. Bull. Environ. Contam. Toxicol. 24:460-462.

Gasiewicz, T.A., Olson, J.R., Geiger, L.H. and Neal, R.A. 1983. Absorption, distribution and metabolism of 2,3,7,8-tetrachlorodibenzo-p-dioxin (TCDD) in experimental animals. Environ. Sci. Res. 26:495-525.

Hobson, L.B., Lee, L.E., Gross, M.L. and Young, A.L. 1983. Dioxin in body fat and health status: A feasibility study. Extended Abstracts, Division of Environmental Chemistry, American Chemical Society 23:91-93.

Kociba, R.J., Keyes, D.G., Beyer, J.E., Carreon, R.M., Wade, C.E., Dittenber, D.A., Kalnins, R.P., Frauson, L.E., Park, C.N., Barnard, S.D., Hummel, R.A. and Humiston, C.G. 1978. Results of a two year chronic toxicity and oncogenicity study of 2,3,7,8-tetrachlorodibenzo-p-dioxin in rats. Toxicol. Appl. Pharmacol. 46:279-303.

Kutz, F.W. 1981. Chemical exposure monitoring in the EPA Office of Pesticides and Toxic Substances. Prepared statement to the Veterans Administration Advisory Committee on Health Effects of Herbicides, November 19, 1981, Washington, D.C., 10 p.

Reggiani, G. 1981. Medical survey techniques in the Seveso TCDD exposure. J. Appl. Toxicol. 1 (6):323-331.

Rose, J.Q., Ramsey, J.C., Wintzler, T.H., Hummel, R.A. and Gehring, P.J. 1976. The fate of 2,3,7,8-tetrachlorodibenzo-p-dioxin following single and repeated oral doses to the rat. Toxicol. Appl. Pharmacol. 36:209-226.

Ryan, J.J. and Williams, D.T. 1983. Analysis of human fat tissue from the Great Lakes Area for 2,3,7,8-tetrachlorodibenzo-p-dioxin and -furan residues. Extended Abstracts, Division of Environmental Chemistry, American Chemical Society, 23 (2):157-158.

Shadoff, L.A. and Hummel, R.A. 1978. The determination of 2,3,7,8-tetrachlorodibenzo-p-dioxin in biological extracts by gas chromatography mass spectrometry. Biomed. Mass. Spectrom. 5 (1):7-13.

Stalling, D.L., Smith, L.M., Petty, J.D., Hogan, J.W., Johnson, J.L., Rappe, C. and Buser, H.R. 1983. Residues of polychlorinated dibenzo-p-dioxins and dibenzofurans in Laurentian Great Lakes fish. Environ. Sci. Res. 26:221-240.

Thalken, C.E. and Young, A.L. 1983. Long-term field studies of a rodent population continuously exposed to TCDD. Environ. Sci. Res. 26:357-372.

Wipf, H.K. and Schmid, J. 1983. Seveso-an environmental assessment. Environ. Sci. Res. 26:255-274.

Young, A.L. 1974. Ecological studies on a herbicide-equipment test area (TA C-52A), Eglin AFB Reservation, Florida. Air Force Technical Report AFATL-TR-74-12, Air Force Armament Laboratory, Eglin AFB, Florida. 146 p. Available from the National Technical Information Service, Springfield, Virginia.

Young, A.L. 1980. The chlorinated dibenzo-p-dioxins. In The Science of 2,4,5-T and Associated Phenoxy Herbicides. R.W. Bovery and A.L. Young. Wiley-Interscience, New York, pp 133-205.

Young, A.L. 1983. Long-term studies on the persistence and movement of TCDD a natural ecosystem. Environ. Sci. Res. 26:173-190.

Young, A. L. and Cockerham, L.G. 1983. A long-term study of 2,3,7,8-TCDD. In Chemicals in the Environment. Proceedings of an International Symposium. Lyngby-Copenhagen, Denmark, October, 1982. Ed. K. Christiansen, B. Kock and F. Bro-Rasmussen, pp.200-225. Available from DIS Congress Service, Unde Alle 48, DK-2720 Vanlose, Denmark.

Young, A.L., Thalken, C.E. and Ward, W.E. 1975. Studies of the ecological impact of repetitive aerial applications of herbicides on the ecosystem of Test Area C-52A, Eglin AFB, Florida. Air Force Technical Report AFATL-TR-75-142, Air Force Armament Laboratory, Eglin AFB, Florida. 127 p. Available from the National Technical Information Service, Springfield, Virginia.

Young, A.L., Calcagni, J.A., Thalken, C.E. and Tremblay, J.W. 1978. The toxicology, environmental fate and human risk of Herbicide Orange and its associated dioxin. Air Force Technical Report OEHL-TR-78-92, USAF Occupational and Environmental Health Laboratory, Brooks, AFB, Texas. 247 p. Available from the National Technical Information Service, Springfield, Virginia.

Young, A.L., Thalken, C.E. and Harrison, D.D. 1979. Persistence, bioaccumulation and toxicology of TCDD in an ecosystem treated with massive quantities of 2,4,5-T herbicide. Paper presented to the Symposium on the Chemistry of Chlorinated Dibenzodioxins and Dibenzofurans. American Chemical Society, 178th National Meeting, September 14, 1979, Washington, D.C., 24 p.

Chapter 12

PREDICTION OF THE ENVIRONMENTAL FATE OF TETRACHLORODIBENZODIOXIN

Theodore Mill
Physical Organic Chemistry Department
Stanford Research Institute

INTRODUCTION

Dioxins are now widely distributed in the environment and have caused great concern because of the extreme toxicity of some of the congeners, particularly TCDD. The polychlorinated dioxins (PCDD) appear to be formed in the manufacturing of chlorinated intermediates and pesticides and in the incineration of chlorinated wastes; the application of pesticides containing trace quantities of TCDDs does not appear to be a significant source of these compounds in the environment although further study of this issue probably is required. During the past ten years, environmental chemists have developed increasingly reliable methods for measuring rates and pathways for the movement and transformation of organic chemicals in air, water, and soil. The objective of this paper is to outline the framework that has been established and to review the data available for TCDD. From these, predictions can be made about the environmental fate of TCDD and, by analogy, the fate of its congeners. Toxicity, distribution in the environment, and analytical methods for TCDD and other chlorinated dioxins are treated in other papers in this volume as well as in numerous other publications and has been summarized by Hutzinger et al. (1982).

Environmental fate estimates are used to provide a sound basis for evaluating the possible hazard associated with the production and/or release of a particular chemical into some compartment of the environment. In Figure 1, the relationships between environmental fate estimates, biological effects and hazard assessments are indicated. Ideally, it would be possible to quantitatively predict the rates of movement and transformation within a compartment and between different compartments and the variation in concentration of a chemical in a particular compartment with time. However, there are usually too few reliable data available from which to make very precise or quantitative estimates. Investigators typically circumvent this difficulty by using model compounds or structure activity relationships (SAR) to obtain reliable data for such estimates.

Models for aquatic or atmospheric systems can be used to integrate fate data over time and space to obtain estimates of concentration as functions of location, time and environmental variations. Evaluative environmental models (such as EXAMS) can be applied to a particular locale only imprecisely but they can be valuable screening tools for problem chemicals such as TCDD.

One of the key data elements needed for reliable fate estimates is the rate of input of the chemical into the environmental compartment of concern. Input can arise from adventitious losses during production, from use or from movement from one compartment to another by volatilization or sorption. Unfortunately, production data

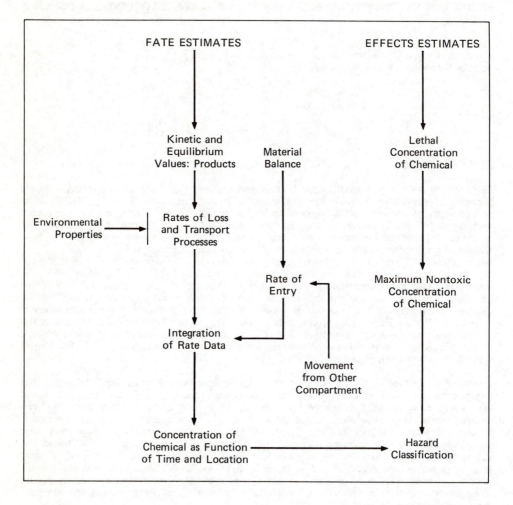

FIGURE 1. Hazard Assessment: Relation of Chemical Fate and Effects

for commercial chemicals and probable losses associated with manufacture and subsequent use are often unreliable and inaccurate. Figure 2 illustrates a material balance on a hypothetical chemical which is manufactured in large amounts, utilized in a variety of end products and lost to the environment at each step in the manufacturing and use cyle. If large amounts are produced and small fractions are lost to the environment, these estimates tend to be imprecise because material balances are based on differences between large numbers, none of which are known accurately.

In the case of TCDD, which occurs in pesticides and chlorinated intermediates as a contaminant at the ppm level and at lower levels in incinerator emissions, the task of estimating input to the environment is even more difficult because of the variety of inputs and the wide variation in contamination levels. What can be done, however, is to ask the following: If a known amount of TCDD is introduced into a particular environmental compartment, how will TCDD become distributed within the compartment and among different compartments and how rapidly and by what routes will TCDD be transformed in each compartment? This question can be answered in semi-quantitative terms if there is detailed information available about the structure and chemistry of the environment and the response of TCDD to these environmental factors.

Table 1 lists the major environmental processes that affect the movement and transformation of organic chemicals. This information can be used, in conjunction with a base set of physical and chemical data for TCDD, to evaluate both its movement and transformation in air, water or soil. Figure 3 illustrates how this process can lead to estimates of a variety of other important properties which affect movement of chemicals within and among different environmental compartments. The most important physical property data are solubility in water (S), vapor pressure (P) and the octanol-water partition coefficient (K_{ow}).

TABLE 1.

Environmental Processes

Air

    Meteorological transport
    Photolysis
    Oxidation
    Fallout

Soil/Sediment

    Sorption
    Bio-uptake
    Run-off
    Volatilization
    Leaching
    Transformations   Hydrolysis
                                     Oxidation
                                     Photolysis
                                     Reduction
    Biodegradation

Water

    Sorption
    Bio-uptake
    Volatilization
    Photolysis
    Hydrolysis
    Oxidation
    Biodegradation

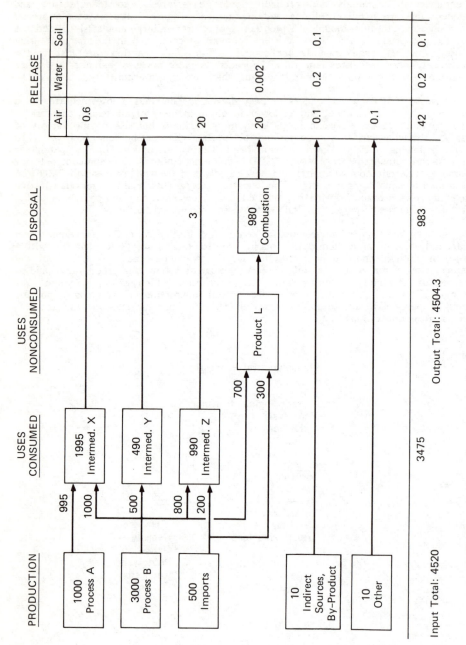

FIGURE 2. General Material Balance Scheme for Volatile Organic Chemical

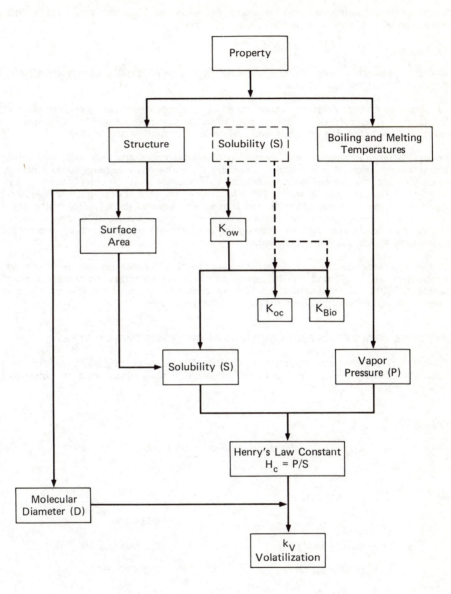

FIGURE 3. Relation of Molecular Properties and Physical Transport Constants

From water solubility we can estimate the value of K_{ow} (or vice versa) through a regression equation such as that of Yalkowsky (1983)

$$\log K_{ow} = -\log S(M) - 0.01\ MP + 0.7 \tag{1}$$

Similar relationships exist among the other primary physical property data as will be shown in the following sections.

To determine the relative importance of various chemical transformations, rate constants for hydrolysis, oxidation by radical and molecular oxidants, photochemical reactivity (including the uv spectrum) and possibly reduction are needed.

Because a large number of different environmental processes may influence movement and transformation of a particular chemical it can be advantageous to do a preliminary evaluation of the probable equilibrium distribution of a chemical among different compartments. Mackay (Mackay, 1980; Mackay et al., 1983) developed an equilibrium, or fugacity approach to calculate distribution which requires data for solubility and vapor pressure and assumes that the chemical is in equilibrium among all compartments. With this information, focus can be placed on the most important transformation processes for a chemical within that compartment.

In the following sections, the influence of physical properties on the environmental distribution of TCDD and the influence of chemical structure on transformation rate constants within the important equilibrium departments will be discussed. In addition, these data will be used to synthesize an overall fate scheme.

PHYSICAL PROPERTIES AND EQUILIBRIUM DISTRIBUTION FOR TCDD

Table 2 lists the physical properties of TCDD. The high melting point and the very low solubility in water make it evident that the value of K_{ow} estimated from equation 1 will be very large: $K_{ow} = 1.3 \times 10^7$

TABLE 2.

Physical Properties of TCDD

mol. wt.	322[a]
m.p., °C	303-305[a]
Solubility in H_2O	0.2 ppb (6 x 10^{-10}M)[a]
Vapor Press. torr	7.2 x 10^{-10}[b]
log K_{ow}	6.839[c]

[a] Crummett and Stehl (1973).
[b] Jaber and Podoll (1983).
[c] Johnson (1982).

This is in good agreement with the value of K_{ow} calculated by Johnson (1982) using fragment additivity. K_{ow} serves as a useful index of how much TCDD will partition to organic phases such as those found in sediment. The actual value of the partition coefficient for sediment sorption, K_{oc}, may be estimated from the relation of Chiou et al. (1979) assuming the solubility of TCDD is 6×10^{-10} M (Table 2).

$$\log K_{oc} = -0.557 \log S + 4.277 \tag{2}$$
(S in μ moles/L)
$$K_{oc} = 1.1 \times 10^6$$

This value is somewhat smaller than K_{ow} or the value of K_{oc} from Karickhoff et al, (1979) which is derived from the following equation:

$$\log K_{oc} = 1.00 \log K_{ow} - 0.21 \tag{3}$$
$$K_{oc} = 8 \times 10^6$$

We can safely assume that TCDD will partition between sediment or biota and water in a concentration ratio between 10^6 and 10^7. Experiments show that TCDD is strongly bound to soil or sediment and leaches into the water column only at an extremely low rate (Wipf et al., 1978). Actual rate constants for sorption or desorption of TCDD from sediments or soil samples are not available; however, we can extrapolate from measurements reported by Karickhoff (1983) on sorption of polycyclic aromatic compounds such as pyrene and methylchloranthrene. Rates of desorption of these compounds from sediments are a function of the length of contact between the chemical and the sediment and exhibit an unusual time dependence (t½). This is due to a complex process in which the rate controlling step may be diffusion into and out of sediment pores. For methylcholanthrene, increasing the contact time from 5 days to 56 days prior to desorption led to an almost ten-fold decrease in the rate of desorption of the compound into pure water. From these results it can be inferred that TCDD in continuous contact with sediments and soils will reequilibrate with water or leach from soil at an extremely low rate; the likelihood that TCDD will leach into groundwater is probably fairly remote. Complete equilibration between sediment and water should require hundreds of days.

Volatilization

Volatilization of TCDD from soil surfaces or from water can be treated fairly accurately using simple relationships based upon vapor pressure and water solubility. Jaber and Podoll (1983) recently measured the vapor pressure of pure TCDD at 25°C (Table 2). Their method, which relies on measuring the amount of ^{14}C-labeled TCDD trapped on an activated carbon trap from saturated vapor gave a value of $(7.6 \pm 0.4) \times 10^{-10}$ torr.

This low vapor pressure means that TCDD will volatilize slowly from soils, with a half-life of many months or years, in the absence of intervening transformation processes. Under some circumstances, volatilization of TCDD and its congeners from soils may be rapid enough to compete with photolysis but additional research is needed to establish this point.

Volatilization of chemicals from water is controlled by diffusion both in the water column and in the gas phase directly above the water surface. Theoretical models for volatilization were developed by Liss and Slater (1974), Mackay and Leinonen (1975) and Smith et al., (1981, 1983). The first order volatilization rate constant, k_v, is given by the relation:

$$k_v = \frac{1}{L} \left(\frac{1}{k_w} + \frac{RT}{Hk_a} \right)^{-1} \tag{4}$$

where L is the depth of the water column, k_w is the coefficient for mass transfer in the water phase and k_a is a corresponding constant for mass transfer in the atmosphere, and H is Henry's constant. Henry's constant is defined as the ratio of P, vapor pressure (in torr),to S, solubility (in moles per liter)

$$H = P/S \qquad (5)$$

As it stands, equation (4) is difficult to use for a particular environmental situation without knowing the values of k_a and k_w. However, Smith et al. (1981) made some simplifying assumptions for limiting cases of very volatile or very nonvolatile chemicals. Using equation (5), Henry's constant for TCDD can be calculated to be 1.1, which means that TCDD is relatively nonvolatile.

$$H = 7.6 \times 10^{-10}/6.2 \times 10^{-10} = 1.1$$

Smith et al. (1981) have shown that if H is less than 40 torr M^{-1}, which corresponds to less than 25% liquid-phase mass transport resistance control, the volatilization half-life of the chemical will be greater than ten days. From their Figure 1, Henry's constant for TCDD corresponds to a half-life of about 200 days in a lake or pond or about ten days in a river.

These volatility estimates critically depend on the value of H, which in turn depends on the measured values of solubility and vapor pressure. The reported solubility for TCDD is extremely small, is difficult to measure and in fact may be a lower limit of the true value. Thus, the Henry's constant estimate is the upper bound and the corresponding half-life in the water body is the lower bound.

No experimental details were provided for the solubility estimate; however, an estimate of the solubility of TCDD based on its molecular structure, using the method of Irmann (1965) as elaborated in Lyman et al. (1982), gives a value of about 8×10^{-9} M. Yalkowsky's correlation of K_{ow} and S in equation (1) (and the calculated value of K_{ow} from Table 2) gives $S = 3 \times 10^{-10}$ M. These estimates probably bound the true value and suggest that the solubility of TCDD is indeed less than 1×10^{-8} M. Thus, volatilization of TCDD from soil will be very slow because of its low solubility in water (high K_{oc}) and low vapor pressure, both of which act to retain it in the soil phase over a range of soil water content.

Bioaccumulation

Of great concern to environmental scientists is movement of TCDD into the food chain thus exposing a wide range of biological populations, including humans, to the compound. Data cited thus far suggest that TCDD is a highly lipophilic, relatively non-volatile chemical. It will move into sediments, soils and biological systems providing a mechanism exists for transfer from one compartment to another. An estimate of the equilibrium conditions can be made using from one of several equations relating log K_{ow} and log BCF (bioconcentration factor). Lyman et al (1982) list several equations, one of which, applicable to chlorinated aromatics, relates BCF to solubility (in ppm):

$$\log BCF = -0.564\log S + 2.791 \qquad (6)$$
(S in ppm)
$$\log BCF = 0.564(3.699) + 2.791 = 4.9$$

The large values for log K_{ow} and log BCF show that TCDD will be almost completely sequestered in sediment and biota. However, the mass ratio of biota to the water column is very small and the equilibrium distribution may not be achieved rapidly compared to other processes that may move or transform TCDD. Experiments conducted with microcosms in which TCDD was introduced in sediments and followed in sediment, biota and water showed slow equilibration over a period of 5-15 days with the ratio between biota and water approaching 10^4 (Isensee and Jones, 1975). Smaller BCFs were observed by Matsumura and Benezet (1973) using shorter exposure times.

Equilibrium Distribution

The foregoing analysis of the physical properties and transport of TCDD in aquatic and soil systems suggests that near equilibrium most TCDD will be sorbed to sediments or soil and only a very small proportion will be dissolved in the water column. However, because the mass of the water column in most aquatic systems is orders of magnitude larger than the available sediment, a significant fraction of total TCDD will be found in the water column.

If PCDDs are initially emitted into the atmosphere through incineration, their equilibrium distribution probably will occur by sorption of vapor to atmospheric particulates. Heicklen (1980) has calculated that chemicals with vapor pressures below 10^{-7} torr probably will aggregate or sorb rather than remain in the vapor phase. PCDDs vaporizing from soil, in the absence of a significant particulate load, may remain in the vapor phase for long periods of time. In fact, volatilization of soil-borne PCDD into the vapor phase, followed by photolysis, could represent a significant loss pathway for PCDD and other chlorinated dioxins (see below). If sorption is fast, then slow deposition of the PCDD-containing particulate onto soil and water surfaces will occur and the material will become incorporated into the larger mass of sediment or soil.

CHEMICAL TRANSFORMATIONS

General Considerations

The molecular structures of TCDD and its congeners do not lend themselves to facile chemical reactions. Bond strengths for aromatic C-Cl bonds are about 85 kcal/mol and these linkages are not particularly susceptible to hydrolysis at temperatures below 150-200°C. Oxidation by oxidants found in surface waters or on soil are probably immeasureably slow (Mill et al., 1980). However, oxidation in the atmosphere by hydroxyl radicals might be an important pathway. Photolysis both in the atmosphere and in surface waters is probably important. The photochemical reactivity of TCDD and its congeners has been studied extensively in organic solvents but not in water (Crosby et al., 1971; Plimmer et al., 1973; Crosby and Mailanen, 1977; Wong and Crosby, 1978; Choudhry and Hutzinger, 1982). However, neither oxidation nor photolysis of TCDD in the gas phase have been reported. Estimates of rate constants suggest that oxidation by air could be an important process (Davenport et al, 1984). Reduction of aromatic C-Cl bonds in anaerobic sediments is possible but there are no experimental data nor theoretical models on which to base reliable estimates of rate constants. The next section indicates some features of TCDD photochemistry in both and surface waters and the atmosphere and provides estimates of atmospheric oxidation rate constants.

Photochemistry of TCDD

Photochemical studies of TCDD in solution, in suspension and on surfaces have been prompted in a large part by the hope that photochemical transformation to less chlorinated homologs would offer a rapid and safe technique for decontaminating large areas such as those at Seveso, Italy. The report of Crosby et al. (1971) and others that photolysis of TCDD in organic solvents leads to successive reductions of chlorine atoms to form lower homologs is encouraging because of the significantly lower toxicity of the 2,3,7- and 2,8-chlorodioxins (McConnell and Moore, 1978). Studies by Wong and Crosby,

Akermark, Liberti et al., and Wipf et al. (all 1978) suggest that, in field situations on soils or leaf canopies, TCDD can photolyze fairly rapidly in sunlight. Studies at Seveso following the widespread distribution of TCDD in the surrounding soil and air showed that the TCDD content of grass growing in soil plots exposed to sunlight over a period of ten days in September 1976 decreased as much as ten-fold (Wipf et al, 1978). Control experiments in the dark confirm that photolysis, not volatilization, was the cause of the decrease.

In 1971, Crosby and his coworkers reported a study of the photolysis of TCDD in solution and in the solid phase (Crosby et al., 1971). Their findings and those of subsequent workers have been summarized in detail by Choudhry and Hutzinger (1982). The UV photoreaction of TCDD and its isomers and homologs resembles that of other chlorinated aromatics; in organic solvents C-Cl bonds are reduced to C-H bonds with formation of HCl via a free radical mechanism.

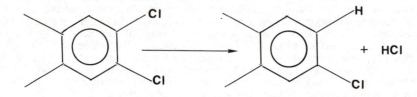

Several workers, including Crosby et al.(1971), Desideri et al. (1979) and Buser (1979) reported that the first step in the photolysis of TCDD is formation of 2,3,7-trichlorodibenzodioxin and that this is followed by rapid photolysis to the dichloro, monochloro and parent dibenzodioxin. Experiments carried out in sunlight indicate that the half-life of TCDD in alkanes and methanol is about 3-4 hours. Dobbs and Grant (1979) reported that the photolyses of more chlorinated dioxins in sunlight gave half-lives ranging from 5 to 47 hours, while Desideri et al. (1979) reported that tri- and dichlorodioxins photolyzed much faster than TCDD. The maximum yields of these products were only 6 to 8% in alkane solvents.

Rapid photolysis of TCDD to the parent dioxin and possibly simpler structures is encouraging evidence for rapid environmental transformation of TCDD to much less toxic compounds. However, direct comparison of the rates of photolysis of various TCDD homologs and isomers is difficult because the quantitative information needed to estimate these rates under standard conditions of sunlight generally is not available.

At this point it is useful to briefly review the kinetics of photochemical processes in surface waters or in the atmosphere and to estimate photolysis rate constants for TCDD in air or water. For dilute solutions of light-absorbing chemicals the rate of photolysis is given by the relation (Zepp and Cline, 1977):

$$d[C]/dt = 2.3\phi I_A = 2.3\phi I_0 \epsilon [C] \tag{7}$$

where I_A or I_0 is the absorbed or incident light in units of photons or einsteins/cm^2, ϵ is the absorption coefficient at a particular wavelength, ϕ is the quantum yield or efficiency of the photo process and [C] is the concentration of the chemical.

Thus, the rate constant for photolysis of chemicals in dilute solutions depends on the absorption coefficient of the chemical, the quantum yield and the light intensity at wavelength. In sunlight, the rate of photolysis is given by the relation:

$$d[C]/dt = \phi(\Sigma_\lambda \epsilon_\lambda L_\lambda) [C] \tag{8}$$

where the summation sign indicates that the total rate in sunlight is the sum of individual rates for each wavelength interval in the solar spectrum where the chemical absorbs light. In general, the quantum yield, ϕ, is independent of wavelength. The light intensity term $2.3I_a$ is referred to as L_λ (Mill and Mabey, 1984).

Recently experiments were performed to measure the quantum yields of TCDD in water and hexane (Mill et al., 1983). Figure 4 is the UV spectrum of 5×10^{-5} M TCDD in acetonitrile showing a maximum at 304-309 nm; in hexane the intensity of the spectral maximum is the same but the peak is shifted slightly to lower wavelengths. Table 3 lists UV intensities of TCDD in acetonitrile for the range of 297-340 nm.

TABLE 3. UV Spectral Listings for TCDD in Acetonitrile and Hexane

Acetonitrile		Hexane	
λ, nm	ϵ^a, M-1 cm-1	λ, nm	ϵ^b, M-1 cm-1
299	6130	299	4870
304	7020	304	5640
309	7020	309	5480
313	6020	313	4640
314	6020	314	4570
319	3590	319	2630
324	1160	324	670
340	0	340	0

a [TCDD] = 1.81×10^{-5} M.
b [TCDD] = 1.68×10^{-5} M.

The quantum yields, measured in sunlight and at 313 nm for 3×10^{-7} M TCDD in 75% water-acetonitrile using a p-nitroanisole/pyridine actinometer (Dulin and Mill, 1982), were 0.00068 and 0.0022 respectively. The quantum yield in hexane at 313 nm is 0.04, about twenty times larger than in water. The half-life of aqueous TCDD in sunlight over four seasons at 40°L can be calculated from equation (8) with appropriate L_λ values and ϕ= 0.0022, (the 313 nm value in which we have more confidence). Table 4 summarizes these results. Half-lives in sunlight vary from 130 h in winter to 20 h in summer in surface waters under clear skies. These half-lives are longer by a factor of 20 than would be observed in hexane.

TABLE 4. Calculated Sunlight Photolysis Rate Constants for TCDD at 40°L a

Season	$L_\lambda \epsilon_\lambda$	10 k_{pE}, d-1	$t_{1/2}$, h b
Winter	63	0.13	130
Spring	267	0.58	28
Summer	364	0.81	20
Fall	147	0.32	52

a From equation (8) with spectral data from
 Table 3, ϕ= 0.0022 and L_λ from Mill et al. (1982).
b Averaged for 24-hr day.

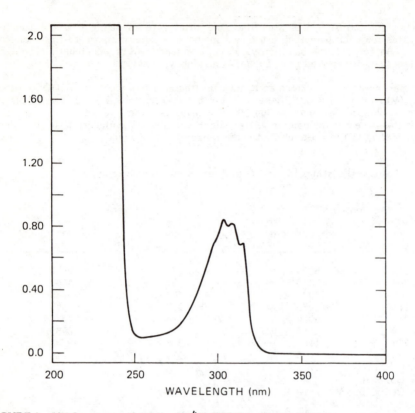

FIGURE 4. UV Spectrum of 1.81 x 10⁻⁴M TCDD in Acetonitrile

One possible explanation for the much faster photolysis rates in organic solvents than in water: acetonitrile mixtures or in emulsions is the very low solubility of TCDD in these aqueous mixtures resulting in formation of microcrystalline TCDD which is not particularly susceptible to photolysis (Crosby et al., 1971).

The proposed pathway for photolysis of TCDD in organic solvents involving reduction of C-Cl bonds to C-H bonds is paralleled in simpler chloro-aromatic systems. For example, photolyses of chlorobenzene, chlorobiphenyls and chlorobiphenyl ethers in organic solvents, such as hexane or methanol, all proceed with replacement of the chlorine by hydrogen (Bunce, 1982). However, in aqueous systems the same chloroaromatics photolyze with nearly the same efficiencies (quantum yields) but follow completely different pathways to give the corresponding phenols (Mill et al., 1983). TCDD photolysis products in water have not been detected but, by analogy to other systems, it is believed that the corresponding phenol is formed.

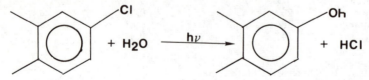

The mechanism for photolysis of chlorinated aromatics (including chlorodioxins) involves excitation of the chloroaromatic to a singlet and/or a triplet excited state from which homolytic cleavage of the carbon-chlorine bond proceeds to form a radical pair. The fate of the radical pair depends on the physical and chemical environment. For example, a radical pair formed in a highly viscous medium, such as a crystalline solid, will probably collapse immediately to the parent compound. This leads to low values of ϕ and probably accounts for the apparent high stability of surface films of solid TCDD (Crosby et al., 1971).

In highly fluid environments the radical pair can dissociate and the ultimate products depend on the composition of the solvent. In water, the radical pair undergoes electron transfer to form an ion pair and subsequently reacts with water, to form, in most cases, the phenol (Mill et al., 1983). Scheme 1 illustrates the dual pathway.

$$Ar\text{-}Cl \xleftarrow{\quad h\nu \quad} {}^1ArCl$$

$${}^1Ar\text{-}Cl \longrightarrow {}^3ArCl$$

$${}^1ArCl \text{ or } {}^3ArCl \longrightarrow Ar\cdot Cl\cdot$$

$$Ar\cdot Cl\cdot \xrightarrow{\quad HR \quad} Ar\cdot + Cl\cdot$$

$$Ar\cdot Cl\cdot \xrightarrow{\quad H_2O \quad} Ar^+Cl^-$$

$$Ar\cdot Cl\cdot \longrightarrow ArCl$$

$$Ar\cdot + HR \longrightarrow ArH + R\cdot$$

$$Ar^+ + OH_2 \longrightarrow ArOH + H^+$$

(Superscripts refer to singlet or triplet states)

SCHEME 1. Photolysis Pathways for Chloroaromatics

To summarize, there is now some fairly reliable quantitative information on the photochemical kinetics for TCDD as well as an abundant literature on the photolytic behavior of TCDD and its congeners in soils and water columns. There is no information about chemical pathways in sediment or gas phase systems (see below).

Air Chemistry

The low vapor pressure of TCDD suggests that some of the PCDDs emitted to the atmosphere from incineration sources will sorb to particulates and either remain in suspended particulates or return to the soil and surface waters by dry deposition. That fraction of TCDD remaining in the vapor phase can undergo photochemical transformation in the same way as TCDD dissolved in the water column. Kinetic rate laws governing the photolysis of chemicals in the atmosphere are virtually identical to those for photolysis of dilute aqueous solutions except for a change of nomenclature designating the light intensity as J_λ instead of L_λ. The spectral properties and photolysis quantum yield of TCDD vapor probably are similar to those of TCDD in hexane. Therefore, rate constants and photolytic half-lives for TCDD vapor in sunlight should follow the relation:

$$k_{pE} = (0.04)\Sigma\epsilon_\lambda J_\lambda \tag{9}$$

where k_{pE} is the rate constant in sunlight. Using ϵ_λ values from Table 3 and J_λ values for summer sunlight at 40°L from Peterson (1976) a value of $k_{pE} = 1.2 \times 10^2$ min^{-1}, corresponding to $t_{1/2} = 56$ min, is obtained.   Thus TCDD vapor appears to be very transient in the atmosphere. It is not known how fast TCDD will photolyze if it is strongly sorbed to particulate; the photolysis rate may be quite different from that in the vapor phase. Townsend (1983) investigated the change in isomer distribution of polychlorinated dioxins in the atmosphere at various sites. These results suggest that airborne microparticulates transport and mix the low volatility chlorinated dioxins and that a major loss process for these may be photochemical.

The major transformation process in the environment for most organic chemicals is oxidation by OH radical (Atkinson et al., 1982). Aromatic compounds react with OH radical in air to form phenols by the following mechanism:

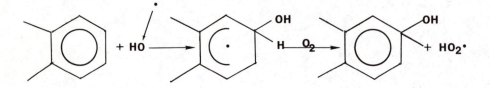

Rate constants for the reaction of OH radical with aromatics are usually large ($> 1 \times 10^8$ M^{-1} s^{-1}) (Darnall et al., 1976) and reactivity usually closely follows the type of substitution on the ring (Hendry and Kenley, 1979). Zetsch (1982) has shown that there is a good correlation of rate constants with the σ or σ^* constants for ring substituents and that constants are additive for multiple substituents. Using chlorine and phenoxy substituents (Davenport et al., 1984), the rate constant for the reaction of TCDD vapor with OH radical is approximately 2×10^8 M^{-1} s^{-1}. The half life for TCDD in the atmospheric vapor phase can be estimated using an average concentration of OH radical in the atmosphere of 3×10^{-15} M (Singh, 1977) as the basis for calculating a first order rate constant of 6×10^{-7}s^{-1}. This rate constant corresponds to a half life of 320 hours and applies only to the vapor phase reaction; there is no data with which to evaluate the rate of oxidation of TCDD sorbed to atmospheric particulate but we suspect that the rate constant will be appreciably smaller. These estimates show that photolysis is the dominant process in the tropospheric vapor phase as well as in surface waters.

BIOTRANSFORMATION

Microbial transformations of TCDD appear to be very slow and are restricted to a few strains of organisms which transform TCDD only in anaerobic sediments (Ward and Matsamura, 1977).   Other studies failed to find evidence of microbiological transformations in anaerobic microcosms (Isensee and Jones, 1975). This loss pathway, although very slow, is possibly important in the long-term because it effects transformations under conditions where other processes may be slower still.

Czuczwa and Hites (1983) have shown that PCDD concentrations in Lake Huron sediments increased steadily from 1940 onward and parallel chlorinated herbicide production and use. Of special interest is the isomer and congener distribution of PCDDs in sediment cores. Czuczwa and Hites (1983) note that these PCDDs are rich in the octachloro congener and contain relatively little TCDD in contrast to reports (Gross, 1984) that particulates near incineration sources have a flat congener distribution. These observations, if confirmed, can be explained either by selective biotransformation of the lower chlorinated congeners in the soil or sediments or selective photochemical transformation of the particulates prior to deposition. Townsend (1983) has interpreted these changes in congener distribution as resulting from photochemistry; however, too few data are available to unambigiously resolve the problem. This observation provides an explanation for the extremely slow transformation of sediment sorbed TCDD in deep lakes where scouring is very slow and light penetration is limited to a few meters.

ENVIRONMENTAL FATE ASSESSMENT

The data developed in each of the preceeding sections for transformation and transport of TCDD are summarized in Table 5 and are assembled in Scheme 2 in the form of a screening fate assessment. This can be used to deduce the major processes affecting distribution and transformation of TCDD. TCDD introduced into the water column will equilibrate with sediment and biota and also volatilize to the atmosphere. Photochemistry will be the dominant transformation process for the small fraction of TCDD in the water column in equilibrium with sediment-sorbed TCDD and will have a half life of about 50 days. The rate of volatilization of TCDD in soil or in the water column also is fairly slow with a half-life of 50-200 days and both processes are slowed further by the fact that a major fraction of TCDD is sorbed to sediment and biota. TCDD in the troposphere as vapor will photolyze very rapidly ($t\frac{1}{2} \sim 1$ h) but will oxidize with OH radical slowly enough that redeposition on particulates will compete ($t\frac{1}{2} \sim 200$ h) (Heicklen, 1982). Photolysis of TCDD sorbed to suspended sediment or particulate may be quite important but no data is available.

TABLE 5. Transport and Transformation Constants for TCDD

Process Constant		Value
	Transport	
H[a]		1.1 torr/mole
k_v		0.07 - 0.03 d^{-1}
K_{OW}		6 x 10^7
K_{OC}		(1.1-8) x 10^6
K_{BIO}		7.9 x 10^4
	Transformation	
ϕ (313, water)[a]		0.0022
ϕ (313, Hexane)[a]		0.04
k_{pE} (sunlight, water)[a]		0.58 d^{-1} (6.7 x 10^{-6} s^{-1})
k_{pE} (sunlight, air)		1.4 hr^{-1} (3.9 x 10^{-4} s^{-1})
k_{OH} (atmosphere)		2 x 10^8 M^{-1} s^{-1}
k_{BIO} (sediment)		<0.002 d^{-1}

[a] Measured value.

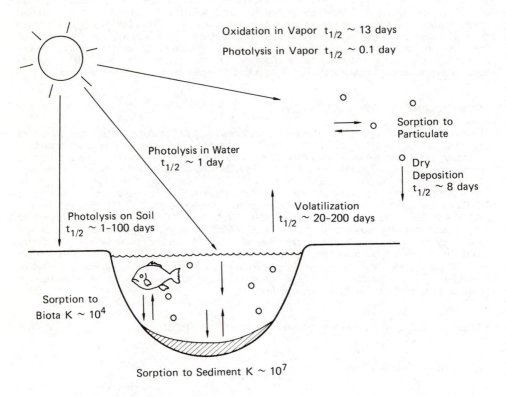

Oxidation in Vapor $t_{1/2} \sim 13$ days

Photolysis in Vapor $t_{1/2} \sim 0.1$ day

Sorption to Particulate

Dry Deposition $t_{1/2} \sim 8$ days

Photolysis in Water $t_{1/2} \sim 1$ day

Photolysis on Soil $t_{1/2} \sim 1$-100 days

Volatilization $t_{1/2} \sim 20$-200 days

Sorption to Biota $K \sim 10^4$

Sorption to Sediment $K \sim 10^7$

SCHEME 2. Pathways for Movement and Loss of TCDD in the Environment

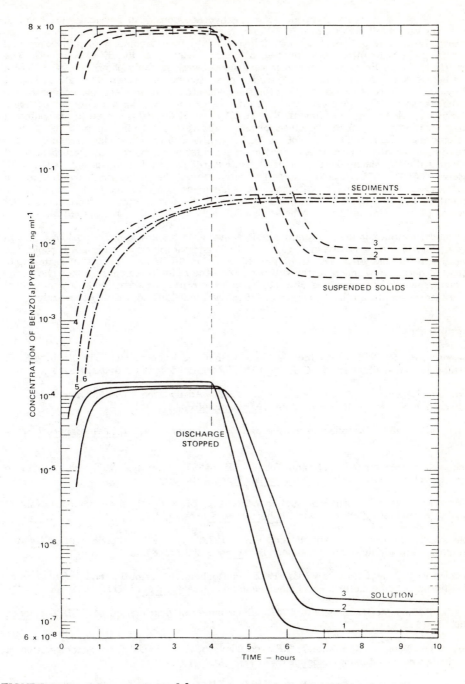

FIGURE 5. Persistence of Benza[a]pyrene in a Partially Mixed River System

The behaviors of several polycyclic aromatic hydrocarbons with physical and chemical properties very similar to that of TCDD (Smith et al., 1978) have been modeled.   Figure 5 shows the result of modeling benzo(a)pyrene (BP) in a 9-compartment hypothetical river using the SRI multicompartment aquatic model (similar to the EXAMS model). The half life of BP in the water column is very short owing to rapid photolysis (t½ ~ 0.5 h); nonetheless, after introduction of BP from a point source has ceased, the rate of loss of BP (which is controlled largely by photolysis) decreases with time and the concentration approaches some very low concentration in the water column. This behavior results from buffering by BP sorbed to sediment; like TCDD most of the BP is sorbed to the sediment and desorption rather than photolysis becomes the rate controlling step in the overall loss process. The rate at which BP or TCDD will desorb from sediment depends on the rate of resuspension of bottom sediment in a particular water body; rapid resuspension of bottom sediment should lead to more efficient reequilibration of sorbed TCDD with dissolved TCDD. TCDD which is sorbed to the biota will be such a small fraction of the total sorbed TCDD that it will make no significant contribution to the equilibrium amount of TCDD present in the water body or in the sorbed state. For example, the fraction of BP estimated to be sorbed to biota is only 0.1% of the total sorbed BP.

This model assumes that sorbed material is unavailable for any transformations. Should this assumption prove incorrect for sorbed TCDD and photolysis on sediment is rapid, the overall rate of loss of TCDD from the water column will be appreciably faster than indicated here. How much faster will depend on the actual rate constant for photolysis on the suspended sediment and other features of the natural water body which control the transmission of light in the region of 310 nm where TCDD absorbs light strongly.

REFERENCES

Akermark, B. 1978. Photodechlorination of haloaromatic compounds. In Dioxin, eds. F. Cattabeni, A. Cavallaro and G. Galli, p. 191, SP Medical Scientific Books, New York.

Atkinson, R., Lloyd, A.C. and Winges, L. 1982. An updated chemical mechanism for hydrocarbon/NO_x/SO_2 photooxidations. Atmos. Environ. 16:1341.

Bunce, N.J. 1982. Photodechlorination of PCBs: Current Status. Chemosphere 11:701-714.

Bunce, N.J., DeSchutter, C.T. and Toone, J.E. 1983. Photolysis of ortho-methylated monochlorobiphenyls. J. Chem. Soc. Perkin Trans. II (in press).

Buser, H-R. 1979. Formation and identification of chlorodioxins from photolysis to isomeric hexachloro dibenzodioxins. Chemosphere 8:251-257.

Chiou, C.T., Peters, L.J., and Freed, V.H. 1979. A physical concept of soil-water equilibria for nonionic organic compounds. Science 206:831-832.

Choudhary, G.G. and Hutzinger, O. 1982. Photochemical formation and degradation of polychlorinated dibenzofurans and dibenzodioxins. Residue Rev. 84:115-161.

Crosby, D. and Moilanen, K.W. 1977. Environmental degradation of TCDD. Science 195:1337-1338.

Crosby, D., Wong, A.S., Plimmer, J.R. and Woolson, E.A. 1971. Photodecomposition of chlorinated dibenzodioxins. Science 173:748-749.

Crummett, W.B. and Stehl, R.H. 1973. Determination of dibenzodioxins and dibenzofurans in various materials. Environ. Health Perspect. 15:230.

Czuczwa, J.M. and Hites, R.A. 1983. Sources and fates of dioxins and dibenzofurans as told by sediment cores. Abstracts Div. Environ. Chem. 23:74.

Darnall, K.R., Lloyd, A.C., Winer, A.M. and Pitts, J.N. 1976. Reactivity scale for atmospheric hydrocarbons based on reaction with hydroxyl radical. Environ. Sci. Tech. 10:692-696.

Davenport, J., Gu, C.-L., Hendrey, D.G. and Mill, T. 1984. Estimation of rate constants for reactions of hydroxyl radical with organic compounds. Manuscript in preparation.

Desidiri, A., Dominico, A.D., Vanzati, R.,Tancioni, P. and Muccio, A.D. 1979. Photolysis of TCDD in isooctane, hexane and cyclohexane. Chim. Farm. 118:274.

Dulin, D. and Mill, T. 1982. Development and evaluation of sunlight actinometers. Environ. Sci. Technol. 16:185.

Heicklen, J. 1982. The removal of atmospheric gases by particulate matter. In Heterogeneous Atmospheric Chemistry, ed. D.R. Schryer, Geophysical Monograph No. 26, American Geophysical Union, Washington, D.C.

Hendry, D.G. and Kenley, R.A. 1979. Atmospheric reaction products of organic compounds. EPA Final Report, 560/12-79-001.

Hutzinger, O., Frei, R.W., Merian, E. and Reggiani, eds. 1982. Chlorinated dioxins and related compounds. Chemosphere 12:425.

Irmann, F. 1965. A simple correlation between water solubility and structure of hydrocarbons and halohydrocarbons. Chem. Ing. Tech. 37:789.

Isensee, A.R. and Jones, G.E. 1975. Distribution of TCDD in aquatic model ecosystems. Environ. Sci. Technol. 9:668-672.

Jaber, H. and Podoll, T. 1983. SRI. Unpublished results.

Johnson, H. 1982. In Aquatic Fate Process Data From Organic Priority Pollutants, Mabey, W.R., ed. EPA Final Report, EPA Contract No. 68-01-3867.

Karickhoff, S.W. 1983. Sorbtion kinetics of hydrophobic pollutants in natural sediments. Abstracts Div. Environ. Chem. 23:188.

Karickhoff, S.W., Brown, D.S. and Scott, T.A. 1979. Sorption of hydrophobic pollutants on natural sediments. Water Res. 13:241.

Liberti, A., Brocco, D., Allegrini, I. and Bertoni, G. 1978. Field photodegradation of TCDD by ultraviolet radiation. In Dioxin, eds. F. Cattabeni, A. Cavallaro and G. Galli, p. 195,SP Medical Scientific Books, New York.

Liss, P.S. and Slater, P.G. 1974. Flux of gases across the air-sea interface. Nature 247:181-184.

Lyman, W. J., Reehl, W.F. and Rosenblatt, D.H., eds. 1982. Handbook of Chemical Property Estimation Methods. McGraw-Hill Book Company, New York.

Mackay, D. 1980. Solubility, partition coefficients, volatility and evaporation rates, Vol.2, Part A. In The Handbook of Environmental Chemistry, ed. O. Hutzinger, pp. 31-45, Springer-Verlag, Berlin.

Mackay, D. and Leinonen, P.J. 1975. Rate of evaporation of low solubility contaminants from waterbodies to the atmosphere. Environ. Sci. Technol. 9:1178-1180.

Mackay, D., Paterson, S. and Joy, M. 1983. Application of fugacity models to the estimation of chemical distribution and persistence in the environment. Amer. Chem. Soc. Symp. Ser. 225:175.

Matsumura, F. and Benezett, H.J. 1973. Studies on the bioaccumulation and microbial degradation of TCDD. Environ. Health Perspect. 5:253-258.

McConnell, E.E. and Moore, J.A. 1978. The toxicopathology of TCDD. In Dioxin: Toxicological and Chemical Aspects, eds. F. Cattabeni, A. Cavallaro and G. Galli, pp. 137-142, SP Medical and Scientific Books, New York.

Mill, T., Drossman, H., Combes, D. and Spanggord, R. 1983. SRI. Unpublished results.

Mill, T., Dulin, D. and Drossman, H. 1983. Photolysis of chloroaromatic compounds in water. EPA Draft Final Report. EPA Contract 68-03-2981, Task 20.

Mill, T. and Mabey, W. 1984. Photochemical transformations. In Exposure to Chemicals in the Environment, eds. B. Neeley and G.H. Blau, CRC Publishers. (In press).

Mill, T., Mabey, W.R., Bomberger, D.C., Chou, T.W., Hendry, D.G. and Smith, J.H. 1982. Laboratory protocols for evaluating the fate of organic chemicals in air and water. EPA Final Report 600/3-82-022.

Peterson, J.T. 1976. Calculated actinic fluxes (290-700 nm) for air pollution photochemistry applications. EPA Final Report 600/4-76-025.

Plimmer, J.R., Klingbiel, U.I., Crosby, D.G. and Wong, A.S. 1973. Photochemistry of dibenzodioxins. Adv. Chem. Ser. 120:44.

Singh, H.B. 1977. Preliminary estimation of average tropospheric HO concentrations in the northern and southern hemispheres. Geophys. Res. Lett. 4:453.

Smith, J.H., Mabey, W.R., Bonohos, N., Holt, B.R., Lee, S.S., Chou, T-W, Bomberger, D.C. and Mill, T. 1978. Environmental pathways of selected chemicals in freshwater systems. Part II: Laboratory studies. EPA Final Report 600/7-78-074.

Smith, J.H., Bomberger, D.C. and Haynes, D.L. 1981. Volatilization of intermediate and low volatility chemicals. Chemosphere 10:281.

Smith, J.H., Mackay, D. and Ing, C.W.K. 1983. Volatilization of pesticides from water. Residue Rev. 85:74.

Townsend, D.I. 1983. Change of isomer ratio and fate of polychlorinated dioxins in the environment. Chemosphere 12:637.

Ward, C. and Matsumura, F. 1977. Fate of 2,4,5-T contaminant, 2,3,7,8-TCDD aquatic environments. US NTIS, PB Rep. PB-264187.

Wipf, H.K., Homberger, E., Neuner, N. and Schenker, F. 1978. Field trials on photodegradation of TCDD on vegetation. In Dioxin, eds. F. Cattabeni, A. Cavallaro and G. Galli, p. 201, SP Medical Scientific Books, New York.

Wong, A.S. and Crosby, D.G. 1978. Decontamination of TCDD by photochemical action. In Dioxin, eds. F. Cattabeni, A. Cavallaro and G. Galli, p. 185, SP Medical Scientific Books, New York.

Yalkowsky, S.H. 1983. Physical chemical parameters relating to sorption and partitioning. Abstracts Div. Environ. Chem. 23:186.

Zepp, R.G. and Cline, D.M. 1977. Rates of direct photolysis in aquatic environments. Environ. Sci. Technol. 11:359-366.

Zetsch, C. 1982. In XV Informal Conference on Photochemistry, Abstracts A-1129.

Chapter 13

THE DEGRADATION AND DISPOSAL OF CHLORINATED DIOXINS

Donald G. Crosby
Department of Environmental Toxicology
University of California - Davis

INTRODUCTION

The degradation and disposal of chlorinated dioxins is feasible. Although the word "dioxin" has become associated in the public's mind with inescapable danger, almost supernatural toxicity, and negative impact of technology on a helpless populace (news media refer to "the monstrous chemical"), dioxins are only chemicals. There certainly is nothing supernatural or monstrous about them. By understanding their properties, technology can also bring about their control and removal.

The degradation and disposal of dioxins have been previously reviewed (Crosby, 1978; Esposito et al., 1980; Crosby, 1983; Shaub and Tsang, 1983; Taft et al., 1983). The present article will relate the physical and chemical properties of the dioxins to the theoretical practical methods of achieving these goals. The purpose is not to provide an exhaustive review, but rather, to stimulate thinking in this important but neglected area.

PHYSICAL PROPERTIES

Most of the attention has focused on TCDD--2,3,7,8-tetrachlorodibenzo-p-dioxin. The TCDD molecule is symmetrical and essentially planar, and the shorter than normal C-Cl bonds (Boer, et al., 1973), as well as the calculated electron-distribution (Miller et al, 1977; Veerkamp et al., 1983), show that the aromatic rings are electron-deficient. The symmetry also is revealed by the melting point of 307°C, compared to 180°C in the 1,3,7,8-isomer (Table 1). Like the similarly symmetrical DDT and hexachlorobenzene molecules, the aqueous solubility of TCDD is extremely low; even its solubility in organic solvents is not great. However, the large difference between the aqueous and organic solubilities results in a high octanol-water partition coefficient (K_{ow}) and, of course, substantial bioconcentration.

The vapor pressure of TCDD has been variously reported to fall between 10^{-7} to 10^{-10} torr (Mill, 1983), resulting in a low (but definite) volatility; the low vapor pressure and low solubility combine to give a small but respectable Henry's Law constant on the order of 1.5×10^{-6} atm-m^3/mole (similar to that of pentachlorophenol). TCDD's partitioning characteristics assure a high degree of soil adsorption (K_f), although desorption from soil could be hindered by both electrostatic attraction from the dioxin's electropositive nature and by physical trapping within clay crystal lattices because of its planarity. In organic solvents, TCDD absorbs ultraviolet light strongly; the wavelengths of maximum absorption (λ_{max}) lying within the sunlight region (above 295 nm) (Table 1).

Table 1. Physical Properties of TCDD

m.p. °C		305-307°
Solubility, mg/L	Water	0.0002
	Methanol	10
	Chloroform	370
	Benzene	570
Vapor pressure, Torr.		7×10^{-10}
K_{ow}		7×10^{6}
K_f		4×10^{4}
λmax^{nm}		310 (ϵ5590)

CHEMICAL PROPERTIES

The chemical reactions of TCDD and other chlorinated dioxins (Table 2) are dominated by their low electronegativity and solubility. Free-radical oxidation, an electrophilic reaction so facile for many organic compounds, is hard to achieve with the dioxins at ambient temperatures. However, at high temperatures (800-1000°C), air oxidation occurs rapidly (Shaub and Tsang, 1983). In laboratory tests, 99.5% of a TCDD sample was oxidized in 21 seconds at 800°C, while only about 50% reacted at 700°C (Esposito et al., 1980).

Table 2. Chemical Properties of Dioxins

1.	Oxidation	Oxygen (combustion)
		Ozone (in water)
		Ruthenium tetroxide
		Radical ion (H_2SO_4)
2.	Reduction	Photochemical (H-abstraction)
		Catalytic (H_2/Pt)
		Electrolytic
3.	Nucleophiles	Alkoxides
		Chloro-iodides
4.	Other Reactions	Electron-impact

However, more powerful oxidizing agents can attack TCDD. Both ozone and ruthenium tetroxide have been reported to react with TCDD (Cavolloni and Zecca, 1977; Wong and Orbanosky, 1979; Ayres, 1981), although products have not yet been identified. In addition, the protonated form of TCDD and other dioxins, which exist in concentrated sulfuric acid or other strong acids, can be air-oxidized to the corresponding blue-purple radical ion (Yang and Pohland, 1973), a reaction already utilized for colorimetric dioxin analysis. Aerobic biodegradation represents a special form of oxidation. Several species of mammals and bacteria have been shown to degrade TCDD or its homologs, and the principal product identified from TCDD is 1-hydroxy-2,3,7,8-tetrachlorodibenzodioxin (Ramsey et al., 1982; Poiger et al., 1982; Philippi et al., 1982; Quensen and Matsumura, 1983). This indicates that oxidative enzymes can attack TCDD, and suggests that reagents generating hydroxyl radicals could also hydroxylate it at the 1-position. Introduction of even a single hydroxyl group can be expected to destablilize the ring and lead to further oxidation and eventual cleavage of the dioxin ring system.

Both electrolytic and catalytic reduction of dioxins have been reported (Esposito et al., 1980; Harrison and Wilkinson, 1981; Harrison et al., 1982). However, most reports concern the photochemical reduction of TCDD and other chlorinated dioxins in organic solvents (Crosby et al., 1971; Plimmer et al., 1973a; Choudhry and Hutzinger, 1982). Photoreduction of octachlorodibenzodioxin (OCDD) has even been used for the preparation of chlorodioxin isomers which otherwise might be very difficult to synthesize (Buser, 1976). The reduction takes place rapidly even in dilute solution (in methanol, for example) (Crosby et al., 1971); chlorines are replaced stepwise by hydrogen, with each stage of dechlorination resulting in increasingly more rapid reduction. Ultraviolet radiation from either a mercury arc (254 nm), fluorescent black-light (300-360 nm), or sunlight energizes the reduction, presumably by generation of a free-radical followed by H-abstraction from the solvent; no reduction occurs in pure water or in crystalline films of TCDD on glass (Plimmer, et al., 1973a). Ionizing radiation (gamma rays) produces the same result (Fanelli, et al., 1978; Buser, 1976). Electron impact in the ionization chamber of a mass spectrometer leads to both dechlorination and loss of carbon monoxide (Plimmer et al., 1973b).

Nucleophiles can react with TCDD. Both alkoxides (such as sodium hydroxide in ethylene glycol) and alkali metal hydroxides or carbonates can react at 140-220°C to convert organic chloride to inorganic chloride (Howard and Sidwell, 1982). Surprisingly, there appear to be no reports of reactions with other powerful nucleophiles, such as amines or thiols, and likewise no evidence for photonucleophilic reactions have been reported. Quaternary ammonium chloroiodides in aqueous media degrade TCDD, and it is possible that a nucleophilic reaction is involved (Botre et al., 1979).

POSSIBLE DISPOSAL PROCEDURES

The physical and chemical properties of TCDD suggest a variety of possible disposal procedures. Oxidative combustion above 800°C is effective, provided that the total residence time is sufficiently long for complete reaction to take place. Satisfactory combustion processes are regularly used by chemical industries and are becoming established elsewhere. While the processes are practical for disposal of chemical wastes or other organic matter, they seem highly impractical for the decontamination of soil and water.

However, the dioxin rings are not immune to other oxidative attack. Ozonolysis presents an attractive possibility for purification of water, even water containing low levels of suspended sediment, while use of the expensive ruthenium oxide might be largely restricted to the purification of fixed streams of air. While the low solubility and low volatility of dioxins render these oxidizing agents unsuitable for general environmental cleanup, removal of these contaminants from recirculating or limited-distribution systems (such as in air conditioning or drinking water) might be more feasible.

Oxidation by living organisms ("metabolism") is another possibility. It seems probable that the natural loss of TCDD from subsurface soil is due largely to microbial action (Young et al., 1976; Ward and Matsumura, 1978; Matsumura et al., 1983). The process is slow among soil microorganisms, perhaps because of the difficult access to the adsorbed dioxins, and attempts to genetically introduce a specific ability to degrade dioxins have so far been unsuccessful (Chakrabarty, 1983). However, TCDD is enzymatically hydroxylated in vivo. This suggests that studies looking at reagents and chemical processes which might be applied to dioxin degradation in vitro, and at the addition of soil modifiers, including moisture and nutrients, may uncover other possible degradation methods (Kearney et al., 1972).

Both catalytic and electrolytic reduction of TCDD offer the possibility of specific decontamination methods by dechlorination of dioxin in solution. However, by far the most applicable reductive dechlorination procedure is photochemical (Crosby, 1983; Wong and Crosby, 1978). The less-chlorinated products are more reactive and less toxic, and the reduction of TCDD is rapid and complete within a matter of hours. The dioxins absorb light above 295 nm, so sunlight can serve as a light source; about half of the effective UV energy reaching the earth's surface comes from the open sky, so exposure to direct sunlight is not necessary.

Three criteria must be met in order for TCDD photolysis to be practical: The wavelengths of incident light must correspond to appreciable absorption by TCDD; the light must penetrate the medium to contact the TCDD; and a source of abstractable hydrogens must be present (water will not do, but herbicide esters or formulating solvents will) (Crosby and Wong, 1977). In practice, this has meant that TCDD degradation was accomplished by exposure to ultraviolet radiation in an organic solvent. Originally, TCDD was thought to be stable in sunlight, because the experiments were conducted in a greenhouse (the window glass filtered out the UV). Thin films of crystalline TCDD were not photolyzed in a glass dish (no H-donor). And once the surface layer of TCDD solution on soil was degraded, no further action occurred in deeper soil (no UV penetration). However, as shown in the next section, in many circumstances the use of UV light for dioxin decontamination is still practical.

Attack on TCDD by nucleophiles represents another possibility. Destruction by alkoxide (such as sodium hydroxide in ethylene glycol) and chloroiodide (as a quaternary ammonium salt) have been demonstrated, and the latter has been observed to reduce TCDD levels in soil by over 50% (Botre et al., 1979). Surprisingly, no application of other nucleophiles such as amines or mercaptans has been reported, and photonucleophilic reactions have received scant attention. As it is effective in aqueous media and near ambient temperature, the chloroiodide procedure holds promise and thus needs more thorough investigation.

Radiolysis by high-energy radiation from radioactive waste presents still another possibility (Buser, 1976). No products have been reported to date; however, high-energy electrons in the ion source of a mass spectrometer produced both dechlorination and TCDD ring decomposition with loss of carbon monoxide (Plimmer et al., 1973b). Both energy sources could conceivably be used to decontaminate wastes or process streams. In addition, there are no reports on the effect of ultrasonic energy on TCDD, a technique which might be applied to soil and sediment.

A review of TCDD degradation and disposal would not be complete without a final solution: do nothing, and let Nature take its course. There is evidence (Bumb, et al., 1980) that dioxins are formed during natural combustion processes. While this source may seem trivial compared to man's input, some detectable buildup over geologic time would be expected if TCDD were completely stable. That this seems not to have happened suggests that combined forces of microbial action, volatility, photolysis, and ozonolysis eventually may destroy low levels of TCDD, as shown by Nash and Beall (1980).

SPECIFIC DISPOSAL EXAMPLES

Laboratory-scale Disposal

Several suggestions have been offered for laboratory disposal of small amounts of dioxins such as may be formed during or left over from experiments (Taft et al., 1983). Experience at UC-Davis has shown that photodegradation is by far the most convenient means for destruction of most TCDD waste (Wong and Crosby, 1978). Small volumes of TCDD solutions in organic solvents (analytical standards, unused sample extracts, etc.) are placed in a jacketed reaction flask or tube (such as a commercial photoreactor) and irradiated with a short-wavelength mercury arc lamp.

Larger volumes (as from equipment rinsing or bench-wiping), containing much additional organic solvent (alcohol), are placed in a closed borosilicate flask or jar in a large Transite cylinder (Crosby and Wong, 1973) and irradiated overnight with "fluorescent blacklights" such as GE F40 BL or Sylvania SF-10. Appropriate solvents for bench cleanup are cellosolves, and lower alcohols make good dilution solvents for the photodegradations; TCDD at 5 mg/L is completely degraded within a few hours, depending on the light intensity (Crosby et al., 1971). While it is not necessary that solutions be colorless, or even transparent, the larger the amount of 310 nm-absorbing interferences present, the longer the dioxin degradation will require. Photochemically reactive solvents must be avoided, and low-boiling solvents (such as ether) could present a fire hazard.

Large-scale Photochemical Degradation

Approximately 4300 gallons of liquid waste from trichlorophenol manufacture was discovered at a Verona, Missouri factory (Sawyer, 1982) and found to contain 343 ppm of TCDD--a total of about 13 pounds. After extensive preliminary examination, it was found that the dioxin could be successfully extracted from the aqueous sludge with hexane and continuously degraded with mercury arc (UV) radiation (Exner et al., 1982). Addition of a small amount of isopropyl alcohol avoided fouling of the lamps with photochemical polymer. This plant-scale operation succeeded in reducing the TCDD level to less than 0.3 ppm, or over 99.9%; complete removal undoubtedly would have been possible had recirculation of the hexane extracts continued for a longer time. The principal hazard was possible ignition of hot solvent rather than TCDD, and careful precautions were taken to avoid and prepare for fire.

Incineration

Complete destruction of TCDD by incineration is theoretically feasible. The largest-scale attempt to date was the incineration of over 2 million gallons (more than 20 million pounds) of contaminated Herbicide Orange--a mixture of liquid butyl esters of 2,4,5-trichlorophenoxyacetic and 2,4-dichlorophenoxyacetic acids containing ppm-levels of TCDD. As overland transport of the mixture to incinerators was precluded by public sentiment, the mixture was combusted at sea in two large furnaces aboard the ship Vulcanus (Esposito et al., 1980).

The herbicide was stored in more than 40,000 steel drums on Johnson Island, several thousand miles southwest of Hawaii. It was pumped aboard, the drums rinsed with diesel fuel, which was added to the rest, and the material burned at an average of 1500°C with sufficient air to provide a 3% excess in the stack gas. Three burn-trips were required for disposal of all of the herbicide (Ackerman et al., 1978).

Despite a combustion efficiency of over 99.9% and the small amount of TCDD involved (a total of under 50 grams), traces of the TCDD were detected in one set of wipe samples from the ship's metal plates and required additional decontamination. However, the principal hazard was the potential for a herbicide spill rather than TCDD itself, and that hazard remains a threat in any similar large-scale disposal attempt.

TCDD Disposal at Seveso

Certainly, one of the most extensive TCDD contamination problems in history occurred because of an industrial accident in a trichlorophenol manufacturing plant in Seveso, Italy, in July of 1976. An estimated 2000 kg of sodium trichlorophenate, containing 100-300 g of TCDD (50-150 ppm) was carried downwind and descended on open grassy fields, small copses of trees, tiled-roof dwellings, and streets in and near the village of Seveso (Pocchiari et al., 1983).

TCDD residues on the most heavily contaminated buildings amounted to many micrograms/m^2; on soil, occasionally over 1 mg/m^2; and on leaves, up to several mg/m^2. The first--and, perhaps, the only-- attempt to destroy the dioxin took place during the month following the accident. The ability of sunlight to degrade TCDD in the presence of a hydrogen-donor had already been established (Crosby et al., 1971). Hand application of a solvent emulsion to a tile roof in Seveso caused complete disappearance of the TCDD in a full day's sunlight. Next, a 400 L/ha spray application of 40% aqueous emulsion of olive oil to a highly-contaminated field resulted in removal of almost 90% of the TCDD within 9 days, reducing the level from 26.2 to 5.2 µg/m^2 (Crosby, 1978; Wipf et al., 1978); repetition of the measurements undoubtedly would have shown eventual complete destruction of TCDD residues. Related experiments also were reported (Liberti et al., 1978).

It is important to note that initially most of the TCDD was present in a thin film on accessible surfaces -- leaves, masonry, roadways -- and loosely bound in a water-soluble sodium trichlorophenate matrix. There was very little on the exposed soil. Besides photochemical destruction, other suggestions for disposal included close mowing of the pastures, defoliation of trees with subsequent incineration of the cuttings, and wet-vacuuming of impervious surfaces with detergent and water-soluble organic solvent followed by exposure of the washings to sunlight.

Needless to say, none of the approaches were attempted, although some scrub-down of interior surfaces was accomplished. At that time, the favorite remedial alternatives were construction of the world's largest cement kiln at Seveso to "burn" all the contaminated soil, or removal of the soil to abandoned salt-mines. Winter came; the leaves, grass, and other surfaces yielded their dioxin to the soil, and the people of Seveso were required to leave their homes. The eventual disposal, initiated in 1980, was accomplished by removal of the top layer of the most contaminated soil and interment in a large, plastic-lined, water-impervious "tomb" covered with a thick layer of reinforced concrete (Noe, 1983), as though dealing with long-lived radioactivity.

CONCLUSIONS

The distinction between dioxin destruction and mere physical removal is important. The people of Lombardy still have their toxic TCDD, and will continue to have it long into the future. It has been hidden away under conditions which assure that it will not break down into nontoxic products. It is merely waiting for another generation of Italians.

Destruction--degradation to less toxic products--is the only solution that makes sense for such a dangerous and persistent substance. As we have seen, methods often are available to at least reduce dioxin levels in the environment, yet more money and effort have been spent on plans for moving toxic residues than has been devoted to seeking and improving methods for their destruction.

The increasing recognition that no-effect exposure levels exist for dioxins in humans and other animals (Cordle, 1983) is extremely significant. It means that complete removal from a location, while desirable, may not be absolutely necessary. Removing 99.9% of a residue usually is much more practical than removing all of it. This makes the accurate detection and measurement of dioxin residues even more important in order to estimate possible exposures and the effort required for reduction of residues to a tolerable level.

Unfortunately, known contamination sites, as well as those yet undiscovered, will provide many opportunities for exploring new methods of dioxin degradation and disposal. In addition, although most of the attention has been focused on the tetrachlorodibenzodioxins, the hexa- and heptachloro-isomers--which come from completely different sources--also are highly toxic and persistent, and the chlorinated dibenzofurans, hexachlorobenzene, and several PCB isomers have some unsavory characteristics in common with dioxins.

Obviously, the circumstances of dioxin occurrence and contamination vary greatly, and each situation has its own individual characteristics. In retrospect, conditions for a major reduction of dioxin levels at Seveso probably were almost ideal, certainly in comparison with those at Times Beach or Binghamton. However, each situation has its own possible avenues for remedy; what we will need is an arsenal of serviceable methods rather than a single "master plan".

This may all sound very simplistic. It is not intended to be so. Under even the best conditions, dioxin contamination presents difficult ameliorization problems. Not least among them has been a strong political and emotional component which on occasion has paralyzed action at the time when it was needed most. In defense of the action finally taken at Seveso, public confidence sometimes may require a "monument"--something people can look at and feel satisfied that action was taken and that problem was solved.

As scientists, we should not confuse the political realities with scientific ones. Dioxins are only chemicals, and they obey discernable physical and chemical laws. The degradation and disposal of chlorinated dioxins are both scientifically and practically possible. If that fact could be accepted more widely, we would be much closer to coming to terms with dioxins in the environment.

REFERENCES

Ackerman, D.G., Fisher, H.J., Johnson, R.J., Maddalone, R.E., Matthews, B.J., Moon, E.L., Scheyer, K.H., Shih, C.C. and Tobias, R.F. 1978. At-sea incineration of Herbicide Orange onboard the M/T Vulcanus, EPA-600/2-78-086, pp. 263, April, Washington, D.C.

Ayres, D.C. 1981. Destruction of polychlorodibenzo-p-dioxins. Nature (London) 290:323-324.

Boer, F.P., Neuman, M.A., Van Remoortere, F.P., North, P.O. and Rinn, H.W. 1973. X-ray diffraction studies of chlorinated dibenzo-p-dioxins. Adv. in Chem. Ser. 120:14-25.

Botre, C., Memoli, C.A. and Alhaique, F. 1979. On the degradation of 2,3,7,8-tetrachlorodibenzodioxin (TCDD) by means of a new class of chloroiodides. Environ. Sci. Technol. 13:228-231.

Bumb, R.R., Crummett, W.B., Cutie, S.S., Gledhill, J.R., Hummel, R.H., Kagel, R.O., Lamparski, L.L., Luoma, E.V., Miller, D.L., Nestrick, T.J., Shadoff, L.A., Stehl, R.H. and Woods, J.S. 1980. Trace chemistries of fire: A source of chlorinated dioxins. Science 210:385-390.

Buser, H.R. 1976. Preparation of qualitative standard mixtures of polychlorinated dibenzo-p-dioxins and dibenzofurans by ultraviolet and gamma-irradiation of the octachloro compounds. J. Chromatog. 129:303-307.

Cavolloni, L. and Zecca, L. 1977. La decomposizione del TCDD mediante ozono. Med. Termalee Climat. 34:73-74.

Chakrabarty, A.M. 1983. University of Illinois-Chicago. Personal communication. November, 1983.

Choudhry, G.G. and Hutzinger, O. 1982. Photochemical formation and degradation of chlorinated dibenzofurans and dibenzo-p-dioxins. Residue Rev. 84:113-161.

Cordle, F. 1983. Use of epidemiology in the regulation of dioxins in the food supply. In Accidental Exposure to Dioxins, eds. F. Coulston and F. Pocchiari, pp. 245-256, Academic Press, New York.

Crosby, D.G. 1978. Conquering the monster: The photochemical destruction of chlorinated dioxins. ACS Symposium Ser. 73:1-12.

Crosby, D.G. 1983. Methods of photochemical degradation of halogenated dioxins in view of environmental reclamation. In Accidental Exposure to Dioxins, eds. F. Coulston and F. Pocchiari, pp. 149-161, Academic Press, New York.

Crosby, D.G. and Wong, A.S. 1973. Photodecomposition of 2,4,5-trichlorophenoxyacetic acid (2,4,5-T) in water. J. Agr. Food Chem. 21:1052-1054.

Crosby, D.G. and Wong, A.S. 1977. Environmental degradation of 2,3,7,8-tetrachlorodibenzo-p-dioxin (TCDD). Science 195:1337-1338.

Crosby, D.G., Wong, A.S., Plimmer, J. and Woolson, E.A. 1971. Photodecomposition of chlorinated dibenzo-p-dioxins. Science 173:748-749.

Esposito, M.P., Tiernan, T.O. and Dryden, F.E. 1980. Dioxins, EPA 600/2-80-197, pp. 257-270, Cincinnati, OH.

Exner, J.H., Johnson, J.D., Ivins, O.D., Wass, M.N. and Miller, R.A. 1982. Process for destroying tetrachlorodibenzo-p-dioxin in a hazardous waste. In Detoxication of Hazardous Waste, ed. J.H. Exner, pp. 269-287, Ann Arbor Science Publishers, Ann Arbor, MI.

Fanelli, R., Chiabrando, C., Salmona, M., Garattini, S. and Caldera, P.G. 1978. Degradation of 2,3,7,8-tetrachlorodibenzo-p-dioxin in organic solvents by gamma-ray irradiation. Experientia 34:1126-1127.

Harrison, J.M. and Wilkinson, R.G. 1981. Electrochemical degradation of persistent organic compounds with harmful or potentially harmful properties. Eur. Pat. Appl. 27,745, April 29; C.A. 95:85851.

Harrison, J.M., Inch, T.D. and Wilkinson, R.G. 1982. The electrochemical decomposition of TCDD. Chem. Ind. (London) 1982:373.

Howard, K.S. and Sidwell, A.E. 1982. Chemical detoxification of toxic chlorinated aromatic compounds. U.S. Patent 4,327,027, 27 April 1982; C.A. 97.

Kearney, P.C., Woolson, E.A. and Ellington, C.P. 1972. Persistence and metabolism of chlorodioxins in soils. Environ. Sci. Technol. 6:1017-1019.

Liberti, A., Brocco, D., Allegrini, C. and Bertoni, G. 1978. Field photodegradation of TCDD by ultraviolet radiation. In Dioxin: Toxicological and Chemical Aspects, eds. F.

Cattabeni, A. Cavallaro, and G. Galli, p. 195, SP Medical and Scientific Books, New York.

Matsumura, F., Quensen, J. and Tsushimoto, G. 1983. Microbial degradation of TCDD in a model ecosystem. In Human and Environmental Risks of Chlorinated Dioxins and Related Compounds, eds. R.E. Tucker, A.L. Young, and A.P. Gray, pp. 191-219, Plenum Press, New York.

Mill, T. 1983. SRI International, Menlo Park, CA. Personal communication, December, 1983.

Miller, G.C., Sontum, S. and Crosby, D.G. 1977. Electron-acceptor properties of chlorinated dibenzo-p-dioxins. Bull. Environ. Contam. Toxicol. 18:611-616.

Nash, R.G. and Beall, M.L. 1980. Distribution of Silvex, 2,4-D, and TCDD applied to turf in chambers and field plots. J. Agr. Food Chem. 28:614-623.

Noe, L. 1983. Reclamation of the TCDD-contaminated Seveso area. In Accidental Exposure to Dioxins, eds. F. Coulston and F. Pocchiari, pp. 69-77, Academic Press, New York.

Philippi, M., Schmid, J., Wipf, H.K. and Huetter, R. 1982. A microbial metabolite of TCDD. Experientia 38:659-661.

Plimmer, J.R., Klingebiel, U.I., Crosby, D.G. and Wong, A.S. 1973a. Photochemistry of dibenzo-p-dioxins. Adv. Chem Ser. 120:44-54.

Plimmer, J.R., Ruth, J.M. and Woolson, E.A. 1973b. Mass spectrometric identification of the hepta- and octachlorinated dibenzo-p-dioxins and dibenzofurans in technical pentachlorophenol. J. Agr. Food Chem. 21:90-93.

Pocchiari, F., DiDomenico, A., Silano, V. and Zapponi, G. 1983. Environmental impact of the accidental release of tetrachlorodibenzo-p-dioxin (TCDD) at Seveso (Italy). In Accidental Exposure to Dioxins, eds. F. Coulston and F. Pocchiaro, pp. 5-35, Academic Press, New York.

Poiger, H., Buser, H.R., Weber, H., Zweifel, U. and Schlatter, C. 1982. Structure elucidation of mammalian TCDD-metabolites. Experientia 38:484-486.

Quensen, J.F. and Matsumura, F. 1983. Oxidative degradation of 2,3,7,8-tetrachlorodibenzo-p-dioxin by microorganisms. Environ. Toxicol. Chem. 2: in press.

Ramsey, J.C., Hefner, J.G., Korbowski, R.J., Braun, W.H. and Gehring, P.J. 1983. The in vivo biotransformation of 2,3,7,8-tetrachlorodibenzo-p-dioxin (TCDD) in the rat. Toxicol. Appl. Pharmacol. 65:180-184.

Sawyer, C.J. 1982. Environmental health and safety considerations for a dioxin detoxication process. In Detoxication of Hazardous Waste, ed. J.H. Exner, pp. 289-297, Ann Arbor Science Publishers, Ann Arbor, MI.

Shaub, W.M. and Tsang, W. 1983. Physical and chemical properties of dioxins in relation to their disposal. In Human and Environmental Risks of Chlorinated Dioxins and Related Compounds, eds. R.E. Tucker, A.L. Young, and A.P. Gray, pp. 731-747, Plenum Press, New York.

Taft, L.G., Beltz, P.R. and Garrett, B.C. 1983. Laboratory handling and disposal of chlorinated dioxin wastes. In Human and Environmental Risks of Chlorinated Dioxins and Related Compounds, eds. R.E. Tucker, A.L. Young, and A.P. Gray, pp. 717-729, Plenum

Press, New York.

Veerkamp, W., Serne, P. and Hutzinger, O.   1983.   Prediction of hydroxylated metabolites in polychlorodibenzo-p-dioxins and polychlorodibenzofurans by Hueckel molecular orbital calculations. J. Chem. Soc., Perkin Trans. 2:353-358.

Ward, C.T. and Matsumura, F.   1978.   Fate of 2,3,7,8-TCDD in a model aquatic environment. Arch. Environ. Contam. Toxicol. 7:349-357.

Wipf, H., Homberger, E., Neuner, N. and F. Schenker.   1978.   Field trials on photodegradation of TCDD on vegetation after spraying with vegetable oil. In Dioxin: Toxicological and Chemical Aspects, eds. F. Cattabeni, A. Cavallaro, and G. Galli, pp. 201-207, SP Medical and Scientific Books, New York.

Wong, A.S. and Crosby, D.G. 1978. Decontamination of 2,3,7,8-tetrachlorodibenzodioxin (TCDD) by photochemical action. In Dioxin: Toxicological and Chemical Aspects, eds. F. Cattabeni, A. Cavallaro, and G. Galli, pp. 185-191, SP Medical and Scientific Books, New York.

Wong, A.S. and Orbansky, M. 1979. Ozonation of 2,3,7,8-tetrachlorodibenzo-p-dioxin (TCDD) in water. Abstr. 178th National Meeting, ACS, Washington, D.C. PEST 83.

Yang, G.C. and Pohland, A.E.   1973.   Cation radicals of chlorinated dibenzo-p-dioxins. Adv. in Chem. Ser. 120:33-43.

Young, A.L., Thalker, C.E., Arnold, E.L., Cupello, J.M. and Cockerham, L.G. 1976. Fate of 2,3,7,8-tetrachlorodibenzo-p-dioxin (TCDD) in the environment: Summary and decontamination recommendations. USAFA-TR-76-18, USAF Academy, Boulder, Co.

Chapter 14

PANEL DISCUSSION - SECTION 3

FREEMAN:	This is for Dr. Mill. You reported a vapor pressure of 7 times 10^4. What is the temperature associated with that point?
MILL:	7×10^{-10}. At 25°.
CYNAR:	This question is directed primarily to Dr. Gross, but perhaps Dr. Crosby might be willing to include an answer. Much information was given this morning and yesterday on municipal incinerators. As far as your study is concerned, what method of incineration was used; what temperatures were these incinerators operated at; did they or did they not include fluidized bed combustion? Is it not true fluidized bed incineration or combustion at or near 1000^oC will destroy dioxins?
GROSS:	The data I reported were taken principally from the literature although the data did include some results from our own laboratory. The results from our own laboratory were not from fluidized bed combustors. I believe, and Dr. Hutzinger is here and perhaps he can verify, one of the incinerators from Sweden sampled by Rappe is a fluidized bed and that incinerator showed the lowest levels. In fact, it showed not detectable levels of some of the PCDD congeners although there were detectable but low levels of all PCDF congeners. I tried to make the point that a whole spectrum of emission levels exist starting perhaps with what you might call very sloppy forms of incineration, solid waste incineration, not fluidized bed, and extending through coal combustion. There were examples of wood combustion reported by Dow that showed very, very low levels of dioxins. There is, indeed, a very large spectrum of emissions. I also tried to make the point that, in many cases, these should be regarded as preliminary results since it's very difficult to make comparisons because not all of the conditions are known, and cannot be found in the literature reports.
RODGERS:	Dr. Crosby, do you have anything to add?
CROSBY:	Of course, for any of these industrial scale processes, and incineration is one of them, in putting through a large volume of material, whatever escapes from the stack is going to depend on a complex mix of parameters. As I pointed out in the case of the photochemical destruction of the Missouri waste TCDD, we could

have kept going past 0.3 parts per million but the rates of destruction decrease and the hazard increases. The same thing could be said in relation to your questions about incineration combustion. It probably would be possible to completely remove dioxins, or any other organics, from stack gases if recirculation was carried out long enough. For each particular batch, it gets to be a question of how hot are you going to heat it and what is going to be the acceptable amount of effluent. These are difficult questions to try to decide.

CULLUM: Dr. Young, I'd like for you to comment, if you would, on a recent report I saw in Natural History. It's an editorial comment by a faculty member of the State University of New York, who was trapping field mouse-type rodents around the perimeter fence of Love Canal. Did you happen to see that?

YOUNG: No, go ahead, please.

CULLUM: Using some skeletal parameters to determine the age of the animals, he found fewer animals than in adjacent areas not on the perimeter fence and he also found that the animals that were there had a shorter lifespan, and both of those were statistically significant, I believe. I don't know if it was TCDD that he was looking at specifically. I don't know that he did fat pad deposits. I don't remember. Could you comment?

YOUNG: Well, Love Canal certainly didn't just have dioxins. I think you recognize that it was a hodgepodge of material. I don't know the particular habits of the mouse in the study you referenced, but I can assure you that we did, in fact, have a very large control population as well as an exposed population and we didn't just make one year of observation. We have followed them for many years, and I think any good field study has to be done that way. You're going to have to let this individual get out and publish it somewhere outside the newspaper, I suspect, so that we can really evaluate it.

CULLUM: I don't think that the journal of the American Museum of Natural History is a newspaper.

YOUNG: I can't comment on it. I don't know how scientifically valid they report the work. I'm simply saying that I think we've got to see a little more data.

CULLUM: The point was that he checked the skeleton to determine how long the mice were living.

YOUNG: We did all those measurements, too. We didn't see anything.

CULLUM: I just want a comment from you on that.

YOUNG: I didn't see the data, I'm sorry. We have looked at bone length, we've looked at skeletal anomalies, and we did look very hard for those. I think Dr. Gross made a very interesting observation of the Eglin animals, that there is a lack of other compounds in them. They're very, very clean animals; almost pristine except for TCDD. The site had not received any DDT. It had been set aside by the military since 1930 and that site had been almost exclusively for the dissemination of herbicide as part of the equipment-developing program. The 2,4-D and the 2,4,5-T had long disappeared, so we had an opportunity not to be confused with other compounds.

LOWER: There are about 500,000 tons of contaminated soil currently known in Missouri. We figure that pyrolysis or what has been classically looked at as solvent extraction would cost between a half billion and 5 billion dollars just to eradicate the current problem in Missouri. My question to the panel is: Can you discuss, and perhaps rank order in your own minds, procedures which might be followed or lines of investigation to develop alternative methods for the destruction of dioxin and other chemicals?

CROSBY: I'm going to bring out what is my very obvious prejudice in all this. I think it would be worthwhile to look at trying to use sunlight. Now this time of year is not the ideal time but perhaps this is something that could be applied in the coming year. I think both Al Young's and our own group have carried out some experiments; in our case so limited that we've not published them. These were on the effectiveness of treating the surface of contaminated soil with a low volatility solvent. We like diethylene glycol for several reasons; it is non-toxic (low,low toxicity), doesn't evaporate easily, is sticky, viscous, and sticks to the surface, and you put it on in a very, very thin layer. That allows the photolysis of whatever TCDD is on the surface. Then in a matter of days or weeks, you lightly till the soil, turn it over, and if necessary, again apply a very, very thin spray of diethylene glycol. After several tries, we were able to substantially decrease the dioxin level. I think Al has done it by adding soil amendments of one sort or another to organic material in the soil. Now, are these highly developed methods that you could walk right in and use? No, they certainly are not. It would be worth trying some experiments of this sort before you resort to destroying the environment by scraping up the soil and burning it. That would be just one possibility. Another possibility that we have not tried and others have not tried is to steam the soil. We have evidence, and many others do too, that dioxin, TCDD, is steam-volatile to a limited extent; it co-distills. It may be possible to steam the stuff out or at least lower the level. Again, I'm prejudiced in that I don't think that you have to get down to zero detectable at the part per trillion level but that some level could be set as tolerable.

YOUNG: I would just like to add one comment. The problem we have is time and the public concern. If we only had the time to do some experiments with those soils and try various methods, we probably would be successful. What I fear is that in such a situation as Missouri, one does not very often get enough time. The public demands immediately that we do something and I know that they do plan to put it in a large basin. They're proposing that and as much as I would hate to say it, that may be the poorest solution scientifically. As someone who's concerned about public policy, I suggest that you've got to remove it from the public's sight. They don't want to see their community with large piles of dioxin-contaminated soil. What worries me is that we're not going to be given, I don't think, much time to play with their yards. I think they're going to ask us to lift up that soil, get rid of it, put new soil down, and experiment with it at the location where we put it.

CROSBY: There's another point that I'm reminded of in defense of the decision at Seveso. That is, in considering the public's reaction to this, there is importance in having a monument. I'm absolutely serious in that. The people don't understand all this stuff we're talking about and they can see that concrete dome out there and say, "By gosh, my problem is solved. There's where it is." And I'm sympathetic with that.

GASIEWICZ: I'd like to address this to Dr. Young concerning the Eglin mice. Since there's a large body of evidence which shows the inter- and intraspecific differences in sensitivity to the compound, and since it was many years after the initial spraying at the Eglin Air Force Base by the time you looked at the mice that were present in the population, is it possible that any sensitive population may have been wiped out or you missed the reproduction effects that may have occurred within the first few years and you were essentially looking at an insensitive population of mice?

YOUNG: I think that's a realistic possibility. I would say, however, we didn't fail to consider it, but this was a field study. We didn't have the luxury of doing all the things you like to do in the laboratory, so what we did was to go out a couple of miles from the site, set up cages and we began to trap animals to understand their movement. We even went so far as to tag animals and document that new individuals were coming into the test range during the time we were doing our work. So, although we were removing mice, the mice were being replaced by others coming to the site. The question I wonder about is: Did some of the originally exposed mice move out and with the change of habitat outside come back into this nice bare area because beach mice have to have bare area? It's the nature of the habitat and when it gets to be too much vegetation, as is now occurring at Eglin, the beach mouse moves or dies out. He can't excape his predator when there's too much vegetation.

GASIEWICZ: Have you rated the relative sensitivities compared to other species that are considered as mammalian?

YOUNG: Where we have really failed is not doing an LD_{50} of the beach mouse and submitting it to someone like you to do the enzymatic work-up of the livers.

TSCHIRLEY: Dr. Young, you inferred that a large number of plant samples were analyzed, but is it indeed true that you did analyze plant samples and were there negative results from them?

YOUNG: The seeds of many of the grass and small herbaceous plants were negative at the detection limit of about 1 ppt. But, Fred, we did in fact select a specific site in cooperation with Mike Gross and we've never published much of this information, unfortunately. In connection with Mike, we attempted to extract roots, culms in the case of the grasses, stems in the case of the herbaceous plants, and leaves. Yes, we did find TCDD in them, and they varied by orders of magnitude as you went up. We found 600 and 700 ppt in the roots growing in the soils that contained 600 and

700 ppt. The problem was, as Mike and I found, that we couldn't remove the soil from the roots, and so we weren't sure whether we were measuring more soil; but it does appear that there was some in the roots. The next level up went from 600 to about 60. We dropped by order of magnitude in the leaves and in the stems. Again, Mike and I could not show that these were free of soil. In the leaves we saw very, very low levels -- parts per trillion, 6 ppt or less.

TSCHIRLEY: Did you have any fruit of those plants analyzed?

YOUNG: We never found any TCDD in any of the seeds of the species. We felt that the deer and the rabbits that we observed feeding on that vegetation should have been contaminated and yet they were not. I can't explain to you why they weren't other than to say you can't keep a rabbit on a 32-acre area if you don't have a fence around it, and we didn't. We actually put radio collars on a whole herd of deer; monitored them coming in and monitored coming out. They obviously spent only a small amount of their time on the test range. When you have an unlimited amount of resources, you can do a whole lot. We had a lot of money into this one.

STALLING: I'd like to express an opinion and also address a question that is related. First, Dr. Crosby, I think the problem with containment of these contaminated soils is one that demands some kind of action, i.e., to minimize the potential for dispersement through the environment. With that possibility in mind, I wonder if you are aware of or would care to comment on the possibility of combining two problems. We have a large amount of radioactive materials available: Have you considered the use of ionizing radiation as a source of energy to activate the dechlorination or destruction of these materials? When we were doing Agent Orange, we proposed some work on the destruction of these materials on carbon. As a first step, we sent several grams to Scandia and asked them to put that in a cobalt pile and irradiate it. To our surprise, when it came back, I think we had about 95% of the TCDD recovered after just intensive radiation. This suggests that some type of electronic coupling occurs on the carbon surface in the adsorption process. What I don't know is whether adding an organic compound, such as a hydrogen donor, to that kind of sample or to the soil with your ethylene glycol and then irradiating would prove feasible. I'd like to have you speculate on that.

CROSBY: That's about all I can do is speculate. We haven't done any work with ionizing radiation. There is work reported in the literature; half a dozen papers and patents indicating an effect of radiation on TCDD. Another indication of an effect has been found, interestingly enough, in a mass spectrometer. You bombard TCDD molecules with moderately high energy electrons, 50 electron volts or something like that, and then look at what happens electronically. Of course the product of that is what we refer to as a mass spectrum. What has happened is a chemical reaction has taken place and the fragments that you see, in addition to the molecular ion, indicate the sequential loss of chlorines and the loss of carbon monoxide. Since this is a vacuum, the carbon monoxide can only come from the carbon and the oxygen that's in dioxin. It seems to me that radiolysis would be a very good possibility and an interesting and important thing to look at.

SUSKIND: Those of us who are concerned with adverse health effects are always interested in knowing what the biologic outcomes are in terms of availability of toxic agents within the body. I would like to ask the panel, since one of the notable biological outcomes happens to be cutaneous, whether there's any good information other than that presented by Dr. Young on the hides of the mice, about the analysis of the skin -- not the liver, not the brain, not the lung -- for TCDD or its metabolites. If we think of the metabolism of the polycyclic aromatic hydrocarbons and its relation to lung cancer, we think of how the lung metabolizes benzpyrene, for example, and what the lung does in biotransforming the benzpyrene to epoxides and diols, etc. I'm curious to know whether there is similar interest on the part of the analytic chemist, not to ignore the toxicologist from whom we're going to hear this afternoon. I would like to hear from the chemists about their knowledge of TCDD and its metabolites in the skin.

YOUNG: We were very interested in finding out if TCDD was passing through the skin of the beach mouse. And were there any anomalies on the skin of the beach mouse that we might attribute to the chemical exposure? To that end, we did remove the skin and it was looked at by patholgists at the Armed Forces Institute of Pathology. In addition, we separated the skin out. The problem is we didn't shave it. So one still has the pelage on it, the fur, and the skin analysis with the fur is what I reported on the table. We did look at some muscle samples and found no TCDD in the muscle suggesting that at least it wasn't accumulating right there. We didn't do enough work to really be able to answer your question. We didn't see any gross lesions on the skin.

SUSKIND: Absorption of dioxin is not necessarily through the skin. There's lots of evidence -- Seveso, Nitro, you name it -- where the portal of entry was the skin and the gastrointestinal tract and the respiratory tract, but it got to the skin as well. The target organ was the skin.

YOUNG: I see. You're suggesting coming through and coming back to the skin. Perhaps.

SUSKIND: Well, at least an active agent which affects the skin and a variety of components of it.

YOUNG: As a weeds man, I can't answer that one.

ROGERS: My question is probably to Dr. Crosby, and probably is not a question; just some comments on alternate methods for treatment of haloorganics. In January this past year, we conducted some studies with Wright State University on the use of glycols and earlier, someone mentioned ethylene glycol. In laboratory tests, both EPA and extramural, we determined that the monoglycol is not as effective as the high molecular weight glycols as a nucleophile for removing chlorine atoms from haloorganics. We determined that these reagents, with molecular weights of 350 to 400, will dehalogenate TCDD and other compounds under ambient conditions. The EPA is interested in developing methods for in situ destruction of these compounds. I agree with you that it's probably a waste of funds to immediately cart out these soils when there's a distinct possibility that they might be decontaminated in place. When we tested the reagent in solutions of around 510 nanograms of TCDD, the chemical was completely destroyed within a matter of 48 hours and could not be detected by the Wright State people in parts per trillion. When we tested the reagents with TCDD contaminated soils, there was initially a reduction in TCDD. However, that ceased, and I think the problem is that of desorption. If anyone can help with or can provide information on desorbing this material, I think we can then destroy the material in soils.

CROSBY: Were you referring to the use of something like diethylene glycol as a hydrogen donor for photolysis?

ROGERS: Yes, I'm thinking about the nucleophilic substitution.

CROSBY: Did you use a sodium derivative, for example?

ROGERS: A sodium alkali base derivative as a nucleophile.

CROSBY: I'm surprised it goes that fast, and I'm delighted to hear that.

AUDIENCE MEMBERS CONTRIBUTING TO THE PANEL DISCUSSION: Raymond Freeman, Monsanto Chemical Company, 800 N. Lindberg, St. Louis, MO 63167; David Cynar, Resource Recovery, Warren Waste to Energy Associates, 30100 Van Dyke, Warren, MI 38093; Malford E. Cullum, Food Science and Human Nutrition, Michigan State University, East Lansing, MI 48824; William Lower, University of Missouri, ETSRC-Route #3, Columbia, MO 65201; Thomas Gasiewicz, University of Rochester, Department of Biology, Rochester, NY 14642; and Charles Rogers, U.S. Environmental Protection Agency, 26 W. St. Clare, Cincinnati, OH 45268.

Section 4
Toxicology of Dioxins

Chapter 15

BIOLOGICAL EFFECTS OF DIOXINS AND OTHER HALOGENATED POLYCYCLICS

Edward A. Smuckler
University of California - San Francisco

INTRODUCTION

Society has dealt with purposeful animal intoxication, be it human or other lower forms, especially those carried out with evil intent, since time began. The days of the royal "taster" have been replaced by an extensive investigative network to approach both accidental and intentional poisonings. The post-World War II period with its intensive and extensive means of environmental modification produced an improved quality of life, but carried with it an explosive growth in the synthetic chemical industry necessary to provide the means for this improvement. By-products as well as formulated chemicals with specific design were introduced, intentionally and unintentionally, into our ecosystem.

One outgrowth of the technical advances and our increased understanding of injury was the recognition that we had also produced another series of diseases related to the very agents that improved our lot. Perhaps nowhere else is this so well recognized as in occupational exposure to hazardous chemicals and the exposure to the public at large to the same agent either during use or following their manufacture. For substantiation of this claim one need only peruse the daily newspaper, or for that matter, look at the list of meetings, such as this one, directed to dioxins alone (Coulston and Pocchiari, 1983). Markedly controversial positions have been taken, from impending doom to an absence of cause for concern (Epstein, 1983; Anonymous, 1983b).

Many other reviews have developed from these meetings, and extensive discussions of the effects of these several chemicals on a variety of animal species, including man, have taken place (Fox, 1983; National Academy of Sciences, 1979; Epstein, 1979). A major task that still confronts us is how to extrapolate animal study findings to mankind, and to do so with the human epidemiological studies as a background. These extrapolations pose a number of inherent problems besides the species differences, such as exposure (duration, amount, etc.), the agents involved (purity, contaminants), and man himself (a poorly inbred species subject to a variety of other environmental factors including his diet). A brief review of the chemicals, the animal data, and the problems related to man's exposure seems to be in order.

CHEMICALS INVOLVED

Dioxins are only one group of polycyclic halogenated carbon-oxygen ring structures that have widespread animal responses (Harris et al., 1973). Even within the chlorinated dioxins, isomers have markedly different potencies as toxins. Some of these chemicals arise as products of directed synthesis (PCBs, PBBs); others are the by-products of this synthetic process (dioxins, dibenzofurans). The major sources of the latter inadvertent by-product are the synthesis of phenoxy herbicides, and polyhalogenated biphenyls used as poorly flammable dielectrics or hydraulic fluids. In point of fact, it was only in the last several decades that the technology for the detection of these contaminants was perfected. Furthermore, the toxicity of these chemicals became apparent through safety testing on lower animals and observation of the results of accidental exposure to man. The recognition of hazard prompted regulation of synthesis and use. At the present time, further manufacture of most of the chemicals has ceased and a concomitant decrease in environmental and animal levels has been noted (National Academy of Sciences, 1979; Anonymous, 1983a). That these chemicals produce diseases has stimulated considerable interest in the mechanisms of action of the group in animal species and the potential hazard to man. Extensive analyses by Poland, Kimbrough, Kociba, and Neal have pointed to the fact that the polyhalogenated biphenyls, the dibenzofurans, and the dibenzodioxins have very similar responses in animals (Poland and Knutson, 1982; Kimbrough, 1974). In fact, these agents are more potent than the phenoxy herbicides, and, of the dioxins, at least one isomer has been claimed to be one of the most potent poisons (teratogen and carcinogen) to which man is exposed. Poland, on the basis of structure-function relationships, has suggested that their toxic properties be considered together and suggests that a similar receptor may be responsible for the cellular changes produced by each. This raises two major problems that make understanding human illness difficult:

1.   The very similar, if not identical, responses seen with these several agents can be interpreted to mean that they all have the same modality for producing injury (Poland and Knutson, 1982; Andres et al., 1983). It must also be recalled that the purity of the materials used in the testing can be called into question, and the effects may be those of a minor but particularly potent agent. Additionally, the principal agent may augment the effect of other toxic agents present in lesser quantity. These considerations seem less likely with the materials employed in laboratory studies, but certainly must be considered when technical grade material is used for toxicology testing and, importantly, in the real world situations where diverse, potentially toxic, compounds act together. Also, the period of time at which the studies were undertaken is important since the purity of the desired product has been improved, and contaminants such as dioxins have been reduced.

2.   Epidemiological studies in man are complicated by the fact that the workers and the public at large are rarely exposed to a single chemical. This synthetic potpourri complicates the studies by the diversity of agents to which they are exposed at work, and additionally, by their own dietary and social habits (e.g. alcohol consumption and smoking) which further modify their physical well being and their responses to exogenous stimuli. It should be noted that subtle differences did occur in the exposure to similar PCBs that occurred in Japan and Taiwan (Kuratsune et al., 1972; Li et al., 1981).

ANIMAL EFFECTS

The effects of this group of polycyclics on diverse animal species has been reviewed by Poland (Poland and Knutson, 1982), gathering together the data on PCBs, PBBs, dibenzodioxins, and dibenzofurans. Remarkable species differences occur in response to any one or many of these potential toxicants, and a carry-over still exists in many diverse species (see Table 1). To summarize briefly:

TABLE 1. Histological Lesion Produced by TCDD, PCB, PBB or Dibenzofurans

Epithelial Changes	Hyperplasia and/or metaplasia of gut epithelium in monkey, cow, hamster, and of:
	... urinary tract in monkey, cow, guinea pig ... bile duct and/or gall bladder of monkey/cow/mouse ... skin of monkey, cow, rabbit and mouse
Liver Lesion	Monkey, guinea pig, rat, mouse, rabbit, chicken and hamster
Hemato-/Lympho-proliferative Depression in	Monkey, guinea pig, cow, rat, mouse, chicken and hamster
Edema (Vascular change?)	Monkey, mouse, rabbit, chicken and hamster
Wasting	All species

Acute Lethality

The guinea pig seems to be the most sensitive animal; between 1 and 2 µg/kg will cause the demise of 50% of a subject population. Chick embryos are somewhat more resistant; 20 µg/kg are required to reach an LD_{50}, and hamsters are the most resistant species tested requiring between 2000-5000 µg/kg to achieve a similar level of lethality. In spite of a very critical series of examinations, the cause of death in these animals is not known. Hepatic necrosis has been implicated in rats; yet this alone seems temporally unrelated to the demise, much in the same manner that CCl_4 and thioacetamide poisoning produce diverse effects in addition to liver injury (Barker and Smuckler, 1973; Barker and Smuckler, 1974). Although a variety of organ responses have been described, no single one of them seems to be the basis of lethality. Even supportive nutritional supplementation does not provide protection against death (Gasiewicz et al., 1980).

There are no data to provide a realistic estimate of human sensitivity, but the more recent Seveso accident suggests that mankind is more, rather than less, resistant (Coulston and Pocchiari, 1983). This notion is further supported by both the Japanese and the Taiwanese cooking oil exposures (Kuratsune et al., 1972; Li et al., 1981).

Lymphoid Involution

Animals exposed to these halogenated hydrocarbons show a thymic and lymphoid involution, a change that is suggested to be an indirect effect. Clearly, the injury associated with a single dose capable of causing somatic death can also cause stress suffecient to stimulate the adrenal-pituitary axis and, indirectly, cause this change (Harris et al., 1973).

Liver Changes

In all species tested there is a liver enlargement. This is associated with increases in the quantity of ergastoplasm in the hepatocyte as well as an increased level of activity of the mixed function oxidase system, and a hepatic based porphyria (Kimbrough, 1974; Poland and Kende, 1976; Parkinson et al., 1983; De Verneuil et al., 1983). Only mice, rats, and rabbits show cell death, the former as a central necrosis, the latter as a scattered hepatocyte loss (Poland and Knutson, 1982).

Epithelial Change

The stratified squamous epithelium show an increased activity with both a hyperplasia and a hyperkeratosis (see Fig. 1). This affects the skin appendages as well, and results in the Meibomian gland changes in the eyelids, chloracne, and even produces changes in the respiratory epithelium. Although mice are supposedly resistant to this change, a distinct hyperkeratosis follows the skin painting.

Gastrointestinal Changes

In monkeys, cows, and hamsters, there is hyperplasia of the glandular element of the GI tract.

Chick Edema

Chickens exposed to dioxins develop acites and a hydropericardium. The mechanism underlying these changes, and especially the integrity of the vascular system, has not been investigated. It should be noted that rabbits also develop edema when treated with dioxin, and that this modification occurs on the anterior thoracic wall.

Carcinogenicity

There is little question that these agents are carcinogenic in rats. In point of fact, they produce both squamous cell carcinomata of the upper respiratory tract and liver cell cancers. Recent studies point to TCDD as a promoter more than as an initiator (Poland and Knutson, 1982).

Reproductive Effect

Reproductive effects of long term feeding of these agents have been described in monkeys, including testicular changes and fetotoxicity. Teratogenic responses have been seen in rodents.

Mutagenicity

Initial surveys of mutagenicity failed to reveal a response in bacterial species. More recent and extensive surveys have shown a possible mutagenic effect (Anonymous, 1983b).

These data point to several target organs that deserve continued scrutiny. Regardless of route of administration, a significant stimulus for epidermal growth occurs. The change is not associated with an alteration in maturation, merely excessive keratinization

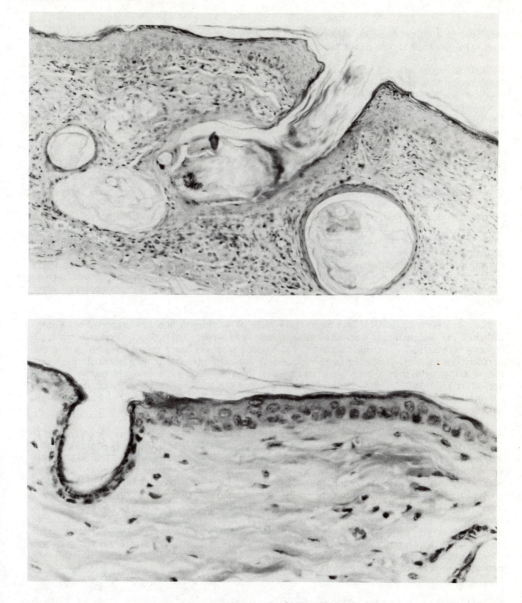

Figure 1: These are micrographs of mouse skin. The upper photo is from a mouse exposed to 2,3,7,8-tetrachlorodibenzo-p-dioxin. Notice the thickened and hypercellular epithelium. (Reduced from magnification about X200.) In addition, the follicles could become plugged with the exuberant formation of keratinized material. This histologic pattern is identical to the one seen in humans exposed to the same material. Compare this to the lower photo of the normal structure of mouse skin. (Reduced from magnification X250.) Note the thin, multilayered epithelium and the hair shaft cut tangentially. The geometric appearance of the hair shaft may suggest a plugged follicle, but in reality it is not.

resulting in a chloracne-like picture. In fact, chloracne may be a marker for exposure in man. Only in rodents (to date) have epithelial-derived neoplasms been found.

Hepatic changes are also marked. In fact, TCDD is a recognized inducer of the mixed-function oxidase system, of cytochrome P450s, and additionally increases the efficacy of bilirubin excretion and results in porphyria. These observations point to a potentially more widespread effect, in this sense, similar to phenobarbital. Perhaps the liver changes are more a growth stimulus, like phenobarbital. How many of these animal data carry over to human beings?

HUMAN EXPOSURE EXPERIENCE

Several accidents have provided us with considerable information concerning acute and subacute exposure to dioxins and polyhalogenated biphenyls (Zach and Suskind, 1980; Coulston and Pocchiari, 1983). Oral ingestion of related but not identical polychlorinated biphenyls occurred in Japan and Taiwan. The human response involved epithelial tissue with alteration in Meibomian glands, acneiform eruptions, skin pigmentation and neurological changes, including headache, dizziness, and paresthesias. Effects on reproduction are more difficult to separate. Some incidence of premature pregnancy termination was seen in women with particularly high levels of PCBs, and babies born to exposed women were frequently hyperpigmented, but even these changes resolved after birth.

Human exposure to TCDDs has been the result of accidents and few exposed have been followed for a significant period of time (since 1953 with publication as recently as 1983) (Thiess et al., 1983). In this instance, 74 exposed workers were identified, 70 during the accident and 4 more involved in the cleanup. As controls, the populations of the town, the district, and the county were used. Notably, 66 of the 74 had chloracne. In the period of study (1953-1980) the mortality rate for the exposed workers was the same as for the control groups, (21/74 compared to 18/74 and 19/74). By way of contrast, a small, but significant, increase in stomach cancer was found.

A second accident study with a 10-year survey period also reported 74 workers exposed to TCDDs following an industrial accident (May, 1982). None had chloracne prior to the incident. Following the accident other workers were exposed, totaling 79 in all. These were compared with a group of executives and office workers without exposure possibility (n=31), a second group that might have had some exposure (n=54), and finally a group who had exposure and chloracne (n=79). No overall differences in clinical disease were noted in these groups; particularly no differences in reproductivity were noted. The exposed group (the last listed above) did have lower levels of serum bilirubin, increased levels of gamma-glutamyl transpeptidase and increased serum triglyceride levels. The intermediate group also showed smaller but similar alterations. It was concluded that these changes might not be specific, since differences were small and extraneous social factors might also contribute to these changes.

What Have We Learned From These Human Exposures?

There are two different types of exposure provided for our scrutiny, one in which PCBs were ingested over a short period of time, and a second set in which a single large and then lower level of TCDD exposure occurred. In both instances, the major targets seemed to be the skin, the nervous system, and liver. In spite of rather significant levels of TCDD exposure, especially in Seveso, mankind seems more resistant than lower vertebrates, more like hamsters. Also, it is suggested that the principal route of absorption in man is the GI tract and skin. Pulmonary absorption is not considered significant. No clear-cut reproductive effects have been shown. Further support for this notion comes from fertility studies of wives of the chemical workers (Townsend et al.,

1982). Mobilization and loss of the toxicant from the body occur. Finally, the most sensitive indication of exposure is in the epithelial change. In fact, from 1949-1973, 579 cases of chloracne had been identified, and Seveso added another 175. In a self-imposed study, Schultz and coworkers found 50-100 µg of the dioxin were required to develop chloracne in themselves, and suggested its basis as an occupational disease (Kimmig and Schultz, 1957).

The carcinogenicity of these halogenated chemicals in rodent species raises the question of their carcinogenicity in man. A small but significant increase in stomach cancers was noted in a worker population (Thiess et al., 1983; May, 1982). A study of Swedish workers exposed to phenoxy herbicides (and, hence, possible dioxins) purported to show increased numbers of "soft tissue" tumors (Axelson et al., 1979; Hardell and Sandstrom, 1979). More recently, the carcinogenic potential of the pesticide in the workers' environment has been called into question (Coggan and Acheson, 1982; Blair et al., 1983), and the Swedish study itself is noted to have problems of interpretation (Rawls, 1983). If nothing else, this points to the very real problems of extrapolating from mice to man (Smuckler, 1983). Certainly the dose and its duration of use are very different.

It would be scientifically unsound to suggest that this group of chemical agents--PCBs, PBBs, benzodioxins, and benzofurans--are not toxicants and potential carcinogens. It is probably also unwise to suggest that dioxins are "the most toxic chemicals recognized by mankind." Substantiation for this claim on the basis of single species response by its very self admits the diversity of the change in other species and the fact that overstatement may be considered. What is clear is that any chemical agent, including water in sufficient amounts, is capable of producing physiological and, in fact, pathological modulations in any given organism.

It seems apparent that one of the most easily identified changes that result from these diverse agents is an epithelial modification called chloracne. In point of fact, it has been shown that it takes between 50-100 µg of dioxin to produce chloracne in man (Kimmig and Schultz, 1957). Although the disease is disfiguring, it apparently is a reversible one. It is in those instances, in which humans have been exposed to dioxin and chloracne produced, that removal of the agent has been associated with resolution of the epithelial change (Coulston and Pocchiari, 1983). What chloracne does provide is a marker, a very simple assay system to determine whether or not there has been sufficient exposure to mankind to produce any of the putative modifications with which we are concerned. The presence of chloracne would obviate the necessity for a determination of body loads of the biphenyls, furans, or dioxins as a first-step.

The lack of evidence of any long-term disability in workers exposed to the dioxins also suggests that the agents are not associated with any specific change in man. Even the high levels of exposure to PCBs in cooking oils, in large part, have been associated with resolution of the disease. Reproductive effects have not been demonstrated to be of significance in the Oriental studies, or among the chemical workers. Even in soldiers exposed to Agent Orange, a putative carrier of TCDD (LaVecchio et al., 1983; Lipson, 1983), the production of neoplastic disease is subject to some scrutiny. The initial identification of soft-tissue tumors in Swedish railroad workers exposed to phenoxy herbicides has recently been subject to critical review and no correlation found. The identification of increased levels of stomach cancer in chemical workers is a repeated and confounding response, but not necessarily related to dioxins and furans. Rather, this seems to be a hazard unique to this group of workers.

CONCLUSIONS

Taken together, these data suggest that, although these materials are hazardous and produce disease in laboratory and wild animals as well as man, if man and rodents are compared, a margin of safety exists for mankind. Furthermore, although acute lethality and long-term lethal diseases, such as neoplasia, have not been seen in humans, disease, in this sense an aberration of the well-being of an individual, can occur. This can be the result of the chemical or the human perception of potential injury, even one that does not exist. Chloracne, disfiguring as it is, can also be considered to have greater impact than the skin lesion itself. It is unfortunate that a non-scientific forum is being used to explore, and exploit, real and imaginary changes resulting from exposure to these agents, since this type of response will only cloud rather than clarify the information available for us to understand the nature of these diseases. This understanding is both scientifically necessary and required for an evaluation of what we may be willing to pay for progress.

REFERENCES

Andres, J., Lambert, I., Robertson, L. Bandiera, S., Sawyer, T., Lovering, S. and Safe, S. 1983. The comparative biological and toxic potencies of polychlorinated biphenyls and polybrominated biphenyls. Toxicol. and Appl. Pharmacol. 70:204-215.

Anonymous, 1983a, PCB levels fall in striped bass in Hudson River, November 20, 1983. The New York Times.

Anonymous, 1983b, Symposium updates health effects of dioxins, benzofurans, September 12, 1983. C & EN, pp. 26-30.

Axelson, O., Edling, C., Kling, H., Andersson, K., Hogstedt, C. and Sundall, L. 1979. Updating of the mortality among pesticide-exposed railroad workers. Lakartidnengen 76:3305-3306.

Barker, E.A. and Smuckler, E.A. 1973. Non-hepatic thioacetamide injury: I. Thymic cortical necrosis. Am. J. Pathology 71:409-418.

Barker, E.A. and Smuckler, E.A. 1974. Non-hepatic thioacetamide injury: II. The morphologic features of proximal renal tubular injury. Am. J. Pathology 74:575-590.

Blair, A., Grauman, D.J., Lubin, J.H. and Fraumeni, J.F. 1983. Lung cancer and other causes of death among licensed pesticide applicators. J. Natl. Cancer Inst. 71:31-37.

Coggan, D. and Acheson, E.D. 1982. Do phenoxyherbicides cause cancer in man? Lancet, 1057-1059.

Coulston, F. and Pocchiari, F. 1983. Accidental exposure to dioxins: Human health aspects. Academic Press, New York and London.

De Verneuil, H., Sassa, S., Kappas, A. 1983. Effects of polychlorinated biphenyl compounds, 2,3,7,8-tetrachlorodibenzo-p-dioxin, phenobarbital and iron on hepatic uroporphyrinogen decarboxylase. Biochem. J. 214:145-151.

Epstein, S.S. 1979. The Politics of Cancer. Anchor Press/Doubleday, Garden City, NY. Revised Edition.

Epstein, S.S. November, 1983. Agent Orange Diseases. Trial, pp. 91-138.

Fox, J.L. 1983. Dioxin's health effects remain puzzling. Science 221: 1161-1162.

Gasiewicz, T.A., Holscher, M.A. and Neal, R.A. 1980. The effects of total parenteral nutrition on the toxicity of 2,3,7,8-tetrachlorodibenzo-p-dioxin in the rat. Toxicol. and Appl. Pharmacol. 54:469-488.

Hardell, L. and Sandstrom, A. 1979. A case control study: Soft tissue sarcoma and exposure to phenoxy acetic acid or chlorophenols. Brit. J. Cancer 39:711-717.

Harris, M.W., Moore, J.D., Vos, J.G. and Gupta, B. 1973. General biological effects of TCDD on laboratory animals. Environ. Health Perspect. 5:101-109.

Kimbrough, R.D. 1974. The toxicity of polychlorinated polycyclic compounds and related chemicals. CRC Crit. Rev. Toxicology 2:445-498.

Kimmig, J. and Schultz, K.H. 1957. Berlufliehe Akne (Sog Chlorakne) dureh chloriente, aromatische zyklishe aether. Dermatologia 115:540-546.

Kuratsune, M., Takesumi, M., Matsuzaka, J. and Yamaguchi, A. 1972. Epidemiologic study on Yusho, a poisoning caused by ingestion of rice oil contaminated by a commercial brand of polychlorinated biphenyl. Environ. Health Perspect. 1:119-128.

LaVecchio, F.A., Pashayan, H.M. and Singer, W. 1983. Agent Orange and birth defects. New England J. Med. 308:719-720.

Li, W.-M. et al. 1981. PCB poisoning of 27 cases in 3 generations of a large family. Clin. Med. (Taipei) 7:23-27.

Lipson, A. 1983. Agent Orange and birth defects. New England J. Med. 309:491.

May, G. 1982. Tetrachlorodibenzo-p-dioxin: A survey of subjects 10 years after exposure. Brit. J. Ind. Med. 39:128-135.

National Academy of Sciences, 1979, Polychlorinated Biphenyls, National Academy Press, Washington, D.C.

Parkinson, A., Robertson, L.W. and Safe, S.H. 1983. Induction of rat microsomal cytochrome P-450 by 2,3',4,4',5,5', hexachlorobiphenyl. Biochem. Pharm. 32:2269-2279.

Poland, A. and Kende, A. 1976. 2,3,7,8-Tetrachlorodibenzo-p-dioxin: Environmental contamination and molecular problems. Fed. Proc. 35: 2404-2411.

Poland, A. and Knutson, J.C. 1982. 2,3,7,8-Tetrachlorodibenzo-p-dioxin and related halogenated aromatic hydrocarbons: Examination of the mechanism of toxicity. Ann. Rev. Pharmacol. Toxicol. 22:517-554.

Rawls, R. October 31, 1983. Worker study casts doubt on cancer-dioxin link. C&EN, p.24.

Smuckler, E.A. 1983. Chemicals, cancer and cancer biology. Western J. Med. 139:55-74.

Thiess, A.M., Frentzel-Beyme, R. and Link, R. 1983. Mortality studies of persons exposed to dioxin in a trichlorophenyl process accident that occurred in BASF AG on November 17, 1953. Am. J. Ind. Med. 3:179-181.

Townsend, C., Bodner, R.M., van Peenen, P.F.D., Olson, R.D. and Cook, R.R. 1982. Survey of the reproductive events of employees exposed to chlorodioxins. Am. J. Epidemiology 115: 695-713.

Zack, J.A. and Suskind, R. 1980. The mortality analysis of employees engaged in the manufacture of 2,4,5-T. J. Occupational Med. 22: 11-14.

Chapter 16

THE CLINICOPATHOLOGIC CHANGES IN VARIOUS SPECIES OF ANIMALS CAUSED
BY DIBENZO-P-DIOXINS

Ernest E. McConnell
National Toxicology Program
National Institute of Environmental Health Sciences

INTRODUCTION

When considering the lesions caused by 2,3,7,8-tetrachlorodibenzo-p-dioxin (TCDD) one
has to realize that it is only in the laboratory setting that this is possible. In the "real
world" exposure to animals or humans is never only to TCDD. Other chlorinated
dibenzo-p-dioxins (CDD) congeners and isomers are invariably present as well as starting
chemicals and/or the chemicals in which they are a contaminant. Additionally, other
related classes of chemicals may also be present, such as chlorinated dibenzofurans
(CDF), polychlorinated biphenyls (PCB), chlorinated biphenylenes (CB) and chlorinated
napthlenes (CN).

This apparently complex situation becomes more manageable when one accepts the most
important principle in the study of the clinicopathologic changes caused by these
chemicals. Namely, the spectrum of lesions induced within a given species of animal is
essentially the same for all of these classes of chemicals. The amount (dose) of one of
these classes or a given isomer or congener within the class needed to cause toxicity will
vary, but once a comparable toxic dose is achieved, the spectrum of lesions within that
species of animal will be similar (McConnell, 1980). To put this principle in proper
context it must be remembered that some congeners and isomers are relatively nontoxic
and it therefore may be impossible to induce the full spectrum of lesions or any lesion at
all.

To study the relative toxicity of each class of compound would require that the most
toxic isomer/congener of each class be given to the same animal species using an
identical protocol. This has been done in vivo (McConnell et al., 1978) and in vitro
(Poland and Glover, 1973; 1977). The results of these investigations show a relative
ranking of toxicity as follows: CDD (most toxic) > CDF >> PCB > CN. These authors
have also demonstrated that a brominated isomer is somewhat more toxic than its
chlorinated counterpart. It is also becoming apparent that the various isomers and/or
classes may act in an additive or synergistic manner to each other (McKinney and
McConnell, 1982; McKinney et al., 1984).

ANIMAL SPECIES SENSITIVITY

There is a considerable difference in the sensitivity of various species of animals to
these compounds. However, in most cases if a given species of animal is more sensitive
than another to a given class of compound, i.e., PCB, this species of animal will also be
more sensitive than other species to the other classes of chemicals, i.e., CDDs, CDFs,
etc. This concept is sometimes less clear, in chronic exposures because the biological
half-lives of various isomers/congeners within these classes of chemicals vary markedly.
For example, rhesus monkeys exposed to relatively equitoxic levels of 2,3,7,8-TCDF and

2,3,7,8-TCDD have shown marked recovery to the former (McNulty et al., 1982) but not the latter (Allen et al., 1977). This would suggest that TCDD is much more toxic than TCDF but acute exposures suggest that the difference is not that great (McConnell et al., 1978; Moore et al., 1979).

While there are a limited number of studies where the protocols are comparable, the general impression is that chickens (and possibly other avian species) and guinea pigs are the most sensitive species of animals to intoxication with these classes of chemicals. In contrast, hamsters and amphibians appear to be fairly resistant to the toxic effects, at least to TCDD.

Another concept of toxicity derived from the study of these chemicals is that in most instances young animals are more sensitive than adults and females more sensitive than males. The age and sex difference has been best documented in environmental exposures in monkeys (Altman et al., 1979; McConnell et al., 1978) and mink (Aulerich et al., 1971) exposed to PCBs.

CLINICAL SIGNS

The clinical signs of intoxication in animals from exposure to dibenzo-p-dioxins are limited. At acutely lethal doses the main clinical sign in most species of animals is a progressive loss of body weight followed by weakness, debilitation, and finally death. This is accompanied by decreased food and water intake which accounts for some (Seefeld et al., 1984) but not all of the weight loss (McConnell et al., 1978). These may be the only signs observed in rats, mice, guinea pigs, rabbits, mink, and poultry after ingestion or oral administration. However, acne-like lesions and hyperkeratosis have been reported in monkeys (Allen and Carstens, 1967), hairless mice (Inagami and Koga, 1969) and in the ears of rabbits after local application (Vos and Beems, 1971). At times, poultry and mice may show a terminal increase in body weight, but this is due to a pathologic accumulation of fluids within the body (subcutaneous edema, ascites, hydrothorax and hydropericardium) (Firestone, 1973; McConnell, 1980).

It is difficult to describe acute signs of toxicity in non-human primates because they do not die "acutely". The time to death is from one to three months even at doses several times the LD_{50}. The time to death in most species of animals is from several days to weeks even at super lethal exposures (McConnell, 1980). In addition to body weight loss, the clinical syndrome in monkeys (McConnell et al., 1978) and cattle (Olafson, 1947) is characterized by skin and eyelid lesions and abnormal finger and toe nails or hooves. The cutaneous abnormalities in monkeys are follicular dermatitis (acne) of the face, neck, and forearms, enlarged tortuous Meibomian glands in the eyelid, exuberant atypical secretions in the ear canal, and overgrowth and loss of nails of the hands and feet. Alopecia may be present, particularly in the areas of the body showing dermatitis. The skin of cattle is thickened and dry, particularly over the neck, shoulders and back. Eyelids may show similar lesions to those in monkeys but of a lesser severity. The hooves of intoxicated cattle may be overgrown with associated lameness.

Signs of poor fertility and fetal wastage are hallmarks of the disease syndrome in chronic sublethal exposures. These may be the main clinical features in "environmental" exposures, particularly in monkeys (Altman et al., 1979), mink (Aulerich et al., 1971), and cattle (Jackson and Halbert, 1974). The reproductive problems appear to be primarily attributable to toxicity to the female in these species.

ORGAN WEIGHT EFFECTS

In those studies where organ weights have been measured, there are only two organs that show a consistent weight effect in most species of animals (McConnell, 1980). The thymus shows a dramatic decrease in weight (actual and relative to body weight), often only 25% of normal. It should be remembered that reduced thymic weight is difficult to assess in adult animals since the thymus normally involutes with age. In contrast, the liver is usually increased in weight. The degree of this change is variable between species of animals. A decrease in the weight of the gonads has been reported but this may be a reflection of debilitation rather than a direct toxic effect.

PATHOLOGY

The organ which consistently shows lesions from toxicity to these classes of chemicals in all species of animals studied is the thymus (McConnell, 1980). Additionally, the thymus usually shows changes at doses lower than those required to cause morphologically perceptable lesions in other organs. The primary lesion is a loss of cortical lymphocytes. In animals lethally exposed to these compounds only a remnant of the cortex may be present. This is often accompanied by necrotic debris in the medulla. At less toxic doses the thymus may look normal histopathologically while being one half normal size. (This emphasizes the reason organ weights are so useful in evaluating the toxicopathology of these chemicals.) The mechanism involved in this lesion appears to be a reduction in a maturation hormone produced in the medulla (Greenlee et al., 1984).

The liver varies in its response to these classes of chemicals depending on the animal species being investigated. In avian species (Vos and Koeman, 1970), and in rabbits (Vos and Beems, 1971), severe hepatocellular necrosis and hemorrhage are the hallmarks of lethal intoxication. In fact, death in these species has been ascribed to severe liver pathology. Prominent but lesser degrees of pathology are observed in rats and mice while the liver is only minimally damaged (anatomically) in guinea pigs, cattle, and monkeys (McConnell, 1980). Intrahepatic bile duct hyperplasia has been described in rodents and monkeys but is a more prominent feature in chronically exposed animals.

Marked epithelial hyperplasia of the extrahepatic bile duct and gall bladder have been described in monkeys (McConnell et al., 1978) and cattle (McConnell et al., 1980). The height and number of epithelial cells is increased yet more striking is the papillary appearance of the mucosa. It is so prominent that macroscopically the bile duct may be two to three times its normal diameter. Epithelial erosions, ulcers and inflammation are often part of the lesion.

Hyperplasia of the transitional epithelium lining the urinary tract has been described in guinea pigs, cattle and monkeys (McConnell, 1980). The lesion extends from the renal pelvis to the urinary bladder stopping at the level of the urethra. The histologic appearance of the epithelium appears normal in all respects except that the number of cell layers may be 2 to 3 times that observed in normal animals. The parenchyma of the kidney does not show microscopic pathology, although an increased severity of chronic progressive nephropathy (a common disease related to aging) has been described in rats exposed chronically to PCBs (Kimbrough, 1979) and PBBs (Gupta et al., 1983).

The stomach of monkeys exposed to these classes of chemicals exhibits a proliferative lesion which may be pathognomonic and has been referred to as "Simian Gastropathy" (Scotti, 1973). The lesion may be so prominent that it often appears as a fungoid-like mass suggesting neoplasia. The basic lesion is that the chief (acid producing) cells are replaced by hyperplastic mucous producing cells. In more chronic exposures, the hyperplastic change becomes more pronounced and at times appears to invade subjacent tissues. Whether this represents true invasion is questionable since it is usually admixed with ulcerative processes and inflammation. The lesion has never been shown to metastasize and will regress if exposure to those chemicals with a relatively short biological half-life ceases (McNulty et al., 1982). A similar but much less severe lesion has been described in rats exposed to PBBs (Gupta et al., 1983). The large intestine also shows hyperplastic changes in monkeys chronically exposed to these chemicals. This has been referred to as "colitis cystica profunda" (Scotti, 1975).

The skin and associated structures of monkeys, rabbits (ears), and certain strains of mice show characteristic lesions when the animals are exposed to these classes of chemicals. In monkeys the lesion is characterized microscopically by epithelial hyperkeratosis and severe atrophy of sebaceous glands and hyperkeratosis of their ducts (McConnell et al., 1978). The ducts become occluded with keratinaceous debris and macroscopically the lesion resembles acne. A lesion of comparable morphology is observed in the Meibomian glands of the eyelid and ceruminous glands of the external auditory canal. These modified sebaceous glands are severely affected and may be morphologically the most sensitive indicators of intoxication to these classes of compounds.

While most strains of mice do not show skin lesions, certain "hairless" (actually not hairless since remnants of hair follicles are present) strains show a similar skin lesion to that in monkeys (Poland et al., 1982). Again, the lesion appears to be related to atrophic and metaplastic changes in the sebaceous glands and hyperplastic changes in their ducts. The inner surface of a rabbit's ear also shows acne-like lesions if these compounds are applied directly to the surface. In fact, this toxic response provides a fairly rapid (7-14 days) bioassay for the detection of these classes of chemicals (Jones and Krizek, 1962). Cattle also show a characteristic skin disease (X-disease) when exposed to these compounds. Historically, one of the earliest environmental intoxications of these classes of chemicals involved dairy cattle which showed severe hyperkeratosis, particularly on the face, neck and over the shoulders. The disease was caused by exposure to CNs in axle grease which the cattle ingested (Olafson, 1947).

Accumulation of fluid in the subcutis, abdominal cavity, thorax and pericardial sac is a characteristic feature of intoxication in avian species. The original recognition of a possible dioxin problem in animals was a disastrous episode in chickens which was referred to as "chick edema disease" (Firestone, 1973). It resulted in the death and destruction of hundreds of thousands of chickens and eggs.

Other lesions have been ascribed to intoxication with these classes of chemicals (McConnell, 1980). These include hemorrhage of the adrenal, atrophy of the zona glomerulosa of the adrenal cortex, germ cell atrophy of the testicle and ovary and amyloidosis. Whether these are primary effects or merely a reflection of severe cachexia in severely intoxicated animals or exacerbation of aging lesions is debatable. These lesions are observed primarily in animals which die or which are killed in a mortibund condition. In addition, similar lesions are sometimes found in animals extremely sick from other causes or in aged animals.

DISCUSSION

The clinicopathologic syndrome associated with exposure to these classes of chemicals is fairly characteristic for a given species of animals. Fortunately or unfortunately, in a diagnostic situation it is impossible to differentiate between PCBs, CDDs, CDFs, PBBs or CNs. Chemical analysis of tissue samples is required for a definitive etiological diagnosis. Even then it is usually impossible to ascribe the severity of intoxication to a given level of the chemical in various tissues. In most cases, the presence of the chemical in tissues means only that the animal was exposed to that chemical. The presence of the characteristic clinicopathologic syndrome is required for a presumptive diagnosis of intoxication. For this reason, a careful post mortem examination is required with collection of an appropriate set of tissues. Diagnosis is also confounded, in many instances, by the presence of secondary infectious disease(s). This may be related to the subtle effects these chemicals have on the immune system.

REFERENCES

Allen, J.R., Barsotti, D.A., Van Miller, J.P., Abrahamson, L.J. and Lalich, J.J. 1977. Morphological changes in monkeys consuming a diet containing low levels of 2,3,7,8-tetrachlorodibenzo-p-dioxin. Food Cosmet. Toxicol. 15:401-410.

Allen, J.R. and Carstens, L.A. 1967. Light and electron microscopic observations in Macaca mulatta monkeys fed toxic fat. Am. J. Vet. Res. 28:1513-1526.

Altman, N.H., New, A.E., McConnell, E.E. and Ferrell, T.L. 1979. A spontaneous outbreak of polychlorinated biphenyl (PCB) toxicity in rhesus monkeys (Macaca mulatta): Clinical observations. Lab. Animal Sci. 29:661-665.

Aulerich, R.J., Ringer, R.K., Seagren, H.L. and Youatt, W.G. 1971. Effects of feeding coho salmon and other Great Lakes fish on mink reproduction. Can. J. Zool. 49:611-616.

Firestone, D. 1973. Etiology of chick edema disease. Environ. Health Perspect. 5:59-66.

Greenlee, W.F., Dold, K.M. and Irons, R.D. 1984. 2,3,7,8-Tetrachlorodibenzo-p-dioxin (TCDD) inhibits the induction by thymic epithelial (TE) cells of T-lymphocyte mitogen responsiveness. The Toxicologist, Vol. 4, No. 1, March, 1984 Abstracts, No. 751.

Gupta, B.N., McConnell, E.E., Moore, J.A. and Haseman, J.K. 1983. Effects of a polybrominated biphenyl mixture in the rat and mouse. II. Lifetime study. Toxicol. Appl. Pharmacol. 68:18-35.

Inagami, K. and Koga, T. 1969. Experimental study of hairless mice following administration of rice oil used by a "Yusho" patient. Fukuoka Acta Med. 60:548-553.

Jackson, T.F. and Halbert, F.L. 1974. A toxic syndrome associated with the feeding of polybrominated biphenyl-contaminated protein concentrate to dairy cattle. J. Am. Vet. Med. Assoc. 165:437-439.

Jones, E.L. and Krizek, H.A. 1962. A technic for testing acnegenic potency in rabbits applied to the potent acnegen 2,3,7,8-tetrachlorodibenzo-p-dioxin. J. Invest. Dermatol. 39:511-517.

Kimbrough, R.D. 1979. The carcinogenic and other chronic effects of persistent halogenated compounds. Ann. N.Y. Acad. Sci. 320:415-418.

McConnell, E.E. 1980. Acute and chronic toxicity, carcinogenesis, reproduction, teratogenesis and mutagenesis in animals. In Halogenated Biphenyls, Terphenyls, Naphthalenes, Dibenzodioxins and Related Compounds, ed. R.D. Kimbrough, pp. 109-190, Elsevier, New York.

McConnell, E.E., Moore, J.A. and Dalgard, D.W. 1978. Toxicity of 2,3,7,8-tetrachlorodibenzo-p-dioxin in rhesus monkeys (Macaca mulatta) following a single oral dose. Toxicol. Appl. Pharmacol. 43:175-187.

McConnell, E.E., Hass, J.R., Altman, N. and Moore, J.A. 1979. A spontaneous outbreak of polychlorinated biphenyl (PCB) toxicity in rhesus monkeys (Macaca mulatta): Toxicopathology. Lab. Animal Sci. 29:666-673.

McConnell, E.E., Moore, J.A., Gupta, B.N., Rakes, A.H., Luster, M.I., Goldstein, J.A., Haseman, J.K. and Parker, C.E. 1980. The chronic toxicity of technical and analytical pentachlorophenol in cattle. I. Clinicopathology. Toxicol. Appl. Pharmacol. 52:468-490.

McConnell, E.E., Moore, J.A., Haseman, J.D. and Harris, M.W. 1978. The comparative toxicity of chlorinated dibenzo-p-dioxins in mice and guinea pigs. Toxicol. Appl. Pharmacol. 44:335-356.

McKinney, J.D., Chae, K., McConnell, E.E. and Birnbaum, L.S. 1984. Structure-induction versus structure-toxicity relationships for polychlorinated biphenyls and related aromatic hydrocarbons. Environ. Health Perspect. (In press).

McKinney, J.D. and McConnell, E.E. 1982. Structural specificity and the dioxin receptors. In Chlorinated Dioxins and Related Compounds: Impact on the Environment, eds. O. Hutzinger, R.W. Frei, E. Merian and F. Pocchiari, pp. 367-381, Pergamon Press, New York.

McNulty, W.P., Pomerantz, I.H. and Farrell, T.J. 1982. Chronic toxicity of 2,3,7,8-tetrachlorodibenzofuran for rhesus macaques. In Chlorinated Dioxins and Related Compounds: Impact on the Environment, eds. O. Hutzinger, R.W. Frei, E. Merian and F. Pocchiari, pp. 411-418, Pergamon Press, New York.

Moore, J.A., McConnell, E.E., Dalgard, D.W. and Harris, M.W. 1979. Comparative toxicity of three halogenated dibenzofurans in guinea pigs, mice and rhesus monkeys. Ann. N.Y. Acad. Sci. 320:151-163.

Olafson, P. 1947. Hyperkeratosis (X-disease) of cattle. Cornell Vet. 37:279-291.

Poland, A. and Glover, E. 1973. Chlorinated dibenzo-p-dioxins: Potent inducers of #-aminolevulinic acid synthetase and aryl hydrocarbon hydroxylase. II. A study of the structure-activity relationship. Mol. Pharmacol. 9:736-747.

Poland, A. and Glover, E. 1977. Chlorinated biphenyl induction of aryl hydrocarbon hydroxylase activity: A study of structure-activity. Mol. Pharmacol. 13:924-938.

Poland, A., Palen, D. and Glover, E. 1982. Tumour promotion by TCDD in skin of HRS/J hairless mice. Nature 300:271-271.

Scotti, T. 1973. Simian gastropathy with submucosal glands and systs. Arch. Pathol. 96:403-408.

Scotti, T. 1975. Colitis cystica profunda in rhesus monkeys. Lab. Animal Sci. 25:55-60.

Seefeld, M.D., Corbett, S.W., Keesey, R.E. and Peterson, R.E. 1984. Characterization of the wasting syndrome in rats treated with 2,3,7,8-tetrachlorodibenzo-p-dioxin. Toxicol. Appl. Pharmacol. (In press).

Vos, J.G. and Beems, R.B. 1971. Dermal toxicity studies of technical polychlorinated biphenyls and fractions thereof in rabbits. Toxicol. Appl. Pharmacol. 19:617-633.

Vos, J.G. and Koeman, J.H. 1970. Comparative toxicologic study with polychlorinated biphenyls in chickens with special reference to porphyria, edema formation, liver necrosis and tissue residues. Toxicol. Appl. Pharmacol. 17:656-668.

Chapter 17

THE HEALTH EFFECTS OF 2,4,5-T AND ITS TOXIC CONTAMINANTS

R.R. Suskind
Institute of Environmental Health
University of Cincinnati

I am grateful to Drs. McConnell and Smuckler who preceded me. They have provided an excellent scientific introduction to the story of workplace events and their adverse health effects from the production of 2,4,5-T which started in 1949.

In October, 1949, my colleagues and I, at the the Kettering Laboratory, were asked to examine four workers who had become ill following an industrial process accident which occurred in March of that year in a plant making 2,4,5-T. A kettle, in which trichlorophenol was being made, overheated and developed excessive pressure and part of the contents was emitted through a safety valve and broken pipe connector into the plant building and its surroundings. We did not know it at the time, but 2,3,7,8-TCDD was a toxic component of that kettle effusion. The medical community was first alerted to the health problems arising from the manufacturing process of 2,3,5-T through this accident.

Those employees involved in the clean-up of the building and the restoration of equipment to resume production developed acute symptoms involving the respiratory tract; they complained of skin and eye irritation, headache, dizziness and nausea. These symptoms subsided within one to two weeks. They were followed by an acneform eruption, severe muscle pain affecting the extremities, thorax and shoulders, fatigue, nervousness and irritability, dyspnea, complaint of decreased libido and intolerance to cold. The first four persons we examined had severe generalized chloracne, hepatic enlargement and tenderness, peripheral neurities, a delayed prothrombin time, and an increase in total serum lipids (Ashe and Suskind, 1949-1950). Transaminase tests were not yet developed at that time. Histological exam of a nerve biopsy in a worker with pedal sensory loss showed myelin degeneration.

All of them had severe generalized chloracne involving face, trunk, genitalia, upper and lower extremities (Figure 1-4).

A total of 36 subjects were followed, in a series of examination, until 1953. By that time, the symptoms and findings observed in 1949 and 1950 referable to the liver and nervous system had subsided. There was some persistence of the acne but considerable improvement was noted in most cases (Suskind, 1953).

The toxic contaminant of the 2,4,5-T process was identified in 1957 as 2,3,7,8-tetrachlorodibenzo-p-dioxin (TCDD) (Kimmig and Schulz, 1957). A considerable amount of research has been carried out in the past ten years on the nature of its toxic action in animals. It is, as many of you know, the most potent acnegen on record.

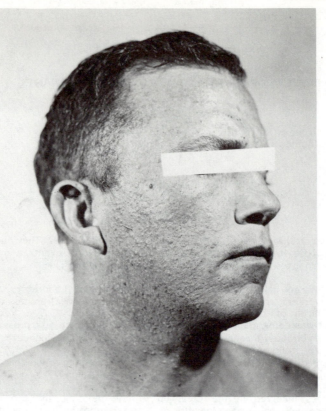

FIGURE 1.

In 1955 we   were able to demonstrate that the cellular events which are the consequence of the cutaneous exposure to contaminated trichlorophenol include:

1. Initial hyperkeratinization of the opening of the sebaceous gland into the follicle lumen followed by hyperkeratinization of the follicle orifice.
2. Modulation of the undifferentiated cells lining of the sebaceous acinus and instead of differentiating into sebum producing cells, they differentiate into keratinocytes.
3. The above process (2) produces the comedo and eventually an inclusion keratin cyst or closed comedone.
4. The above process also results in disappearance of sebaceous elements and the hair follicles which are replaced by the comedo and/or keratin cyst.

In 1978 we were able to return to the scene. A standard mortality analysis was conducted on the workers exposed to the runaway reaction materials (Zack and Suskind, 1980). As of 1979, the SMRs for all causes of death was 0.69 with 32 deaths observed and 46.41 expected. For the categories of cancer and cardiovascular diseases, the SMRs were 1.00, and 0.68 respectively. Because of the small size of the cohort and small numbers of deaths, the results cannot be regarded as conclusive, but suggest no significant difference from expected death rates. We pause here to comment and question. Here is a cohort which was heavily exposed to TCDD. Disabling health effects were observed acutely, subacutely, and subchronically. If risks were substantial for

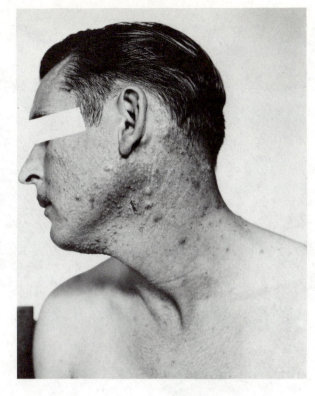

FIGURE 2.

hepatic, cardiac, pulmonary disease and cancer, we should have detected them even in this small cohort in the mortality analysis. One of this group died of a malignant fibrous histiocytoma, originating in the skin. It is classified as a soft tissue sarcoma. Another, not in this accident group but exposed to the process and who had chloracne, died of a liposarcoma. The frequency data of soft tissue sarcomas for the general population is inadequate since those occurring in specific organ systems are classified under ICD # for tumors of the stomach, or CNS, or kidney, or where ever they are found. The clear association of soft tissue sarcomas and TCDD is still to be determined.

We then returned to the plant site and carried out a clinical study on 436 employees of this plant to determine and identify the possible long-term effects of chemicals associated with the production of 2,4,5-T including TCDD, and to determine the increased risk for the adverse effects which have been observed in the subacute phase in man, as well as those noted in experimental animals. The examination program attempted to determine possible increased risk for cutaneous, pulmonary, cardiovascular, gastrointestinal, hepatic, renal, neurobehavioral problems, reproductive and birth defect problems, effects on lipid metabolism and the possibility of increased risk for cancer. The population included those exposed to the process accident, as well as those exposed to the normal processes of manufacturing and included chemical operators, service employees, such as pipefitters, mechanics, etc. The controls were never associated in any way with the 2,4,5-T process or its materials.

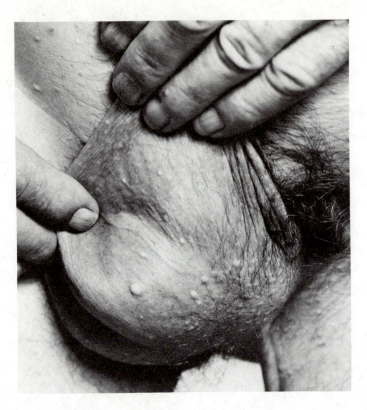

FIGURE 3.

The cohorts consisted of the following:
204 - Exposed
163 - Not Exposed
 51 - Of Questionable Exposure

The examination included: an interview, clinical laboratory examination of blood and urine, pulmonary function tests, ECG, chest x-ray, nerve conduction velocity measurements, and a complete physical examination, including skin examination by dermatologists. During the dermatological examination biopsies and skin scrapings were taken as deemed appropriate by the physician. The nerve conduction velocity measurements were obtained for most subjects from two nerves: the peroneal nerve for motor function and the sural nerve for sensory function.

Clinical laboratory analyses included: blood calcium, phosphorous, BUN, creatinine, BUN/creatinine ratio, uric acid, glucose (CS), total protein, albumin, globulin, albumin/globulin ratio, total bilirubin, direct bilirubin, Transaminase SGO, Transaminase SGP, alkaline phosphatase, LDH, cholesterol, iron, total lipids, sodium, potassium, chloride, G-glutamyl transpeptidase, triglycerides, CBC and differential, thyroxine R.I.A., thyroxine binding globulins. Urinalysis included routine examination as well as coproporphyrins and uroporphyrins. Blood serum lipid fraction was analyzed for plasma cholesterol, plasma triglyceride, plasma HDL, and estimated plasma LDL.

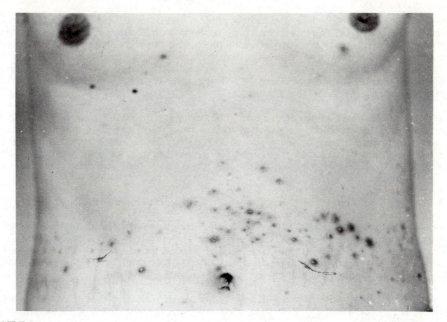

FIGURE 4.

A few words about the characteristics of the cohorts. Because of the time interval between the beginning of the process (1948), when it was terminated (1969), and the examination itself (1979), it was not possible to match the exposed and not exposed group for age and employment status. There was a 10 year mean age difference between the exposed and not exposed groups. There was a greater percentage of retired and terminated persons in the exposed than the not exposed. 86% of the not exposed were active employees; 55% of the exposed were active employees.

The following factors were considered in the analysis of the data - exposed versus not exposed versus questionably exposed: relationship to age, history or presence of chloracne - the hallmark of absorption and biological response; smoking, alcohol, other exposures than 2,4,5-T, (e.g. mining, welding, farming, etc).

As to drinking and smoking habits, there were no significant differences in alcohol consumption in the two groups. When smoking habits were compared by pack years the exposed gorup was significantly higher. There was a 19 pack year difference between the exposed and not exposed for present smokers and a 7 pack year difference between the exposed and not exposed in former smokers. This is a reflection of the difference in age (10 years) and smoking habits of the older age group.

When illnesses elicited by medical history were compared, the differences are found in the history of chloracne, acne vulgaris and peptic ulcer. Chloracne occurred in 86.27% of the exposed but did not occur in the not exposed and questionable exposure group. History of acne vulgaris occurred more frequently in the not exposed group than in the exposed group. A history of upper gastrointestinal ulcer occurred almost 4 times more frequently in the exposed group than in the not exposed ($p < 0.005$). When the medical history of the exposed and not exposed are compared for two (2) age groups, less than 50 vs. 50 years and older skin cancer and cerebrovascular accidents, hypertension, and coronary artery disease were related to age not exposure. Exposure, not age, appears to be associated with a history of gastrointestinal ulcer.

Since chloracne appeared to be the prime clinical indicator of exposure, a marker of absorption and biological response, the study subjects were further classified into three sub-groups within the exposed populations: those who never had developed chloracne, those who only had a history of chloracne, and those whose chloracne persisted and noted on clinical examination. As in the exposed versus not exposed group, the history of hypertension, cerebrovascular accident (CVA) and coronary artery disease were clearly age-related not chloracne related.

In the physical examination no differences in blood pressure findings were noted between the exposed and not exposed groups. The following criteria for abnormal systolic and diastolic values were used: for the groups < 50 (140/90) and for the groups > 60 (160/95). There were no significant differences in % of exposed or not exposed population with diastolic 80 or less, between 80-89, 80-94 and those considered abnormal, >90 for <59, ≥95 for ≥60.

52.7% of those who were clearly exposed were found to still have chloracne. Among the exposed 59.1% were found to have actinic elastosis in contrast to 30.1% among the not exposed. There is a significant difference in the occurrence of actinic elastosis between the exposed and not exposed in both age groups even though age is a factor in this clinical finding. Actinic elastosis is a problem found in persons of light coloration exposed over many years to sunlight (farmers skin, sailors skin). It is characterized by swelling and fragmentation of the elastic tissue elements of the skin.

It was observed that actinic elastosis is found predominately in the subjects with persistent chloracne (74.8%) but it also occurs significantly in those with a history of chloracne only 47.1%.

The frequency of abnormal plasma lipid findings were compared for exposed, not exposed and questionably exposed. No significant differences were noted in cholesterol, triglycerides, HDL and LDL levels. Smoking appeared to have no effect on the differences between these groups. Logistic regression was used to detect associations of abnormal lipid findings with exposure. After adjusting for pack years smoked, no significant differences between exposed and not exposed could be found.

When the lipid levels of the exposed group only are examined in relation to the occurrence of chloracne, the HDL levels in those with persistent chloracne are found to be somewhat lower than of the group with a history only of chloracne or those who never had chloracne. It is also interesting to note that those who had a history only of chloracne have somewhat higher LDL levels than those who had chloracne currently or never. I cannot comment on the real significance of this. The numbers are small.

No differences in mean values or out-of-range values for alkaline phosphatase, SGOT, SGPT, Gamma GT were found when the exposed were compared to the not exposed or those with chloracne were compared to those who only had a history of the skin problem or no history of chloracne.

Consistent differences in abnormal pulmonary function values (FEV_1, FVC, FEV_1/FVC and FEF_{25-75}) were found between the exposed and not exposed groups. Among present smokers only there was a significant difference in pulmonary function values between the exposed and not exposed group. There are no differences in pulmonary function values among persons who have formerly smoked or among persons who have never smoked when the exposed were compared to the non exposed.

Nerve conduction velocity determinations were made. All subjects reporting diabetes or reporting a high weekly alcohol intake were eliminated from the data analysis (high weekly alcohol intake was defined as greater than or equal to 35 oz. alcohol per week). After these deletions, there were 319 with complete sural examination and 336 with complete peroneal examination remaining. The data from the nerve conduction velocity study were adjusted according to the deJesus method.

Using analysis of covariance after adjusting for age as well as using the Z score method, there appeared to be no differences in nerve conduction velocity, in latency or in amplitude ratios for peroneal and sural nerves.

In presenting the information on reproductive and birth defects, it should be understood that all of the data depended on personal recall of such information as number of pregnancies, miscarriages, live births, stillbirths, infant mortality, etc. Factors which affect accuracy are obvious - e.g. interviews of male subject only, age of subject, and change in cultural attitudes about reproductive matters. It is also influenced by the fact that the pregnancies, miscarriages, and stillbirths were not designated in a time period related to exposure e.g., pre, during, or post exposure.

Fisher's exact test was used to compare the reported occurrence or reproductive anomalies in the exposed group to the not exposed group. The data on reproductive and birth defect findings indicated no significant differences were found in either the frequencies or miscarriages, in the rate of birth defects or of stillbirths.

From this study one can conclude that for those exposed to the 2,3,5-T process persistent effects are cutaneous and involve the pilosebaceous apparatus and the elastic tissue of the dermis. Chloracne may persist for as long as 30 years.

The data are suggestive that for the exposed there was an increased risk for upper gastrointestinal ulcer; that in those who currently smoke and have been exposed to 2,4,5-T process materials there may be an association of abnormal pulmonary function findings when compared to those who smoke but who were never exposed; that among those in whom chloracne persists there is (although numbers are small) an association with low HDL levels and further for those with only a history of chloracne there is an association with higher LDL levels.

There is no evidence from this study population that there are identifiable long-term effects on the cardiovascular system, on the liver, on renal or on peripheral nerve function. From recall of medical problems there is no indication of an increase risk for infections. There is no indication, on the basis of historical information (recognizing all of its weaknesses) that there was a greater risk for miscarriages, stillbirths, or birth defects among the families in which the male parent was exposed.

Finally, it is appropriate to summarize the acute, subacute or subchronic and long-term effects of TCDD from trichlorophenol or 2,4,5-T contamination. I have assembled these in three tables (Tables 1-3). Workers exposed to TCP runaway reactions or from poor plant hygiene may initially develop eye, respiratory, skin and gastrointestinal irritation, as well as headache and malaise. Ten days to several weeks after this initial exposure, one observes the subacute and eventually sunchronic features which include: chloracne, peripheral neuritis, liver dysfunction, hyperpigmentation, hirsutism of the face, irritibility and nervousness. Porphyria cutanea tarda, and/or uroporphyrinuria have not been observed in populations which have only been exposed to trichlorophenol or 2,4,5-T; but only in mixed exposures as in the New Jersey (Bleiberg et al., 1964) and Czechoslovakian (Jirasek et al., 1973) incidents. The laboratory findings in the subacute or subchronic state include: peripheral nerve, myelin damage, elevated SGOT, GGTP, triglyceride and total lipids. In our very early observations of subacute effects there was an increased prothrombin time found.

The long-term health effects have been described in the major part of this presentation and are summarized in Table 3.

TABLE 1. Human Health Effects - TCDD

	Clinical Features	Acute - (Following TCP Runaway Reaction and/or Poor Plant Hygiene)
		Eye, respiratory, skin and GI irritation
		Headache
		Malaise

TABLE 2. Human Health Effects - TCDD - Subacute or Subchronic

	Clinical Features	Laboratory Findings
Constant	Acne	
Inconstant	Neuromuscular symptoms, pain in skeletal muscles, chest, extremities = peripheral neuritis fatigue	Myelin degeneration on biopsy
Inconstant	Enlarged tender liver	Elevated SGOT Elevated GGTP Elevated prothrombin in time Elevated triglyceride Elevated total lipids
Rare	Porphyria cutanea tarda (only in mixed 2,4,5-T and 2,4-D exposures)	Uroporphyrinuria
Inconstant	Hyperpigmentation	
Inconstant	Hirsutism of face	
Inconstant	Irritability and nervousness	

TABLE 3. Human Health Effects

	Clinical Findings	Laboratory or Test Findings
Common	Persistent chloracne	
	Increased frequency of actinic elastosis associated with chloracne	
	Malar hirsutism	
Suggestive	Increased frequency upper GI ulcer	Abnormal PFT among present smokers
		Abnormal HDL among those with persistent chloracne

REFERENCES

Ashe, W.F. and Suskind, R.R. 1949-1950. Reports on chloracne cases. Monsanto Chemical Company, Nitro, West Virginia. Reports of the Kettering Laboratory, December 1949 and April 1950.

Bleiberg, J. Wallen, M., Brodhen, R. and Applebaum, I.L. 1964. Industrially acquired porphyria. Arch. Dermatol. 89:793-797.

Jirasek, L. Kalensky, J. and Kubek, K. 1973. Acne chlorina and porphyria cutanea tarda during the manufacture of herbicides. Cesk Dermatol. 48:306-315.

Kimmig, J. and Schulz, K.H. 1957. Occupational acne (so called chloracne) due to the chlorinated aromatic cyclic esters. Dermatologica 115:540-546.

Suskind, R.R. 1953. A clinical and environmental survey, Monsanto Chemical Company, Nitro, West Virginia. Report of the Kettering Laboratory, July 1953.

Zack, J.A. and Suskind, R.R. 1980. The mortality experience of workers exposed to tetrachlorodibenzodioxin in a trichlorophenol process accident. J. Occupational Med. 22(1):11-14.

Chapter 18

ADVERSE HEALTH EFFECTS IN HUMAN POPULATION EXPOSED TO 2,3,7,8-TETRACHLORODIBENZO-PARA-DIOXIN (TCDD) IN SEVESO: AN UPDATE

Franco Merlo
Istituto Nazionale per la Ricerca sul Cancro
Genova, Italy

INTRODUCTION

On July 10, 1976, an explosion at the Industrie Chimiche Meda Societa Azionaria (Icmesa) plant in the Northern Italian town of Meda released a cloud of aerosol which contaminated the surrounding area. The aerosol contained 2,4,5-trichlorophenol (TCP), sodium hydroxide and the by-product, 2,3,7,8-tetrachlorodibenzo-para-dioxin (TCDD). Starting in 1947, the Icmesa plant produced a variety of chemicals (acetates, benzyl chloride, benzyl cyamide, phthalates, etc.). In 1970, pilot production of TCP began, and in 1974 full scale operation of TCP was set up. The incineration of production wastes was done by a very rudimentary combustion oven without any environmental control. During the years before the accident, many animal deaths were observed but local authorities were never informed about these. Moreover, local authorities were never informed about the TCP production at the Icmesa plant despite the fact that the TCP operation was considered notifiable by Italian Environmental-Occupational Laws (Acts of Parliamentary Commission, 1978).

THE ACCIDENT

The accident occurred six and a half hours after the Icmesa factory had closed down for the weekend. It is generally accepted that there was a "runaway reaction" in the reactor producing TCP. The pressure increased as the reaction became exothermic and reached the critical limit, causing the safety disk to rupture and the discharge of the reactor contents. The safety valve, situated outside the plant, discharged the aerosol directly into the atmosphere and it then drifted over a highly inhabited area.

THE AREA

The affected area (92.85 km^2) was subsequently divided into three zones on the basis of gas chromatography-mass spectrometry analysis of soil samples (Fig. 1) (di Domenico et al., 1980). Zone A, an area of about 1.2 km^2 in the town of Seveso just south of the plant, was contaminated with the highest levels of TCDD (from .75 to 20,000 μg/m^2). Zone B, covering about 2.3 km^2, was contaminated with lesser amounts: 5 to 50 μg/m^2 of TCDD in the soil was found. Zone R (14.8 km^2), further south and including both Zone A and B, usually had a concentration of less than 5 μg/m^2 of TCDD in the soil.

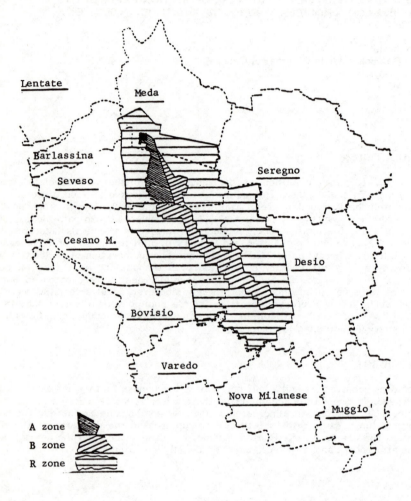

Figure 1. Map of the Contaminated Area by Polluted Zones

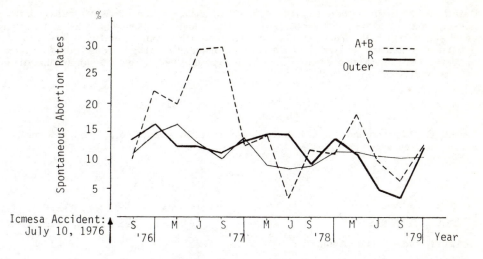

Figure 2. Time trends of spontaneous abortion rates by quarters and by polluted zones (1976-1979) (Strigini et al., 1982).

POPULATION(S) AT RISK BASED ON TCDD SOIL CONTENTS

By the end of July 1976, 16 to 23 days after the accident, 735 people were evacuated from Zone A, and the area was fenced off. About 4,300 people lived in Zone B and 40,000 in Zone R. None of the people died from acute exposure to TCDD, but of the people who were exposed to TCDD, about 500 were treated for acute skin irritation. From September to December 1976, 44 children were diagnosed with chloracne. To date, the number of cases of chloracne amounts to a total of 193. No cases of chloracne were observed among the Icmesa workers, even though they continued to work for one week following the accident.

SPONTANEOUS ABORTIONS AND BIRTH DEFECTS

A health monitoring program (HMP) was established in July 1976 by the local regional authorities. The data collected during a five-year follow-up by the obstetric and gynecologic teams have been analyzed (Strigini et al., 1982). Due to the lack of abortion baseline values prior to the accident, only a backward analysis of the embryotoxic effects in different areas has been possible. A statistically significant increase in the spontaneous abortion rate has been detected in those areas in which higher levels of TCDD were found (areas A and B). This temporary rise in spontaneous abortions, as shown in Figure 2, reached a peak in the second half of 1977, about one year after the accident. This rise in the abortion rate among exposed pregnant women was observed despite the fact that more than 90 pregnant women from those areas obtained a clinical abortion.

Data from the Birth Defects Registry established during 1978 do not show an association between malformations and exposure to TCDD except for hemangiomas and benign neoplasms (Table 1).   This association becomes statistically significant ($x^2 = 5.97$, $p<0.05$) when data are analyzed considering the distribution of chloracne rates (see later in text) as risk markers for potential TCDD exposure instead of the simple analytical detection of TCDD on the soil.

TABLE 1. Observed and expected birth defect cases by area of residence of the mother during the pregnancy (1976-1980)

	Cases		
	Whole Area	Zones A+B+R	
Congenital Anomalies		Observed	Expected*
Central Nervous System Anomalies	27	6	5.19
Central Nervous System and Eye Anomalies	39	8	7.49
Anomalies of the Ear	27	4	5.19
Heart Anomalies	44	6	8.45
Heart and Circulatory System Anomalies	53	8	10.18
Anomalies of Respiratory System	14	3	2.69
Hypospadias	39	8	7.49
Hip Dislocation	38	8	7.30
Talipes Equinovarus	27	4	5.19
Polydactyly, Syndactyly	16	3	3.07
Anomalies of Integument	30	6	5.76
Benign Neoplasm - Hemangiomas	228	50	43.81
Chromosomal Anomalies	27	4	5.19
Anomalies of the Musculoskeletal System	19	3	3.65
All others	30	4	5.76
Total	587		

* On the basis of the birth defect rates in the whole area

CHLORACNE GROUPS

In order to establish adverse health effects among people who developed chloracne as a consequence of TCDD absorption, 164 affected children and 182 children of the same age, living in A, B, and R areas and without chloracne, were studied. The results of this study were published in 1981 (Caramaschi et al., 1981). Unfortunately, the "control" group was not randomly selected: only children having medical examinations and without skin irritation became part of the "control" group. The children selected as a comparison group were not representative of the unexposed children. They were a self-selected group of people who voluntarily submitted to the health monitoring program established by the Regional Health Minister to assist and test people living in the contaminated area. Recognizing the bias in selection, higher frequencies of GGT, GPT and Ala-U abnormalities were detected in the chloracne group when compared to the "control" group (Table 2).

TABLE 2. Frequency of subjects with abnormal values among chloracne and "control" group*

Test	Threshold Values	Chloracne Group	no=164	"Control" Group	no=182	P Value
GGT	>37 U/L	2.8%	(4/141)	---	(-/138)	<0.001
GPT	>27 U/L	3.5%	(5/141)	---	(-/138)	<0.005
ALA-U	>6.1 mg./L	24.1%	(33/137)	5.2%	(7/135)	<0.001

* Reproduced with permission from Caramaschi et al., 1981.

The response rate to the health monitoring program decreased from 1976 through 1980 among the chloracne group, as well as among the general population and the occupational groups followed. In late 1982, 6 years after the accident, a 3 year prospective follow-up study of the whole chloracne group (193 people) and of a comparison group (193 people matched by age, sex and history of exposure to TCDD) began. One of the major efforts in this study was to define unpolluted areas from which the comparison group was selected.

In early 1982, at the time the study design was prepared, the epidemiologic team in charge asked the Scientific Governmental Commission to follow at least two controls for each chloracne case in order to avoid problems due to a possible refusal to participate in the study. As of today, because of the low response rates to the first calls (November 1982 - March 1983) for the medical examination among chloracne and control groups (82.4% and 67.9% respectively), it is difficult to analyze and interpret the data.

OCCUPATIONAL STUDIES

An occupational health surveillance, according to the HMP was established soon after the accident. Its prevailing clinical characteristics and the lack of adequate study design limited any conclusions from the large amount of data collected from 1976 through 1980. Table 3 indicates the groups of people with potential occupational exposure to TCDD as specified by the HMP and the response rate to the control calls in 1980 among these groups. Although such initial participation followed by discontinuous participation to the clinical follow-up do not allow any epidemiological processing, in five out of 23 ex-cleanup workers hospitalized from October 1976 to May 1981, a diagnosis of liver disease suspected to be of toxic origin was made (Table 4).

TABLE 3. Occupational groups potentially exposed to TCDD and their response rates in 1980

Groups	Subjects	Examination Response Rate in 1980
Icmesa workers	191	62%
Encol workers*	92	75%
Public Service employees	2035	50%
Soldiers	342	61%
Clean-up workers	926	47%

* Response rate in 1981

TABLE 4. Liver diseases diagnosed among 23 ex-cleanup workers hospitalized from October 1976 to May 1981

Diagnosis	Number of Subjects
Virus hepatitis	15
Alcoholic liver disease	2
Liver diseases (negative HBSAg)	1
Liver diseases suspected of toxic origin	5
Total	23

The participation of the Icmesa workers in the medical monitoring program decreased over time. This drop in the response rate makes the follow-up evaluation difficult. The five year time trends have been analyzed. Statistically significant downward trends for GGT and alkaline phosphatase were seen (Table 5). These results seem to indicate that since 1976, for the study population, those conditions which caused the observed high frequency of abnormal liver function tests just after the accident, ceased.

TABLE 5. Frequency of subjects with abnormal laboratory values among the Icmesa workers with one clinical examination every year

Year	Alkaline Phosphatase cut-off = 50 U/L *	Gamma GT cut-off = 50 U/L *
1976	22.22%	27.77%
1977	8.89%	24.44%
1978	8.63%	22.47%
1979	8.63%	20.00%
1980	8.53%	15.93%
Chi square for the Trend	8.23	4.23
P level	.005 > P > .0001	.01 > P > .005

* Suggested by the International Steering Committee

A neurologic study done by the Clinica del Lavoro Luigi Devoto of Milano (Ghezzi, 1981) indicated that among the ICMESA workers there were four cases of slight polyneuropathy in the lower limbs with clinical and electrophysiological alterations. Three subjects showed a reduction of the motor and/or sensory nerve conduction velocity. Another 16 subjects presented subclinical signs of neuropathy of the distal muscles of the limbs. Interpretation of these findings is not possible because of the lack of a control group and because alcohol consumption and/or history of diabetes was not determined.

In late 1980, a cross-sectional study was designed to evaluate hepatotoxic and neurotoxic effects in the Icmesa population (188 subjects). A control group was identified consisting of 305 workers of a metallurgical and mechanical industry out of the polluted area and in which there were no known hepatoneurotoxic risk factors. Clinical examinations were carried out among all the workers at the Occupational Health Department of Desio Hospital. A standardized questionnaire was administered at the time of this examination by trained interviewers in order to investigate universal variables, confounders and/or modifiers. Lung function tests (FVC, FEV$_1$), SPE and ulnar nerve electromyography, SGOT, GGT, alkaline phosphatase, total bilirubin, cholesterol serum level, triglycerides, total serum protein and electrophoresis, prothrombin time, hematocrit, hemoglobin, WBC and differential and total urinary porphyrin were carried out in both groups. The response rate was higher than 90% for the Icmesa workers and reached 100% for the control group. No statistically significant differences were found between the two groups examined. This means that five years after the July 1976 Icmesa accident, no particular health effects were detected in the Icmesa workers compared with a selected control group.

A mortality study on the 1947-1976 Icmesa cohort, consisting of 746 workers employed for at least six months, began in late 1980. Two control groups were composed of 1,659 people who worked for at least six months in two plants located in an unpolluted area. It was difficult to trace the Icmesa workers because of the unusually high turnover in this plant. The causes of death among the Icmesa workers are shown in Table 6. An interpretation of significance can only be made after a mortality analysis of the control group is completed. In 1980, a study was initiated to evaluate the effectiveness of the safety measures adopted during the cleanup of the highest polluted sub-area A$_1$. The lack of relevant differences between the cleanup workers and a selected control group make it possible to assume the effectiveness of the safety measures used. However, long-term adverse health effects related to a potential TCDD exposure can not be excluded (Ghezzi et al., 1982).

TABLE 6. Causes of Death Among the "1947-1976 Icmesa Cohort"

ICD Code 9th Revision		
(140-208)	Malignant neoplasms including neoplasms of lymphatic and hematopoietic tissues	42
(162, 163)	Cancer of trachea, bronchus, lung and pleura	16
(161)	Cancer of larynx	2
(200-208)	Cancer of lymphatic and hematopoietic tissue	3
(140-149)	Cancer of lip, oral cavity and pharynx	1
(150-159)	Cancer of digestive organs and peritoneum	14
(155)	Cancer of liver and intrahepatic bile ducts	3
(151)	Cancer of stomach	5
(191)	Cancer of brain	3
(189.2)	Cancer of ureter	1
(172, 173)	Cancer of skin	2
(310-448)	Major cardiovascular diseases	43
(571)	Chronic liver diseases and cirrhosis	19
(E800-E949)	Accidents and adverse effects	17
	All others	22
	Total	143

TABLE 7. All causes of death: Age adjusted rates per 100,000 inhabitants by residence, sex and year of death (1975-1980)

Years		1975		1976		1977		1978		1979		1980	
Zones		C.R.	A.R.	C.R.	A.R.	C.R.	A.R.	C.R.	A.R.	C.R.	A.R.	C.R.	A.R.
A and B	M	265.60	362.22	763.61	960.96	697.21	834.24	464.81	565.36	630.81	763.13	830.01	996.14
	F	307.06	427.81	341.18	492.82	307.06	395.01	341.18	434.18	409.42	565.96	375.30	455.67
R	M	692.21	764.71	803.46	909.18	679.85	778.55	852.90	952.33	781.10	915.61	630.41	749.45
	F	606.50	731.18	624.77	738.18	630.04	740.17	600.51	705.36	582.31	688.33	630.84	751.29
Outer Area	M	891.17	871.33	892.30	868.38	870.07	847.90	867.60	844.62	883.32	859.54	900.17	875.60
	F	701.95	776.99	792.35	766.61	689.19	666.46	729.60	704.45	692.30	669.15	700.88	677.23
Whole Area	M	847.29	847.29	075.90	875.90	837.13	837.13	856.52	856.52	862.98	862.98	857.34	857.34
	F	678.47	678.47	759.33	759.33	672.30	672.30	701.38	701.38	668.78	668.78	681.99	681.99
Italy 1975	M	1076.71	785.28	1076.71	785.28	1076.71	785.28	1076.71	785.28	1076.71	785.28	1076.71	785.28
	F	906.33	721.73	906.33	721.73	906.33	721.73	906.33	721.73	906.33	721.73	906.33	721.73

C.R. = Crude Rate
A.R. = Adjusted Rate
M = Male
F = Female

TABLE 8. Causes of death: Malignant tumor of larynx, trachea, bronchus and lung (I.C.D. 8th; 161,162): Crude and adjusted rates per 100,000 inhabitants by zone of residence, sex and year of death (1975-1980)

| Years | | 1975 | | 1976 | | 1977 | | 1978 | | 1979 | | 1980 | |
Zones		C.R.	A.R.	C.R.	A.R.	C.R.	A.R.	C.R.	A.R.	C.R.	A.R.	C.R.	A.R.
A and B	M	0	0	33.20	48.77	66.40	83.96	33.20	40.66	33.20	40.66	66.40	83.96
	F	0	0	34.12	53.92	0	0	0	0	0	0	0	0
R	M	61.80	68.82	98.89	106.78	49.44	56.33	55.72	62.84	74.17	84.05	37.08	41.23
	F	12.13	12.24	0	0	6.07	6.87	12.13	13.96	24.26	28.64	6.07	7.59
Outer Area	M	62.85	61.51	71.83	70.09	81.93	79.96	70.71	69.05	93.16	91.09	97.65	94.96
	F	5.32	5.11	9.57	9.30	7.44	7.20	10.64	10.25	11.70	11.34	12.76	12.50
Whole Area	M	60.92	60.92	74.96	74.96	76.61	76.61	67.38	67.38	88.61	88.61	85.84	85.84
	F	6.17	6.17	8.81	8.81	7.05	7.05	10.57	10.57	13.22	13.22	11.45	11.45
Italy 1975	M	67.58	53.48	67.58	53.48	67.58	53.48	67.58	53.48	67.58	53.48	67.58	53.48
	F	8.56	7.29	8.56	7.29	8.56	7.29	8.56	7.29	8.56	7.29	8.56	7.29

C.R. = Crude Rate
A.R. = Adjusted Rate
M = Male
F = Female

MORTALITY STUDY AND CANCER REGISTRY

In order to set up a mortality study and a cancer registry, the population living in the area at the time of explosion has been computed starting from residents in 1979 and going back to July 10, 1976. This was possible with the cooperation of the eleven Municipalities' Demographic offices. The "July 10, 1976 Seveso Cohort" was identified retrospectively, and since 1979 it has been kept up-to-date prospectively month by month. The completeness of the mortality data collected from 1975 through 1980 was more than 99% of the deaths. In the analysis, the mortality rates of the polluted areas were compared with the 1975 Italy mortality rates (the most recent available). The total population of 22,837 in the eleven Municipalities up to December 31, 1979, has been used as a standard population for making the age adjustment. In Table 7, mortality rates for all causes of death refer to the subdivision by zones of residence at the time of death. With regard to those long-term health effects correlated with TCDD exposure based on observation in animals and humans, it is obvious that no conclusion can be reached five years after the Icmesa accident due to their long latency period. However, an increasing trend has been detected in 1979-1980 in the age adjusted mortality rates for cancer of the larynx, trachea, bronchus and lung (Table 8). A statistically significant difference was also observed in the time trend for the eleven Municipalities between 1976 and 1980 in mortality rates for hypertension.

More suggestive data comes from the "Seveso Cancer Registry" established on January 1981. A statistically significant excess has been found in the incidence of soft tissue sarcomas in the population living in Zone R. Eight histologically confirmed cases have been observed from 1977-80; the expected number based on the population of eleven Muncipalities was 3.23 with a risk ratio of 2.48. Comparison with national mortality rate was excluded due to the varying quality of the data.

It has to be pointed out that no conclusions can be drawn from the cancer data because of the recognized latency period for cancer induction and the fact that in this instance the risk-assessment base used only one risk marker (TCDD in the soil). There are at least three other possible markers of exposure: chloracne, acute skin irritation and animal deaths occurring as a consequence of the accident. The geographical distributions of these TCDD related adverse health effects are shown in Figures 3, 4 and 5. In order to define the real population potentially exposed to TCDD, the whole area has been divided into sub-areas of one square kilometer (Figure 6). Chloracne, acute skin irritation and animal mortality rates have been computed for each sub-area. In this approach, high rates for these adverse effects must be considered to define sub-areas in which a high risk of TCDD related health effects would be expected. Differences in rates for the markers considered are shown in Figures 7, 8 and 9.

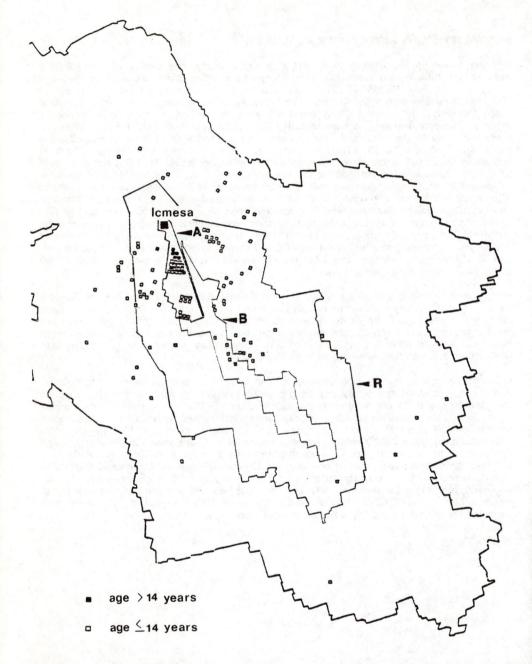

Figure 3. Geographical distribution of chloracne cases (males) notified after July 10, 1976 in the polluted area.

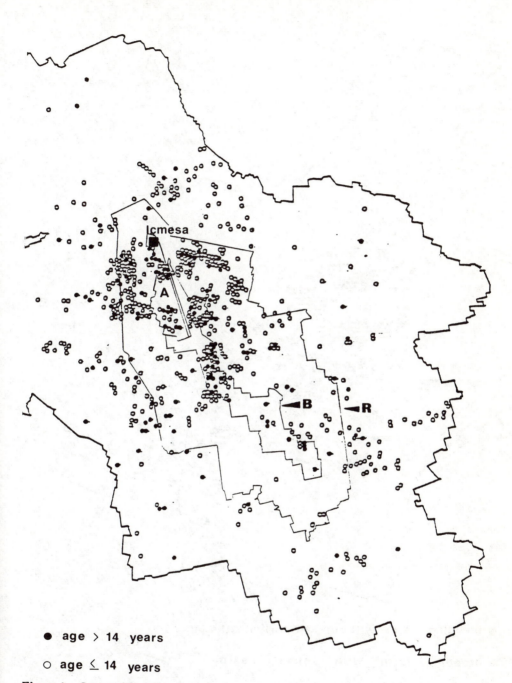

● age > 14 years

○ age ≤ 14 years

Figure 4. Geographical distribution of acute skin lesion cases (males) notified after July 10, 1976 in the polluted area.

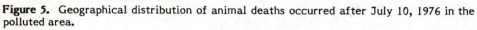

Figure 5. Geographical distribution of animal deaths occurred after July 10, 1976 in the polluted area.

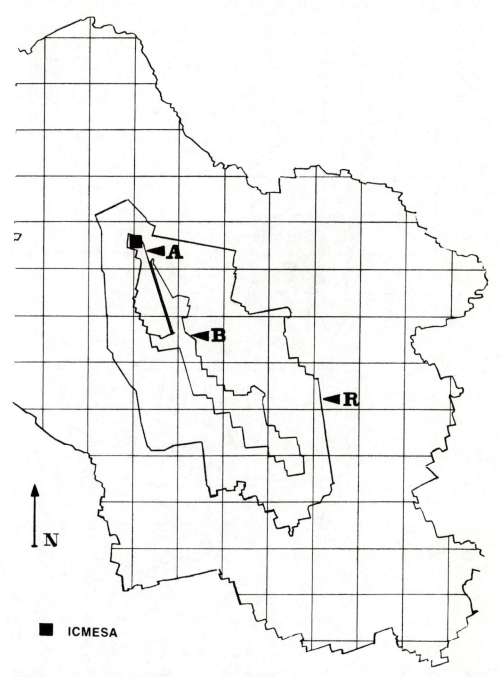

Figure 6. Map of the Seveso area by square kilometers

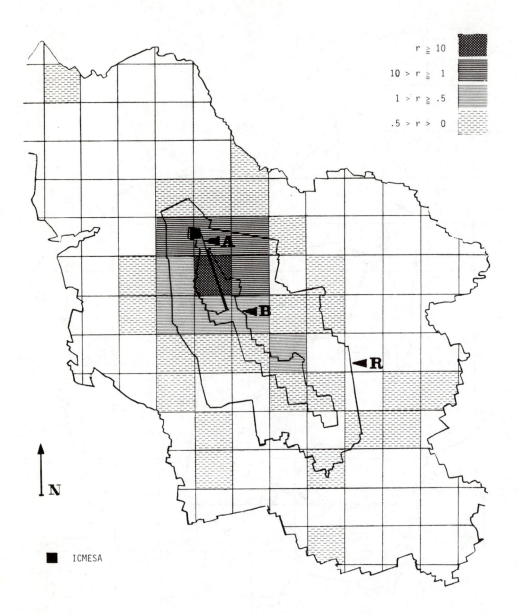

Figure 7. Geographical Distribution of Chloracne Rates (r) x 1000 per Km²

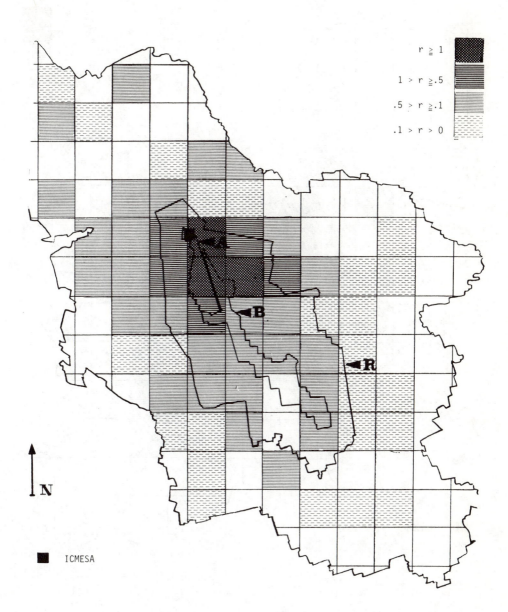

Figure 8. Geographical Distribution of Acute Skin Lesion Rates (r) x 1000 per Km^2

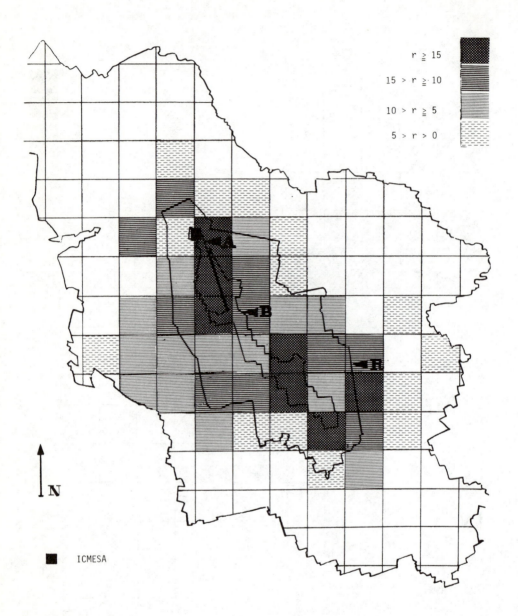

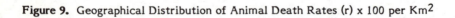

Figure 9. Geographical Distribution of Animal Death Rates (r) x 100 per Km^2

CONCLUSION

Knowledge of the adverse health effects of TCDD comes from animal studies and human occupational exposures occurring during the manufacture of trichlorophenol. Short term effects have been identified. Long term effects are still under study.

The high persistence of TCDD bound to the soil, and its absorption and translocation in vegetables and fruit trees, represent serious problems in Seveso. In this highly populated area, two major kinds of exposure occurred after the accident: 1) an acute high-level exposure in which larger quantities of TCDD were probably absorbed directly and through the food chain; 2) a chronic low-level TCDD exposure that could still be present in those subjects who have lived and are still living in areas that were never cleaned up such as Zones B and R. Several efforts have been made in the last two years to identify the populations most likely exposed to TCDD in order to plan methodologically correct studies for mid and long term effects. There is an urgent need to define and quantitate exposure in order to improve the quality of the epidemiological investigation. In Seveso, no systematic analyses of human tissue were done. Only one analysis of TCDD in human tissues was carried out among the thousands of people exposed (Fachetti et al, 1980). This was from an autopsy of a woman who lived in Seveso's highly polluted Zone A. She died in October 1976 of pancreatic cancer. It has to be underlined that she was a grandmother of two of the more severe cases of chloracne that occurred and that she never developed either chloracne or skin irritation. 2,3,7,8-TCDD was detected in all tissues at levels ranging from 6 to 1840 pg/g (Caramaschi et al., 1981). It is clear that although chloracne is an indicator of absorption and biological effects, it is not a sensitive marker of TCDD exposure. Other parameters have to be considered to identify exposed and control groups.

Unfortunately, due to the lack of proper studies in the early phase of the "Seveso Program", reevaluation of these data, such as has been done with the Hiroshima and Nagasaki study records, has to be excluded.

Only well designed carefully executed epidemiologic studies will enable us to draw conclusions about the occurrence of chronic health effects and their relationship to TCDD exposure.

REFERENCES

Acts of Parlamentary Commission for the Seveso Accident. 1978. Atti Parlamentari - VII Legislatura, Rome, Doc. XXIII, No. 6.

Caramaschi, F., Del Corno, G., Favaretti, C., Giambelluca, S.E., Montesarchio, E. and Fara, G.M. 1981. Chloracne following environmental contamination by TCDD in Seveso, Italy. International Journal of Epidemiology 10, 2:135-143.

di Domenico, A., Silano V., Viviano, G. and Zapponi, G. 1980. Accidental release of 2,3,7,8-TCDD at Seveso, Italy: TCDD distribution in the soil surface layer. Ecotoxicology and Environmental Safety, 4:293-320.

Facchetti, S., Fornari, A. and Montagna, M. 1980. Distribution of 2,3,7,8-TCDD in the tissue of a person exposed to the toxic cloud at Seveso. In Forensic and Environmental Application, Institute of Petroleum 61:1405-1414.

Ghezzi, I. 1981. Lecture presented at the meeting: Five Years of Epidemiology in the Seveso Area, Milano, November 13-14.

Ghezzi, I., Cannatelli, P., Assennato, G., Merlo, F., Mocarelli, P., Brambilla, P. and Sicurello, F.   1982.   Potential 2,3,7,8-TCDD exposure of Seveso decontamination workers: A controlled prospective study.   Scand. J. Work Environ. Health 8, Suppl. 1:176-179.

Strigini, P., Blanco, G. and Formigaro, M.   1982.   Gli aborti spontanei.   Sapere,   June-August:64-65.

Chapter 19

THE MECHANISM OF ACTION OF DIOXIN

Fumio Matsumura
Pesticide Research Center
Michigan State University

TOXIC EFFECT OF TCDD

There is no question that TCDD is a very unique poison. The first time I gave TCDD to animals I expected to see some immediate symptoms. We waited and waited and we could not see usual signs of toxicity. The animals did look a little quieter but there was no obvious toxicity until about thirty days later; at that point the animals just died. In addition, we could find no clear-cut dose response. Even when we gave high doses, not all animals died and we had no idea what the difference was among the population. Not only are there differences within species, there are very large differences between species as Dr. McConnell pointed out (McConnell, 1984).

TCDD is also different in not showing organ specific toxicity. Although it does produce organ damage, the target organs differ from species to species (Moore, 1973). In addition, you cannot say what effect leads to the death of the animal. If you give something like DDT, the animal starts showing convulsions so you suspect that the nervous system must be affected. But in the case of TCDD you cannot say why they die. It is really a mysterious compound.

ENZYME INDUCTION

Now, some good news. There has been significant progress in one area; the area of induction. TCDD is a very potent inducer of certain detoxification enzymes, particularly in the liver, which is the detoxifying organ for foreign compounds. When you administer a small quantitiy of TCDD you notice that the liver (hepatocyte) microsomes start increasing. This is the first step in the increase of the detoxification enzymes which reside in the microsome. Several groups, especially Dr. Poland's and Dr. Nebert's groups, have contributed to the understanding of TCDD's mechanism of action. It appears that TCDD binds with a receptor in the cytosolic portion of the cell and this complex migrates into the nucleus. This somehow activates the synthesis of the detoxifying enzymes: cytochrome P448 and related systems. There is a pleiotropic response; that is, one change (TCDD-receptor complex) leads to many, many different changes (induction of many proteins) (Poland et al., 1974; Nebert, 1979).

Although phenomenal progress has been made in this area, there is one problem: induction, per se, probably has nothing to do with toxicity. There are many other compounds, such as DDT, phenobarbital, 3-methylcholanthrene, which are good inducers but do not cause the same symptoms as TCDD (Madhukar and Matsumura, 1981). They are toxic but they do not cause weight loss, chloracne and other signs of toxicity which are specific to TCDD-type compounds. The best evidence for the lack of relationship of induction and toxicity is the case of the guinea pigs. Guinea pigs are the most sensitive animals to TCDD but liver induction is not seen. In fact, when you look at the liver of the guinea pigs, you hardly see any effects of TCDD even at the time of death (Gupta et al., 1973; McConnell et al., 1978).   This is not to say that induction studies are unimportant; they reflect some profound biochemical changes that are taking place. However, what I would like to emphasize here is that we still do not have the whole picture.

PLASMA MEMBRANE ALTERATIONS

In the absence of a clear understanding of TCDD's toxicity, our group started looking at the problem from a different angle. Around 1975-77, I had the pleasure to work with Dr. Dick Peterson and his group which had found that the excretion of neutral substrate in the liver was hampered by TCDD (Yang et al., 1977). This phenomenon was confirmed by Dr. Curt Klaassen's group.   Not knowing about the mechanisms of neutral substrate transport in the liver, we suspected that it could be due to sodium-potassium ATPase. We found that after about 10 days of TCDD administration the level of ouabain transport starts to decrease.   At the same time, sodium-potassium and magnesium ATPase also start decreasing.   It was a beautiful correlation.   Unfortunately, we also found that sodium-potassium ATPase had nothing to do with the transport of neutral substrate, since by using steroid hormone analogs the ouabain transport activity could be uncoupled from that of ATPases (Peterson et al., 1979a; Peterson et al., 1979b).

However, we later realized that sodium-potassium ATPase is a good marker for plasma membrane; i.e., cell surface membrane as opposed to any other membrane. This came to our attention when we were studying the isolated hepatocytes. When you start culturing the hepatocytes from an animal treated with TCDD, you realize that those cells do not stick to each other in contrast to normal hepatocyte cultures where the cells are attached to each other. In addition, normal cells start forming a monolayer so that when you pour off the supernatant, you can see beautiful layers formed. This is not observed in cells from TCDD-treated animals. Thus we started to suspect that there was some change in the plasma membrane around 1979.

At that point, we started to look at the plasma membrane and fortunately there is a good biochemical method for isolating relatively pure plasma membrane from the rat liver. When we examined SDS gel-electrophoretograms of the plasma membrane proteins we noticed that some of the protein bands started disappearing after TCDD treatment. There wasn't much effect in the first few days but by the tenth day, intensities of some bands started decreasing. We used one band, at 48,000, as a marker, because it is a structural protein which always gives two or three percent of the total protein. We sometimes used markers at the microsomal enzymes and, so that if there is any contamination there, we will find it. Using these markers, you can see a great decrease in some of the bands, particularly after day 20. It was clear that some profound changes were taking place in the plasma membranes (Brewster et al., 1982).

LIPOPROTEIN ACTIVITY

At the same time, other investigators were looking at various biochemical changes in the guinea pig in an attempt to better understand the mechanism of toxicity. One noticeable sign of TCDD's toxicity is an unusual accumulation of cholesteryl ester and triglyceride carrying lipoproteins in the serum; particularly low-density lipoproteins (LDL) and very low-density lipoproteins (VLDL) (Swift et al., 1981). In light of the known alterations in plasma membranes due to TCDD administration, and the presence of low-density lipoprotein receptors in liver cell plasma membranes, we decided to look at this phenomenon more closely.

We administered TCDD by injection to the guinea pigs and isolated their hepatocytes ten days later. We first looked at the uptake of low-density lipoprotein by these cells as compared to cells from untreated animals. We found that there was a significant decrease in both the rate of uptake and total uptake in the cells from the TCDD-treated animals. The next step was to try to see why this reduction in uptake was occurring. To approach this, we looked at how the different liver cell fractions responded to low-density lipoprotein. It was clear that the greatest reduction in lipoprotein uptake occurred in the plasma membrane fraction (Bombick et al., 1984).

A further refinement was to isolate the plasma membranes from both TCDD-treated and untreated guinea pigs and also treated and untreated rats (which also show increased serum cholesterol in response to TCDD administration). There was a clear decrease in low-density lipoprotein binding in both guinea pig and rat hepatic plasma membranes. To ensure that these decreases were not due to changes in nutritional status (i.e. TCDD poisoned animals eat less),we also looked at untreated animals which were fed exactly the same amount of food as the treated ones. Again, the results were the same (Bombick et al., 1984).

RECEPTOR SYSTEMS

As a check on these findings, we decided to look at the internalization of low-density lipoprotein receptors in hepatocytes. It is known that when low-density lipoprotein interacts with its receptor, it is then carried inside the cell where it is metabolized. Thus, if there is less uptake and thus fewer lipoprotein-receptor complexes, there should be less low-density lipoprotein internalized. Studies of cells from TCDD-treated animals and untreated animals showed that this was, indeed, the case. There was a significant decrease in internalization in the treated as compared to the untreated animals (Bombick et al., 1984).

Although it appears clear that there is an association between TCDD and low-density lipoprotein receptor activity, it might be argued that this is a secondary effect resulting from the increased cholesterol levels (i.e., "down regulation"). We do not feel this is the case for a number of reasons. One is the low level of TCDD at which the binding decreases occur in the guinea pig and the lack of overt toxic signs at these levels. It would thus appear we are seeing the early toxic effects of TCDD rather than some indirect action. Second, if the reduction of LDL receptors is due to down regulation there should be a decrease in VLDL production by the liver, whereas VLDL levels in TCDD treated guinea pigs are elevated, rather than depressed. There are a number of observations which support our theory that serum low-density lipoprotein can increase as a result of a reduction in the activity of low-density lipoprotein receptors. This has been seen not only in animals such as rabbits (e.g., Watanabe rabbit) (Goldstein et al., 1983) but also in humans who have a genetic disorder known as familial hypercholesterolemia.

These results are obviously of interest in providing clues as to the mechanism of action of TCDD. Moreover, they also tie in with the possible hypercholesterolemia in humans exposed to TCDD that was mentioned earlier in Dr. Suskind's presentation (Suskind, 1984). Although this link is based on epidemiological data from limited populations, the similarity of effect found in experimental animals suggests the need for further studies in this area.

We are continuing to look at the plasma membrane to see if we can detect other changes which might reflect TCDD's mode of action. We have looked at several enzyme systems and have found that many are affected, mostly depressed. One which seems to show an increase in activity is the group of protein kinases.

In addition, we are looking at receptor systems other than the low-density lipoprotein receptors. Again, we find effects which seem to be related to TCDD. For example, the insulin receptor seems to be stimulated at lower doses but depressed at higher ones. The epidermal growth factor (EGF) receptor also seemed to show a marked depression after TCDD administration. Indeed, EGF receptor was the one which was most sensitive, i.e., that showed an effect at the lowest TCDD dose so far as we have studied. We are presently following up on that finding.

Even if we do find these changes, we are still faced with the task of determining if these are related to toxicity and, if so, in what way. What we are seeing so far are little hints or clues to keep us going. We are far from an understanding of the unique action of TCDD but we are hoping that the combined efforts of many biochemical toxicologists will eventually provide the answers we seek.

REFERENCES

Bombick, D.W., Matsumura, F. and Madhukar, B.V. 1984. TCDD (2,3,7,8-tetrachlorodibenzo-p-dioxin) causes reduction in the low density lipoprotein (LDL) receptor activities in the hepatic plasma membrane of the guinea pig and rat. Biochem. Biophys. Res. Comm. 118:548-554.

Brewster, D.W., Madhukar, B.V. and Matsumura, F. 1982. Influence of 2,3,7,8-TCDD on the protein composition of the plasma membrane of hepatic cells from the rat. Biochem. Biophys. Res. Comm. 107:68-74.

Goldstein, J., Kita, T. and Brown, M. 1983. N. Engl. J. Med. 309:288-296.

Gupta, B.N., Vos, J.G., Moore, J.A., Zinkl, J.G. and Bullock, B.C. 1973. Pathologic effects of 2,3,7,8-tetrachloro-p-dioxin in laboratory animals. Environ. Health Perspectives 5:125-140.

Madhukar, B.V. and Matsumura, F. 1981. Differences in the nature of induction of mixed function oxidase systems of the rat liver among phenobarbital, DDT, 3-methylcholanthrene and TCDD. Toxicol. Appl. Pharmacol. 61:109-118.

McConnell, E.E. 1984. This volume.

McConnell, E.E., Moore, J.A., Haseman, J.K. and Harris, M.W. 1978. The comparative toxicity of chlorinated dibenzo-p-dioxins in mice and guinea pigs. Toxicol. Appl. Pharmacol. 44:335-356.

Moore, J.A. 1973. Chlorinated dibenzodioxins and dibenzofurans. Environ. Health Perspectives, Issue No. 5, pp. 313, National Institute of Environmental Health Sciences, Research Triangle Park, NC.

Nebert, D.W. 1979. Genetic differences in the induction of monooxygenase activities by polycyclic aromatic compounds. Pharmacol. Ther. 6:395-417.

Peterson, R.E., Madhukar, B.V., Yang, K.H. and Matsumura, F. 1979a. Depression of ATPase activity in isolated liver surface membranes of 2,3,7,8-tetrachlorodibenzo-p-dioxin-treated rats. J. Pharmacol. Exp. Ther. 210:175-282.

Peterson, R.E., Hamada, N., Yang, K.H., Madhukar, B.V. and Matsumura, F. 1979b. Reversal of 2,3,7,8-tetrachlorodibenzo-p-dioxin-induced depression in ouabain biliary excretion by pregnenolone-16α-carbonitrile and spiranolactone in isolated perfused rat livers. Toxicol. Appl. Pharmacol. 50:407-416.

Poland, A., Glover, E., Robinson, J.R. and Nebert, D.W. 1974. Genetic expression of aryl hydrocarbon and hydroxylase activity. Induction of monooxygenase activities and cytochrome P-450 formation by 2,3,7,8-tetrachlorodibenzo-p-dioxin in mice genetically "nonresponsive" to other aromatic hydrocarbons. J. Biol. Chem. 249:5599-5606.

Suskind, R.R. 1984. This volume.

Swift, L.L., Gasiewicz, T.A., Dunn, G.D., Soule, P.D. and Neal, R.A. 1981. Characterization of the hyperlipidemia in guinea pigs induced by 2,3,7,8-tetrachlorodibenzo-p-dioxin. Toxicol. Appl. Pharmacol. 59:489-499.

Yang, K.H., Croft, W.A. and Peterson, R.E. 1977. Effects of 2,3,7,8-tetrachlorodibenzo-p-dioxin on plasma disappearance and biliary excretion of foreign compounds in rats. Toxicol. Appl. Pharmacol. 40: 485-496.

Chapter 20

PANEL DISCUSSION – SECTION 4

GASIEWICZ: A very intriguing talk, Dr. Matsumura. But I have a couple of questions. First of all, do compounds other than TCDD, that decrease the concentration of EGF receptors, have the same type of toxicity as TCDD?

MATSUMURA: They don't.

GASIEWICZ: So a decrease in concentrations of EGF receptors clearly does not, by itself, explain the differences in toxicity. The second question is: Did you do pair-fed control animals in your studies?

MATSUMURA: Yes, we did. There's no effect of pair-feeding. As to your comment, I hope I have made it very clear that we cannot say that the toxicity is directly related to EGF.

GASIEWICZ: The third question is: At what doses did you get decreases in EGF receptor concentrations and how are these related to lethal concentrations?

MATSUMURA: We have found the effect in the hamster at dose concentration ranges starting at 100 micrograms per kilogram, which is low compared to the lethal dose. However, toxic symptoms can certainly be observed; you can start seeing the changes in the liver and all that.

CROSBY: I have a question for Dr. Suskind. I wonder if you could briefly outline the possible treatments available for chloracne, including skin grafting?

SUSKIND: The treatment of chloracne, to begin with, has to be differentiated from the treatment of acne vulgaris. Most of the traditional medications and the modalities used for acne vulgaris are really contraindicated in chloracne except for the retinoic acid derivatives. This includes the kerolytic agents like salicylic acid, resorcin, and especially ultra violet light. The other modalities, which years ago we used in acne, were superficial radiation, that is, ionizing radiation (x-ray) and this also caused hyperpigmentation and didn't cause improvement of the chloracne. In the last ten years, however, the emergence of retinoic acid, and especially the cis-retinoic acid (Isotretinon) which is marketed as Accutane, has in some instances been very beneficial. And it's interesting what effect retinoic acid has on the cell. It inhibits sebaceous gland function and keratinization. It affects the rapidity with which the squamous cell becomes keratinized. There have been, for example, outbreaks of chloracne from chlorinated azoxybenzene, and in these instances, topical retinoic acid has been very useful. I think that's all we really have to offer at the moment. I must say that in the group we recently examined, we were epidemiologists, not therapists, so we had no way to offer therapeutic modalities. But, I would think that if a good therapeutic study were done, it could be done on a population like this.

YOUNG: Dr. Suskind, in terms of the exposure time on the individuals that you reported, specifically on the 204 that did develop chloracne, am I to understand that once they developed it they were not continually exposed; or were they, in fact, in the plant where they continued to work for many years and where they could have continued to have a low level of exposure?

SUSKIND: The exposure period in the exposed group varied anywhere from one month or less to 15 years and more.

YOUNG: So when we say that the chloracne has persisted over 30 years, we've got to be careful to bring that in, then, is that right? I guess I'm concerned that some people have been saying, once you've had this acute exposure, you may show chloracne for 30 years, and I'm not sure that's what your data are telling us.

SUSKIND: What I'm saying is that in this group in which we have not been able to identify or quantitate actual levels of exposure, we do not know how much dioxin any one of these individuals was exposed to. We may know a little bit about duration of exposure, but even then the amount of dioxin to which a worker would have been exposed from 1949 to 1953 was very different than for the group which initially was exposed in 1960, because the hygienic conditions were very different. As a matter of fact, the building in which the accident occurred was ostensibly cleaned up, but acne was still occurring in new assignees who were getting into the building and working there. So they destroyed the building, and built new ones; first one to make trichlorophenol and another one to acidify it and make the 2,4,5-T, and finally they built a third building which incorporated both the synthesis of trichlorophenol and the synthesis of 2,4,5-T. The hygiene in that third building was superior to the initial one so that the degree of exposure was very different in different areas during that period from 1948 to 1969.

YOUNG: One last question. Recently the Mt. Sinai group, Dr. Singer specifically, published an article relating to part of the same population you studied, and discussed the issue of nerve conduction and potential damage from exposure. Would you care to comment on this?

SUSKIND: Well, my only comment is, that if you take seriously the expertise of those who know most about nerve conduction, nerve conduction velocity measurements have to be made under extremely controlled conditions. It's not a field measurement. It has to be done under controlled conditions of temperature, of humidity, and the application of the electrode to the skin has to be uniform. The individual who does it has to be very expert at it and in the view of such experts as Schaumberg and Spencer, it does not provide a method to detect, for example, changes that you could not really detect by a good thorough neurological examination.

YOUNG:

Dr. Merlo, I noted that in Seveso there were reports of changes in nerve conductivity. Would you care to comment on that?

MERLO:

There were many doubts about the quality of those data. The International Scientific Advisory Committee (a group of scientists in charge of supervising and reviewing the Seveso research) was particularly critical about the control group the investigators chose. From these studies we cannot draw strong conclusions but also we can't reject a possible cause-effect relationship. Some subclinical effects (changes in nerve conduction) were detected more frequently among TCDD exposed people when compared with the control, thus, we can't keep our eyes closed.

SUSKIND:

We tried to get the best help that we could and we got the assistance of the NIOSH group that had probably the most up-to-date equipment and really the most experienced technical people, particularly Mr. Boyd. He was with us at the time and, from our results, we didn't find any differences, remembering that all of these have to be age-corrected. In addition, you have to eliminate your diabetics; you have to eliminate your alcoholics; and you have to eliminate all those in which neuropathy is possible. We did all of these things and we found no differences.

GILMAN:

Dr. Merlo, there's been a lot of confusion, I think, over the adverse pregnancy outcome issue from TCDD exposure. The situation in Seveso is a little cloudy. I'm wondering whether or not you can make any comments on more up-to-date findings. What about stillbirths, spontaneous abortions, congenital anomalies?

MERLO:

A Birth Defects Registry was set up in late 1978. Actually, final data are available and the statistical analysis has shown that hemangiomas are the only abnormalities that have reached statistical significance. About the occurrence of spontaneous abortion in this area, one can find information and evaluation in an Italian scientific journal (these data were never published in an international journal). A significant increase in abortion rate has been observed in 1977 in the A and B areas (the more contaminated by TCDD), and not in the less polluted zones (R and outer). Some people are actually working to investigate whether or not the observed increase in abortion rates may be related to psychological problems rather than to an embryotoxic effects. It is my opinion that the higher frequency of spontaneous abortion has been the consequence of a direct toxic effect of TCDD on the embryo.

BERNARD:

I think that dioxin provides the scientific community, and perhaps society as a whole, with really a unique opportunity to study some of the basic problems that exist in the relationship between science, congressional action, and regulatory action. I know that in my work I am faced many times with regulatory activity occurring based on a paucity of data. I think what we've heard today is quite a bit of animal evidence as to what dioxin does, but I haven't heard, really anything that indicates that over the past 30 years a real problem exists with dioxin with regard to humans. We know 30 years ago we had chloracne problems. We have indications that on high acute exposures, we have liver problems. But after extensive expenditures and very careful studies we still have no evidence that a problem exists, much less are we able to quantify the risk that does exist; yet we are moving ahead. One estimate is that we are talking about spending up to five billion dollars to deal with a problem in Missouri. I think this is an extremely good example where regulatory activity and congressional activity have so leaped beyond any scientific basis that it behooves us to look at that very carefully. One question that I do have for the panel is: We obviously have a number of instances where humans have been acutely exposed to extremely high levels of dioxin, and yet we have no evidence that that has caused any long-term harm. How could one relate those acute high level exposures to possible chronic, very low-level exposures of living in a place such as Times Beach?

MATSUMURA: Dr. Smuckler, would you like to answer that?

SMUCKLER: You can't and the reason you can't is that there is a remarkable reserve on the part of the human body. You think how we, as a group, abuse ourselves, yet we respond and live 70 years without any problem; how we can be subject to mutilating surgical procedures and still survive. A single episode with the healing capacity of the human body provides us with evidence of that great reserve. Let me also second what you've said. We have had a number of examples in which the inability of our government as well as ourselves to handle hazardous problems leads me to some concern. In 1961 we attempted to have carbon tetrachloride removed from household fire extinguishers. There, we had plenty of human data. We didn't need rats to turn up their feet to heaven. We had humans that did it. The allied chemical industries were intransigent. They thought this was the most absurd thing they'd ever heard even though they admitted that it was a problem. Fortunately, we were able to remove the material. On the other hand, the evidence that Red Dye #2 had ever produced any disease in human beings is interesting. It was introduced into our own food chains shortly before World War I, and in the late '60s the average human being in the United States consumed 18 milligrams a day. Yet you don't find any red M&M's any more, do you? The problem is one that we've addressed here in part, and I think the difficulty is that our concept of injury is archaic, our understanding of injury is miniscule, and in large part, we have not expended the energy we should in attempting to understand interactions of chemicals with cells. We've done a better job with viruses and even there we don't know what's happening. We have no idea what the cell origin of a cancer is and need only ask: Is it monoclonal or polyclonal? - and you'll get into a family argument. We don't know what an acute effect is. As Dick Recknagle pointed out, until we can understand how a simple, symmetrical, saturated haloalkane like carbon tetrachloride can kill a liver cell, how can we expect something as complex as TCDD to become manifest?

McCONNELL: I would like to respond to that and take a little bit different tack.

I would agree that it's hard to compare a Nitro, West Virginia, or an acute exposure in an animal to a Times Beach situation because the former are single exposures. I think people may or may not have been exposed in Times Beach, but if they were exposed, they were exposed chronically. Now, how do you compare that? We have shown in animals that chronic low-level exposures in several species of animals appear to be more potent than a single equivalent dose. In other words, it takes less of the TCDD, spread out over a period of time to produce a given effect than it does in a single exposure; just the opposite of what occurs with many, many chemicals. So, I am not sure that following the Nitro group in a negative sense will be able to predict anything in terms of a chronic exposure. If I did find something in a Nitro group, I certainly would look for it in the Times Beach people, but I might expect to find something different in the Times Beach exposed population.

BERNARD: I guess what I was saying is that all of the lectures presented today indicate that if there is a problem, it certainly is one we've had great difficulty identifying in humans. And if this is the case, how is the scientific community going to get across to the lay public, and perhaps more importantly to the regulatory agencies, that we are spending such vast sums of money on a problem which we are not sure really exists?

SUSKIND: May I answer the comment made by the last speaker. I'm not altogether sure I heard him correctly, that you couldn't draw some conclusions about chronic exposure from a group of humans, many of whom were exposed for 15 to 20 years. These were not people who were exposed once. This was not an LD$_{50}$ experiment. This was a regular plant operation in which people were exposed continuously for as long as 15 or 20 years or as short as a month or a week, and I think that you can learn a great deal from it.

BERNARD: I think you can, too, but what I'm saying is: Those who were exposed for a week or a month, and there were significant numbers of those, were the people who were exposed to the highest levels. Correct?

SUSKIND: I think that if they were exposed - let's say from 1965 to 1969 - their exposure levels were not nearly as high as those people who were exposed in 1948 and 1949, so that their dose levels were different.

BERNARD: What I'm saying, though, is if you find something in that group, that certainly is something pertinent to look for in a group somewhere else. However, I would not be entirely surprised if I found something in another group that was chronically exposed that you did not observe.

SUSKIND: Yes, but from the standpoint of biological information, you have a whole range of exposures in that relatively small population: 204. Incidentally, that represents about 60% of the estimated people who were exposed, not the whole population, and even that is a kind of a bias, epidemiologically, but that's the best we could do. I think that one does learn a great deal from this group, a small group with a wide range of exposure, which is even applicable to the Times Beach population in which the bioavailability of the dioxin is very limited.

YOUNG: I'd like to ask just one very short question for Gene McConnell. In the literature, we see a reference to one particular animal study that came up with some soft tissue sarcomas. Would you care to comment on that particular study?

McCONNELL: The animal study that came up with the soft tissue sarcomas? I question that study as to whether those are real or not. However, I do feel that the liver tumors are real.

YOUNG: I'm referring to the work of Van Miller. That study is being cited a great deal to show that soft tissue sarcomas have occurred in an exposed animal population; therefore, one should expect to see them in exposed humans.

McCONNELL: No, I agree with you. There's a lot of other questionable literature. For example, I have referenced studies for many years that said that all that weight loss in dioxin-intoxicated animals is due to something other than not eating. I think it's now clear that a majority of the weight loss is due to not eating or not drinking. There are other examples of misleading literature, but this is not unique to this subject.

MATSUMURA: I hate to terminate such interesting discussions, but time is up, and I'd like to thank you all very much.

AUDIENCE MEMBERS CONTRIBUTING TO THE PANEL DISCUSSION: Thomas Gasiewicz, University of Rochester, Department of Radiation Biology, Rochester, NY 14642; and A. Gilman, National Health & Welfare, Canada, Tunney's Pasture, Ottawa, Ontario K1A 0L3.

PART II
WORKSHOP
SUMMARIES

Section 1
Public Policy on Dioxins

PUBLIC POLICY ON DIOXINS - WORKSHOP SUMMARY

Co-chairmen: Daniel Bronstein
                 Dennis Wint

Panel Members

Bruce Bernard	William Lowrance
William Cooper	Alexander B. Morrison
Joseph DiMento	William Rustem
John Gannon	Michael Slimak
John Hesse	Fred Tschirley
Larry Holcomb	Bernard Wagner
Harold Humphrey	Alvin Young

INTRODUCTION

The dioxin issue exemplifies the problems faced by scientists with many other of the toxic agents. The layman looks to academia, government and institutional agencies for answers, for "the truth", yet only rarely can "the truth" be provided. Public policy, then, has to be created despite these unrealistic expectations of the public and the scientist's uncomfortable awareness of the limitations of the available data.

Ethical constraints prevent the use of humans in most studies where adverse effects are suspected; thus, most of our evaluations of human health effects come from extrapolation of animal data or from epidemiological studies. The extrapolation of results from animal studies to humans, in the ideal setting, becomes significant when the mechanisms of action are understood. Yet these mechanisms are often elusive and conclusions or decisions must be made without them. For instance, the mechanism of cigarette-induced lung cancer still remains a mystery after forty years of investigations. Although direct causality cannot unequivocably be proven, the correlation is strong enough to warrant public policy on the carcinogenicity of cigarettes.

Epidemiological studies also have certain inherent limitations. Dose response curves cannot normally be constructed; quantitative measurements of exposure are usually not available. Results from epidemiological studies are limited by the size of change we are looking for (ie. if the change is less than 10% of the norm it will not be detected). This is more significant with epidemiological than with other types of studies, as variables are more difficult to define and control. In addition, the study of the toxic effects of any one chemical on a human population is hampered by the fact that humans are exposed to a large and diverse mixture of chemicals, making it difficult to determine the causative agents.

Ideally, public policy with respect to human health effects should be guided by a complete data base, but this data is often not available. The public needs to understand that it is sometimes necessary to make decisions without all of the facts and generally the regulatory system is based on "best available" data and not "perfect" knowledge. In light of these concerns, the following issues will be the focus of this summary: dioxin as a public policy priority, research areas needed, public education and the transfer of information from scientists to the public.

PUBLIC POLICY PRIORITY OF DIOXINS

The currently available data on the toxicity of 2,3,7,8-TCDD indicates that this compound is an animal carcinogen. However, the human studies conducted to date do not prove dioxin to be as serious a threat to humans as was initially feared. Most of our current information on the health effects of dioxins on humans is based on epidemiological studies subsequent to industrial accidents such as the Nitro, W.Va. incident (Suskind, 1984) and the Seveso, Italy incident (Merlo, 1984). However, as was pointed out by Dr. Merlo, who is conducting the Seveso study (Merlo, 1984),these epidemiological studies are fraught with many problems. The conclusion of the Human Health and Toxicity workshop at this conference was that there is insufficient epidemiological evidence to suggest that TCDD is a human carcinogen, and we concur in this.

There are many ongoing studies of the human health effects of TCDD which are attempting to overcome the limitations of these earlier studies. The Agent Orange Working Group, a group which coordinates many of the programs related to dioxins and the health studies associated with them, is responsible for a total of 26 such studies. Among these are the Air Force "Ranch Hand" Study (Panel on the Proposed Air Force Study of Herbicide Orange, 1980), which claims to have well documented exposure histories and a massive veterans study with a cohort of 60,000. The Public Policy Workgroup did not review these protocols and took no position on them, but did conclude that properly designed and executed epidemiological studies of such populations should be able to answer some of the issues regarding low dose effect of TCDD on humans.

The Source, Distribution and Fate Workshop looked at parameters critical to the assessment of dioxin as a public priority: distribution, persistence, bioaccumulation, quantity and sources. The bioaccumulation of dioxins, unlike that of DDT, has not proven to be a problem in terrestrial areas and dioxins although quickly becoming ubiquitous are distributed in very minute quantities. They concluded that although TCDD is a hazardous toxin, it shows limited distribution, generally low concentrations, relative immobility and limited sources. Combining this with the health and environmental data to date, the Public Policy Workshop concluded that dioxins are not an exceptionally high priority public policy issue.

RESEARCH RECOMMENDATIONS

Although dioxin should not have a high national priority, it is recognized that dioxin can be a regional or local problem. An example of this is the recent episode in Times Beach, Missouri (Sun, 1973) where large quantities of TCDD were inadvertently distributed. The concentration of 2,3,7,8-TCDD in this area is cause for concern. It is important that all such "hot spots" be identified and mapped out because the potential for individual risk is high.

As was pointed out during this conference, there are many congeners of dioxin which are known to exist and which should be evaluated for their toxicity. Octachlorodibenzodioxin is one of these isomers which is known to be released into the environment during the manufacture of pentachlorophenol. Efforts should continue to quantitate these isomers and to study their toxicological properties.

The dibenzofurans are another class of compounds which, like the dioxins, are formed as a by-product of some processes. These compounds are being released into the environment and the impact of this release should be investigated.

In summary, research areas which need to be addressed include:

1. ambient levels of dioxin nationwide with focus on regions of high concentrations

("hot spots"),
2. continued investigation regarding the sources, both natural and man-made, of dioxins and dibenzofurans,
3. continued investigations on the toxicity of other isomers of dioxins,
4. continued emphasis on mechanistic studies, and
5. continued investigations in areas of chemical runoff (eg. water and aquatic organisms) to determine if there are additional significant results.

Resources should be allocated for these types of studies but not at the expense of other, more significant, environmental and human health issues.

PUBLIC EDUCATION

Any public policy regarding regulation must include policy on public input and education. As was demonstrated in a recent formaldehyde conference (National Center for Toxicological Research, 1983), consensus among the scientific community is not something which is done quickly. Science is too diverse and it would be erroneous to expect the scientific community to deal quickly with immediate issues. The PBBs incident in Michigan (Dunckel, 1975) is an example where public policy decisions are sometimes needed even before basic data, such as compound identification, are obtained.

The key to public policy is public education. Recently, in the state of Missouri during the Times Beach incident, it was demonstrated that early, active participation by public representatives was an effective method of public education. A task force, which served as a liaison between the scientific community, the government and the public, was formed (Governor's Dioxin Task Force, 1983). This task force included citizens and scientists and through its active participation in decision making and dissemination of information it alleviated some public concerns and dispelled misperceptions. A similar situation has occurred in Midland, Michigan where public representatives actively participated in decision making regarding monitoring of soil samples for dioxin (Peterson, 1983). It is clear, therefore, that given the opportunity, the public will act responsibly. In addition, it was suggested by the workshop that education of key groups in the community would also increase public trust.

In summary, any public policy for dealing with chemical contamination of the environment should also include a plan to educate, not only the public, but also key individuals such as legislators, legislative aides, key community leaders, and the media .

INFORMATION TRANSFER

The problem of piecemeal accumulation of data, which is inherent to all properly conducted scientific studies, and the release of this information in the same piecemeal fashion was discussed. Controversy in the medical field currently exists relating to the release of information before peer review. Dr. Engelfinger, a former editor of the New England Journal of Medicine, to prevent dissemination of data before peer review, established the policy whereby a press release was considered prior publication; thus any material previously released to the press would not be considered for publication.

One must also consider, however, the public's rights and demands to know "the facts". Two case studies, demonstrating opposite extremes in methods of information transfer to the public, are representative of what can happen. In the Chesapeake Bay Kepone incident (Cohn et al, 1976), the attorney general issued a restraining order prohibiting the premature release of information. The public reaction to this order was very negative and had many repercussions. At the other extreme, during the PBBs incident (Dunckel, 1975), the state of Michigan opted for an "open" approach. This resulted in the piecemeal dissemination of information, in many cases by unqualified personnel, and led to a similar chaotic environment and public confusion. The soft tissue sarcoma controversy (Cook, 1983; Eriksson et al., 1981), which the Agent Orange Working Group seeks to shed light on, is an example related to dioxin where data that was incomplete and unverified was generally accepted by the public as a "truth" related to dioxins.

Therefore, the premature dissemination and reporting of data too often is a significant deterrent to the education of the public about chemical and environment problems. Efforts should be made to report scientific data in its totality as well as by knowledgeable and responsible individuals. However, there must be a release of data immediately when a serious problem exists which can affect human and environmental health.

SUMMARY

1. In light of our review of the currently available data and the conclusions of the Human Health Effects and Fate and Transport groups, 2,3,7,8-TCDD is not a chemical rating an exceptionally high public policy priority which diverts resources and public attention from other more wide-spread and dangerous chemical compounds. However, in those "hot spots", places where major sources exist or major concentrations are found in the environment, appropriate epidemiological and environmental system studies are worthwhile. Thus, sampling and monitoring to locate such "hot spots" should continue. Toxicological mechanism research is also important as it can lead to a fuller understanding of how the classes of dioxins and furans interact with biological systems in man and the environment.

2. Studies involving issues of public concern in identified specific populations or geographical areas should seek the participation of representatives of the affected public. The design should be such that all data are quality controlled before dissemination and that only complete data sets are released. Public representatives should be part of the group evaluating the data and the data should be released to the affected group at the same time they are released to the research team.

3. Regulatory actions should seek to protect the aggregate population at risk as well as high-risk populations.

4. Information transfer from scientists to the public should clearly state what is known, what is unknown, and what is uncertain. This recommendation stems from our perception that the public is often inadequately informed on knowns and unknowns and accordingly is unable to deal with uncertainty.

5. A public policy addressing chemical contamination should also include a plan to inform and educate not only the public but also key target audiences such as legislators and legislative aides, community leaders, and media representatives.

REFERENCES

Cohn, W.J., Blanke, R.V., Griffith, F.D. Jr. and Guzelian, P.S. 1976. Distribution and excretion of Kepone in humans. Gastroenterology 71: 901.

Cook, R.R. 1983. Soft tissue sarcomas: Clues and caution. In Human and Environmental Risks of Chlorinated Dioxins and Related Compounds, eds. R.E. Tucker, A.L. Young and A.P. Gray, pp. 613-617, Plenum Press.

Dunckel, A.E. 1975. An updating of the polybrominated biphenyl disaster in Michigan. J. Am. Vet. Med. Assoc. 167:838-841.

Ericksson, M., Hardell, L., Berg, N.O., Moller, T. and Axelson, O. 1981. Soft tissue sarcomas and exposure to chemical substances: A case-referent study. Br. J. Ind. Med. 38:27-33.

Governor's Dioxin Task Force. 1983. Final report of the Missouri Dioxin Task Force. Submitted to Governor Christopher S. Bond.

Merlo, F. 1984. Adverse health effects in human population exposed to 2,3,7,8-Tetrachlorodibenzo-p-dioxin in Seveso: An update. (In Chapter 19 this volume).

National Center for Toxicological Research, 1983. National consensus conference on formaldehyde. Chemical Regulation Reporter 7(29): 893-895 Oct 14 1983.

Panel on the Proposed Air Force Study of Herbicide Orange. 1980. Review of U.S. Air Force Protocol: Epidemiologial investigation of health effects in Air Force personnel following exposure to herbicide orange. National Academy of Sciences Washington, D.C.

Peterson, I. 1983. Dow announces program to allay fear on dioxin. The New York Times June 2, 1983.

Sun, M. 1983. Missouri's costly dioxin lesson. Science 219: 367-369.

Suskind, R.R. 1984. The health effects of 2,4,5-T and its toxic contaminants. (In Chapter 17 this volume).

Section 2
Human Health and Toxicity

HUMAN HEALTH AND TOXICITY – WORKSHOP SUMMARY

Co-Chairmen: Michael Kamrin
Fumio Matsumura

Panel Members
Ralph R. Cook
Gary Hurlburt
E.E. McConnell
Franco Merlo

Richard E. Peterson
Raymond Suskind
Daniel E. Williams

INTRODUCTION

In considering the toxicity of 2,3,7,8-tetrachlorodibenzo-p-dioxin (TCDD), it is important to note that it is just one member of the family of chlorodibenzodioxins and as such, it shares many properties with a large group of related compounds, which include polychlorinated dibenzofurans, polychlorinated biphenyls, polybrominated biphenyls and polychlorinated naphthalenes. Not only do these compounds have many toxicological and chemical properties in common, they often occur together in the environment. For example, the furans and dioxins are known to be products of combustion (Smith et al., 1982; Buser et al.,1978; Olie et al.,1977). It is thus appropriate to consider these compounds as a group and to utilize data, especially from human exposure, from one group of compounds to make inferences about the other related compounds. In keeping with this, the conclusions will be stated in terms of the most toxic congener 2,3,7,8-TCDD, using this compound as a prototype.

ORGAN TOXICITY

It is well established that TCDD is lethal to some experimental animals at very low doses. The lethal dose varies considerably from species to species with guinea pigs found to be the most sensitive and hamsters the least. Certain toxic signs are observed in most species, provided the dose of TCDD is sufficiently high to produce lethality in that species. Most conspicuous is the wasting syndrome, which is characterized by continual weight loss and associated with decreased food and water intake (Schwetz et al., 1973; Vos et al., 1974; McConnell et al., 1978; Olson et al., 1980; Henck et al., 1981; Kociba et al., 1976; Seefeld et al., 1984).

In addition to this syndrome, a number of different organ systems are affected by TCDD. Thymic involution or atrophy has been consistently observed (Henck et al., 1981; Gupta et al., 1973) and has been associated with immunological suppression in the affected animals (Thigpen et al., 1975; Hinsdill et al., 1980; Luster et al., 1980). Neither thymic atrophy nor signs of immunosuppression have been observed in human populations exposed to compounds containing chlorinated dioxins and benzofurans (Reggiani, 1981).

Another common target organ in laboratory animals is the liver. Liver hypertrophy is found at low doses of TCDD and more severe effects, such as liver necrosis, at higher doses (McConnell et al., 1978; Vos et al, 1974). These effects are accompanied by related changes, such as elevations of serum enzymes (Kociba et al., 1978). Similar serum enzyme elevations have been observed in some exposed human populations (Jirasek et al., 1973; Pocchiari et al., 1979). However, these elevations have not been found consistently so it cannot be concluded that TCDD causes liver damage in humans.

The skin also appears to be susceptible to TCDD damage. Various skin changes including chloracne and hyperkeratinization have been found in animals (Schwetz et al., 1973; McConnell et al., 1978). Chloracne and other skin disorders, such as hyperpigmentation and actinic elastosis, are the most consistent signs of toxicity in humans (Oliver, 1975; Poland et al., 1971; Ashe and Suskind, 1949; Suskind and Hertzberg, 1984; Suskind 1953). The first two effects are reversible, at least to some degree, although the severity of each effect and its persistence depend on the level of exposure and a number of idiosyncratic variables (Crow, 1981; Theiss et al., 1982). Elastosis is not reversible.

A number of other conditions have been found in some animal species and in some human populations exposed to dioxin-containing mixtures. These include porphyria (Goldstein et al., 1982; Kociba et al., 1976; Jirasek et al., 1973; Pazderova-Vejlupkova et al., 1981; Bleiberg et al., 1964), alterations in serum lipoproteins (Dugois and Coulomb, 1957; Cunningham and Williams, 1972; Pazderova-Vejlupkova et al., 1981), and gastrointestinal disorders such as stomach ulcer (Poland et al., 1971; Gupta et al., 1973; Suskind and Hertzberg, 1984).

There are still other conditions for which there is even less conclusive evidence. Limited data in some experimental animals have shown edema (McConnell et al., 1978; Vos et al., 1974) and vascular changes but these have not been found in other species or in human populations. Polyneuropathy, more specifically peripheral neuropathy, has been observed in a number of exposed human populations (Pazderova-Vejlupkova et al., 1981), but has not been detected, directly or indirectly, in other exposed species. Follow-up studies of these conditions, in humans and laboratory animals, are necessary to determine if they are toxic effects from TCDD.

MUTAGENICITY

The mutagenicity of TCDD has been investigated in a number of microbial test systems both with and without activation (Hussain et al., 1972; Seiler, 1973; Geiger and Neal, 1981; Bronzetti et al, 1982). In addition, both in vivo and in vitro DNA binding studies (Poland and Glover, 1979) and investigations of possible chromosomal aberrations have been conducted (Green and Moreland, 1975; Green et al., 1977). The preponderance of evidence seems to indicate that TCDD is either non-mutagenic or very weakly mutagenic.

Some studies of chromosomal aberrations in TCDD-exposed human populations have been performed (Czeizel and Kiraly, 1976; Mottura et al., 1981). Although initially some chromosomal changes were suspected, there is no consistent body of evidence which indicates that TCDD is mutagenic in humans. Additional data from experimental animals and humans will be needed before the association, if any, between TCDD and mutagenicity can be evaluated.

TERATOGENICITY

It has been clearly established that TCDD is teratogenic in certain laboratory animals (Courtney and Moore, 1971; Smith et al., 1976; Giavini et al., 1982). The defects varied among species but cleft palate and kidney anomalies appeared common to a number of different strains of mice (Courtney and Moore, 1971; Neubert and Dillman, 1972). Other observed defects included edema and hemorrhage (Courtney and Moore, 1971; Sparschu et al., 1971; Khera and Ruddick, 1973).

Although there are widely scattered reports of a number of different types of birth defects in humans possibly exposed to TCDD, they are largely anecdotal and the evidence to date is inconclusive. A consistent pattern in birth defects has not been observed or studied; however, a recent study of a highly exposed population in Seveso, Italy suggested that TCDD may increase the frequency of hemangiomas (Bruzzi, 1983). This birth defect was observed only in offspring of women who lived in the most highly contaminated areas. No teratogenic effects were seen in other Seveso residents who lived in the less contaminated regions.

It should be noted that teratogenic effects in experimental animals have been seen only with maternal exposure. Birth defects have not been observed with animal paternal exposure to TCDD (Smith et al.,1976; Lamb et al., 1980; Lamb et al.,1981). Likewise, human birth defects have not been associated with paternal exposure to TCDD (Townsend et al.,1982). This is consistent with the evidence supporting the non-mutagenicity of TCDD. It also suggests that TCDD affects the embryo or fetus directly via placental transfer.

REPRODUCTIVE EFFECTS

Studies in experimental animals, including primates, have shown that TCDD can induce decreases in fertility, fetal loss, decreased litter size and shortened gestational survival (Murray et al., 1979; Allen et al., 1979). As with the teratogenic effects, reproductive effects were found only as a result of maternal exposure and not when exposure was limited to the male animals (Lamb et al.,1981).

Although there have been reports of reproductive toxicity in human populations exposed to TCDD, the epidemiological data are, at present, not supportive (U.S. EPA, 1979; Townsend et al.,1982; Wagner et al.,1979). However, in the Seveso, Italy population, there did appear to be a transient increase in the frequency of spontaneous abortions (Strigini et al., 1982). This occurred only to women who lived in the contaminated areas and was not associated with isolated paternal exposure.

CARCINOGENICITY

The carcinogenic potential of TCDD exposure has been investigated using a number of bioassays, most notable are the studies at Dow Chemical Company and at the National Cancer Institute (Kociba et al., 1978; NTP, 1980). These studies showed that TCDD induced hepatocellular carcinomas. Other tumors were also evident but these varied between species. In animal studies serious toxic effects accompanied the induction of cancer, and thus, these studies might not be applicable to humans; i.e., humans would discontinue exposure at the earliest signs of toxicity and would not receive the high doses thought necessary to induce cancer. However, concomitant toxicity is a common feature of animal bioassays which cannot be automatically extrapolated to humans.

Epidemiological data from human populations exposed to TCDD are difficult to interpret. They are based on accidental or occupational exposures to other chemicals in addition to TCDD and involve poorly quantitated exposure levels and durations. In addition, the end-points may be poorly defined. For example, one cancer of concern, soft tissue sarcoma, is actually a generic term for a heterogenous group of lesions that includes more than 100 different tumors (Hajdu,1981). They are difficult to diagnose and they have gone through a number of reclassifications during the period of concern (Cook,1983; Cook and Cartmill, 1983). Thus, although there have been suggestions that soft tissue sarcomas and stomach cancer may be related to TCDD exposure (Hardell and Sandstrom, 1978; Axelson et al., 1980; Thiess et al., 1982), it is difficult to establish whether TCDD may be the cause of these or other cancers in humans. Others that have been mentioned include Hodgkins, non-Hodgkins lymphoma and nasal-pharyngeal cancer (Hardell et al., 1981). Recent studies conducted by scientists at NIOSH indicate that the incidence of confirmed soft tissue sarcoma is low among the U.S. workers with proven exposure to dioxin and dibenzofuran containing products (Fingerhut, 1983). Long range studies, such as those on the Seveso inhabitants, and more careful examination and follow-up on other populations are needed before this hypothesis can be adequately tested. Thus, while TCDD is an animal carcinogen, these animal data have not been confirmed in humans.

Some studies have examined the effect of TCDD exposure following administration of a known cancer initiator (Pitot et al., 1980; Poland et al., 1982). These studies appear to indicate that TCDD functions as a promoter of carcinogenesis in laboratory animals. As is characteristic of its other toxic effects in experimental animals, TCDD appears to serve as a promoter at very low doses.

MECHANISM OF ACTION

Although a large number of effects have been observed in laboratory animals , it has not been possible to determine how TCDD produces most of these toxic effects. It is known that TCDD is a potent inducer of liver enzymes in animals and, most likely, humans (Kociba et al., 1978; Pocchiari et al., 1979). However, it is not clear that enzyme induction is related to the mechanism of toxic action.

TCDD appears to bind to a cytosolic receptor (Knutson and Poland, 1980; Vecchi et al., 1983) in a TCDD-receptor complex binding step which appears necessary for toxicity. Further, as yet unknown, steps are required before the signs and symptoms of toxicity become evident.

The mechanism of lethality is puzzling. It is clear that the severe loss of body weight which precedes lethality is at least partly related to decreased feed intake (Seefeld et al.,1984) but lethality in TCDD-treated rats is not prevented when the weight loss response is blocked by total parenteral nutrition (Gasiewicz et al., 1980). One hypothesis, currently being tested, is that TCDD exerts it effects through alterations of cell membranes, particularly changes in plasma membrane protein composition (Brewster et al., 1982). More research is needed before this, or other possible modes of action, can be identified as the mechanism(s) by which TCDD produces its various toxic effects. Understanding of the mechanism(s) of action is crucial to understanding the species differences already noted and to predicting effects in human populations.

FUTURE RESEARCH RECOMMENDATIONS

The above discussion of the toxic effects of TCDD in humans and laboratory animals revealed a number of areas where greater research efforts are needed. First, in a negative sense, it would not be profitable to conduct additional LD_{50} studies for 2,3,7,8-TCDD on other species. In a positive vein, animal studies and human epidemiological research suggest that TCDD may induce gastrointestinal lesions, hyperlipidemia, neurological disorders, teratogenesis, spontaneous abortion and specific types of cancer and these need further investigation.

In view of the need for epidemiological studies to assess toxic effects in humans, a number of improvements in methodology need to be pursued. These fall into the general category of techniques necessary for identifying and quantifying human exposure in the past, present and future. For example, biological markers of exposure must be established so that previously exposed individuals in a population can be identified and, ideally, their levels of exposure can be determined. Methodology for quantitating human absorption through various routes of exposure--dermal, oral or inhalation--is needed.

Another research area needing greater attention is the toxicology of furans and dioxins other than 2,3,7,8-TCDD, especially those shown to be entering the environment as by-products of combustion. The relative toxicities of the different congeners should be determined so that the relative risks of each can be estimated. Some of this work may require increased efforts in areas such as environmental monitoring for these congeners.

Last, full understanding of the health effects of TCDD will require a much better understanding of its toxicokinetics and toxicodynamics. Studies of this type may not produce immediate results but their ultimate importance is so great that research in the area should be pursued vigorously. Understanding of the mechanisms of toxicity will allow improved extrapolation from experimental animals to humans.

SUMMARY

TCDD is the prototype of a number of other compounds which produce a variety of toxic effects sometimes referred to as the "halogenated aromatic hydrocarbon syndrome." It is unique in that it produces its effects at much lower doses than many others in these groups of compounds. Although many of these related compounds have been studied in animal models over a number of years, there are a variety of reported toxic effects which remain unconfirmed. Even those which have been confirmed often show great species specificity. As a result of these uncertainties, it is difficult to extrapolate from animal data to predict human toxicity.

Unfortunately, studies directly on humans (i.e. epidemiological studies) also have a number of inherent pitfalls. These include mixed chemical exposures, poor exposure history and difficulty in defining toxicological end-points. In the preceding sections, studies of one particular population, that of Seveso, Italy, has been mentioned specifically as this is one of the few populations where ecologic exposure is known. A number of studies are underway on the Seveso population and it is important that these follow-up studies continue. Another group that is being carefully examined is the cohort of Vietnam war veterans exposed to Agent Orange. The results of these studies will hopefully shed light on possible long-term effects of TCDD in humans.

The last type of study which can provide valuable information is the mechanistic one. Research of this type has just scratched the surface but progress is being made. Ultimately, this research will provide us with an understanding of TCDD action at the molecular level.

The conclusions reached by the workshop participants are given below:

Carcinogenicity

1. The standard bioassay shows that TCDD is an animal carcinogen.
2. Insufficient epidemiological evidence exists to indicate that TCDD is a human carcinogen. Further studies are underway to test this hypothesis.

Mutagenicity

1. While a few studies suggest that TCDD is a weak animal mutagen, the preponderance of data indicate that TCDD is not a mutagen.
2. There is no direct evidence of mutagenicity in humans.

Reproductive Effects

1. TCDD administration can lead to reproductive failure in animals.
2. In Seveso, Italy, a site of massive environmental TCDD contamination, a transient increase in the frequency of spontaneous abortions was observed among women living in the most heavily contaminated areas.

Teratogenic effects

1. TCDD can produce teratogenic effects when administered to pregnant female animals. There is no evidence that it can cause birth defects through paternal exposure.
2. Epidemiological studies have not shown a consistent pattern of birth defects in human populations exposed to TCDD.

Other effects

1. TCDD has been shown to cause a variety of acute effects in laboratory animals including the wasting syndrome and thymic involution, which have not been observed in human populations.
2. TCDD exposure is fatal to common laboratory animal species at low levels but there are great differences in susceptibility between species. Guinea pigs are the most susceptible. Based on the absence of human deaths in TCDD-exposed populations, it appears that humans are not as sensitive as guinea pigs.
3. TCDD has been shown to cause chloracne, actinic elastosis and hyperpigmentation in humans. These effects seem to vary in persistence and severity.
4. There have been less consistent reports of stomach ulcer, porphyria, alteration in serum lipoproteins and neurological disorders in TCDD-exposed humans.

Mechanism of action

1. TCDD is an enzyme inducer in animals and, mostly likely, humans. However, it appears that its toxicity is unrelated to the phenomenon of induction.
2. TCDD appears to bind to a cytosolic receptor but this alone is not sufficient to explain its toxicity.
3. A variety of experimental studies suggest that TCDD is a promotor of carcinogenesis.
4. The mechanism of lethality is still unresolved.

BIBLIOGRAPHY

Allen, J.R., Barsotti, D.A., Lambrecht, L.K. and Van Miller, J.P. 1979. Reproductive effects of halogenated aromatic hydrocarbons on nonhuman primates. Ann. NY Acad. Sci. 320:419-425.

Ashe, W.F. and Suskind, R.R. 1949-1950. Reports on chloracne cases. Monsanto Chemical Company, Nitro, West Virginia. Reports of the Kettering Laboratory.

Axelson, O., Sundell, L., Anderson, K., Edling, C., Hogstedt, C. and Kling, H. 1980. Herbicide exposure and tumor mortality: An updated epidemiological investigation on Swedish railroad workers. Scand. J. Work. Environ. Health 6:73-79.

Bleiberg, J., Wallen, M., Brodbin, R. et at. 1964. Industirally acquired porphyria. Arch. Dermatol. 89:793-797.

Brewster, D.W., Madhukar, B.V. and Matsumura, F. 1982. Influence of 2,3,7,8-TCDD on the protein composition of the plasma membrane of hepatic cells from the rat. Biochem. Biophys. Res. Commun. 107(1):68-74.

Bronzetti, G., Zeiger, E., Lee, I., Suzuki, K. and Malling, H.V. 1982. Genetic effects of 2,3,7,8-tetrachlorodibenzo-p-dioxin (TCDD) in yeast in vitro and in vivo. In Chlorinated Dioxins and Related Compounds: Impact on the Environment, eds. O. Hutzinger, R.W. Frei, E. Merian and F. Pocchiari, pp. 429-436, Pergamon Press, Oxford.

Bruzzi, P. 1983. Birth defects in the TCDD polluted area of Seveso: Results of a four-year follow-up. In Accidental Exposure to Dioxins, eds. F. Coulston and F. Pocchiari, pp. 215-225, Academic Press, New York.

Buser, H.R., Bosshardt, H.P. and Rappe, C. 1978. Identification of polychlorinated dibenzo-p-dioxin isomers found in fly ash. Chemosphere 2:165-172.

Cook, R.R. 1983. Soft tissue sarcomas: Clues and Caution. In Human and Environmental Risks of Chlorinated Dioxins and Related Compounds, eds. R.E. Tucker, A.L. Young and A.P. Gray, pp. 613-618, Plenum Press, New York.

Cook, R.R. and Cartmill, J.B. 1983. Soft tissue sarcoma and dioxin: Putting the data into perspective. Presentation at Rockefeller University Dioxin Conference, New York City, October 19-20, 1983.

Courtney, K.D. and Moore, J.A. 1971. Teratology studies with 2,4,5-T and 2,3,7,8-TCDD. Toxicol. Appl. Pharmacol. 20:396-403.

Crow, K.D. 1981. Chloracne and its potential clinical implications. Clin. Exp. Dermatol. 6(3):243-257.

Cunningham, H.M. and Williams, D.T. 1972. Effect of 2,3,7,8-tetrachlorodibenzo-p-dioxin on growth rate and the synthesis of lipids and proteins in rats. Bull. Environ. Contam. Toxicol. 7(1):45-51.

Czeizel, E. and Kiraly, J. 1976. Chromosome examinations in workers producing Klorinol and Buminol. In The Development of a Pesticide as a Complex Scientific Task, ed. L. Banki, pp. 239-256, Medicina, Budapest.

Dugois, P. and Coulomb, L. 1957. Remarques sur l' acne' chorique (a propos d'une ecolsion de cas provoques par la preparation due 2-4-5 trichlorophenol). J. Med. Lyon. 38:899.

Fingerhut, M. 1983. A platform presentation at "Symposium on Public Health Risks of the Chlorinated Dioxins". Rockefeller University, October 19-20 1983, New York City.

Gasiewicz, T.A., Holscher, M.A. and Neal, R.A. 1980. The effect of total parenteral nutrition on the toxicity of 2,3,7,8-tetrachlorodibenzo-p-dioxin in the rat. Toxicol. Appl. Pharmacol. 54:459-488.

Geiger, L.E. and Neal, R.A. 1981. Mutagenicity testing of 2,3,7,8-tetrachlorodibenzo-p-dioxin in histidine auxotrophs of Salmonella typhimurium. Toxicol. Appl. Pharmacol. 59(1):125-129.

Giavini, E., Prati, M. and Vismara, C. 1982. Rabbit teratology study with 2,3,7,8-tetrachlorodibenzo-p-dioxin. Environ. Res. 27(1):74-78.

Goldstein, J.A., Linko, P. and Bergman, H. 1982. Induction of porphyria in the rat by chronic versus acute exposure to 2,3,7,8-tetrachlorodibenzo-p-dioxin. Biochem. Pharmacol. 31(8):1607-1613.

Green, S. and Moreland, F.S. 1975. Cytogenetic evaluation of several dioxins in the rat. Toxicol. Appl. Pharmacol. 33:161.

Green, S., Moreland, F. and Sheu, C. 1977. Cytogenic effect of 2,3,7,8-tetrachlorodibenzo-p-dioxin on rat bone marrow cells. FDA By-Lines 6:292, U.S. FDA, Washington, D.C.

Gupta, B.N., Vos, J.G., Moore, J.A., Zinkl, J.G. and Bullock, B.C. 1973. Pathologic effects of 2,3,7,8-tetrachlorodibenzo-p-dioxin in laboratory animals. Environ. Health Perspectives 5:125-140.

Hardell, L., Eriksson, M., Lenner, P. and Lundgren, E. 1981. Malignant lymphoma and exposure to chemicals, especially organic solvents, chlorophenols and phenoxy acids: A case-control study. Brit. J. Cancer 43:169-176.

Hardell, L. and Sandstrom, A. 1978. Case-control study: Soft-tissue Sarcomas and exposure to phenoxyacetic acids or chlorophenols. Brit. J. Cancer 39:711-717.

Hajdu, S.I. 1981. Soft tissue sarcomas: Classification and natural history. CA-A Cancer Journal for Clinicians 31(5):271-280.

Henck, J.W., New, M.A., Kociba, R.J. and Rao, K.S. 1981. 2,3,7,8-Tetrachlorodibenzo-p-dioxin: Acute oral toxicity in hamsters. Toxicol. Appl. Pharmacol. 59:405-407.

Hinsdill, R.D., Couch, D.L. and Speirs, R.S. 1980. Immunosuppression in mice induced by dioxin (TCDD) in feed. J. Environ. Pathol. Toxicol. 4(2-3):401-425.

Hussain, S., Ehrenberg, L., Lofroth, G. and Gejvall, T. 1972. Mutagenic effects of TCDD on bacterial systems. Ambio 1:32-33.

Jirasek, L., Kalensky, J. and Kubec, K. 1973. Acne chlorina and porphyria cutanea tarda during the manufacture of herbicides. Cesk. Dermatol. 48:306-315.

Khera, K.S. and Ruddick, J.A. 1973. Polychlorodibenzo-p-dioxins: Perinatal effects and the dominant lethal test in Wistar rats. Adv. Chem. Ser. 120:70-84.

Kociba, R.J., Keeler, P.A., Park, C.N. and Gehring, P.J. 1976. 2,3,7,8-Tetrachlorodibenzo-p-dioxin results of a 13-week oral toxicity study in rats. Toxicol. Appl. Pharmacol. 35:553-574.

Kociba, R.J., Keyes, D.G., Beyer, J.E., Carreon, R.M., Wade, C.E., Dittenber, D.A., Kalnins, R.P., Frauson, L.E., Park, C.N., Barnard, S.D., Hummel, R.A. and Humiston, C.G. 1978. Results of a two-year chronic toxicity and oncogenicity study of 2,3,7,8-tetrachlorodibenzo-p-dioxin in rats. Toxicol. Appl. Pharmacol. 46(2):279-303.

Knutson, J.C. and Poland, A. 1980. 2,3,7,8-Tetrachlorodibenzo-p-dioxin: Failure to demonstrate toxicity in twenty-three cultured cell types. Toxicol. Appl. Pharmacol. 54(3):377-383.

Lamb, J.C.,Moore, J.A. and Marks, T.A., 1980. Evaluation of 2,4-dichlorophenoxyacetic acid (2,4-D), 2,4,5-trichlorophenoxyacetic acid (2,4,5-T) and 2,3,7,8-tetrachlorodibenzo-p-dioxin (TCDD) toxicity with C57BL/6 mice: Reproduction and fertility in treated male mice and evaluation of congenital malformations in their offsprings. National Toxicology Program.

Lamb, J.C., Moore, J.A., Marks, T.A. and Haseman, J.K. 1981. Development and viability of offspring in male mice treated with chlorinated phenoxy acids and 2,3,7,8-tetrachlorodibenzo-p-dioxin. J. Toxicol. Environ. Hlth. 8:835-844.

Luster, M.I, Boorman, G.A. Dean, J.H., Padavathsingh, M.L. and Moore, J.A. 1980. Examination of bone marrow, immunologic parameters and host susceptibility following pre- and postnatal exposure to 2,3,7,8-tetrachlorodibenzo-p-dioxin (TCDD). Int. J. Immunopharmacol. 2:301-310.

McConnell, E.E., Moore, J.A., Haseman, J.K. and Harris, M.W. 1978. The comparative toxicity of chlorinated dibenzo-p-dioxins in mice and guinea pigs. Toxicol. Appl. Pharmacol. 44(2):335-356.

Mottura, A., Zei, G., Nuzzo, F., Crimaudo, C., Giorgi, R., Veneroni, P., Paggini, L., Mocarelli, P., Fraccaro, M., Nicoletti, B. and De Carli, L. 1981. Evaluation of results of chromosome analysis on lymphocytes of TCDD exposed subjects after the Seveso accident. Mutat. Res. 85(4):238-239.

Murray, F.J., Smith, F.A., Nischke, K.D., Humiston, C.G., Kociba, R.J. and Schwetz, B.A. 1979. Three-generation reproduction study of rats given 2,3,7,8-tetrachlorodibenzo-p-dioxin (TCDD) in the diet. Toxicol. Appl. Pharmacol. 50:241-251.

Neubert, D. and Dillman, I. 1972. Embryotoxic effects in mice treated with 2,4,5-trichlorophenoxyacetic acid and 2,3,7,8-tetrachlorodibenzo-p-dioxin. Arch. Pharmacol. 272(3):243-264.

NTP (National Toxicology Program). 1980. Bioassay of 2,3,7,8-tetrachlorodibenzo-p-dioxin for possible carcinogenicity (Gavage study). DHHS publication No. (NIH) 82-1765. Carcinogenesis Testing Program, NCI, NIH, Bethesda, MD and National Toxicology Program, RTP, Box 12233, NC.

Olie, K., Vermeulen, P.L. and Hutzinger, O. 1977. Chlorodibenzo-p-dioxins and chlorodibenzofurans are trace components of fly ash and flue gas of some municipal incinerators in the Netherlands. Chemosphere 8:455-459.

Oliver, R.M. 1975. Toxic effects of 2,3,7,8-tetrachlorodibenzo-p-dioxin in laboratory workers. Br. J. Ind. Med. 32(1):49-53.

Olson, J.R., Holscher, M.A. and Neal, R.A. 1980. Toxicity of 2,3,7,8-tetrachlorodibenzo-p-dioxin in the golden Syrian hamster. Toxicol. Appl. Pharmacol. 55:67-78.

Pazderova-Vejlupkova, J., Nemcova, M., Pickova, J., Jirasek, L. and Lukas, E. 1981. The development and prognosis of chronic intoxication by tetrachlorodibenzo-p-dioxin in men. Arch. Environ. Health 36(1):5-11.

Pitot, H.C., Goldsworthy, T., Campbell, H.A. and Poland, A. 1980. Promotion by 2,3,7,8-tetrachlorodibenzo-p-dioxin of hepatocarcinogenesis from diethylnitrosamine. Cancer Res. 40:3616-3620.

Pocchiari, F., Silano, V. and Zampieri, A. 1979. Human health effects from accidental release of tetrachlorodibenzo-p-dioxin (TCDD) at Seveso, Italy. Ann. NY. Acad. Sci. 320:311-320.

Poland, A. and Glover, E. 1979. An estimate of the maximum in vivo covalent binding of 2,3,7,8-tetrachlorodibenzo-p-dioxin to rat liver protein, ribosomal RNA and DNA. Cancer Res. 39(9):3341-3344.

Poland, A., Palen, D. and Glover, E. 1982. Tumor promotion by TCDD in skin of HRS/J hairless mice. Nature 300(5889):271-273.

Poland, A.P., Smith,D., Metter, G. and Possick, P. 1971. A health survey of workers in a 2,4-D and 2,4,5-T plant with special attention to chloracne, porphyria cutanea tarda, and psychologic parameters. Arch. Environ. Health 22:316-327.

Reggiani, G. 1980. Acute human exposure to TCDD in Seveso, Italy. J. Toxicol. Environ. Health 6(1):27-43.

Schwetz, B.A., Norris, J.M., Sparschu, G.L., Rowe, V.K., Gehring, P.J., Emerson, J.L. and Gerbig, C.G. 1973. Toxicology of chlorinated dibenzo-p-dioxins. Environ. Health Perspect. 5:87-99.

Seefeld, M.D.,Corbett, S.W., Keesey, R.E. and Peterson R.E., 1984. Characterization of the wasting syndrome in rats treated with 2,3,7,8-Tetrachlorodibenzo-p-dioxin. Toxicol. Appl. Pharmacol. 73: 311-322.

Seiler, J.P. 1973. A survey on the mutagenicity of various pesticides. Experientia 29:622-623.

Smith, A.H., Fisher, D.O., Pearce, N. and Chapman, C.J. 1982. Congenital defects and miscarriages among New Zealand 2,4,5-T sprayers. Arch. Environ. Health 37:197-200.

Smith, F.A., Schwetz, B.A. and Nitschke, K.D. 1976. Teratogenicity of 2,3,7,8-tetrachlorodibenzo-p-dioxin in CF-1 mice. Toxicol. Appl. Pharmacol. 38(3):517-523.

Smith, R.M., Hilker, D., O'Keefe, P.W., Kumar, S., Aldous, K. and Jelus-Tyror, B. 1982. Determination of polychlorinated dibenzofurans and polychlorinated dibenzodioxins in soot samples from a contaminated office building. New York State Department of Health Report, Albany, New York.

Sparschu, G.L., Dunn, F.L., Lisowe, R.W. and Rowe, V.K. 1971. Effects of high levels of 2,4,5-trichlorophenoxyacetic acid on fetl development in the rat. Food Cosmet. Toxicol. 9(4):527-530.

Strigini, P., Blanco, G. and Formigaro, M. 1982. Gli Aborti Spontanei. Sapere, June-August:64-65.

Suskind, R.R. 1953. A clinical and environmental survey. Monsanto Chemical Co., Nitro, West Virginia. Report of the Kettering Laboratory.

Suskind, R.R. and Hertzberg, V.S. 1984. Human health effects of 2,4,5-T and its toxic contaminants. JAMA 251:2372-2380.

Theiss, A.M. Frentzel-Byme, R. and Link, R. 1982. Mortality study of persons exposed to dioxins in a trichlorophenol-process accident that occurred in the BASF on November 17, 1953. Am. J. Ind. Med. 3:179-189.

Thigpen, J.E., Faith, R.E., McConnell, E.E. and Moore, J.A. 1975. Increased susceptibility to bacterial infection as a sequela of exposure to 2,3,7,8-tetrachlorodibenzo-p-dioxin. Infect. Immun. 12(6):1319-1324.

Townsend, J.C., Bodner, K.M., Van Peenen, P.F., Olsen, R.D. and Cook, R.R. 1982. Survey of reproductive events of wives of employees exposed to chlorinated dioxins. Am. J. Epidemiol. 115(5):695-713.

U.S. EPA. 1979. Report of assessment of a field investigation of six-year spontaneous abortion rates in three Oregon areas in relation to forest 2,4,5-T spray practice. OTA/EPA.

Vecchi, A., Sironi, M., Canegrati, M.A., Recchia, M. and Garattini, S. 1983. Immunosuppressive effects of 2,3,7,8-tetrachlorodibenzo-p-dioxin in strains of mice with different susceptibility to induction of aryl hydrocarbon hydroxylase. Toxicol. Appl. Pharmacol. 68:434-441.

Vos, J.G., Moore, J.A. and Zinkl, J.G. 1974. Toxicity of 2,3,7,8-tetrachlorodibenzo-p-dioxin (TCDD) in C57BL/6 mice. Toxicol. Appl. Pharmacol. 29:229-241.

Zack, J.A. and Suskind, R.R. 1980. The mortality experience of workers exposed to tetrachlorodibenzodioxin in the trichlorophenol process accident. J. Occup. Med. 22(1):11-14.

Wagner, S.L., Witt, J.M., Norris, L.A., Higgins, J.E., Agresti, A. and Ortiz, M., Jr. 1979. A scientific critique of the EPA Alsea II study and report with November 16, 1979 supplement. Environmental Health Sciences Center, Oregon State University, Corvallis, Oregon, October 25, 1979.

Section 3
Source, Distribution and Fate

SOURCE, DISTRIBUTION AND FATE - WORKSHOP SUMMARY

Co-chairmen: James Petty
              Paul Rodgers

Panel Members
Donald Crosby   Ross Norstrom
Jean Czuczwa   William Richardson
John Giesy   Thomas Rohrer
Otto Hutzinger   David Stalling
Theodore Mill

INTRODUCTION

In the past, encounters with chemicals similar to dioxins (e.g. DDT and PCBs) were with compounds known to have certain properties which made them useful to society. Dioxins, however, do not serve our society in any capacity. They are formed as inadvertent by-products of chemical production and combustion processes. Although the compounds with which dioxins are associated are useful, technology is now available to essentially preclude dioxin contamination. Therefore, scientists need not weigh their benefits against their risks but, instead, must evaluate the risk of their presence and then judge the desirability of removal and prevention. For an accurate risk assessment, it is necessary to evaluate their toxicity, understand how they enter our environment, determine their transport and distribution, and ascertain how their fate can be managed given various remedial alternatives. Evaluation of these and related issues are so complex that investigators have to rely on a variety of sources including theoretical expectations, interpretation of process specific data, inferences from field data and lessons learned from previous encounters with similar chlorinated hydrocarbons. A constraint in understanding the behavior of dioxins in the environment is that many of our past research and present regulatory efforts have focused on a single dioxin isomer, 2,3,7,8-TCDD. Some aspects of the behavior of other dioxins can be inferred from knowledge of 2,3,7,8-TCDD, but caution should be exercised when making inferences based on limited data. Participants of this workshop session relied on a broad range of experience to accomplish the goals of the workshop which were to summarize our present state of knowledge on dioxin presence and persistence, discuss areas of uncertainty and present research recommendations. These deliberations are summarized by identifying known sources, describing observed distribution, and discussing the factors which determine the fate of dioxins in the environment.

SOURCES

A great deal of effort has been exerted, thus far, to identify the sources of dioxins in the environment. In 1980, the EPA reviewed in detail the possible sources, including organic chemical production and emissions from combustion sources (Esposito et al., 1980). These studies identified the production of herbicides, the disposal of wastes, and combustion as important sources of dioxins.

Recently, the EPA initiated a "Dioxin Strategy" (USEPA, 1983) as mandated by Congress. As part of this multi-million dollar strategy the EPA identified seven "study tiers", based on their decreasing potential for contamination, which will be monitored for dioxins. Four of these study tiers are aimed at sites that might be contaminated with 2,4,5-

trichlorophenol (2,4,5-TCP). Various herbicides and pesticides are manufactured using 2,4,5-TCP, including the well known herbicide 2,4,5-T. The chemical name for 2,4,5-T is 2,4,5-trichlorophenoxyacetic acid and is a major constituent of the exfoliant "Agent Orange" used in Vietnam. Herbicides containing esters of 2,4,5-T are contaminated with dioxins at varying levels. Elevated levels of dioxins in the environment are most often observed at manufacture sites of these herbicides, or at the disposal sites of their waste products (USEPA, 1983). This is particularly true for the more highly toxic dioxin, 2,3,7,8-TCDD (Weerasinghe and Gross, 1984).

The significance of dioxin contamination of herbicides can be found in bioconcentration studies. Uptake of 2,3,7,8-TCDD by biota in areas treated with 2,4,5-T herbicides has been observed in some studies (Harless et al., 1981; Young, 1974; Ryan et al., 1974), while other studies have not detected this bioconcentration (Shadoff et al., 1977; Kocher et al., 1978). Human bioconcentration of dioxins due to exposure to herbicides containing 2,4,5-T (Agent Orange) has been suspected in Vietnam Veterans. A joint study by the University of Nebraska and the U.S. Veterans Administration to monitor adipose tissue of a select group of Vietnam Veterans found a range of TCDD levels from non-detectable to 99 ppt. Confirmation analysis of the same samples by EPA laboratories measured the highest level at 173 ppt (Gross et al., 1984). These results indicate that humans and certain animals bioconcentrate dioxins in their tissues. This observation is important in analyzing human risk due to exposure because toxic effect is presumably related to concentration.

The disposal sites of 2,4,5-T wastes have repeatedly been identified as sites of dioxin contamination. The most prominent of these sites, Love Canal, had levels in local sewers reported in a range of 670-9570 ppb (USEPA, 1982). Leakage from disposal drums containing a variety of organic chemicals is a suspected source of dioxins in the environment in many disposal sites around the nation. A recent rash of litigation purporting dioxin contamination from local waste sites and a review of "Superfund" sites attest to the legacy of dioxin contaminated wastes left by past production of 2,4,5-TCP and its progeny herbicides and pesticides.

Disposal of wastes by industrial and municipal incineration is a prominent method of waste management. These combustion processes have been identified worldwide as sources of dioxins and furans. Dioxins have been identified in fly ash and flue gases in the Netherlands (Olie et al., 1977), Switzerland (Buser and Bosshardt, 1978), various locations in the United States (ASME, 1980), Canada (Eiceman et al., 1979) and elsewhere (Olie et al., 1982).

Other combustion sources of dioxins have been reported, including coal and wood combustion, automobile emissions, and accidental fires (Weerasinghe and Gross, 1984; Bumb et al., 1980). Two factors, however, have emerged as important requirements to the production of dioxins by combustion. First, the appropriate chemical precursors must be present. For example, wood treated with chlorophenols for weather and mold protection will be more likely to produce dioxins than non-treated wood. Secondly, certain incinerator conditions of temperature and residence time will favor dioxin formation, while other conditions actually inhibit or preclude dioxin formation. Combustion temperatures between 180-400°C favor dioxin formation. Temperatures in excess of 1000°C, with dwell times of at least 2 seconds, are needed for efficient destruction of dioxins and related chemicals in municipal and industrial incinerators (Wilkinson et al., 1978).

Once dioxins are identified in the environment it can be difficult to conclusively trace their origin. Long range transport of combustion products can lead to contamination of environments well removed from the original source. An analytical technique, called "fingerprinting", was once believed to be a method for assigning sources to contamination sites. Fingerprinting compares the congener distribution of the environmental sample to the source sample, the concept being that a relative match identifies the culprit. However, experience has shown that the variability of incineration and production processes, as well as the interim environmental transformations of one congener to another, makes fingerprinting impractical. Probably the primary method by which to assign responsibiltiy of source is classical data interpretation. For example, elevated dioxin levels in fish and sediment samples will be in the vicinity of or downriver from the responsible source. Diffuse sources, like widespread combustion, will rarely be responsible for elevated levels identified in a location having well defined boundaries.

DISTRIBUTION

The distribution of dioxins may be dealt with in two parts. The first is an inventory of how dioxins are distributed among physical compartments - air, soil and water. The second is an important exposure factor known as biomagnification. Biomagnification is evident when dioxins are more concentrated in successively higher trophic levels of biota (e.g. insects<fish<predatory birds). These two aspects of dioxin distribution are summarized herein.

Airborne transport of dioxins has been identified as a major force in the distribution of dioxins over wide areas and is perhaps responsible for the now nearly ubiquitous distribution. Air particulates from municipal areas have been measured at the part per billion (ppb) level and are enriched with octa-dioxins (Czuczwa and Hites, 1984). In one area, Midland, Michigan, where combustion of chemical wastes occurred nearby, parts per million (ppm) levels of hepta- and octa-chlorodioxins were observed in dust samples from a research building.

Soils are the most frequently sampled physical compartment for the analysis of dioxins. In Times Beach, Missouri, the action level for the EPA to define the boundaries of evacuation and buy-out, as defined by the Centers for Disease Control, was based on soil levels in excess of 1 ppb of 2,3,7,8-TCDD. Soils having 2,3,7,8-TCDD levels in excess of this have been observed in a number of areas, but all having locally attributable sources (Esposito et al., 1980). Because dioxins are highly hydrophobic they are partitioned to soils and are relatively immobile. Studies using different soil types indicate that migration of TCDD is very slow, especially in soils high in organic content (Kearney et al., 1973; Matsumura and Benezet, 1973). These observations suggest that contamination of groundwater supplies through percolation of contaminated soils is unlikely and that soil contamination boundaries are rather stable.

Knowledge regarding levels of dioxins in natural waters is nearly nonexistent. A number of samples have been measured at detection limits of parts per trillion (ppt) and reported as not detected. Wastewater effluent samples from Dow Chemical measured by the US EPA indicated that 2,3,7,8-TCDD was present at 50 parts per quadrillion (ppqd) prior to entering the Tittabawassee River, Michigan. The capability and experience necessary to measure water samples at the parts per quadrillion (ppqd) level has been so rare historically that Dow Chemical Company used reported biomagnification factors (e.g. 6,600) to infer water concentrations from indigenous fish data (Forney, 1983) and thereby estimated levels of 6 ppqd of TCDD in the Tittabawassee River. The Connecticut Department of Environmental Protection recently reported levels of approximately 140 ppqd in an initial sample from a "test well" drilled through a disposal site (Laurel Park, Inc. et al. v. Stanley J. Pac, Commissioner). This level has not been replicated in subsequent samples following standard procedures. It is necessary that the investigator assessing water samples be prepared for the extraordinarily vigorous quality assurance demands of sampling and measuring dioxins at the parts per quadrillion level.

The concept of biomagnification is critically important in determining the exposure levels in a risk assessment. Evidence of bioconcentration has been presented (see Sources) and is a widely accepted phenomenon. However, bioconcentration alone implies only that biota incorporate dioxin from environmental sources within body tissues.

Biomagnification would further indicate that biota could accumulate dioxin levels many times greater than the levels to which they were exposed. This characteristic would be expected to be more pronounced as the investigator assessed higher trophic levels of biota. Evidence for biomagnification is most often found when comparing one trophic level (e.g. rodent, fish) with its local environment (Esposito, 1980). Fish samples, when detected, are often measured at the part per trillion level (Forney, 1983) - many times the ambient water concentrations - thereby indicating biomagnification. Certain other studies also identify organisms at a single trophic level as having dioxin levels higher than their local environment or immediate food source. For example, Harrison et al. (1979) found that meadowlark livers from an Air Force study area were measured at 1020 ppt TCDD while the local soil and insects were measured at 46 and 40 ppt, respectively. However, the literature does not indicate a study of a single ecosystem conclusively demonstrating progressively higher concentrations of dioxins for progressively higher levels of trophic organisms. Assessing the potential for biomagnification is complicated because very little is known about the availability of dioxins in environmental samples. Since man consumes many game fish and animals it is desirable to have more specific information regarding biomagnification in order to confidently assess long term risks.

FATE

To forecast risk or evaluate alternative remedial actions requires knowledge of environmental fate. The fate of dioxins and related chemicals in the environment is determined by operative physical, biological and chemical processes. These processes have impact on three important aspects of environmental fate, namely 1) longevity; 2) transport; 3) chemical state. Because of our scientific experience with chemicals similar to dioxins, we are knowledgeable of many of the natural processes which most likely determine the fate of dioxins in the environment. However, very little specific process information is available and, therefore, our discussion is largely limited to the general concepts of chemical fate, given our state-of-the-art knowlege of dioxins. Recommentions for supplying dioxin specific fate data are also made.

Longevity of dioxins in a given environmental compartment (e.g. atmosphere or water body) is determined by transformation and transport processes. Transformation processes are capable of detoxifying dioxins and are important in natural environments and in designing disposal techniques. Transformation processes which may determine persistence or longevity of dioxins include biodegradation, photolysis, oxidation and reduction. Transformation processes may result in the complete destruction of a dioxin molecule, or in the conversion of a higher chlorinated dioxin molecule to a lesser chlorinated dioxin molecule. This conversion may alter the original characteristics of the dioxin molecule, including its toxicity and further transformation potential.

Transport processes affect on physical movement or relocation of dioxins in the environment. Processes which most frequently dominate pollutant transport include advection, dispersion, and solids dynamics (e.g. sedimentation and resuspension). An important consideration in analyzing transport and longevity is the chemical state of a pollutant. Two characteristics are inferred here regarding chemical state. First, the congener type or degree of chlorination of the dioxin molecule is crucial to the expected chemical behavior and toxic effect. The specific structure of the dioxin molecule will be primarily determined by the source and its exposure to transformation processes. A second aspect of chemical state is whether the dioxin molecule is in true solution (freely available) or if it is associated with other solution constituents (e.g. solids). Hydrophobic/lipophilic chemicals, like dioxin, are often associated with biotic solids or found in high levels in biota and are usually transported by these organisms. The solution status of dioxins in a natural environment will depend on adsorption/desorption kinetics. Although investigators have gained empirical and theoretical insight into the partitioning of organic pollutants onto solids, the kinetics of these physicochemical processes remain uncertain.

Defining and projecting pollutant transport, chemical state and longevity is often best approached through mathematical modeling. These models use chemical and site specific data to develop a reliable simulation of environmental fate. Toxicity information based on exposure is required to interpret results. Together, the data, the mathematical model chosen, and the toxicology of the compound enable a risk assessment to be quantitatively made which can guide resource management decisions designed to protect human and environmental health.

RESEARCH RECOMMENDATIONS

The workshop participants identified areas of research required to better define human and environmental risk due to exposure to dioxins. The greatest volume of information regarding dioxins addresses significant sources or contaminated sites of 2,3,7,8-TCDD. The present federal and state emphasis in studying dioxins is to monitor possible contaminant sites. These monitoring programs are essential in evaluating the extent of the problem and in identifying potential health problems. However, many other aspects of dioxins as they interact with the environment are essential to a reliable risk assessment and prudent regulatory action. These recommendations are focused on the need to supply information on exposure and persistence of dioxins in the environment.

Knowledge of biological availability is presently lacking in many of our scientific and regulatory evaluations. For instance, do soils contaminated with dioxins continue to contaminate plants and animals for many years or are they substantially removed from biological availability through adsorption? Likewise, are dioxins biologically available from aquatic solids and sediments? Answering questions of bioavailability requires appropriately designed laboratory studies and subsequent verification by field observations. These answers ultimately define actual exposure and refine our interpretation of dose/response toxicity evaluations.

Additional laboratory studies required to better understand environmental fate include defining important process kinetics. This means actually measuring the volatilization, adsorption/desorption, and relevant transformation rates for which little empirical information is available. The experimental techniques and indications of applicability to specific environmental sites can be derived from past studies on similar chemicals. Since dioxins are so potentially toxic and diverse these process studies must be conducted with special care and a commensurate level of support.

When possible, risk assessments and regulatory actions should be based on a quantitative interpretation of the many factors which impact fate, exposure and toxic effect. A useful tool for making quantitative assessments is a mathematical model which represents the relevant processes, based on state-of-the-art knowledge. These models have analyzed fate issues for many toxic contaminants. Thus far, our knowledge of dioxins has not been integrated into a physicochemical fate model and tested against site specific data. An appropriate site to test a dioxin model and its representation of relevant processes would be characterized by data indicating both temporal and spatial trends in dioxin levels. In addition, support for development of a quantitative framework or model that addresses the dioxin issue from the source, through its distribution to its expected toxic effect would be especially desirable. Such an effort would supply both research and remedial insight.

Dioxins are yet another group of chemicals that have been distributed in our environment which may be responsible for human or environmental health effects. There have been others before, many others are now being studied, and still others will be recognized in years to come. The workshop participants strongly recommend that a policy for supporting research of toxicants be a proactive policy and not merely a series of reactive efforts. Long term goals need to be established and widely recognized. Research to support these specific goals to protect human health ought to be long term as well.

WORKSHOP SUMMARY

The final task of the workshop participants was to issue a joint statement regarding the issues discussed during the proceedings and examined herein. These are the unanimous opinions of this workshop session regarding six areas of inquiry. These statements were read to the press and public at the conclusion of the workshop.

1. Sources

In locations where dioxins are observed at elevated levels their presence is attributable to local sources. This is indeed noteworthy; even though the worldwide total amount of dioxins may originate from many sources, high levels in water, soils and fish are invariably associated with a local source. Therefore, if toxic effects are of concern, these locations and sources would be of special concern. Furthermore, we concluded that the major source of dioxins in terms of elevated levels are typically manufacturers of chemicals which are contaminated with dioxins. This would include the manufacturers' disposal sites. On the other hand, proper application of low concentrations of herbicides that are contaminated with dioxins does not pose a significant contamination event.

2. Distribution of Dioxins

Dioxins and similar chemicals such as furans have or are approaching ubiquitous distribution. These chemicals can be distributed to remote areas by atmospheric transport. The introduction of dioxins to the atmosphere occurs due to incineration of wastes and wood, as well as transfer from contaminated soils to the atmosphere. In addition, it was noted that dioxins from incineration are typically composed primarily of less toxic forms of dioxin.

3. Fate of Dioxins

The workshop participants demonstrated that scientists do know the factors which influence the fate of dioxins and furans in our environment and food sources. The problem, however, is that we cannot now quantify the relative importance of these factors. In particular, the field and laboratory data are not available to accurately measure these factors. Fulfillment of these needs, therefore, would require well focused field monitoring programs and laboratory studies.

4. Risk Assessment

In reviewing the process of evaluating how dioxins or other chemicals from a source might impact a human population we found that many of the requirements of assessment are indeed recognized and that related programs are underway. However, there are specific links in our chain of clearly defining human risk which are missing or inadequate. For instance, in the soils of contaminated areas such as Times Beach, Missouri, and Midland, Michigan, we do not know the exposure levels or the bioavailability of dioxins once exposure occurs.

5. Remedial Alternative

While there have been a number of mitigative actions proposed for sites contaminated with dioxins, including incineration of soil, disposal of soil and containment of site, the working group recommended that on-site methods of dioxin destruction or decontamination should be examined thoroughly. The session further noted that the contaminated sites at Times Beach, Missouri would be an ideal site for the testing and refinement of on-site methods of dioxin decontamination. A method of on-site dioxin decontamination meriting further investigation included sunlight assisted destruction.

6. Conclusion

Our understanding of the environmental problems posed by dioxin compounds in the environment is based on a basic understanding of environmental processes and previous experience with related coumpounds such as PCBs. To respond rationally and timely to problems like dioxin contamination requires a long-term commitment to a strong environmental infrastructure. Only with a scientific understanding of production, sources, fate, and effects of toxic substances will we be able to prevent future environmental crises. In the meantime, we should continue to locate sources of toxic contamination, monitor their impacts, and then eliminate, decontaminate, remove, or seal sites depending on site specific evaluations.

REFERENCES

American Society of Mechanical Engineers (ASME) research communication on industrial and municipal wastes. 1980. Study on State of the Art of Dioxins from Combustion Sources.

Bumb, R.R., Crummett, W.B., Cutie, S.S., Gledhill, J.R., Hummel, R.H., Kagel, R.O., Lamparski, L.L., Luoma, E.V., Miller, D.L., Nestrick, T.J., Shadoff, L.A., Stehl, R.H. and Woods, J.W. 1980. Trace chemistries of fire: A source of chlorinated dioxins. Science 210:385-390.

Buser, H.R. and Bosshardt, H.P. 1978. Polychlorinated dibenzo-p-dioxins, dibenzofurans, and benzenes in the fly ash of municipal and industrial incinerators. Mitt. Geb. Lebensmittelsunters Hyg. 69(2):191-199.

Czuczwa, J.M. and Hites, R.A. 1984. Dioxins and dibenzofurans in air, soil and water. In Dioxins in the Environment, eds. M. Kamrin and P.W. Rodgers, Hemisphere Publishing Corp. (This volume).

Eiceman, G.A., Clement, R.E. and Karasek, F.W. 1979. Analysis of trace organic compounds in fly ash from municipal incinerators. Anal. Chem. 51:2243.

Esposito, M.P., Tierman, T.O. and Dryden, F.E. 1980. Dioxins, Environmental Protection Technology Series, Document EPA/600/2-80-197, November. Available from the National Technical Information Service, Springfield, VA.

Forney, J.C. 1983. Summary of dioxin contamination in Michigan. A staff report by the Toxic Chemical Evaluation Section, Michigan Department of Natural Resources, March 10.

Gross, M.L., Lay, J.O., Jr., Lyon, P.A., Lippsteu, D., Kangas, N., Harless, R.L., Taylor, S.E. and Dupuy, A.E., Jr. 1984. 2,3,7,8-Tetrachlorodibenzo-p-dioxin levels in adipose tissue of Vietnam veterans. Env. Research 33:261-268.

Harless, R.L., Lewis, R.G., Dupuy, A.E. and McDaniel, D.D. 1981. Analysis for 2,3,7,8-TCDD residues in environmental samples. Paper presented at Arlington, VA in October.

Harrison, D.D., Miller, C.I. and Crews, R.C. 1979. Residual levels of 2,3,7,8-

tetrachlorodibenzo-p-dioxin (TCDD) near herbicide storage and loading areas at Eglin Air Force Base, Florida. AFATL-TR-79-20, February.

Kearney, P.C., Woolson, E.A., Isensee, A.R. and Helling, C.S. 1973. TCDD in the environment: Sources, fate and decontamination. Environ. Health Perspectives 5:273-277.

Kocher, G.W., Mahle, N.H., Hummel, R.A., Shadoff, L.A. and Getzendaner, M.E. 1978. A search for 2,3,7,8-tetrachlorodibenzo-p-dioxin in beef fat. Bull. Environ. Contam. Toxicol. 19:229-236.

Laurel Park, Inc. et al. v. Stanley J. Pac, Commissioner, State of Connecticut, Docket No. 289519.

Matsumura, F. and Benezet, H.J. 1973. Studies on the bioaccumulation and microbial degradation of 2,3,7,8-tetrachlorodibenzo-p-dioxin. Environ. Health Perspectives 5:253-258.

Olie, K., Lustenhouwer, J.W.A. and Hutzinger, O. 1982. Polychlorinated dibenzo-p-dioxins and related compounds in incinerator effluents. In Chlorinated Dioxins and Related Compounds: Impact on the Environment, eds. O. Hutzinger, R.W. Frei, E. Merian and F. Pocchiari, pp. 227-243, Pergamon Press, Oxford.

Olie, L., Vermeulen, P.L. and O. Hutzinger. 1977. Chlorodibenzo-p-dioxins and chlorodibenzofurans are trace components of fly ash and flue gas of some municipal incinerators in the Netherlands. Chemosphere 8:455-459.

Ryan, J.F., Biros, F.J. and Harless, R.L. 1974. Proceedings of the 22nd Annual Conference on Mass Spectrometry and Allied Topics, Philadelphia, PA, May.

Shadoff, L.A., Hummel, R.A., Jensen, D.J. and Mahle, N.H. 1977. The gas chromatographic mass spectrometric determination of 2,3,7,8-tetrachlorodibenzo-p-dioxin in fat from cattle fred Ronnel insecticide. Anali di Chimica 67:583-592.

U.S. EPA. 1983. Dioxin Strategy. Prepared by the Office of Water Regulations and Standards and the Office of Solid Waste and Emergency Response in conjunction with the Dioxin Strategy Task Force, November 28.

U.S. EPA. Environmental Monitoring at Love Canal. 1982. A report of the Office of Monitoring Systems and Quality Assurance, ORD, USEPA, Washington, DC.

Weerasinghe, N.C.A. and Gross, M.L. 1984. Origins of polychlorodibenzo-p-dioxins (PCDD) and polychlorodibenzofurans (PCDF) in the environment. In Dioxins in the Environment, eds. M. Kamrin and P.W. Rodgers, Hemisphere Publishing Corp. (This volume).

Wilkinson, R.R., Lawless, E.W., Meiners, A.F., Ferguson, T.L., Kelso, G.L. and Hopkins, F.C. 1978. State-of-the-art report on pesticide disposal research. In Disposal and Decontamination of Pesticides, ed. M.V. Kennedy, pp. 73-80, ACS Symposium Series 73, American Chemical Society, Washington, DC.

Young, A.L. 1974. Ecological studies on a herbicide-equipment test area (TA C-52A), Eglin AFB Reservation, Florida. Air Force Technical Report AFATL-TR-74-12, Air Force Armament Laboratory, Eglin AFB, Florida. 146 p. Available from the National Technical Information Service, Springfield, VA.

Section 4
Sampling and Analytical Techniques

Section 6
Sampling and Statistical
Techniques

SAMPLING AND ANALYTICAL TECHNIQUES - WORKSHOP SUMMARY

Chairman: Matthew Zabik

Panel Members
Warren Crummett
Robert Harless
Swiatoslav Kaczmar

Douglas Kuehl
Lewis Shadoff
V. Elliott Smith

The group of chemical compounds which include the dioxins represent a unique challenge to the analytical chemist. There are many congeners for each (75 for the dioxins); they occur in a wide variety of matrices; and some congeners are toxic at very low concentrations. As a result of these characteristics, great care must be exercised in choosing sampling and analytical techniques that are reproducible and combine a high degree of sensitivity and selectivity. This workshop summary describes how some of these problems have been solved and the areas that need to be addressed.

Before discussing the individual facets of analytical methods, some general principles should be mentioned. First, the purpose of each study must be clearly stated before any steps, including sampling, are performed. All facets of analysis are sensitive to the aim of the study; e.g. qualitative vs. quantitative or congener-specific vs. non-specific. The second principle is that the analytical chemist should be directly involved in the planning of any study which involves analysis of these compounds. The analytical chemist can then help to insure that the results are valid and can be used for the stated purpose.

SAMPLING

Since dioxins are found in most physical environment compartments as well as in living organisms, many sampling issues are specific to particular matrices; e.g. sediments. However, there are three basic areas of concern: collection, transportation and storage. The number, size and distribution of samples that are collected are determined by the purpose of the study and statistical considerations. Thus, grab samples might be appropriate for screening while carefully determined individual samples might be necessary to reveal the concentration variation over the whole site. High standards of cleanliness are required and only certain types of containers; (e.g. glass or teflon) should be utilized. In addition, samples should be indelibly labeled and information about how and where the samples were collected should accompany each sample.

The main considerations in transportation and storage are to protect the identity of the sample and to avoid changes in the sample between the site of collection and the site of analysis. As a general rule, biological samples should be frozen and other samples cooled, if possible. It appears that dioxins are not easily degradable, in the absence of light and hydrogen donors, so that conditions which minimize these factors will help to maximize the integrity of the sample.

ANALYSIS

The analysis of dioxins and related compounds at concentrations down to the part per trillion and part per quadrillion range, is a complex and time consuming process. As a result, there are only a limited number of laboratories which can undertake such measurements. The analytical techniques used in each of these laboratories have evolved rapidly during the past decade and have followed somewhat different paths. The resulting variety in extraction and cleanup procedures, and measurement devices and techniques have led to questions about the comparability of results obtained in these different laboratories. In view of this, the scientists involved in performing and interpreting analysis of these types of compounds have worked together in the past few years to examine the issue of comparability.

A number of steps have been taken and continue to be taken to assure the comparability and validity of studies performed in different laboratories. One of these is the comparison of results from several laboratories. The Canadian/American study (Ryan et al., 1983) examined a number of fish-analyses from different facilities and concluded that the procedures of each laboratory, although different, led to accurate determinations of part per trillion levels of one of the dioxins--2,3,7,8-TCDD. Other studies have confirmed this finding. While these results are reassuring, further studies are needed to validate any results from new laboratories which undertake the analysis of dioxin and related compounds.

To insure comparability requires the analysis of blind quality assurance samples during test sample analysis. Fifteen to twenty percent of the total samples should be blind. In addition, control samples should be from both field and laboratory and contain the congener(s) of interest and others which are blanks.

Another step taken to insure validity is to establish basic analytical criteria for both identification and quantification of specific congeners. These criteria have evolved over the past few years and remain an important way to maintain the validity and credibility of the results.

As a result of these measures taken during the past few years, it is clear that despite the complexity of methods, and the selectivity and sensitivity required, analyses performed by different laboratories and by different methods can be comparable and valid. This provides a solid basis for future analytical studies of these compounds.

RESEARCH NEEDS

Although the state of the art is quite advanced, most of the quality control investigations have been performed with a limited number of congeners. The main reason is that the congener, 2,3,7,8-TCDD, is currently of most interest toxicologically and so has been measured most commonly. However, some analytical studies would be helped if standard congeners which have not yet been synthesized became available. It would be especially useful if radiolabeled versions of these congeners were made available to investigators in this field.

As mentioned earlier, congener-specific analyses are very expensive and time-consuming. In order to minimize the need for this procedure, better screening methods should be developed. Both biological and chemical screening procedures have been investigated but more work is needed to develop these into routine techniques.

SUMMARY

The present analytical methodology allows definitive analysis for all dioxins and dibenzofurans for which reference standards are available. These analyses can be carried out at a high level of confidence at the part per trillion level for most matrices and part per quadrillion level for waters. Several analytical schemes have been used to achieve these detection limits. However, it is recognized that in order to analyze and validate such samples, extraordinarily vigorous quality assurance procedures (multi-laboratory) must be employed.

We feel confident that all the dioxin and furan congeners can be determined as soon as reference materials become available. It is of primary importance that the analytical chemist be involved in the inital planning of studies and that a concise set of goals be included as part of the protocol for each study. There is a need for continuing collaborative studies for all laboratories involved in dioxin and furan analyses.

For instance, it is possible to determine a single isomer such as 2,3,7,8-TCDD with a minimum of expenditure of time and money, but if the goal is to determine sources, then all isomers must be determined at a greatly increased expenditure of cost and time.

BIBLIOGRAPHY

ACS Committee on Environmental Improvement. 1980. Data acquisition and data quality evaluation in environmental chemistry. Anal. Chem. 52:2242-2249.

Blaser, W.W., Bredeweg, R.A., Shadoff, L.A. and Stehl, R.H. 1976. Determination of chlorinated dibenzo-p-dioxins in pentachlorophenol by gas chromatography/mass spectrometry. Anal. Chem. 48:984-986.

Buser, H.R. and Rappe, C. 1980. High-resolution gas chromatography of the 22 tetrachlorodibenzo-p-dioxin isomers. Anal. Chem. 52:2257-2262.

Crummett, W.B. 1979. Fundamental problems related to validation of analytical data elaborated on the example of TCDD. Toxic. Environ. Chem. Rev. 3:61-71.

Crummett, W.B. 1982. Analytical methodology for the determinatin of PCDDs and PCDFs in products and environmental samples: An overview and critique. In Human and Environmental Risks of Chlorinated Dioxins and Related Compounds, ed. R.E. Tucker, A.L. Young and A.P. Gray, pp. 45-63, Plenum Press, New York.

Crummett, W.B. 1983. Status of analytical systems for the determination of PCDDs and PCDFs. Chemosphere 12:429-446.

Crummett, W.B. and Taylor, J.K. 1982. Guidelines for data acquisition and data quality evaluation in environmental chemistry. In IUPAC Collaborative Interlaboratory Studies in Chemical Analysis, ed. H. Egan and T.S. West, pp. 63-65, Pergamon Press, Oxford and New York.

Erk, S., Taylor, M.L. and Tiernan, T.O. 1979. Determination of 2,3,7,8-tetrachlorodibenzo-p-dioxin residues on metal surfaces. Chemosphere 8:7-14.

Harless, R.W. and Lewis, R.G. 1982. Quantitative determination of 2,3,7,8-tetrachlorodibenzo-p-dioxin residues by gas chromatogrphy/mass spectrometry. In Chlorinated Dioxins and Related Compounds: Impact on the Environment, ed. O. Hutzinger, R.W. Frei, E. Merian and F. Pocchiari, pp. 25-35, Pergamon Press, Oxford.

Harless, R.W. Oswald, E.O., Wilkinson, M.K., Dupuy, A.E., Jr., McDaniel, D.D. and Han Tai. 1980. Sample preparation and gas chromatography/mass spectrometry determination of 2,3,7,8-tetrachlorodibenzo-p-dioxin. Anal. Chem. 52:1239-1245.

Harless, R.L., Oswald, E.O., Lewis, R.G., Dupuy, A.E., McDaniel, D.D. and Han Tai. 1982. Determination of 2,3,7,8-tetrachlorodibenzo-p-dioxin in fresh water fish. Chemosphere 11:193-198.

Jensen, D.J., Hummell, R.A., Mahle, N.H., Kocher, C.W. and Higgins, H.S. 1981. A residue study on beef cattle consuming 2,3,7,8-tetrachlorodibenzo-p-dioxin. J. Agric. Food Chem. 29:265-268.

Lamparski, L.L. and Nestrick, T.J. 1980. Determination of tetra-, hexa-, hepta-, and octachlorodibenzo-p-dioxin isomers in particulate samples at parts per trillion levels. Anal. Chem. 52:2045-2054.

Lamparski, L.L. and Nestrick, T.J. 1981. Synthesis and identification of the 10 hexachlorodibenzo-p-dioxin isomers by high performance liquid and packed column gas chromatography. Chemosphere 10:3-18.

Lamparski, L.L., Mahle, N.H. and Shadoff, L.A. 1978. Determination of pentachlorophenol, hexachlorodibenzo-p-dioxin, and octachlorodibenzo-p-dioxin in bovine milk. J. Agri. Food Chem. 26:1113-1116.

Lamparski, L.L., Nestrick, T.J. and Stehl, R.H. 1979. Determination of part-per-trillion concentrations of 2,3,7,8-tetrachlorodibenzo-p-dioxin in fish. Anal. Chem. 51:1453-1458.

Lamparski, L.L., Nestrick, T.J. and Stenger, V.A. 1984. Presence of dioxins in a sealed 1933 sample of dried municipal sewage sludge. Chemosphere, in press.

Langhorst, M.L. and Shadoff, L.A. 1980. Determination of parts-per-trillion concentrations of tetra-, hexa-, hepta- and octa-chlorodibenzo-p-dioxins in human milk samples. Anal. Chem. 52:2037-2044.

McLeod, H. (Chairman), Panel of Associate Committee on Scientific Criteria for Environmental Quality. 1981. Polychlorinated dibenzo-p-dioxins: Limitations to the current analytical techniques. National Research Council of Canada, NRCC No. 18576.

Mieure, J.P., Hicks, O., Kaley, R.G. and Michael, P.R. 1977. Determination of trace amounts of chlorodibenzo-p-dioxins and chlorodibenzofurans in technical grade pentachlorophenol. J. Chromatogr. Sci. 15:275-277.

Norstrom, R.J. and Simon, M. 1983. Preliminary appraisal of tetra- to octachlorodibenzodioxin contamination in eggs of various species of wildlife in Canada. In Pesticide Chemistry: Human Welfare and the Environment, Vol. 4, ed. J. Miyamoto, P.C. Kearney, R. Greenhalgh and N. Drescher, pp. 165-170, Pergamon Press, Oxford.

Norstrom, R.J., Hallet, D.J., Simon, M. and Mulvihill, M.J. 1982. Analysis of Great Lakes herring gull eggs for the tetrachlorodibenzo-p-dioxins. In Chlorinated Dioxins and Related Compounds: Impact on the Environment, ed. O. Hutzinger, R.W. Frei, E. Merian and F. Pocchiari, pp. 173-181, Pergamon Press, Oxford.

O'Keefe, P., Meyer, C., Hilker, D., Aldons, K., Jelue-Tyror, B., Dillon, K. and Donelly, R. 1983. Analysis of 2,3,7,8-tetrachlorodibenzo-p-dioxin in Great Lakes fish. Chemosphere 12:325-332.

Ryan, J.J., Pilon, J., Conacher, H.B.S. and Firestone, D. 1984. Interlaboratory study on determination of 2,3,7,8-tetrachlorodibenzo-p-dioxin in fish. J. Assoc. Off. Anal. Chem. 66:700-707.

Shadoff, L.A. and Hummel, R.A. 1978. Determination of 2,3,7,8-tetrachlorodibenzo-p-dioxin in biological extracts by gas chromatography mass spectrometry. Biomed. Mass

Spectrom. 5:7-13.

Tiernan, T.O.   1983.   Analytical chemistry of polychlorinated dibenzo-p-dioxins and dibenzofurans: A review of the current status.   In Chlorinated Dioxins and Dibenzofurans in the Total Environment, ed., G. Choudhary, L.H. Keith, and C. Rappe, pp 211-237, Butterworth Publishers, Boston.

Zabik, M.E. and Zabik, M.J.   1980.   Dioxin levels in raw and cook liver, loin steaks, round, and patties from beef fed technical grade pentachlorophenol.   Bull. Environ. Contam. Toxicol. 24:344-349.

LIST OF PARTICIPANTS AND CONTRIBUTORS

Bruce Bernard, Director, Scientific Resource Association, Inc., 200 St. Lawrence Drive, Silver Springs, MD 20901

* M.V.D. Berg, Laboratory of Environmental and Toxicological Chemistry, University of Amsterdam, THE NETHERLANDS

Daniel Bronstein, Professor, Resource Development, Michigan State University, East Lansing, MI 48824

* John E. Cantlon, Vice President for Research and Graduate Studies, Michigan State University, East Lansing, MI 48824

* Lorris G. Cockerham, Lt. Col., USAF, Ph.D., Armed Forces Radiobiology Research Institute, Bethesda, MD 20814

Ralph R. Cook, Director of Epidemiology, Dow Chemical Company, Midland, MI 48640

William E. Cooper, Chairman, Department of Zoology, Michigan State University, East Lansing, MI 48824

* Donald Crosby, Professor, Department of Environmental Toxicology, University of California at Davis, Davis, California 95616

* Warren Crummett, Technical Manager, Senior Research Scientist, Dow Chemical Company, Midland, MI 48640

* Jean M. Czuczwa, Graduate Student, School of Public and Environmental Affairs, Indiana University, Bloomington, Indiana 47401

Joseph DiMento, Professor, University of California at Irvine, Irvine, California 92717

* W.J. Dunn, III, University of Illinois Medical Center, Chicago, IL

John Gannon, International Joint Commission, International Association for Great Lakes Research, Windsor, Ontario, CANADA N9A 6T3

John Giesy, Associate Professor, Pesticide Research Center, Michigan State University, East Lansing, MI 48824

* Michael L. Gross, Professor, Department of Chemistry, University of Nebraska at Lincoln, Lincoln, NE 68588

Robert Harless, U.S. Environmental Protection Agency, Research Triangle Park, NC 27711

John Hesse, Michigan Department of Public Health, Center for Environmental Health Sciences, P.O. Box 30035, Lansing, MI 48909

* Ronald Hites, Professor, Chemistry Department, Indiana University, Bloomington, Indiana 47401

Larry Holcomb, Executive Director, Michigan Toxic Substance Control Commission, Washington Square Building, Suite 815, 109 West Michigan Avenue, P.O. Box 30026,

Lansing, MI 48909

Harold E.B. Humphrey, Michigan Department of Public Health, Center for Environmental Health Sciences, P.O. Box 30035, Lansing, MI 48909

Gary Hurlburt, Michigan Department of Natural Resources, Environmental Services Division, Toxic Chemical Evaluation Unit, P.O. Box 30028, Lansing, MI 48909

* Otto Hutzinger, Professor, University of Bayreuth, Chair of Ecological Chemistry and Geochemistry, Postfach 3008, D-8580, Bayreuth, GERMANY

Swiatoslav Kaczmar, Environmental Toxicologist, O'Brien and Gere Engineers, Inc., 1304 Buckley Road, Syracuse, NY 13221

Michael Kamrin, Professor, Center for Environmental Toxicology, Michigan State University, East Lansing, MI 48824

Douglas Kuehl, U.S. Environmental Protection Agency, Environmental Research Laboratory, 6201 Congdon Boulevard, Duluth, MN 55804

* L.L. Lamparski, Analytical Laboratories, Dow Chemical Company, Midland, MI 48640

Robert W. Leader, Acting Director, Center for Environmental Toxicology, Michigan State University, East Lansing, MI 48824

* William Lowrance, Professor, Life Sciences and Public Policy Program, The Rockefeller University, York Avenue at 66th, New York, NY 10021

* Fumio Matsumura, Professor and Director, Pesticide Research Center, Michigan State University, East Lansing, MI 48824

* E.E. McConnell, National Toxicology Program, National Institute of Environmental Health Sciences, P.O. Box 12233, Research Triangle Park, NC 27709

* D. Franco Merlo, Department of Epidemiology and Biostatistics, Scientific Institute for Research on Cancer, University of Genova, Genova, ITALY

* Theodore Mill, Department of Physical Organic Chemistry, Stanford Research Institute, Menlo Park, CA 94025

* Alexander B. Morrison, Assistant Deputy Minister, Health Protection Branch, Department of Health and Welfare Canada, Health Protection Branch Building, Tunney's Pasture, Ottawa, Ontario, CANADA K1A 0L2

* T.J. Nestrick, Analytical Laboratories, Dow Chemical Company, Midland, MI 48640

Ross J. Norstrom, Head, Environmental Chemistry Section, Wildlife Toxicology Division, Canadian Wildlife Service National Wildlife Research Center, Ottawa, Ontario, CANADA K1A 0E7

* K. Olie, Laboratory of Environmental and Toxicological Chemistry, University of Amsterdam, THE NETHERLANDS

* A. Opperhuizen, Laboratory of Environmental and Toxicological Chemistry, University of Amsterdam, THE NETHERLANDS

Richard E. Peterson, Associate Professor, Pharmacology and Toxicology, School of Pharmacy, University of Wisconsin, 425 N. Charter Street, Madison, WI 53706

* J.D. Petty, U. S. Department of the Interior, Fish and Wildlife Service, Columbia National Fisheries Research Laboratory, Route 1, Columbia, MO 65201

William L. Richardson, U.S. Environmental Protection Agency, 9311 Groh Road, Grosse Ile, MI 48138

Paul Rodgers, Vice President of Research and Development, LIMNO-TECH, Inc., 15 Research Drive, Ann Arbor, MI 48103

Thomas K. Rohrer, Aquatic Biologist, Toxic Chemical Evaluation Section, Environmental Services Division, Department of Natural Resources, P.O. Box 30028, Lansing, MI 48909

William R. Rustem, Executive Director, Center for the Great Lakes, 135 South LaSalle Street, Chicago, IL 60603

* S. Safe, Department of Veterinary Physiology and Pharmacology, College of Veterinary Medicine, Texas A & M University, College Station, TX 77843

Lewis Shadoff, Dow Chemical Company, Midland, MI 48640

Michael Slimak, Chief, Exposure Assessment Section, Monitoring and Data Support Division (WH-553), U.S. Environmental Protection Agency, Washington, D.C. 20460

* L.M. Smith, U.S. Department of the Interior, Fish and Wildlife Service, Columbia National Fisheries Research Laboratory, Route 1, Columbia, MO 65201

V. Elliott Smith, Cranbrook Institute of Science, 500 Lone Pine Road, Box 801, Bloomfield Hills, MI 48013

* Edward Smuckler, Professor and Chairman, Pathology Department, HSW 501, University of California-San Francisco, San Francisco, CA 94143

* David L. Stalling, Chief Chemist, U.S. Department of the Interior, Fish and Wildlife Service, Columbia National Fisheries Research Laboratory, Route 1, Columbia, MO 65201

* Raymond Suskind, Professor, Institute of Environmental Health, University of Cincinnati, 3223 Eden Avenue, Cincinnati, OH 45267

Fred Tschirley, Professor, Department of Botany and Plant Pathology, Michigan State University, East Lansing, MI 48824

Bernard Wagner, Department of Pathology, Overlook Hospital, Summit, NJ 07901

* N.C.A. Weerasinghe, Department of Chemistry, University of Nebraska at Lincoln, Lincoln, NE 68588

Daniel E. Williams, Michigan Department of Public Health, Center for Environmental Health Sciences, P.O. Box 30035, Lansing, MI 48909

Dennis M. Wint, Director, Cranbrook Institute of Science, 500 Lone Pine Road, Box 801, Bloomfield Hills, MI 48013

* Alvin L. Young, Senior Policy Analyst for Life Sciences, Executive Office of the President, Office of Science and Technology Policy, Room 5005, New Executive Office Building, Washington, D.C. 20506

Matthew W. Zabik, Professor and Associate Director, Pesticide Research Center, Michigan State University, East Lansing, MI 48824

*Authors of papers published in this book.

SUBJECT INDEX

Accidental Fires 14,118,119 (See Sources of PCDD)

Adipose Tissue 134,137,138,154-159 (See TCDD levels)

Agent Orange 9,12,38,39,137,140,147,155-157,209

Alsea, Oregon 39,135,137

Aryl Hydrocarbon Hydroxylase (AHH) 16-20,77

Assays
   aryl hydrocarbon hydroxylase (AHH) induction assay 16-20,77
   cytosol receptor assay 16-20,52,77
   enzyme induction 35,52
   fat 34
   keratinization 77
   mass spectrometry 77
   radio immunoassay 35,77

Atmospheric Transport 93-95,175

Benzo(a)pyrene 190

Binghamton, New York 118,119,201

Birth Defects 137,243

Bioaccumulation of PCDD and PCDF 14,158,169,180,243,259

Bioavailability 169

Biomagnification 133,136,138

Biotransformation 186,187

Carcinogenesis 15,35,51,52,101,218,220,221,232,233,248-251,259

Chemical Waste 12,21,87,88,94,97,133,138-141,153,241

Chemometrics 108-122

Chick Edema 16,39,217,226,228

Chloracne 15,35,218,221-223,226,228,237,243,244,251,252,256,259,261
   and liver function 245
   and pancreatic cancer 259

Cigarette Smoke 141

Clean Air Act 47 (See Regulatory Acts)

Clean Water Act 37 (See Regulatory Acts)

Coal Combustion 95-97